Things of Darkness

THINGS OF DARKNESS

Economies of Race and Gender
in Early Modern England

KIM F. HALL

Cornell University Press

ITHACA AND LONDON

First published 1995 by Cornell University Press.

Printed in the United States of America

⊗ The paper in this book meets the minimum requirements of the
American National Standard for Information Sciences—Permanence
of Paper for Printed Library Materials, ANSI Z39.48–1984.

Library of Congress Cataloging-in-Publication Data

Hall, Kim F., 1961–
    Things of darkness : economies of race and gender in early modern England / Kim F.
Hall.
        p.   cm.
    Includes bibliographical references (p.   ) and index.
    ISBN 0-8014-3117-4 (cloth : alk. paper) — ISBN 0-8014-8249-6 (paper : alk. paper)
    1. English literature—Early modern, 1500–1700—History and criticism.   2. Race in liter-
ature.   3. Feminism and literature—England—History.   4. Literature and society—
England—History.   5. Women and literature—England—History.   6. Sex role in
literature.   7. Blacks in literature.   I. Title.
PR428.R35H35 1995
820.9'353—dc20   95-36592

for my parents,
Lawrence H. Hall and Vera P. Webb Hall

Contents

List of Illustrations   ix

Acknowledgments   xi

Introduction   1
   Who Is English? The Black Presence in England   11
   Pirates, Poets, and Traders: England and African Trades   16

1 A World of Difference: Travel Narratives and the
    Inscription of Culture   25
   Writing Africa: Native Informants and Narrative Anxiety   28
   Enterprise and Conversion: Ordering the World in Hakluyt
     and Purchas   44

2 Fair Texts/Dark Ladies: Renaissance Lyric and the Poetics
    of Color   62
   Astrophel and Stella: "New Found Tropes with Problemes
     Old"   73
   The Traffic in Fairness: Cosmetics and Blackness   85
   Sunburn: Anxieties of Influence/Anxieties of Race   92
   Washing the Ethiope White: The Song of Songs   107
   Aethiopissa and Her Sisters   116

3 "Commerce and Intercourse": Dramas of Alliance
    and Trade   123
   The *Masque of Blackness* and Jacobean Nationalism   128
   Marriages of State: *The Tempest* and *Antony and
     Cleopatra*   141
   Colonialism and the Economics of Marriage   160

4 The Daughters of Eve and the Children of Ham: Race and
   the English Woman Writer   177
      The "Other" Woman: Beauty, Women Writers, and
         Cleopatra   178
      Blackness and Status in the *Urania*   187

5 "An Object in the Midst of Other Objects": Race, Gender,
   Material Culture   211
      Male Portraits, Property, and Colonial Might   226
      Beauty, Colonialism, and the Female Subject   240

   Epilogue: On "Race," Black Feminism, and White
   Supremacy   254

   Appendix: Poems of Blackness   269
   Works Cited   291
   Index   309

Illustrations

1. Peregrine Bertie, Lord Willoughby d'Eresby   5
2. Arms of Sir John Hawkins   20
3. "Aethiopem lavare," from Geoffrey Whitney's *A Choice of Emblemes*   68
4. Engraving from Bulwer's *Anthropometamorphosis*   88
5. Lady Raleigh as Cleopatra   186
6. Gem with scarabs   216
7. Moor and emperor cameo   217
8. Black cameo   218
9. Diana cameo   219
10. Gresley jewel—outer locket   220
11. Gresley jewel—inside view   221
12. Drake jewel   223
13. Drake jewel—inside view   224
14. Sir Francis Drake, by Gheeraerts   225
15. Prince Rupert, by Mytens   229
16. William Fielding, first earl of Denbigh, by Van Dyck   231
17. Cecil Calvert, by Soest   233
18. George Calvert, by Mytens   234
19. Charles I and Henrietta Maria, by Mytens   236
20. *Machomilia en Turk*, engraving by Diepenbeck   237
21. Anne of Denmark, by van Somer   239
22. *Woman in an Arched Stone Aperture*, anonymous portrait by Netscher   243
23. Anonymous woman by Gignes   245

24. Barbara Villiers, duchess of Cleveland, by Lely   246
25. Portrait by Wissing, possibly of Hortense Mancini de la
    Porte, duchess of Mazarin   249
26. Louise Renée de Kéroüalle, duchess of Portsmouth, by
    Jacques D'Agar   250
27. Louise Renée de Kéroüalle, duchess of Portsmouth, by
    Mignard   252

Acknowledgments

One benefit of working on a project over an extended period of time is that it increases one's opportunities to refine and, one hopes, improve ideas through the alchemy of conversation. It has been my great fortune to work on this project with three fine groups of scholars and to have benefited from their insight and support.

This book began while I was at the University of Pennsylvania, where I had the benefit of an energetic Renaissance discussion group that included Greg Bredbeck, Rebecca Bushnell, Juliet Fleming, Gwynne Kennedy, Janet Knepper, Cary Mazer, Robert Turner, Wendy Wall, and Georgianna Ziegler. This group also included Margreta deGrazia, whom I thank for her unwavering critical eye; Maureen Quilligan, for showing me that there was a place for me in the academic community when I was ready to give up and for her unwavering support and complete enthusiasm when I went into the then-untested waters of race in the Renaissance; and Phyllis Rackin, for many things, but most of all for showing me that excellent scholarship does not have to come at the sacrifice of politics, humanity, or integrity.

A postdoctoral fellowship from the Ford Foundation afforded me the opportunity to think and learn about visual culture and to work in the English Department at Columbia University in 1992–93. I am grateful to the Renaissance faculty and graduate students there who made me a part of their community for the year. Special thanks go to Jean E. Howard for serving as my official mentor and for generously giving me her time and friendship as well as challenging my thinking in countless ways, and to

John Michael Archer for reading my work and sharing his own research with me.

My Georgetown colleagues old and new, faculty and students, have been invaluable sources of intellectual community and friendship: Valerie Babb, Gay Gibson Cima, Pamela Fox, Lindsay Kaplan, Patricia O'Connor, Connie M. Razza, Amy Robinson, Jason Rosenblatt, Lisa Silverberg, Bruce Smith, and Norma Tilden. I am particularly thankful for the sustaining friendships of Leona Fisher, who unselfishly served as my sounding board and who kept up her enthusiasm for the book even when my own was fading, and of Michael Ragussis, who gave me the benefit of his unerring critical judgment, sound advice, and excellent pasta in equal and generous proportions. My chair, James Slevin, has been a staunch supporter of mine since I came to Georgetown. I was able to complete much of this work with the help of summer grants from Dean Robert Lawton, S.J., and the graduate school. Tiffany Gill, Marsha Fausti, Janelle Walthour, Bonnie Billman, and Brigette Craft lent invaluable assistance at crucial times.

Many people have shared with me their discoveries about race and I thank them for their material and their insights; even items that did not make it into the book were nonetheless helpful. My colleague Dennis Todd, whose findings often took me into new areas of inquiry, and Gwynne Kennedy, who kept me supplied with new things to think about and always had time to listen to those thoughts, have been particularly outstanding in this regard. Jennifer Brody's thinking on this subject has been influential in subtle and profound ways.

I also thank my Cornell editor, Bernhard Kendler, for his unfailing patience, and the manuscript readers, Peter Erickson and Mary Ellen Lamb, for their speed, enthusiasm, and excellent advice. The staffs of the Folger Shakespeare Library, the National Portrait Gallery Archives, and the Courtauld Institute of Art have been unfailingly generous.

Denise Albanese, Alison Byerly, Ellen Garvey, Robert Gibbs, Steve Jensen, Jacqueline Jones, Caren Kaplan, Alison Lane, Kimberly Robinson Morton, Carmen Sanchez, Eric Smoodin, and Susan Zlotnick are all friends whom I see too little of, yet they enrich my life beyond measure.

My immediate family, Reginald Lawrence Hall, Ranota Hall, and Andrew Lawrence Hall, always remind me that life is not only about work while respecting the time needed for the work. My extended family and what my grandmother called "family connections" are too many and support me in ways too numerous to mention here, but they are always in my thoughts. I thank them all for overlooking the missed family events, the distraction, and the (I hope only occasional) thoughtlessness caused by my involvement in this project.

Sections of chapters 3 and 4 have appeared in "Guess Who's Coming to Dinner? Colonization and Miscegenation in *The Merchant of Venice*," *Renaissance Drama* 23 (1992): 87–111; "Sexual Politics and Cultural Identity in *The Masque of Blackness*," in *The Performance of Power*, ed. Sue-Ellen Case and Janelle Reinelt (Iowa City: University of Iowa Press, 1991), 3–18; and " 'I rather would wish to be a Black-moore': Race, Rank, and Beauty in Lady Mary Wroth's *Urania*," in *Women, "Race," and Writing*, ed. Margo Hendricks and Patricia Parker (London and New York: Routledge, 1994), 178–194.

In the interests of clarity, I have silently changed *f* to *s*, *y* to *i*, and *v* to *u* throughout and slightly modernized the least accessible texts.

K. F. H.

Things of Darkness

Introduction

Or when we deride by plaine and flat contradiction, as he that saw a
dwarfe go in the streete said to his companion that walked with him:
See yonder giant: and to a Negro or woman blackemoore, in good sooth
ye are a faire one . . .
                     —George Puttenham, *The Arte of English Poesie* (1589)

He that cannot understand the sober, plain, and unaffected stile of the
Scriptures, will be ten times more puzzl'd with the knotty Africanisms,
the pamper'd metaphors, the intricat, and involv'd sentences of the
Fathers . . .
                     —John Milton, *Reformation Touching Church Discipline* (1641)

In Shakespeare's *A Midsummer Night's Dream*, Lysander rejects his
"dark" lover, shouting, "Away, you Ethiop!" and "Out, tawny Tartar"
(3.2.257 and 263).[1] Typically, scholars have replicated Lysander's dismissal of the "Ethiop" by refusing to consider such remarks in the context
of the elements of race, sexual politics, imperialism, and slavery, which
form a prominent set of "subtexts" to the play (Jameson 81). A survey of
scholarly editions of Shakespeare's works demonstrates how modern literary criticism remystifies the appearance of blackness in literary works by
insisting that references to race are rooted in European aesthetic tradition
rather than in any consciousness of racial difference. For example, Harold
Brooks, editor of the Arden edition of the play, is typical in seeing Lysander's gibes as only a commentary on Hermia's beauty: "Hermia is conscious of what in unsympathetic eyes may be considered her 'bad points'
. . . and Lysander has attacked one of them, her unfashionable dark complexion."[2]

Similar evocations of blackness—with similar critical effacement—occur
with startling regularity throughout a broad range of Renaissance texts.

1. All references are to *The Riverside Shakespeare* unless otherwise noted.
2. *A Midsummer Night's Dream*, ed. Harold Brooks, cviii.

From Puttenham's early example of antiphrasis through Milton's admonitions against the "knotty Africanisms" of biblical commentary lies a broad discursive network in which the polarity of dark and light articulates ongoing cultural concerns over gender roles and shifting trade structures.[3] I argue that descriptions of dark and light, rather than being mere indications of Elizabethan beauty standards or markers of moral categories, became in the early modern period the conduit through which the English began to formulate the notions of "self" and "other" so well known in Anglo-American racial discourses. This argument complements Winthrop Jordan's landmark contribution, *White over Black: American Attitudes toward the Negro*, both by refining his contention that the language of dark and light is racialized in this period and by examining the ways in which gender concerns are crucially embedded in discourses of race. More significant, the following chapters suggest a crucial interrelationship between race and gender that is deeply embedded in language deployed in the development of the modern—that is to say, white, European, male—subject. Frequently the "dark" side of this polarity is figured in specific geographic and racial terms, as in Puttenham's use of "Negro or woman blackemore" and Milton's rebuke against "Africanisms" in biblical exegesis. In this Introduction I first outline the political import of what I am calling tropes of blackness and then examine the evidence for England's involvement with dark-skinned Africans. I conclude by returning to my opening text, *A Midsummer Night's Dream*, to discuss the questions raised by an acknowledgment of its racialized language.

If, as poststructuralists have argued, part of the process of stabilizing meaning is the "identification of difference as polarity" (Belsey, "Disrupting Sexual Difference" 177), the binarism of black and white might be called the originary language of racial difference in English culture.[4] The deconstructionist Barbara Johnson has insightfully noted that binary oppositions undergird Western culture's logic about both race and sex. This binarism certainly pre-dates the Renaissance, but during this period it becomes increasingly infused with concerns over skin color, economics, and gender politics. It is perhaps no coincidence that the *Oxford English*

3. Milton's work is particularly interesting in this regard because it is part of a larger diatribe against obscurantism in biblical commentary, in which he draws heavily upon the language of dark and light. For example, he claims that the difficulties of Scripture are attributable to the nature of man rather than to the text itself: "The very essence of Truth is plainnesse, and brightnes; the darknes and crookednesse is our own" (566). In his *Blank Darkness*, Christopher Miller analyzes the word "Africanism," particularly in its 'difference from "Orientalism" (14).

4. Interestingly, the dichotomy of black and white seems to be one of the few not taken up in deconstructive analysis. See, for example, Catherine Belsey, "Disrupting Sexual Difference: Meaning and Gender in the Comedies."

Dictionary locates the first use of "fair" as a term of complexion in Thomas Wilson's manual *The Rule of Reason*.[5] It defines his use of "faire" as "Of complexion and hair: Light as opposed to dark" and, with some puzzlement, states that this meaning is "apparently not of very early origin," therefore suggesting that this opposition between fair and dark, typical in discussions of beauty, happens in the 1550s. This semantic shift appears just at the moment of intensified English interest in colonial travel and African trade.[6] That moment also happens to be a time when England itself had a heightened nervousness about group identity and power and, as Peter Fryer maintains, was thus ripe for the development of race prejudice:

> But race prejudice . . . is specially persistent in communities that are ethnically homogeneous, geographically isolated, technologically backward, or socially conservative, with knowledge and political power concentrated in the hands of an elite. Such communities feel threatened by national or racial differences, and their prejudices serve to reassure them, to minimize their sense of insecurity, to enhance group cohesion. England in the sixteenth and seventeenth centuries was a classic instance of such a community—though its geographical isolation was rapidly being overcome and its technology was about to leap forward. (133)

Although Fryer pays less attention to England's movement out of its isolation and into its great development as a naval power, I would suggest that it is England's sense of losing its traditional insularity that provokes the development of "racialism."[7] This moment of transition—England's

5. For a more detailed discussion of this moment in Wilson, see my essay " 'I rather would wish to be a Black-moore': Race, Rank, and Beauty in Lady Mary Wroth's *Urania*," 178–79.

6. Other scholars place England's black presence and its "racial" consciousness much earlier. Paul Edwards finds evidence of blacks in the Romano-British period. Christian Delacampagne sees the origins in European racial discourses in classical antiquity: "Racist discourse, as we have known it in Europe since the nineteenth century, did not appear ex nihilo. It is the fruit—or the inheritor—of other, older discourses, whose first elements can be located in the philosophers of antiquity and whose course can be charted through the theologians and scholars of the Middle Ages" (83). Delacampagne's view silently rebuts the classicist Frank Snowden's more well known position that ancient Greeks did not exhibit race prejudice. Snowden argues that the common association of blackness with death "does not seem to have had a negative effect on the generally favorable view of blacks dating back to the Homeric poems, or to have given rise to a serious anti-black sentiment" (*Before Color Prejudice* 101), and he concludes that "antiquity as a whole was able to overcome whatever potential for serious anti-black sentiment there may be in color symbolism" (101). I do not think that Delacampagne's view necessarily precludes mine. He later states that "the medievals knew nothing of their ancient predecessors" (84). If he is correct, then it would suggest that the humanist project and its revivification of classical antiquity would also promote a belief in "a system of thought that strove to be rational" with its oppressive implications. Allison Blakely has also challenged Snowden's thesis (xviii, 289–90).

7. I borrow the term "racialist" from Anthony Appiah, who sees it forming only in

movement from geographic isolation into military and mercantile contest with other countries[8]—sets the stage for the longer process by which preexisting literary tropes of blackness profoundly interacted with the fast-changing economic relations of white Europeans and their darker "others" during the Renaissance.

The economic expansion of England was a linguistic and, ultimately, an ideological expansion in which writers and travelers grappled with ways of making use of the foreign *materia* "produced" by colonialism. Tropes of blackness were discovered by white English writers (both male and female) to be infinitely malleable ways of establishing a sense of the proper organization of Western European male and female in the Renaissance: notions of proper gender relations shape the terms for describing proper colonial organization. Further, the English/European division of beauty into "white" or "black" not only served aesthetic purposes but supported an ideology that still continues to serve the interests of white supremacy and male hegemony.[9]

This is not to dismiss the traditional association of blackness in conventional Christian symbolism with death and mourning, sin and evil.[10] On the contrary, it is to say that the culture recognized the possibilities of this language for the representation and categorization of perceived physical differences. Thus traditional terms of aesthetic discrimination and Christian dogma become infused with ideas of Africa and African servitude, making it impossible to separate "racial" signifiers of blackness from traditional iconography. For example, in a posthumous portrait of Lord Willoughby d'Eresby (see figure 1), the association of black people with the

---

eighteenth-century scientific notions of race which were rooted in the belief that one "could divide human beings into a small number of groups, called 'races,' in such a way that all members of these races shared certain fundamental, biologically heritable, moral and intellectual characteristics with each other that they did not share with members of any other race" ("Race" 276). While I disagree with Appiah that racialism began in the eighteenth century, I find his term useful because it suggests a way of talking about notions of human difference that have political and social effects and that are different from more institutionalized forms of racism. The idea of absolute separation seems key to this definition, as it is to the black/white binarism.

8. Knorr, in particular, argues that colonial/mercantile theory was rooted in an antagonistic contest based on the common belief that resources were limited and that the gain of resources by one country always meant loss by another.

9. I use the term "white supremacy" with full awareness of its implications. "Racism" does not adequately cover the networks of power and behavior we see in early modern texts that are often not overtly or directly discriminating against or exploiting black people. See bell hooks, "overcoming white supremacy: a comment," and Doris Davenport, "The Pathology of Racism: A Conversation with Third World Wimmin."

10. We should, however, keep in mind that this language is never without political, racial consequences. African-Americans in particular have always been keenly sensitive to the dinigration of black bodies in Western culture.

Figure 1. Anonymous portrait of Peregrine Bertie, lord Willoughby d'Eresby (1555–1601). It is undated but the memento mori carried by the attendant identifies it as posthumous. Willoughby was celebrated for his valor (particularly in the war in the Netherlands) for years after his death. (The Trustees of the Grimsthorpe and Drummond Castle Trust; photograph, Courtauld Institute of Art.)

conflated imagery of blackness and death is quite apparent. The portrait depends on the contrast of white and black and the association of the servant's dark skin with the death indicated by the black *memento mori*. Such images suggest how aesthetic concerns easily become a semiotics of race. Albert Boime suggests in his discussion of nineteenth-century art that "the famous *chiaroscuro,* or light and dark polarity, is intimately associated with the religious dualism of Good and Evil" (2); it is also part of a racial hierarchy in which blackness and black men serve to heighten the whiteness of Europeans. Here, too, the painting works to glorify English whiteness and literally to marginalize blackness as associated with black people. The black figure barely escapes being cut off by the painting's frame. He follows, rather than leads, and is situated not near the rider but behind the bridled horse. Even before the Renaissance, tropes of blackness drew their primary force from the dualism of good and evil and its association with African cultures and peoples.[11] The insistent association of "black" as a negative signifier of different cultural and religious practices with physiognomy and skin color is precisely what pushes this language into the realm of racial discourse.

Despite contemporary disagreement about the very existence of "races" and therefore the viability of "race" as a term in cultural or literary studies, I hold onto the idea of a language of race in the early modern period and eschew the scare quotes so popular in contemporary writings on race. The easy association of race with modern science ignores the fact that language itself creates differences within social organization and that race was then (as it is now) a social construct that is fundamentally more about power and culture than about biological difference. Most theorists of race do agree that racist thought involves a degree of classification and exclusion used to exercise or to justify control over (or exploitation of) people of other cultures.[12] Even in the Anglo-American scientific discourses privileged in analyses of race, "race" has been used invariably to rationalize property interests, either in the use of humans as property, as in slavery, or in the appropriation of land or resources, as in colonization.

The trope of blackness had a broad arsenal of effects in the early modern period, meaning that it is applied not only to dark-skinned Africans

11. John Hodge asserts: "In Western societies dualist justifications typically take a particular form as a consequence of the identification of good with reason, law, and rationality, and bad with emotion, chance, spontaneity and nature" (96).

12. Gerda Lerner is particularly cogent in this regard (although I would add to her formulation that one does not need to use the word "race" for the dynamic to exist): "The essence of racism is to divide the world according to groups with certain political characteristics, call these groups 'races,' and then classify them or rank them according to superiority or inferiority" (92). See also Etienne Balibar, "Racism and Nationalism," who sees classification as a fundamental operating principle in racism and reminds us that "classification is presupposed by any form of hierarchical ranking. And it can lead to such a ranking, for the more or less coherent construction of a hierarchical table of groups which make up the human race is a privileged representation of its unity in and through inequality" (55–56). From both views, one can see the placement of people with dark skins on the lowest levels within a hierarchical system (or the exclusion of them) as a precursor to later, more overtly racist, scientific classification.

but to Native Americans, Indians, Spanish, and even Irish and Welsh as groups that needed to be marked as "other." However, I assert that in these instances it still draws its power from England's ongoing negotiations of African difference and from the implied color comparison therein. Thus the Irish may be called "black" and an English woman may be called "Ethiopian," but these moments always depend on a visual schema that itself relies on an idea of African difference. In practice, this means that although I concentrate primarily on representations of Africa and Africans and descriptions of "black" skin, it is impossible to look solely at a single broad group, for the investigation of one difference inevitably opens up inquiry into other cultural, religious, and ethnic differences. My discussion, therefore, often expands to include Muslims, Native Americans, Indians, white North Africans, and Jews. During the period, the designation "Moor" very often stood alternatively for many of these categories, especially as it became a general term for the ethnically, culturally, and religiously "strange" (Barthelemy 17).

Similarly, I will use "blackness" and "black" to cover both social practices and cultural categories.[13] I also will use the term "black" to refer to Africans and African-descended people in England, the Caribbean, and the Americas. Although this practice might leave me open to the charge of reifying the very binarism I am trying to deconstruct, I prefer to think of my usage of "black" as a term that opposes the dominance of white/light and that foregrounds the role of color in organizing relations of power. Audre Lorde articulates this position with some sympathy but suggests that it is problematic:

I see certain pitfalls in defining Black as a political position. It takes the cultural identity of a widespread but definite group and makes it a generic identity for many culturally diverse peoples, all on the basis of a shared oppression. This runs the risk of providing a convenient blanket of apparent similarity under which our actual and unaccepted differences can be distorted or misused. . . . There must be a way for us to deal with this, if only on the level of language. For example, those of us for whom Black is our cultural reality, relinquishing the word in favor of some other designation of the African Diaspora, perhaps simply *African.* (*Burst of Light* 67)

13. It is perhaps fitting that multicultural coalitions in Britain are adopting "black" as a term of both solidarity across cultures and resistance to cultural hegemony. See, for example, the preface to *Charting the Journey: Radical Writings by Black and Third World Women*, in which the editorial group envisions a solidarity rooted in the experience of exile and colonization: "Thus began the business of transforming transplanted ways of being, seeing and living— ways of life both determined by, and opposed to, colonial domination—into a 'Black British' way of being" (Grewal et al.). See also Stuart Hall's comment on the "Black British" movement and its possibilities for rethinking ideas of race in "New Ethnicities" in Kobena Mercer's *Black Film, British Cinema.*

Even while I agree with Lorde's reservations about the term "black," her suggested alternative, "African," carries similar problems. It replaces a generic term of color with a term of geography that is in fact no less generic when we think about the organization of communities within the continent. This usage is particularly vexed for the early modern period, since Africa, as we see it in modern cartography, did not exist for the writers with whom I am dealing.

Although, as Lorde points out, I risk erasing very real and significant cultural differences, for this project that risk is superseded by the problem of working with representations of diasporic people whose self-determined cultural identity is largely lost to me. "Black" encompasses the peoples of the African diaspora without having to make attributions of nationality and culture that have been erased from historical records or do not obtain in the early period. For example, is an African just brought to the American colonies "African-American"? Similarly, should African slaves brought to England (and expelled) before 1600 be called Afro-English or Afro-British? Rather than negotiate such tangled thickets in this space, I adopt the simple, albeit problematic, nomenclature: "black."

The critical dismissal of an aesthetic of fairness as mere "fashion"— and thus not to be taken seriously—overlooks the ways in which "fashion" also works to circumscribe women.[14] Even scholars of the black presence in the period who have made the link between the language of dark and light and the representations of darker-skinned peoples pay only cursory attention to the ways in which this language, especially in connection to

14. Leslie Fiedler's *The Stranger in Shakespeare* is perhaps the best-known example of a scholarship that insists on the importance of "difference" or "Others" but denies the racial politics of this presence; he resorts to complex verbal gymnastics to "prove" that the black/fair dichotomy is far removed from modern notions of race. In attempting to disassociate *Othello* from American ideas of miscegenation, he somewhat perversely asserts that the use of the word "fair" as an antonym to "black" is precisely what indicates that the language is not racialized. This assertion is bolstered with Fiedler's claim that Shakespeare uses the terms "hue" or "complexion" when speaking of black or fair and that because these terms derive from humoral discourse, they are consequently not racialized. Paradoxically, he reads Othello as African but not as a racial subject: "But this means that for Shakespeare 'black' does not primarily describe an ethnic distinction (though, of course, Othello is meant to be perceived as an African, thick-lipped as well as dusky-hued), but a difference in hue—and temperament—distinguishing from another even what we would identify as members of the same white race" (170–71). Fiedler's attempt to explore the idea of the "stranger" while resolutely denying Anglo-American racial formations politically aligns it with more contemporary strategies of erasing race, a point I will take up in the Epilogue. On the *Othello* question Karen Newman's essay " 'And wash the Ethiop white': Femininity and the Monstrous in *Othello*," in its upfront acknowledgment not only of Othello's "blackness" but of the way ideologies of white and black work together, offers a welcome corrective to Fiedler's approach even though she privileges gender difference over race at the same time that she provides evidence for the profound interaction of the categories.

race, is highly gendered. Frequently, "black" in Renaissance discourses is opposed not to "white" but to "beauty" or "fairness," and these terms most often refer to the appearance or moral states of women, as in Puttenham's derisive example that a black woman is the opposite of fair. This is not to say that men are not "fair" or "black" in this discourse, but that the terms acquire a special force when they are turned to women and that they are most frequently used in relation to women. Peter Fryer, drawing from Winthrop Jordan, begins his discussion of the "demonology of race" with the dark/light polarity: "The very words 'black' and 'white' were heavily charged with meaning long before the English met people whose skins were black. Blackness, in England, traditionally stood for death, mourning, baseness, evil, sin and danger. . . . White, on the other hand, was the colour of purity, virginity, innocence, good magic, flags of truce, harmless lies, and perfect human beauty" (135). Most of the terms associated with white in Fryer's list are also the issues that are primal concerns in early modern culture. Moreover, "white" is attached to values—purity, virginity, and innocence—represented by (or notably absent in) women.

In practice this means that the polarity of dark and light is most often worked out in representations of black men and white women. The black/white opposition posits a special relationship between white femininity and black masculinity that is negotiated in artistic representation, discursive practices, and social modes. This dependence on black men to define fairness appears most startlingly in the black servant portraits I discuss in the last chapter. Concern over the whiteness of English women and the blackness of African men (and the mixture of both) projects onto the bodies of white women the anxieties of an evolving monarchial nation-state in which women are the repository of the symbolic boundaries of the nation (Enloe 42; Yuval-Davis 9–10). When white women bear the symbolic weight of the culture in this way, attention is deflected from the equally vulnerable bodies of white men and the potentially threatening bodies of black women. For example, John Evelyn's diary describes a dinner party with a Moroccan ambassador that "placed about a long Table a Lady betweene two Moores: viz: a Moore, then a Woman, then a Moore &c . . ." (4:268). The practice, as well as Evelyn's description, suggests that whiteness and fairness must be made visible with the addition of "Moores" whenever the opportunity arises and that the black/white binarism shapes social occasions as well as discursive practices. Instead of merely focusing on the dominant conjunction of black men and white women, as in Evelyn's entry, this book questions the ways in which such representations work to configure silently the whiteness and masculinity that, as in the case of Evelyn, controls the representation.

Although this book outlines a semiotics of race in early modern English culture generally, this discursive network manifests itself most obviously within certain literary conventions. I have thus found it advantageous to arrange the chapters by genre, not so much to focus on genre per se as to use the perspectives of different genres to reveal clearly certain themes and tropes. The first chapter grounds the discussion by focusing on travel narratives, particularly descriptions of Africa, and demonstrates that the dissemination of cultural myths of race rests on gendered representations of alien cultures through the submission of those cultures to the discipline of European rhetorical and cultural order. Chapter 2 then turns to lyric poetry, focusing particularly on the language of English Petrarchism that provides the basic "grammar" for the discursive field of race. More specifically, I contend that the English sonnet relies on a process of conversion of black to white that supports English competition for new world trade and that works to alleviate particularly aristocratic anxieties over their unusual involvement in merchant trade as well as more general anxieties over extending traditional patterns of commerce and diplomacy to stranger nations. Sir Philip Sidney's *Astrophel and Stella* is the touchstone of the chapter, and I use the individual poems in the sequence as catalysts for larger discussions of three conceits—sunburn, cosmetics, and whitewashing—which specifically work to introduce and structure racial attitudes. The chapter closes with a survey of later poems that are either specifically on African difference and miscegenation or that trope African difference in striking ways. These poems (reprinted in the appendix) clearly are the heirs to the poetic challenges and the more elusive practices of the sonnet; moreover, their appearance retroactively suggests that poets and their readers understood the racial valences of the sonnet language at its inception.

The third chapter turns to the play of race on stage, suggesting that James I brought to England his own fascination with Africans and exotic commodities and that blackness in the Jacobean period mediates cultural anxieties over England's imperial expansion, particularly the creation of *Great* Britain. Whereas this chapter is more concerned with attempts to bridge the black/white polarity with images of "mixture," the final two chapters focus on ideologies of fairness and the specific ways in which blackness is used to create a value for whiteness. Chapter 4 demonstrates that fairness becomes a necessary medium for shaping the subjectivity of white English women through a reading of blackness in Lady Mary Wroth's *The Countess of Montgomerie's Urania* and points out in Wroth's work a specifically female investment in and resistance to England's imperial project. Chapter 5 examines blackness in visual culture and contends that certain representations draw upon Petrarchan dynamics to negotiate issues of gender and property. It finds in the popular black cameos that circulated in Elizabeth's court a visual analogue to the language of blackness in the sonnets and then turns to a specific genre—the black servant portrait—to examine how Petrarchan poetics and ideas of white power and black servitude are incorporated into this key signifier of white aristocratic wealth and identity.

Who Is English? The Black Presence in England

> I my selfe have seene an Ethiopian as blacke as a cole brought into England, who taking a faire English woman to wife, begat a sonne in all respects as blacke as the father was, although England were his native countrey, and an English woman his mother: whereby it seemeth this blacknes proceedeth rather of some natural infection of that man, which was so strong, that neither the nature of the Clime, neither the good complexion of the mother concurring, coulde any thing alter, and therefore, we cannot impute it to the nature of the Clime.
> —George Best, in Hakluyt, *Principal Navigations*

The evidence for the black presence, particularly in the Tudor period, is often gathered from narratives such as this description of an Ethiopian-English marriage printed in George Best's 1578 description of Frobisher's search for a northwest passage. Since travel and trade with African cultures was often not reciprocal (that is, English traders went to the markets of Guinea and Barbary, but African traders rarely went to England) and blacks were not necessarily recognized even as a marginalized population (unlike servants, the poor, witches, etc.), evidence for an African presence is minimal. There are no extant firsthand accounts from the black Tudor population. However, the status of black people as curiosities or oddities meant that they were considered both as individual "cases" and as emblematic of a larger group. Best's anecdotal evidence that the blackness of this Ethiopian man is due not to exposure to the sun but to an "infection" is less important for its evidence that there was racial intermarriage in England than for its articulation of the cultural anxieties—about complexion, miscegenation, control of women, and, above all, "Englishness"—brought out by the presence of blacks.

Best's attempt to locate the nature of human somatic differences is not an innocent involvement with the "other." This passage demonstrates the "binary system of representation [that] constantly marks and attempts to fix and naturalize the difference between belongingness and otherness" that is typical of racist discourse (S. Hall, "New Ethnicities" 28). There are certain value judgments already at work when Best notes the lack of efficacy of the land and the woman, "neither the good nature of the clime, neither the good complexion of the mother concurring." Both the complexion of the "faire English woman" and the clime are characterized as "good," which immediately positions white/black on the same conceptual grid as the good/evil dichotomy. His formulation also associates England with whiteness, because "the nature of the Clime" is rhetorically associated with the "good complexion" of the mother. To heighten the threat of blackness, it is paradoxically seen as invisible, as an infection, a troping that works to naturalize the difference between the black man and his white wife as well as to demonstrate the seeming vulnerability of female bodies.

That Best's ultimate proof of the power and stability of blackness is found not in Africa but in England, in the marriage of an Ethiopian to a "faire English woman," indicates that blackness for him really has meaning only in relation to whiteness. This particular passage is part of Best's attempt to assure his readers that English adventurers will not be affected by African climates: "Wee also among us in England have blacke Moores, Æthiopians, out of all partes of Torrida Zona, which after a small continuance, can well endure the colde of our Countrey, and why should not we as well abide the heate of their Countrey?" (Hakluyt, *Principal Navigations* 5:172). This anxiety over the significance of whiteness is also linked to his concern over the meaning of Englishness. "England" and "English" are repeated obsessively in the previous passage, and the repetition only heightens the son's exclusion from the category "English" because of his blackness ("although England were his native countrey"). To include him in the nation would be to break the desired homology between land, skin, and group identity, thereby overturning the associations of England with whiteness and fairness. As Paul Gilroy notes for a later period, the passage acts "to reproduce blackness and Englishness as mutually exclusive categories" (55).

These concerns with the nature and origins of blackness crop up again and again in Renaissance texts. Fifty years later, Sir Thomas Browne devotes three chapters of his *Pseudodoxia Epidemica* to "the blackness of Negros," querying "Why some men, yea, and they a mighty and considerable part of mankinde, should first acquire and still retaine the glosse and tincture of blacknesse?" (508). Returning to Best's initial inquiries, Browne uses emergent scientific method to bring to the forefront what was only implied in Best's text: the opposition of blackness to fairness and beauty. He ends his second chapter on blackness with a digression on beauty, indicating that the categories of blackness and beauty are mutually dependent. Although Browne shows a good deal more cultural relativism (for example, he reminds the reader that blackness cannot properly be called a curse, because of its "neither seeming so to them, nor reasonably unto us" [520]), his language is as infused with value judgments related to color as is Best's; he claims that "they of Europe in Candy, Sicily, and some parts of Spaine," while dark, do not deserve "so low a name as Tawny" and that the inhabitants of the "torrid zone" "descend not so low as unto blacknesse" (512). Both Best's and Browne's concerns about the blackness of Africans ultimately spring from larger concerns about the stability of whiteness. They also share the assumption that blackness is an aberration and whiteness the original: in Browne's words, blackness is a trait "acquired" by Africans. The methods of both of these authors suggest that the traditional assumption that the religious difference of "Moors" is the primary threat to English culture does not tell the whole story.[15] Clearly, what interests Best, Browne, and the many writers who participated in this debate, even indirectly, is the problem that dark skin and certain physical features posed for a culture that believed that God made man in his own image.

Africans in early modern England often exist for contemporary readers of the period in the realm of the anecdote. As with Best's description, they appear—in isolated entries of parish records and diaries or in fleeting moments in literary texts—unnamed (or renamed) and stripped of a history of their own. Their personal histories are often replaced with a more overtly symbolic function than is seen in Best. For example, the records of the Sackville family indicate a hundred-year tradition of having a servant who was always named "John Morocco," which suggests that he is valued not so much for his status as laborer as for his symbolic capacity (Sackville-West 191–92).[16] So too, the masque in *Love's Labour's Lost* calls for "blackmoors with music" (5.2), which indicates that their blackness was integral to their performance. Even in moments that would seem to demonstrate that black people were a larger cultural presence, such as

15. This assumption is even more perturbing when it comes from someone who would be expected to think more critically about the problem. See, for example, Anthony Appiah's entry "Race" in *Critical Terms for Literary Study*. He claims, "There is good reason, then, to interpret these Elizabethan stereotypes, which *we* might naturally think of as what I have called "racialist," as rooted far less in notions of inherited dispositions and far more in the idea of the Moor and the Jew as infidels, unbelivers whose physical differences are signs (but not causes or effects) of their unbelief" (278).

16. The diary of Lady Anne Clifford also records a black laundress named Grace Robinson. Obviously, her presence was more directly tied to labor and contributes to her invisibility. For a discussion of this diary and of the intersections of race and gender, see my essay "Reading What Isn't There: 'Black' Studies in Early Modern England."

Elizabeth I's attempted expulsion of the Moors in 1596 and 1601, their significance is belied by their actual numbers.[17] These elusive appearances resonate throughout the texts of English culture and have an importance that is belied by the seeming arbitrariness of their presentation. Just as Toni Morrison discovers in American literature that "even, and especially, when American texts are not 'about' Africanist presence or characters or narrative or idiom, the shadow hovers in implication, in sign, in line of demarcation" (*Playing* 46–47), I find that the impact of the Africanist presence on white English subjectivity can never be fully understood if one focuses only on the texts (such as *Othello*) that are "about" blackness.

In this book I am especially concerned with just those "shadows" and "lines of demarcation" that Morrison outlines rather than with the more obvious Africanist presences. I am more interested in discerning the ways in which the Africanist presence is embedded in language than with proving the nature of the black presence in England. In his recent study of racial imagery in the Dutch world, the historian Allison Blakely finds that "the existence of color prejudice in a predominately 'white' society does not require the presence of racial conflict or even of a significant 'colored' population" (xvi). I too have found that the significance of blackness as a troping of race far exceeds the actual presence of African-descended people in England. Methodologically, the existence of blacks in narrative or fragmentary moments means that this project has been greatly indebted to reading practices grouped under the rubric "new historicism." In particular, the reliance of "new historicism" on anecdotes as narratives with particular cultural weight and resonance has meant that one can bring figures into history whose significance might be lost with traditional literary criticism and historiography.[18]

Ironically, despite their interest in the "alien" or "marginal" in English culture, many of the more prominent new historicists have paid little more than cursory attention to the role that both gender and racial assumptions played in developing notions of identity.[19] Although they have brought

17. For a discussion of the proclamation of expulsion, see my essays "Guess Who's Coming to Dinner? Colonization and Miscegenation in *The Merchant of Venice*" and "Reading What Isn't There: 'Black' Studies in Early Modern England."

18. "Taking their cue from Geertz's method of 'thick description' they [new historicists] seize upon an event or anecdote . . . and re-read it in such a way as to reveal through the analysis of tiny particulars the behavioral codes, logics, and motive forces controlling a whole society" (Veeser xi).

19. See, for example, the opening of Greenblatt's *Renaissance Self-Fashioning*, which outlines the shaping of aristocratic identity against a projected other: "Self-fashioning is achieved in relation to something perceived as alien, strange or hostile. This threatening Other—heretic, savage, witch, adulteress, traitor, Antichrist—must be discovered or invented in order

heretofore unseen populations to literary analysis, they provide little guid-
ance in understanding the complexities of early modern racial discourses.
Thus although my work might be recognizable as new historicist, it is
rooted in feminist practices and is more indebted to the work of women
of color within feminist movement than traditional scholarly forms of recognition would indicate. As Patricia Williams has claimed for her current
work, I, too, have found that "extrinsic sources and intuitive means of
reading may be the only ways to include the reality of the unwritten,
unnamed, nontext of race" (117). Here Williams articulates a practice of
resistant reading that seems key to an enterprise of this sort. To claim
that there is a "text of race" means at times to refuse to accept both the
authority of the writers I work with and to resist the hegemony of white
male knowledge in the academy. I use "intuitive means of reading" in
the sense that my reading of dominant culture is fundamentally shaped
by knowledge that is in fact taught in African-American communities
about "white" culture.[20] I also draw from "extrinsic sources" when I suggest alternative readings and viewpoints regarding the subjects of colonial
rule that are largely absent in the period: these "alternative viewpoints"
rely heavily on black feminists such as bell hooks, Angela Davis, and the
late Audre Lorde, who have been clear voices of opposition to modern
imperialist and racist practices.[21] I argue in the Epilogue for the importance of black feminist methodology in this type of work and here will
simply say that the entire project is built on black feminists' insistence on
both the interconnection of race, gender, and other forms of oppression
and on the need to interrogate whiteness as a social construct.[22]

---

to be attacked and destroyed" (9). His formulation, oddly enough, omits race, even though
it includes almost every other possible category.

20. Patricia Hill Collins speaks more specifically about the "everday" knowledge of black
feminists: "The ideas we share with one another as mothers in extended families, as other-
mothers in Black communities, as members of Black churches, and as teachers to the Black
community's children have formed one pivotal area where African-American women have
hammered out a Black woman's standpoint" (15).

21. Unlike Ronald Sanders, who outlines similar methodological problems in his *Lost
Tribes and Promised Lands*, I do not feel that my viewpoint must be shaped by the materials I
work with as he claims: "Now, in the case of two of our main characters—the Black and the
Indian—such firsthand written material does not really exist from this period. We are forced,
for the most part, to adopt the viewpoint of the oppressive but highly articulate white man"
(xiv). Rather, I adopt from Patricia Hill Collins the reminder that much of the knowledge
produced by the "highly articulate white man" is "permeated by widespread notions of black
and female inferiority" and that these notions make resistant projects such as this one immediately suspect.

22. Toni Morrison has been the most recent advocate of the necessity of analyzing whiteness. In *Playing in the Dark*, she argues: "We need studies of the technical ways in which an
Africanist character is used to limn out and enforce the invention and implications of white-

Pirates, Poets, and Traders: England and African Trades

While the anecdote and "thick description" popularized in literary criticism by Clifford Geertz have proved useful for unearthing a cultural discourse of blackness and discerning its potential significance, they do not
tell the entire story and may imply that black people were viewed only as
singular or strange and were therefore only peripheral to the culture. In
actuality, Africa, particularly the darker peoples of the central interior and
southern portions of the continent, played a key role in the rapid change
of England from "an underdeveloped country" in its own right to the
empire that would dominate the globe for the next two centuries (Rabb
1). This period saw the beginnings of England's exposure to the African
interior that culminated in the later journeys of Stanley and Burton in
the Victorian era.

The rise in English travel and trade and the consequent emergence of
England as a naval power greatly shaped the English character and was
the focus of much of its energies. The historian James Williamson notes,
"The search for markets wider than Europe could offer became a national
duty and instinct" (34). Nonetheless, most work done on early modern
English colonialism, particularly by new historicists, focuses on the newly
discovered lands and colonies in the Americas. While the Spanish-
American trade was massive, it was rivaled in potential by the Portuguese
trade with Africa (Andrews 11). The many ways in which African trade
provided the practice, theory, and impetus for English trade remain un-
remarked. Geographically and conceptually, Africa was crucial to English
travel in the Atlantic. Three of the four major routes to the Americas
involved passage through African waters, and it was the attempt to avoid
the arduous journey around the Cape of Good Hope (a route controlled
by the Portuguese) that generated the frantic search for alternative routes.
Charles Verlinden notes the primacy of Africa in the change from a Mediterranean to an Atlantic economy: "Africa is fatally linked to this zone
by the early and even present maritime transportation systems, since its
economic connections with the rest of the world have been vital to its
existence from the moment when European expansion forced it into contact with the exterior world" (75). The map literally changed almost moment by moment, and although the most interior parts of Africa had not
been explored by the English, more and more of the interior was being
explored and charted by European traders and cartographers.

---

ness" (52). See also Peter Erickson's discussion of *Playing in the Dark* in his essay "Profiles
in Whiteness."

England began its involvement in what was known as the Barbary and Guinea trades during Elizabeth I's reign when merchants who dealt in Iberian trade began to see and act on the weaknesses of Portugal's hold on Africa. In his study of Elizabethan privateering, Kenneth Andrews finds that "in the fifties the commercial penetration of Morocco and Guinea assumed serious proportions, and the leaders of this movement in England were the Iberian traders" (11). Andrews goes on to note that this trade differed from ordinary commercial practices "not only in scale but kind," offering unheard-of profit as well as new goods (11). As we shall see, this sense of wealth and novelty infuses English literature and is tied to representations of race. The region known as Barbary covered most of the coastline between Tripoli and the Atlantic (Willan 92). The meeting ground between the eastern trade and African lands to the south, it was a key route for the ancient trade in black slaves and gold (Clissold 17). After the colonization of the Americas the area known as Barbary increased in importance because it became the site where Spain and Portugal maintained their connections with the "mines of India" evoked with such regularity in English texts.

Both the Barbary and Guinea trades developed sporadically and were unregulated for over thirty years, largely because Portugal still maintained its (repeatedly ignored) entitlement to the trade. Consequently, both trades involved ongoing patterns of complaint and reply from Portugal to England: the Portuguese tended to couple Morocco and Guinea together in their protests against English trade with Africa, but in doing so they laid much greater stress on their claim to a monopoly of the Guinea trade than on their claim to exclude others from the Moroccan trade (Willan 140). Travel in these areas gave rise to both legitimate, negotiated trade and the privateering so characteristic of the age. This is particularly true of the Moroccan trade because it crossed the Spanish routes to the Indies, which meant that English traders would have had access to the slave trade in Spain (Willan 220). As a model that England both followed and distanced itself from, Spain has a particularly complex role: it fostered the lucrative trade in gold and slaves and had its own involvement with a threatening darker "other" through its history of Moorish invasion and conquest. Having no African properties of its own, Spain relied on Portugal for the steady supply of slaves to run the sugar mills and gold mines that were the source of its jealously guarded wealth.

England's increasing involvement with these trades was a source of contention between English traders as well as between England and other European countries. In 1589, one of Walsingham's staff complained about the overabundance of English merchants: "Outbidding one annother in the price of Barbary commodityes thorough the envy and mallice that raigneth among them" (quoted in Willan 268). Although they began as individual ventures, trading voyages into Africa became increasingly regulated during Elizabeth's reign: companies formed by traders and aristocrats were given monopolies for various trades. Most of these ventures were formed by royal charter, and their precarious fortunes culminated in establishment of the Royal Company of Adventurers Trading into Africa in 1663, which was the first such company that had an expressed purpose of slave trading.[23]

The late Tudor–early Stuart periods were the site of "the most striking transformations in economic history" (Rabb 2). These transformations were particularly notable in the wide use of joint-stock companies and the involvement of aristocrats to a degree unprecedented anywhere in Europe. Thus the class that was in great part responsible for the great flowering of vernacular literature in the Elizabethan period was simultaneously involved in laying the groundwork for Britain's future economic advancement. The aristocracy and landowning gentry helped shape England's trade through their involvement in joint-stock companies and their support of privateering ventures (Andrews 11–13). Elizabeth's powerful adviser and noted literary patron, the earl of Leicester, was given unprecedented power in the formation of the Barbary Company in 1585 (Willan 187). One of the century's leading figures, Sir Philip Sidney, attempted to use Sir Francis Drake's voyage to the West Indies as an outlet for his frustrated ambitions. Princes, privateers, and poets were all connected in court and diplomatic politics, and many sought to enrich themselves through encroaching on the Portuguese monopoly on African trade. Although this book does not deal as directly with class differences, it must be said that the discourses of fairness were by and large shaped by this aristocratic class, which may have been anxious over its novel involvement in mercantile adventure.

23. In 1588, rights to the trade of the Guinea Coast between Senegal and the Gambia were granted to a company of London and west-country merchants (Willan 139). The trading giant, the East India Company, began as a modest enterprise in 1600. The West Africa Company was incorporated in 1618 for trading in Guinea and Benin (Lipson 354). In 1631, Charles I began the precarious Royal African Companies, which had as their main purpose the trade in gold and ivory. By the next year, the English had a factory at Winneba, and they began their first fort in Coramantin in 1638 (Davies 115). That company was superseded by the "Company of Royal Adventurers into Africa," formed in 1660, and was itself reformulated—with the first explicit mention of slaving in the company charter—as the Royal Company of Adventurers Trading into Africa in 1663. Although slaving was a by-product of the African trade in the earlier companies, after the Restoration the trade became more dominated by slave trade as merchants attempted to fill the demand for slaves in England's West Indian colonies (Lipson 271).

African voyages were truly the nursery to English seamen. Later maritime luminaries such as Sir Francis Drake and Martin Frobisher got their first sea experience on the African voyages of those founding fathers of the English slave trade—the Hawkins family. African trade became a way for such merchants to rise in class and was early on a marker of wealth and identity. The colonization of the Gold Coast by Portugal began in 1471 with the concession of Sierra Leone to Fernão Gomes, who was rewarded with a title and a coat of arms showing "the heads of three negroes wearing collars and pendants of gold" (Vilar 53). John Hawkins, who demonstrated the weakness of Portugal's hold on those colonies and initiated England's involvement in the slave trade, was similarly rewarded with a coat of arms: "Sable, on a point wavy a lion passant or; in chief three bezants; for a crest, a demi-Moor proper bound in a cord" (Williamson 113–14) (figure 2). The use of not only blackness but black people with badges of slavery is an ongoing way of demarcating status. As we shall see later, many aristocratic portraits included servants also wearing gold or silver collars, bringing to bear a similar set of associations between aristocratic white bodies, black servitude, and foreign wealth.

England was also connected in both direct and indirect ways to the traffic in slaves and the opening of heretofore unknown sections of Africa. That England's first involvement in slave trading occurs in the 1550s suggests that slave trading was from the first an integral part of the African trade. England's domestic politics, economy, and international affairs and the European slave trade in Africa increasingly met and became sites of contest in the Elizabethan period. England's trading practices in Africa soon put it into dispute with Spain and Portugal. Much of the conflict with Portugal over England's African trade centered on English attempts to break into the traffic in slaves. During Mary's reign, the Portuguese dominated African trade, supplying slaves to the Spanish Indies in exchange for gold and goods throughout Europe both by right of first exploration and by military might. This right was also confirmed by papal dispensation, and under the Catholic Mary there was virtually no involvement in slave trafficking. Nonetheless the potential profits of the trade held some allure for Englishmen, and a syndicate of London fitted out five ships to explore the Guinea coast in 1554 (Donnan 9).[24]

24. Elizabeth Donnan notes an early, abortive attempt at the slave trade: "In 1481 rumor reached Portugal that two Englishmen, William Fabian and John Tintam, were equipping an expedition for Guinea trade. John II. of Portugal promptly protested that this violated the terms of his papal privileges, and the voyage was stayed. About the same time Edward IV. of England asked the pope for permission to trade in Africa but nothing came of his request" (1:6).

Figure 2. A re-creation of the Hawkins coat of arms. It was augmented after Sir John Hawkins's (1532–1595) second slave trading voyage with a crest described as "a demi-Moor proper bound in a cord." (Library of Congress.)

It was under Elizabeth that England gained a foothold in the Atlantic trade. In 1552, John Lok sold the first slaves that he captured in Guinea. In 1562, John Hawkins sounded the death knell to Portugal's hold over its trade routes by taking three hundred slaves pirated from Portuguese ships to the West Indies. Afterward, some of Elizabeth's closest advisors, such as Robert Dudley and William Cecil, expressed interest in the trade (Donnan 47), and Elizabeth herself surreptitiously supported the voyages. Of necessity, Elizabeth's reign was characterized by official reticence and actual aggression toward the African trade. Often during the next forty years Portugal complained of English piracy and encroachments. After one such protest, Lord Cecil told the Spanish ambassador, Guzman de Silva, that he was offered a role in the trade, "but that he refused as he did not like such adventures" (de Silva; 5 November 1565 in Donnan 1:59). Likewise, even as Elizabeth officially ordered Hawkins not to attempt the Guinea trade she lent him ships and equipment necessary for his privateering.[25] The Guinea Company, which became the first organized, legitimate venue for the African trade, was formed after Elizabeth's recognition of Don Antonio as king of Portugal (Willan 139).

Unfortunately, the importance of the early slave trade is underdocumented because of its surreptitious nature. However, there is evidence that merchants had detailed knowledge of the mechanics of the trade. The depositions surrounding Hawkins's third voyage reveal specifics of the capture and sale of slaves. Merchant William Fowler of Ratcliffe in 1569 alleged that "the best trade in those places [Vera Cruz and the West Indies] is of Negros" and describes the trade:

> That by the experience of the trade which he hathe had to and at the saide place called Vera Crux and other the cheiffe of the West Indias as is aforesaid this deponent knowethe that a Negro of a good stature and yonge of yeres is worthe and is commonlie bought and soulde there at Mexico and the maine lande of the West Indias for iiiᶜvᶜ and viᶜ pesos. For if a negro be a Bossale that is to say ignorant of the spanishe or Portugale tonge then he or she is commonlye soulde for iiiiᶜ and iiiiᶜ L [450] pesos. (Donnan 1:72)

James I created the Company of Adventurers of London Trading into Parts of Africa in 1618 and granted to Robert Rich "control over the trade on the explored east coast of Barbary" (Donnan 78). This company would build the first English factory in Africa. Between 1624 and 1630 the Guinea trade was legitimized, and by 1637 the Guinea Company complained that another group was infringing on its monopoly: "Resolving under pretence of going to Barbary to trade upon the coasts of Guinea and to take nigers, and to carry them to other foreign parts" (Thirsk and Cooper 489), indicating that slave trading was a lucrative part of their business. Although it was not until the late seventeenth century that England became a major participant in the slave trade, the weakening of Iberian control over the trade meant that the English, the French, and

25. In a letter to Philip II (12 July 1567), the Spanish ambassador Guzman de Silva reports: "I hear that the ships Hawkins is going to take out are being got ready rapidly and I am now told that there are to be nine of them, four of the queen's and five which Hawkins has in Plymouth, where they say the others are to join them" (Donnan 63).

the Dutch began redrawing its configuration and competing for the crucial rights to the slave trade that would provide the necessary labor to buttress their other colonial ambitions.

To return to my opening, how, then, do we read "the unnamed, nontext of race" of *A Midsummer Night's Dream?* Rather than see Lysander's denigration and dismissal of Hermia ("Away you Ethiop"; "Out, tawny Tartar") as an isolated reference to brunette hair, we might look at it in conjunction with the play's concerns with trade and gender politics. Louis Montrose's influential reading of the play has already exposed it as a site of gender struggle that works out anxieties of male subjects to a powerful queen. What is also apparent is that here threatening female sexuality and power is located in the space of the foreign: male, Grecian order is opposed to the dark, feminine world of the forest, which is also replete with Indians, Tartars, and "Ethiops."

A play about marriage and the proper pairing of male and female, *A Midsummer Night's Dream* is rooted in questions about the value of women who are the means for the appropriate transfer of property and forming of bloodlines (Parker 122–23). As Puttenham's remark in my opening epigraph suggests, "black" women—real or rhetorical—are coded as the ultimate in undesirability and thus are not suitable objects of social exchange. Lysander's "Away you Ethiop" assigns a value to women as property and resonates more powerfully than the gibe about Hermia's height (particularly since the now-desired Helena is "this princess of pure white, this seal of bliss!" [3.2.144; Erickson 518]). The Ethiop and the Tartar are undesirable partners in marriage, and the epithet evokes the unlawful mixing that so much of the play is about. None of the women marked with the language of blackness are at that moment desired partners in marriage. Oberon is married to the temporarily disobedient Titania rather than to the "buskin'd warrior"; Theseus is about to be married to a tamed Amazon, and at the moment that he is affected by the drug Lysander characterizes his love as an Ethiop to denote her absolute undesirability as a sexual or marriage partner: "Who will not change a raven for a dove?" (2.2.114). In his study of how the dark/light dichotomy marks Shakespeare's love comedies, Peter Erickson notes that "this language is sharpened by the edge Lysander gives to his dismissal of Hermia" (518). Conversely, at the height of Hermia's desirability, Helena obsessively comments on Hermia's "fairness" as a sign of male approval. In both instances, the evocation of blackness serves to racialize whiteness and make it visible.

As I have attempted to indicate, most tropes of blackness operate within

a larger discursive network; in this play blackness is associated with femaleness, foreignness, political upheaval, and chaos. More specifically, the
"Ethiop" epithet must be read along with the presence of the Indian maid
and the eroticized language of merchant adventure that is associated with
her. "Indian trade" often involved some trade with Africa. For example,
the "East Indies" often took in "the whole littoral of East Africa and of
Asia" in merchant discourse (Furber 7). Furthermore, this eroticized language of merchant adventure appears in conjunction with a disturbance
of traditional wooing and marriage in much the same way that *The Merchant of Venice* interweaves trade with other lands with the traffic in women.

We might then turn to a little-discussed context for the play that suggests a historical use of black people as decorative signifiers. Many of the
play's editors have made the link between the mechanicals' concerns that
Snug's lion would frighten the ladies in the audience and an entertainment at the christening of James I's son, Prince Henry Frederick, which
was planned to include a chariot "which should been drawne in by a
lion" (Scott 179). In the actual entertainment, the lion was removed for
fear he would disrupt the performance: "(but because his presence
might have brought some feare to the nearest, or that the sight of the
lights and torches might have commoved his tameness) it was thought
meete that the Moor should supply that roome" (Scott 179). A "black-
moor" thus became the chief feature of the feast, bringing the last
course, or banquet:

> Now, being thus in a very honourable and comely order set, and after a while,
> having well refreshed themselves with the first service, which was very sump-
> tuous, there came into the sight of them all, a blackmoor, drawing (as it
> seemed to the beholders) a triumphal chariot, (and before it the melodious
> noise of trumpets and hautboyes) which chariot entered the hall; the motion
> of the whole frame (which was twelve feet long, and seven feet broad) was
> so artificial within itself, that it appeared to be drawne in, onely by the
> strength of a Moor, which was very richly attired; his traces were great
> chaines of pure gold. (Scott 179)

> Upon this chariot was finely and artificially devised, a sumptuous covered
> table, decked with all sorts of exquisite delicates and dainties, of patisserie,
> frutages, and confections.
> About the table were placed six gallant dames, who represented a silent
> comedie . . . (Scott 179)

Instead of a tamed lion, this audience is given a "blackmoor," here displayed "with pomp, with triumph and with revelling" (*Midsummer Night's*

Dream 1.1.19). The entertainment demonstrates the "aesthetic" uses of enslaved black people; the man's "traces" or bridle "of pure gold" are merely a more aestheticized version of the chained blackmoors added to Sir William Hawkins's coat of arms. The banquet itself, like Titania's "Indian maid" speech, enacts the desires of merchant trade when the ship enters with Neptune, dressed in "Indian silks," on its bow. Both entertainments rely on a display of women as audience and spectacle; more important, both offer a troping of blackness, a use of difference associated with Africa to express European luxury, wealth, and beauty. The actual appropriation of the Moor's body in James's court resurfaces in the rhetorical evocation of Ethiopes and Tartars in Elizabeth's.

CHAPTER ONE

A World of Difference: Travel Narratives and the Inscription of Culture

> She is spherical, like a globe; I could find
> out countries in her.
>
> — *The Comedy of Errors*

Positioned very early to be interchangeable, tropes of disorder, racial otherness, and unruly sexuality become the terms by which European expansion first appropriates the strange newness of the lands "discovered" in the Renaissance. In the earliest travel narratives, African societies are not automatically dismissed as savage "other," as happens in later colonial narratives, but are judged according to their projected malleability to Eurocentric forces. What cultural chaos the early travelers saw, they perceived primarily in terms of gender: a disorder that, while similar to the full alterity and far more threatening strangeness that postcolonial critic Abdul R. JanMohamed outlines in his discussion of later colonialist literature, would itself have been recognizable by the male European as a disorder more amenable to the imposition of European order.[1] The chief sign of cultural disorder in the earlier texts is gender, specifically a sense of the instability of gender, thus allowing for an easy slippage between the concerns about the alienness of race and the unruliness of women.[2] Issues

---

1. According to JanMohamed, colonialist literature is "an exploration and a representation of a world at the boundaries of 'civilization,' a world that has not (yet) been domesticated by European signification or codified in detail by its ideology. That world is therefore perceived as uncontrollable, chaotic, unattainable, and ultimately evil. Motivated by his desire to conquer and dominate, the imperialist configures his colonial realm as a confrontation based on differences in race, language, social customs, cultural values, and modes of production" (83).

2. Louis A. Montrose makes a comparable argument for new world narratives: "The topic of sexual conduct can become a point of convergence for a multiplicity of discourses—among them, gender, ethnicity, nationality, and social estate" ("Work of Gender" 19).

of cultural propriety and narrative order are mutually inflected in that the concern over both shapes these narratives and their "interpretation" of cultures.

The fantastic tales that first formed the popular conceptions of Africa preserved an image of an Africa that is out of joint with itself, internally chaotic. Even before the first appearance of the 1499 English translation of the popular *Travels of Sir John Mandeville*, some of the most enduring images—the Blemmye and the Anthropophagi, for instance—were those of people who are literally "out of joint":

> . . . and in one of these Iles are men that have but one eye, and that is in the middest of their front, and they eate not but flesh and fish all raw. And in another Ile dwell men that have no heads, and their eyes are in their shoulders, and their mouth is on their breast. In another Ile are men that have no head ne eyes, & their mouth is in their shoulders. And in another Ile are men that have flat faces without nose, and without eyes, but they have two small round holes in stead of eyes, and they have a flat mouth without lips. And in that Ile are men also that have their faces all flat without eyes, without mouth, and without nose, but they have their eyes & their mouth behind on their shoulders. (O2r-O3r)

Bakhtin has suggested that the grotesque bodies of these monstrous races serve in this period to affirm dialectically the ordered, classical body of the European elite (325).[3] Such a fantasized physical difference is only a more extreme embodied sign of an entire set of actual differences by which Europeans constructed a vision of Africa. While Mandeville exhibits a degree of cultural relativism in his views on color (in the same manner as Sir Thomas Browne), the body is still a prime signifier of cultural difference. A reader of Mandeville would see Africa as a place not only of grotesque bodies but of continual abrogation of European models for gender, marriage, and rule. For example, in his introduction to "Ethiopia," Mandeville's description of the country leaves its reader with an overwhelming sense of incontinence and the ambiguity of physical boundaries:

> In this land the rivers and all the waters are troubled and some [yield] salt for the great heate, and men of that land are lightly dronken, and have little appetite to meate, and they have commonly the fl[u]x of body, and they live

---

3. Peter Stallybrass addresses the absence of gender in Bakhtin's analysis and notes the use of the female body in colonization in his "Patriarchal Territories: The Body Enclosed."

not long. In Ethiope are such men that have but one foote, and they go so fast it is a great mervaile, and that is a large foot that the shadow therof covereth the body from Sun or raine when they lye upon their backs, & when their children are first borne they looke like russet, and when they wax old then they bee all black. (L3r–v)

This catalog of geographical, anatomical, and sexual anomalies insists on the absolute difference between the reader and the subject. Like Ethiopia's rivers, the bodies of the natives, who have but one foot and who change color, are unstable and disordered. Such corporeal and geographical transgressions, as anthropologist Mary Douglas has revealed, are often the signs of a threat to a culture's social boundaries (94). Although Douglas is, of course, referring to internal cultural threats, I would argue that in using these cultures to develop a clearer sense of their own identity (which comes to include the ability to master these cultures), Europeans respond to such "outside" threats precisely as though they were internal ones. The noting of physical and geographical "differences" serves only to represent and reinforce African inversions of European social and cultural models. Here the Ethiopians are continually drunk, and both men and women suffer from the "flux." Not just women but an entire society is afflicted with hysteria, a disease associated with females that, as Patricia Parker notes, commonly functioned as a sign of disorders that must be avoided in the larger society (106).

The very geography of Ethiopia is "troubled" and not subject to orderly nature. As we shall see in Chapter 3, this notion of Africa's rivers (chiefly the Nile), which regularly overflow their boundaries, becomes a source of fascination for the English and is often conflated with the sense of Africans as a people who resist boundaries and rule. This pivotal conflation of geographical and human bodies is also found in Pory's prologue to Leo Africanus's *Geographical Historie of Africa,* which features a strange combination of vegetative and human generation. The barrenness of the land of Guinea is equated with the hairless bodies of its inhabitants and their marketing of their own offspring: "The countrey in most places is destitute of trees that beare fruite: neither have the greatest part of the inhabitants any haire on their bodies, save onely a thicke tuft growing upon their heads: they sell their children unto strangers, supposing that their estate cannot possiblie be impaired" (43).[4] The descriptions found in Mandeville are a very early

---

4. Louis Montrose notes a similar homology in Raleigh between natives and land, which allows for the ultimate feminization of the land; however, this association ends with the

constellation of the increasingly complex links between the fear of alien cultures and the destructive powers of sexuality associated with black-ness.[5] Mandeville's use of his classical sources heightens the sense of dif-ference and reproduces it visually in terms of color. Although such exaggerated ambiguity as the Ethiopian children who change from "rus-set" to black is merely fascinating and not particularly threatening, in the later texts printed after the first English involvements in the African slave trade and the exploration of America, there appears a new nerv-ousness about skin color and cultural "disorder."

This heightened sense of disorder seems only fitting at the moment England begins to confront its own power and ability to reorder nature. Disorder, as Mary Douglas has pointed out, symbolizes danger and power; it also provides the basis for the exercise of power: "Granted that disorder spoils pattern; it also provides the materials of pattern. Order implies re-striction; from all possible materials, a limited selection has been made and from all possible relations a limited set has been used. So disorder by implication is unlimited, no pattern has been realised in it, but its potential for patterning is indefinite" (94). The use of Africa and black-ness as signs of disorder is the first step in preparing for Europe's ordering and later exploitation of Africa's human and natural resources. In the ordering of such strange variety, there lies power as well as wealth. At first only a culminating sign of physical oddity and natural disorderliness, blackness begins to represent the destructive potential of strangeness, dis-order, and variety, particularly when intertwined with the familiar, and familiarly threatening, unruliness of gender.

Writing Africa: Native Informants and Narrative Anxiety

Significantly, one of the manuscripts that best epitomizes the Western obsession with African difference and sexuality is that of a converted Moor, Al Hassan Ibn Mohammed Al Wezaz, Al Fasi, now known as Johan-nes Leo Africanus. Leo, a traveler, scholar, diplomat, and possible spy, was captured by pirates, who delivered him to the Vatican. The story goes that the pope, struck by his learning, converted him, became his godfather,

---

effacement of the natives, who are "rendered invisible by a metonymic substitution of place for persons, a substitution of the land for its inhabitants" ("Work of Gender" 12).

5. For a discussion of these elements and their connections with later Victorian notions of disease and madness, see Sander Gilman's *Difference and Pathology: Stereotypes of Sexuality, Race, and Madness*, 136.

and later encouraged him to write the stories of his travels. John Pory's English translation of Leo's work, *A Geographical Historie of Africa*, appeared in 1600 (the same year as the last volume of Hakluyt's *Principal Navigations*). Although it never went through a second printing, it was included in Purchas's collection and became the single most authoritative travel guide on Africa for the next three centuries. Information reputedly from Africanus appears in a variety of Renaissance texts, from maps to conversion narratives to medical treatises. However, the importance of Africanus goes beyond the information that England gleaned from his travels. Not only did Pory's translation of *A Geographical Historie* provide an assessment of Africa's potential for colonization, it contributed to the developing sense of the unruly and diverse sexuality of Africans; and it gave England a model for controlling the "meaning" of Africa and the seemingly inexhaustible difference it represented.

As with the native guides who were captured and converted for the express purpose of escorting European travelers through unknown lands, much of Leo's stature and granted authority comes from both his indigenous status and his seeming absorption of European values.[6] However, there is throughout the Africanus/Pory text a nervousness about where the boundaries of difference lie with this newly converted Christian. Leo brings to the travel narrative a renewed immediacy because of his indigenous status. Like other popular European narratives that begin to equate the experience of writing the narrative with travel itself, *A Geographical Historie* gives the reader the sense that the travels described are almost concurrent with the time of reading; Leo's English translator and editor, John Pory, describes the text as if it were the journey itself, promising a conclusion in these terms: "From which cape we returne toward the north, describing all along the westerne countries and isles of *Africa*, till we have brought our whole descriptions to an end upon the most southwesterly partes of *Barbarie*..." ([A4v]).[7] As I discuss in more detail at the end of this chapter, "description" (repeated twice in this passage) becomes in such texts not a neutral term of observation but an act connoting ownership and control.

Most significantly, both Leo and his English translator, John Pory, insist

6. Christopher Miller discusses the French roots of this text in *Blank Darkness: Africanist Discourse in French* and also notes its mediating function: "The importance of the *Description of Africa* is that it is located precisely on the cusp between Europe and Islam" (12).

7. In a similar vein, William Prat, in his preface to *The Discription of the Countrey of Aphrique* (1554), claims that in writing he acts as a tour guide: "As if I shuld leade the[e] by the hand from one place to an other from one region to an other, or to pointe the[e] with my finger" (34).

on the orderliness of the manuscript and its improvement over earlier narratives in this regard. Pory apologizes for taking so long to publish: "I thought good . . . to bestowe a part of [his spare time] in collecting and digesting, the same" ([A4r]), and he praises Leo because he "hath so largely, particularly, and methodically deciphered the countries" ([A3v]). This emphasis on the ordering and collecting of travel information is quite marked. Unlike Mandeville's text, where the only sense of place is that of the "distance" separating countries from Christianity, Leo's text is ordered according to the actual geography of Africa.[8]

Despite Leo's own sense of proper narrative decorum, the edited version manifests great unease with the idea of Leo's text. Pory's relation to the original narrative is fascinatingly complex. He adds an opening book, "Places undescribed by John Leo"; marginalia; and an addendum that reorders part of the material according to subject. Thus the "original" text is encircled by and interwoven with Pory's text, which at times serves to protect the unwary reader from the narrator. For example, he adds a section on "the religions of Africa" which begins the discussion of Islam with the heading, "Of Mahumet, and of his accursed religion in general" (380). The orderly text, like the converted Leo (or converted guide), becomes a safe conduit through which readers become protected tourists, enjoying the wonders and promised wealth of Africa while safely distanced from its more ominous—and seductive—cultural practices.

Leo seemingly shares with his European audience a disdain for the darkest African peoples, and he introduces judgments that juxtapose negative assessments of their appearance with disapproval of cultural practices. In his general discussion of "the land of Negros" (which is the shortest book and thus evidence that this is still the "least known" part of Africa), he complains of the lack of civilization in the areas surrounding Libya:

> The residue of the said land was found out, being as then inhabited by great numbers of people, which lived a brutish and savage life, without any king, governour, common wealth, or knowledge of husbandrie. Clad they were in skins of beasts, neither had they any peculiar wives: in the day time they kept their cattell; and when night came they resorted ten or twelve both men and

8. Stephen Greenblatt points out that Jerusalem is more than central to Mandeville: "This choice confers upon the Holy Land the highest honor, so that 'among all other lands' it is 'the most worthy land and sovereign of all other.' The world then is organized not simply around a central space, but that space is the space of the greatest honor—as if the whole world were like a royal court with a distribution of rank and title" (*Marvelous Possessions* 42).

women into one cottage together, using hairie skins in stead of beds, and
each man choosing his leman which he had most fancy unto. (284–85)

Again, the seeming absence of known social structures (king, commonwealth, agriculture) is connected to unfamiliar gender arrangements.
Moreover, in a later passage, Leo indicts the inhabitants of Casena (already implicated by default in the previous judgment) for their physical
features: "The inhabitants are all extremely black, having great noses and
blabber lips" (291).

The assumed values that Leo Africanus shares with his reader, however,
do not assure the safety of his text. In not wanting Leo to "appeere too
solitarie upon the stage" ([A4r]), Pory reveals a concern about the Moor's
"deciphering" and the possibility of a direct relationship between reader
and author. Much of the editing, I would suggest, is the result of an anxiety about difference (even, or especially, converted difference) that is not
merely editorial but cultural. Throughout the book, Pory provides the
usual marginalia, pointing out the more interesting oddities such as people who eat ostriches and camels and strengthening terms of opprobrium
when he finds Leo too open-minded. However, the marginalia seem designed to disrupt the reader's relationship with the text. Leo's text assumes an identification with the reader, but Pory's marginal notes serve
to undermine this identification at key points and to reinforce Leo's difference. For example, in describing a mountain people in "Barbarie,"
Leo observes, "They build their houses of the barke of certaine trees, the
rooffe whereof dependeth on slender sparres, fashioned like unto the
hoops environing the lids of such chests or trunks, as the women of Italie,
when they travell, carrie upon their mules. So likewise these people trans-
port their whole houses up and downe by the strength of mules, till they
have found a fit place of aboad" (106). Pory's marginal gloss adds, "These
people live like the Tartars." While one could of course argue that this
note serves to make the text clearer, it may also serve to defamiliarize the
text and thereby subvert the more homely—and more dangerous—analogy likening nomadic Africans to European women.

A similar moment of estrangement occurs when Leo uses another, more
threatening, comparison: "Howbeit the Arabians usually doe blaze their
petigree in daily and trivial songs; which custome as yet is common both
to us, and to the people of Barbarie also" (135). At this point Pory (rather
obviously) identifies Leo as one of the "Moores of Granada." Just at the
moment that Leo aligns himself with a European Christian reader ("is
common both to us"), Pory reinscribes Leo's original difference, thereby
also distancing Arabian "blaze[ing]" and "songs" from European lyric.

As Emily Bartels has noted in relation to the Hakluyt authors, "Part of the point was to retain the unfamiliarity of the native subject and so to create a critical boundary between Africa and England" ("Hakluyt" 523). Leo Africanus himself becomes that boundary, a liminal figure (the converted Moor) who both gives insight into and shields European readers from the threatening difference of Africa.[9]

Pory's attempts at control are even more noticeable given the emphasis on order in the narrative itself. Leo himself insists on describing towns and cities "fully, particularly, largely, and distinctly" (44). *A Geographical Historie* is remarkable for this sense of organization—both geographical and historical—as well as for the insertion of details marshaled by this order. Paradoxically, the very emphasis on an ordered decorum only throws into relief the breaks that do fissure the narrative. On occasion, Leo intrudes into the narrative with a personal anecdote or moralizing commentary. Interestingly, these personal, emotional "breaks" in the narrative inevitably occur when he comments on unruly women. Such fissures in the text make clear to the reader that women (in Africa as well as Europe) are the downfall of family, government, empire, and civilization. The first such address occurs at the end of book 1, where Leo apologizes for maligning his homeland with the observation that the "Negroes" live among harlots:

> Neither am I ignorant, how much mine owne credit is impeached, when I my selfe write so homely of Africa, unto which countrie I stand indebted both for my birth, and also for the best part of my education: Howbeit in this regarde I seeke not to excuse myselfe, but onely to appeale unto the dutie of an historiographer, who is to set downe the plaine truth in all places, and is blame-woorthie for flattering or favouring of any person. And this is the cause that hath mooved me to describe all things so plainly without glossing or dissimulation: wherefore here I am to request the gentle Reader friendly to accept of this my most true discourse, (albeit not adorned with fine words, and artificiall eloquence) as of certaine unknowne strange matters. (42)

9. Keeping in mind Bartels's description of the complementary difference between the use of "Moor" and "Negro" may be instructive here: "Moors appear then as subjects whose customs and beliefs are more knowable and whose civility, particularly since it is put down in writing, is more sure. 'Goodlier' Negroes may allow profitable exchange, but the brevity of reports of successful bargaining and the preponderance of accounts of disaster remind us that their willingness or ability to interact is as limited as their hospitality is unreliable. Despite these important differences, however, Hakluyt also enforces the similarity of the two groups, aligning the most civilized with the most savage in one disenfranchised whole" ("Hakluyt" 529).

These "unknowne strange matters" almost always have to do with uncontrolled sexuality. In attempting to confirm his claims to objectivity, Leo rationalizes at length the inclusion of material he considers unseemly; nevertheless, in rationalizing this "truth," he paradoxically reveals how matters of sexuality undermine the rule of orderliness and propriety that he tries to make the basis of his manuscript. His own claim to a plain style and continued insistence on plain speech hints that his worry about figurative language is of a piece with his attempt to order the disorderliness of Africa, an order threatened by the allure of sexuality and tropic-al language.[10]

Not surprisingly, this "strange matter" stimulates Leo's own most figurative language. He uses not only metaphors but a whole fable to clarify his own estranged detachment from the negative material he recounts; Leo becomes the epitome of the self-fashioner in his ability to rise above being defined by the negative traits of his native country.[11] Thus he describes his own practice by telling the story of a bird, Amphibia, who could "live as well with the fishes of the sea, as with the fowles of the aire" (43):

Out of this fable I will inferre no other morall, but that all men doe most affect that place, where they finde least damage and inconvenience. For mine owne part, when I heare the Africans evill spoken of, I wil affirme my selfe to be one of Granada: and when I perceive the nation of Granada to be discommended, then will I professe my selfe to be an African. But herein the Africans shall be the more beholding unto me; for that I will only record their principall and notorious vices, omitting their smaller and more tolerable faults. (43–44)

The "principall and notorious vices," for which Leo apologizes at length, are those which have to do with the inordinate sexuality of exorbitantly erotic females. Such moments often take the form of Leo's comments on communities that do not exert recognizable control over their women. In describing the inhabitants of Barbarie, for instance, he impugns the fathers of young women as accomplices in their daughters' guilt because they keep no recognizable control over their daughters' sexuality:

10. For a discussion of the relation between sexual propriety and the rules of rhetoric, see Patricia Parker, *Literary Fat Ladies: Gender, Rhetoric, Property*, 97–154.

11. Stephen Greenblatt argues that "in the sixteenth century there appears to be an increased self-consciousness about the fashioning of human identity as a manipulable, artful process" (*Self-Fashioning* 2).

They are a rude people, and (as a man may say) borne and bred to theft, deceit, and brutish manners. Their yoong men may goe a wooing to divers maides, till such time as they have sped of a wife. Yea, the father of the maide most friendly welcommeth her suiter: so that I thinke scarce any noble or gentleman among them can chuse a virgine for his spouse: albeit, so soone as any woman is married, she is quite forsaken of all her suiters; who then seeke out other new paramours for their liking. (41–42)

This passage demonstrates how gender concerns are linked to other social categories—in this case, class. The failure of the patriarchal family to restrict sexual relations before marriage causes troubles in the state as well: no "nobles or gentlemen" can find virgins to wed and thereby guarantee themselves the continuation of an untainted aristocratic bloodline.

These illustrations of the base nature of a people inevitably involve negative judgments about their sexual freedom, and Leo's imposition of European values of family and marriage causes him to make such judgments. Although the realm of sexuality is utterly different from a European order (Gilman 214), it is too important to be ignored, so Leo resorts to a rather plaintive apology for including the material at all. When not fully elaborated, the problem of licentiousness appears as a shorthand for indicting a society: "The Negros likewise leade a beastly kinde of life, being utterly destitute of the use of reason, of dexteritie of wit, and of all artes. Yea they so behave themselves, as if they had continually lived in a forrest among wilde beasts. They have great swarmes of harlots among them; whereupon a man may easily conjecture their manner of living" (42). The mere presence of numbers of prostitutes is a sign of the depravity of society as a whole. The conjunction of harlot with Negro is enough to hint at what is literally unspeakable, and the ease with which Leo assumes a European reader will fill in the gaps indicts that society as well.

Subsequent breaks in the narrative are all marked by such confrontations with the instability of gender. In Fez, for instance, we see a society of men who, Hercules-like, reduce themselves to the status of spinsters. Oddly enough, this passage opens with a consideration of women who themselves occupy a problematically "unmoored" position in society as widows: "In these innes certaine poore widowes of Fez, which have neither wealth nor friends to succour them, are relieved; sometimes one, and sometimes two of them together are allowed a chamber; for which courtesie they play both the chamberlaines and cookes of the inne" (130). Innocent enough at first, this inn then turns into the site of multiple transgressions, which are primarily characterized by gender inversion: "The inne-keepers of Fez being all of one familie called Elcheua, goe apparelled like women, and shave their beards, and are so delighted to imitate women, that they will not only counterfeite their speech, but will sometimes also sit downe and spin" (130). This inversion seems to be the path to all sorts of unacceptable behavior: the companions to these innkeepers are women even more out of control than the brides of Barbarie (whose fathers allow, if not condone, their behavior). Even so, they are maintained as a necessary appendage of the state:

> Each one of these hath his concubine, whom he accompanieth as if she were his owne lawfull wife; albeit the said concubines are not only ill-favoured in countenance, but notorious for their bad life and behaviour. They buie and sell wine so freely, that no man controules them for it. None resort hither but most lewd & wicked people, to the end they may more boldly commit villany. The inne-keepers have a consul over them, and they pay tribute unto the governour of the citie. And when the king hath occasion to send foorth an armie, then they, as being most meete for the purpose, are constrained largely to victuall the campe. (130–31)

Dangerous in any number of ways, these women disrupt family structures (being concubines, albeit ugly ones); more important, they are thriving businesswomen whose very business Leo sees as corrupting the state even as he stresses its structural necessity:[12]

> Had not the streit law of historie enforced me to make relation of the foresaid particulars as they stand, I would much rather have smothered such matters in silence, as tend so extremely to the disgrace of Fez; which being reformed, there is not any citie in al Africa, for the honestie and good demeanour of the citizens, comparable thereunto. For the very companie of these inne-keepers is so odious and detestable in the sight of all honest men, learned men, and merchants, that they will in no wise vouchsafe to speake unto them. (131)

As before, Leo claims that the exigencies of history insist on his recording this unseemly material. Truth forces him to speak about that which the

---

12. This sense of unruly or ungoverned women as a potentially dangerous and yet vital presence in times of war echoes Pory's prologue. While registering his distress at the presence of the Amazons of Monomatopa, Pory simultaneously stresses that these Amazon warriors are "indeed the very sinewes and chiefe strength of all [the king's] militarie forces" (33).

traveler should otherwise suppress. Although it is certainly logical to assume that travelers would want to know about inns, one wonders if the compulsion to describe such transgressions seduces us in two ways—both as an allure and as an invitation to repress uncontrolled sexuality.

Leo turns violent in his opposition to the female soothsayers he encounters. In Fez, he includes in his condemnation of their "deceit" an account of female homoeroticism that disrupts the order of the patriarchal family. The women Leo describes integrate several of the elements of strangeness discussed earlier: these women are not only dark, but demonic and, interestingly, open to men who seek forbidden knowledge:

> The third kinde of diviners are women-witches, which are affirmed to have familiaritie with divels: some divels they call red, some white, and some black divels: and when they will tell any mans fortune, they perfume themselves with certaine odours, saying, that then they possesse themselves with that divell which they called for: afterwards changing their voice, they faine the divell to speake within them: then they which come to enquire, ought with great feare & trembling aske these vile & abominable witches such questions as they meane to propound, and lastly offering some fee unto the divell, they depart. But the wiser and honester sort of people call these women *Sahacat*, which in Latin signifieth *Fricatrices*, because they have a damnable custome to commit unlawfull Venerie among themselves, which I cannot expresse in any modester termes. If faire women come unto them at any time, these abominable witches will burne in lust towardes them no otherwise then lustie yoonkers doe towards yoong maides, and will in the divels behalfe demaunde for a rewarde, that they may lie with them: and so by this meanes it often falleth out, that thinking thereby to fulfill the divels command they lie with the witches. (148–49)

These soothsayers are contrasted with "fair" women who not only are beautiful and lighter in color but are subject to the order of the patriarchal family. They are particularly dangerous because they can seduce "fair" women, causing them to subvert patriarchal rule (although the ideal of the "fair woman" is complicated by the seeming ease with which they are led astray).[13] Not only are these women no longer "well-

---

13. In this sense, the "fair women" might be read as "femmes," in Valerie Traub's use of the term: "In the psychic landscape of the time, 'femmes' would be assumed available to give birth; tribades and sodomites would not. The 'femme' involved with a tribade was seen as 'abused', the not altogether innocent victim of another woman's lust; her crime was correspondingly more minor, her punishment less severe" (164). The witches do not seem to be "tribades" in Traub's use of the term, but they do seem to pose a similar threat in that they too are deliberately nonreproductive.

disposed"—ordered according to patriarchal standards[14]—they reduce
their husbands to the role of pander for female homoerotic desire and
thus demonstrate the "instability of gender within categories of sexuality"
(Traub 151). The man gives over his home to a horde of witches who
turn it into a site of unlawful sexual license:

> Yea some there are, which being allured with the delight of this abominable
> vice, will desire the companie of these witches, and faining themselves to be
> sicke, will either call one of the witches home to them, or will send their
> husbands for the same purpose: and so the witches perceiving how the matter
> stands, will say that the woman is possessed with a divell, and that she can no
> way be cured, unlesse she be admitted into their societie. With these words
> her silly husband being persuaded, doth not onely permit her so to doe, but
> makes also a sumptuous banket unto the dammed crew of witches: which
> being done, they use to daunce very strangely at the noise of drums: and so
> the poore man commits his false wife to their filthie disposition. (149)

Like the earlier innkeepers, the husband assumes a feminized role in the
home marked by his "make[ing] also a sumptuous banket" for the
witches.

Such a passage is also fascinating for its demonstration of one very
persuasive definition of the nature of imperialist power. In his reading
of the Bower of Bliss episode of *The Faerie Queene*, Stephen Greenblatt
argues, "Power may . . . prohibit desire, but it is in its own way a version
of the erotic: the violence directed against Acrasia's sensual paradise is
. . . in itself an equivalent of erotic excess" (*Renaissance* 173). The two
"cures" Leo proposes for female desire are telling in the way they echo
this dynamic of eroticism and power: "Howbeit some there are that will
soone conjure the divell with a good cudgell out of their wives: others
faining themselves to be possessed with a divell, wil deceive the said
witches, as their wives have been deceived by them" (149). A husband
has two options: to exert physical mastery over the wife with a beating
or to "deceive" or seduce the witch, thereby giving into this evocation
of uncontrollable sexuality for the express purpose of putting the man
back on top. These two solutions correspond to the dynamic of imperialist power outlined as well in Greenblatt's reading of Spenser which
maintains that excess force is acceptable in the maintenance of civiliza-

---

14. For a discussion of the links between the rhetorical trope "Dispositio" and the proper
"disposition" of a people, see Patricia Parker's *Literary Fat Ladies*, 98.

tion and that power directed against the erotic can be thought to participate in the erotic.

We see something like this double use of force and eroticism in an earlier digression. Allegedly recounting the story "of a certaine prince called Hebdurrahmam" who "for a greedy and ambitious desire of raigning murthered his owne uncle" (82), Leo actually gives us a cautionary tale of the disintegration of power, which ends up as an indictment of the perfidy of women:

> He had a daughter of most excellent beauty, who falling in love with a certaine courtier (whose name was *Hali*, being sonne unto one *Goesimen*) by the helpe of her mother and her wayting maide enjoyed oftentimes the companie of her paramour. Which when her father had intelligence of, hee rebuked his wife, threatening death unto her, if shee reformed not the manners of her daughter: howbeit afterwarde hee dissembled his furie. But the mother thoroughly knowing her husbandes intent, tolde her daughters paramour that the prince was not to bee trusted, and therefore advised him to take heede unto himselfe. (82)

Narrating in detail a tortuous plot of regicide, civil chaos, overthrow of the Portuguese, and subsequent rebellion, he explains that the Portuguese, the final arbiters of civil order, fail because the Portuguese king is "not acquainted with their customes" (84). Leo summarizes: "Soone after ensued the miserable desolation and ruine, not onely of the citie but of the whole region thereabouts. In this discourse we have beene somewhat tedious, to the end we might shew of how great evill a woman may be the instrument, and what intollerable mischiefes are bred by dissension" (84). Although the actors in this "tedious" drama are all men (the patricidal king, the king-killing courtier, the opportunistic Portuguese), the originators of this civil and international strife are two women: the daughter whose sexuality her father could not control and the disloyal wife who would not support the rule of the father.

A Geographical Historie gives the reader a sense of Africa as a chaotic and disordered land, one badly in need of a sense of order. Accordingly, the narrative reflects the problem of hierarchies of gender that disrupt the ideal of "ordo" and its questions of rule and hierarchy that enforce English societal norms. The earlier *The Discription of the Countrey of Aphrique* (1554) adopts from Herodotus a depiction of Africa as an almost exact inversion of English rule, all through the scrutiny of gender:

> The thinges which be issued out from the *Ethiopiens* shal sufficiently declare the same to us, who hathe ben the inventures of these thinges. . . . Their wives

of an olde & aunciente custome do use to occupy marchaundise, to kepe
hostillerie and utillisinge houses & do also trafike, whereupon the men do
give themselves to make linnen clothe and to cary fardles upon their heades,
where women do not carie but upon their shoulders, as our men do here in
Englande. Moreover, they use to make water against a wall like unto our men
& the men cowringe downe to the ground like as our women do here. (80)

Such gender inversions are fundamental and remain persistent signs of
cultural otherness.

Gender is always included as part of the narrative of alien culture and
race, sometimes intruding almost gratuitously. Thus in a digression from
the main discussion in the prologue to *A Geographical Historie of Africa,* John
Pory recounts:

About the fountaines of Nilus some say, that there are Amazones or women-
warriers, most valiant and redoubted, which use bowes and arrowes, and live
under the governement of a Queene: as likewise the people called Cafri or
Cafates, being as blacke as pitch, and of a mightie stature, and (as some
thinke) descended of the Jewes; but now they are idolators, and most deadly
enimies to the Christians; for they make continuall assaults upon the Abassins,
dispoiling them both of life and goods: but all the day-time they lie lurking
in mountaines, woods, and deepe valleies. (41)

Pory somehow drags the Amazons and the Jews from the Nile basin into
the same rhetorical position as the Cafri so that blackness is seen as inescapably allied to the gender threat. Although idolators, they are made
descendants of even better-known outsiders, the Jews, and therefore are
triply alien to Christians. Last, they are almost part of the threatening
land itself as they "lurk" in the "hidden" parts of the landscape.

The protoimperialist necessity of imposing order on culture and gender
extends into the economic realm as well. Leo Africanus and other travelers continually comment on societies that possess valuable natural resources but do not know how to use them. He notes, for example, that
the people of Hea use their abundance of honey instead of food: "But
the waxe they cast away, little regarding it, because they know not the
value thereof" (45). In like manner, he informs us that in Azaphi, the
"soile is exceeding fertill; but so grosse is their owne unskilfulnes and
negligence, that they [the inhabitants] know neither how to till their
ground, to sow their corne, or to plant vineyards" (284). Thus the commodification that is integral to colonialism becomes yet another factor in
the imposition of order as travelers begin the process of putting these

resources to "proper" use, readying them for absorption into European markets: a process that will ultimately intertwine the commodification of human as well as natural resources when England becomes more fully involved in the slave trade.

A contemporary narrative, Abraham Hartwell's *A Reporte of the Kingdome of Congo* (1597), shares many characteristics of the better-known *Geographical Historie;* however, in its attempt to address some of the primary issues of blackness, it throws into relief some of the movements that I have just outlined. The frontispiece of the manuscript claims to debunk the then-current African myths. In his epistle dedicatory, Hartwell is very open about the value of the narrative for conquest, although less so about the possible motives for conquest: "To the end it might be a president for such valiant English, as do earnestly thirst and desire to atchieve the conquest of rude and barbarous Nations, that they doo not attempt those actions for commodity of Gold and Silver, and for other transitorie or worldly respectes, but that they would first seeke the Kingdome of God, & the salvation of many thousand soules, which the common enemie of mankinde still detayneth in ignorance"(¶3r). For Hartwell, the task of translation is caught up in the task of empire and in the larger enterprise of bringing the unknown to "light." Hartwell states clearly the sense of England's geographic and epistemological isolation that one sees in the other narratives: "To help our *English Nation*, that they might knowe and understand many things, which are common in other languages, but utterly concealed from this poore *Island*" (¶4v).

Although Hartwell is more tolerant of differing social structures, in describing how the manuscript came into his hands he takes up the idea of imposing an order on a "found" manuscript seen in the other works. He creates a small allegory in which the manuscript is acquired through conquest. He finds it on a captured Portuguese ship, and, just as he was about to tear it "into many mo peeces," "*My second wits* stayed me, and advised me, that I should peruse all his *Report*, before I would proceede to execution. . . . I was so bold as to pardon him, and so taught him to speake the *English toung*, In which language . . . hee will tell you many notable observations of divers *Countreys* and peoples inhabiting in *Africa*, whose names have scarce been mentioned in England" (*1r–v). His epistle to the reader anticipates objections to the disorder of the narrative: "And first, they will except perhaps against the *Methode* of the *Author*, because he keepeth no continuate *Order* in this *Report*, but leapeth from one *Matter* to another, without any coherence" (*2r). Although he refuses to reorder the manuscript, Hartwell attributes a great power to the original editor, who, Godlike, wrought a little world out of chaos—and separated light from darkness: "He is rather to be commended, that having so rude and undigested a *Chaos* to worke upon, he could frame so handsome a little world of it as this is. If happily it be further urged, that the Translator should have taken paines to cast him in a new *Mould*, and to make his members hang proportionably one upon another" (*2r). Hartwell provides an interesting perspective in that he is well aware of the pressure for an ordered narrative but insists on reproducing the status of the original manuscript and, if necessary, on banishing the resisting reader to the margins of his text: "But if algates some *Enthusiasme* have come upon our *Critikes*, that hath revealed unto them . . . the certaintie of the *Authors* writing and meaning, to be such as they have confidently set downe, let me be bold to intreate them, that they would muster their conceytes in the Margine (if the Margine will hold them: as I doubt it will not in this *Hypercriticall* world)" (*2v). His refusal to bend to the pressures of narrative order is allied to the narrative's acceptance of blackness as an insoluble mystery. Like *Pseudodoxia Epidemica, A Reporte of the Kingdom of Congo* almost revels in the uncertainty of blackness. The skin itself holds the promise of a yet-undiscovered secret of nature:

> Hee noted that the colour of the skinnes of the inhabitants in both countries was farre different: For in *Congo*, they are generally and for the most parte blacke, and in *India* almost white, that is to say, of a middle colour, betweene white and blacke, which the *Spaniardes* call *Mulato*, Browne, or Darke-Tawney. Whereby he would signifie, that it is not caused by the Sunne, as it hath been recorded of long time, but that it commeth of nature it selfe, who worketh it by some secreat reason, which never yet to this day, either by auncient *Philosopher*, or new writer, hath beene fully set downe or understoode. (173)

Even though Hartwell's text suggests a more expansive notion of human somatic differences, he is still able to express them only within a binarism of black and white ("of a middle colour betweene white and black").

Richard Eden's famous translation, *The Decades of the Newe Worlde* (1555), records a similar dynamic in Francisco Lopez de Gomora's appreciation of diversity: "One of the marveylous thynges that god useth in the composition of man, is colour: whiche doubtlesse can not bee considered withowte great admiration in beholding one to be white an other blacke, beinge coloures utterlye contrary. Sum likewise to be yelowe whiche is betwene blacke and white: and other of other colours as it were of divers liveres" (quoted in Jordan 7). Gomora projects aesthetic appreciation onto human, cultural difference. This is a significant moment: as we shall see, ideas of racial difference become increasingly embedded in aesthetic notions of color, and the traditional opposition of the colors black and white becomes the central trope for expressing fears about the confrontation of cultures in imperial interaction. Indeed, this sense of diversity as a sign of God's wonders all but disappears under the imperative to convert natives and to subsume their religious difference and perceived disorder under Western European Christianity.

Although Hartwell insists on the title page that the text will refute the time-honored notion that blackness proceeds from too much sun, he offers no other "scientific" solution, but declares instead that it springs from "some secreat reason" of Nature, an argument consistent with his continual dwelling on the inexplicable mystery of Africa. Most significantly, Africa is female in its ability to produce monsters: "He will tell you the sundry kinds of *Cattell, Fishes, and Fowles, strange Beasts, and Monstrous Serpents,* that are to be found therein: For *Africa* was always noted to be a fruitfull Mother of such fearfull and terrible *Creatures*" (*1v). While there is a sense here that this is threatening fecundity, it makes Africa rather more productive of the oddities of nature that Hartwell's manuscript is so eager to put before the reader.

In a sense *A Reporte* lessens the effects of such promised variety by comparing African difference with European difference: "The language of the people of *Angola* is all one with the language of the people of *Congo*. . . . Only the difference between them is, as commonly it is betweene two nations that border one upon another, as for example betweene the *Portingalles* and the *Castilians,* or rather between the *Venetians* and the *Calabrians,* who pronouncing their wordes in a divers manner, and uttering them in severall sortes, although it be all one speech, yet do they very hardly understand one another" (57). The *Reporte* is somewhat more generous than other narratives in evaluating African marriage customs. Polygamy, for example, causes no more than a mere passing comment: "This kingdome of *Angola,* is full of people beyonde all credite: For every man taketh as many wives as hee listeth, and so they multiply infinitely: But they doe not use so to do in the kingdome of *Congo,* which liveth after the manner of the *Christians*" (55). However, when Hartwell moves to women beyond male control, such as Amazons, their untrammeled femaleness threatens the very idea of empire.

Hartwell promises to explicate the "*Paradoxe* touching the *Amazones*" along with the mysteries of blackness. The possibility that such a mythical group might still exist proves quite troubling:

I do not see, why it should be counted a *Paradox* to beleeve, that there is such a *Nation,* considering how many *Authors* both *Greeke* and *Latine,* both *Histori-*

ographers and *Cosmographers*, both *Divine* and *Prophane*, have acknowledged that *Nation*, and the *Countrey* wherein it inhabited. But our new Writers say, that a little after *King Alexanders* death it was utterly overthrowne and quite extinguished. . . . But yet suppose some *Hipsiphile*, or *Penthesilea*, or *Thalestris*, or some such other, did wisely conveigh hir selfe away . . . and being guided by some happie *Venus*, arrived in a farre remote *Region*, and there observed the customes and fashions of their owne *Native Countrey*. Might not these three, together with some other women that were desirous of Rule and government, and allured by them to be of their Societie; . . . (*3v–*4r)

If Angolan polygamy is disturbing, it still has women reproduce under patriarchal rule ("they multiply infinitely"). In contrast, Amazons (like Leo's witches) are threatening both because they do not reproduce within patriarchy and because they can attract other women "desirous of Rule and government." The articulation of their threat is intermingled with the idea of Africa as remote and producing hidden wonders: "Might not they (I say) in processe of time, (for it is a long time since *Alexander* died) breede a New Nation of *Amazones*, although we never heard, in what *Climate* they remained?" (*4r). Not only are the Amazons the military threat that they are in Africanus/Pory; here they are the potential colonizers of Europe. Gender becomes the primary threat to empire as Hartwell conjures up of a vision of Amazonian colonization: "Yea it may be for any thing that I know, this latter generation might growe againe to be so populous, that they could send foorth *Colonies* from them into other places, and so plant themselves in divers Countreys" (*4r). Interestingly, Hartwell emphasizes the nature of his own enterprise by conjecturing a threat curiously like the English imperialist project he forwards. So too he concludes by joining this vision of unruliness with another sign of disorder, claiming, "And I hope that in good time, some good *Guianian* will make good proofe to our *England*, that there are at this day both *Amazones*, and *Headlesse men*" (*4r). The paradox of Amazons includes headless men, the visual symbol of the threatening/castrating freedom of Amazons. This threat seems so acute that Hartwell calls for a sympathetic (presumably male) native informant (such as Leo?) to validate his warning.

The worst sort of disorder in this text is cannibalism—not just ordinary cannibalism but familial cannibalism: "True it is that many nations there are, that feede upon mans flesh as in the east *Indies*, and in *Bresill*, and in other places: but that is only the flesh of their adversaries and enemies, but to eat the flesh of their own frendes and subjectes and kinsefolkes, it is without all example in any place of the worlde, saving only in this nation of the *Anzichi*" (36). Even in this case, Africa becomes the repository for the most threatening sort of transgression. In a pinch, it may be acceptable to eat the flesh of outside enemies, but consuming one's "frendes and subjectes and kinsefolkes" implies that the Anzichi have no sense of external/internal boundaries or difference. Such a lack of civilization may authorize England's own economic exploitation of cannibalistic culture in its own ever-increasing merchandizing and consumption of foreign resources.

Enterprise and Conversion: Ordering the World in Hakluyt and Purchas

A more self-conscious process of inscribing order on native culture can be found in Richard Hakluyt's *Principal Navigations, Voyages, and Discoveries of the English Nation*. Hakluyt's work, a compilation of the narratives of English trade and travel, is one of the classics of English travel literature. While Hakluyt brings to these texts a sense of proper order, he does so without the harsher judgments found in *A Geographical Historie*, perhaps because his European sources do not yet see themselves as implicated in the culture in the same way that Leo does. First published in 1589, one year after the Armada, this "prose epic of the modern English nation"[15] had an explicitly political agenda: to put English exploration on the map of European expansion, making England competitive with its European neighbors. Hakluyt's work conveys a rigorous and self-conscious sense of order and method. It is, of course, not surprising for the compiler of such a range of material to emphasize his ordering of it; Hakluyt is unusual, however, in the persistent conflation of his methods of editing the manuscripts and his sense of the destined order of the English empire, a conflation that makes the ordering of these narratives crucial to the success of the burgeoning empire. In the dedicatory epistle to Sir Francis Walsingham in the first edition, he laments that the English are behind in the race for conquest: "I both heard in speech, and read in books other nations miraculously extolled for their discoveries and notable enterprises by sea, but the English of all others for their sluggish security, and continuall neglect of the like attempts especially in so long and happy a time of peace" (1:2).

Hakluyt is at great pains to remind his reader of the immensity of his task, almost as immense as the burden of empire itself. This dual strategy

---

15. For a complete discussion of *The Principal Navigations* as an English epic, see George Bruner Parks, *Richard Hakluyt and The English Voyages*, 187–99.

supports the sense of urgency in his work and makes the writer as important as the traveler to the security of the nation. The rhetoric he uses in
speaking of manuscripts is close to that used by explorers in describing
the difficulties of traveling through these new worlds. Walter Raleigh, in
recounting his voyage to Guiana, bemoans the difficulties of travel: "Of
that litle remaine I had, I have wasted in effect all herein. I have under-
gone many constructions. I have bene accompanied with many sorrowes,
with labour, hunger, heat, sickenes, & perill" (Hakluyt 7:273). For Hakluyt, the task of research is equally arduous: "I call the worke a burden,
in consideration that these voyages lay so dispersed, scattered, and hidden
in severall hucksters hands, that I now woonder at my selfe, to see how I
was able to endure the delayes, curiosity, and backwardnesse of many from
whom I was to receive my originals" (1:3). Hakluyt's juxtaposition of national pride and good order becomes more apparent and more strident
in successive editions of the travels. He begins his preface to the 1598
edition with a vision of an England itself buried in obscurity:

> Having for the benefit and honour of my Countrey zealously bestowed so
> many yeres, so much traveile and cost, to bring Antiquities smothered and
> buried in darke silence, to light, and to preserve certaine memorable exploits
> of late yeeres by our English nation atchieved, from the greedy and devouring
> jawes of oblivion: to gather likewise, and as it were to incorporate into one
> body the torne and scattered limmes of our ancient and late Navigations by
> Sea, our voyages by land, and traffiques of merchandise by both: and having
> (so much as in me lieth) restored ech particular member, being before dis-
> placed, to their true joints and ligaments; I meane, by the helpe of Geogra-
> phie and Chronologie (which I may call the Sunne and the Moone, the right
> eye and the left of all history) referred ech particular relation to the due time
> and place. (1:19)

This ordering of his texts is connected both to the prosperity and fame
of the English and to the protection of England's integrity and security
"from the greedy and devouring jawes of oblivion" (1:19). His use of the
body metaphor yokes the *Principal Navigations* to the aggrandizing body
of state, putting both in their proper order. If the disjointedness of the
monstrous races in Mandeville marks an incapacity of native cultures to
be ordered, later such disjointedness gives way to Hakluyt's ability to put
back the dispersed members of earlier material and shape "England"
through his collection.

A reliance on time and place is critical to Hakluyt's sense of proper disposition. Like his friend John Pory, Hakluyt describes his writing as travel. The compilation of the *Principal Navigations* itself becomes a voyage:

> For the bringing of which into this homely and rough-hewen shape, which here thou seest; what restlesse nights, what painfull dayes, what heat, what cold I have indured; how many long & chargeable journeys I have traveiled; how many famous libraries I have searched into; what varietie of ancient and moderne writers I have perused; what a number of old records, patents, privileges, letters, &c. I have redeemed from obscuritie and perishing; into how manifold acquaintance I have entred; what expenses I have not spared. (1:19)

Just as compiling these manuscripts is a way of traveling, so does traveling become a way of properly ordering the world—subsuming both territorial property and literary propriety to the needs of the state. Hakluyt begins his epistle to the reader with a summary of "the Methode and order" (1:6) used in his work, taking care to say that he attributes each narrative episode to its original source and excoriating previous editors for their sloppiness:

> I have referred every voyage to his Author, which both in person hath performed, and in writing hath left the same: for I am not ignorant of Ptolomies assertion, that Peregrinationis historia, and not those wearie volumes bearing the titles of universall Cosmographie which some men that I could name have published as their owne, being in deed most untruly and unprofitablie ramassed and hurled together, is that which must bring us to the certaine and full discoverie of the world. (1:6)

This "certaine and full discoverie" is achieved only through proper order. Hakluyt himself has "disposed and digested the whole worke into 3. partes, or as it were Classes, not without my reasons"(1.7). Submitting his work to the discipline of rhetorical order, Hakluyt assigns each author his due property. Partitioning his discourse likewise puts each segment in its proper place, simultaneously ordering his work and bolstering the new-found interest in British empire.

In outlining his project, Hakluyt seems to feel that the Americas are the most "well disposed" regions. In the actual narratives, "disposition" is translated into the civil disposition of the people themselves: "Touching the westerne Navigations, and travailes of ours, they succeede naturallie in the third and last roome, forasmuch as in order and course those coastes, and quarters came last of all to our knowledge and experience"

(1:9). In the 1598 Epistle Dedicatory, the Americas become the absolute zenith of order:

> Of this New world and every speciall part thereof in this my third volume I have brought to light the best & most perfect relations of such as were cheife actours in the particular discoveries and serches of the same, giving unto every man his right, and leaving every one to mainteine his owne credit. The order observed in this worke is farre more exact, then heretofore I could attaine unto: for whereas in my two former volumes I was enforced for lacke of sufficient store, in divers places to use the methode of time onely (which many worthy authors on the like occasion are enforced unto) being now more plentifully furnished with matter, I alwayes follow the double order of time and place. Wherefore proposing unto my selfe the right situation of this New world, I begin at the extreme Northerne limite, and put downe successively in one ranke or classis, according to the order aforesaide, all such voyages as have bene made to the said part: which comming all together, *and following orderly one upon another, doe much more lighten the readers understanding, and confirme his judgement, then if they had bene scattered in sundry corners of the worke* (1:48–49; emphasis added).

Just as the much-vaunted American plenitude invites relief of a domestic dearth of commodities, the "plentiful matter" provided by the American voyages allows for the perfect completion of Hakluyt's project.

If the Americas are the most malleable voyages for Hakluyt, allowing him to "lighten the readers understanding," then Africa is the obscure matter that must be muddled through for further discovery. Hakluyt apologizes for the seeming hesitation in British colonialism by making Africa the blocking figure that detained England's arrival as a colonial power. Their less perfect knowledge of Africa prevented English exploration from reaching the same proportions as that of the Portuguese and Spanish:

> Howbeit you will say perhaps, not with the like golden successe, not with such deductions of Colonies, nor attaining of conquests. True it is, that our successe hath not bene correspondent unto theirs: yet in this our attempt the uncertaintie of finding was farre greater, and the difficultie and danger of searching was no whit lesse. For hath not Herodotus (a man for his time, most skilfull and judicial in Cosmographie, who writ above 2000. yeeres ago) in his 4. booke called Melpomene, signified unto the Portugales in plaine termes; that Africa, except the small Isthmus between the Arabian gulfe and the Mediterran sea, was on all sides environed with Ocean? (1:20)

Samuel Purchas exhibits a similar sense of the obscurity of Africa. Before his reprint of *A Geographical Historie*, he includes a map of Africa, "For the Readers greater both pleasure and profit," so that "hee may indeed see, even with both Eyes of Geographie (the Mappe and the Relation) to travell thorow that least knowne part of the Elder-knowne World" (5:303). Africa is so difficult to "discover" and describe that he needs both text and maps to situate the reader.

The language of dark and light aggressively "colors" Hakluyt's text. He invariably refers to his enterprise as a process of bringing England "to light": "But alas our English nation, at the first setting foorth for their Northeasterne discovery, were either altogether destitute of such cleare lights and inducements, or if they had any inkling at all, it was as misty as they found the Northren seas, and so obscure and ambiguous, that it was meet rather to deterre them, then to give them encouragement" (1: 21). In all Hakluyt's own writings, darkness is always connected with the unknown and unordered world. To be known is to be ordered and recognizable according to European standards of propriety and rule. Hakluyt continually speaks of bringing manuscripts from dangerous chaos and oblivion to light: "[I] have brought to light many very rare and worthy monuments, which long have lien miserably scattered in mustie corners, & retchlesly hidden in mistie darkenesse, and were very like for the greatest part to have bene buried in perpetuall oblivion" (1:13–14). When Hakluyt creates the written world of the travel collection, he, like Hartwell, imitates Genesis: "And the earth was without forme & voide, and darknesse *was* upon the deepe. . . . And God said, Let there be light: and there was light. And God sawe the light that it *was good*, and God separated the light from the darkenes" (Genesis 1. 2–4 Geneva). Dividing the light from the darkness seems to underlie Hakluyt's entire enterprise, if not the entire colonial project. The dark/light dichotomy becomes the dividing line for both the "known" and the "civilized" worlds. Although the impulse of the travel narrative is not only to divide the dark from the light but to bring as much as possible "to light," Africa in the Hakluyt narratives remains both unknown and uncivilized because it is written as ultimately "unknowable."[16]

A similar sense of Africa as "unknowable" is combined with a more forthright disdain for African religious difference in Pory's emendations

16. See Emily Bartels's discussion of how Africa is created as the "dark continent" through the Hakluyt narratives: "Through this almost emotionless reporting, the gap in understanding between cultures is rewritten as a gap within the 'other' culture, which thus appears incomprehensible rather than not comprehended, uncivilized rather than civilized in a different (non-European) way" ("Hakluyt" 527).

to *A Geographical Historie*. Pory makes the transition between his discussions of Islam and Christianity in Africa thus: "Now that we have declared the miseries and darkness of Affrik, it remaineth that we set downe that little light of true religion which there is" (389). As I noted earlier, Pory here condemns Islam in terms that heighten the animosity to Islam in the primary text. His evocation of Christianity as a "little light" buried in African darkness not only conflates the spiritual sense of the black/white binarism with cultural and geographic difference, it is also, as I will demonstrate later, a not uncommon colonialist gesture which locates valuable whiteness (in this case, Christianity) in the middle of "dark" Africa.

Just as "lightness" becomes the ideal of English discovery and the mark of successful conquest, so does gender become another term by which cultures are evaluated. Although Emily Bartels notes that "women rarely figure in Hakluyt" ("Hakluyt" 526), in the many tracts collected by Hakluyt, inscribing the vast number of disparate travelers' voices, gender stratification (particularly a culture's adherence to European patriarchal norms) is a key boundary that identifies "civilization."[17] In speaking of the Isle of Fogo, Walter Raleigh significantly notes, "They keepe no order of marriage; but have as many wives as they can buy, or win by force of their enemies, which principally is the cause of all their warres" (8:12). Furthermore, gender and race are still continuously united as in the fascinating alignment of black person and European female in the 1594 voyage of James Lancaster to Brazil. Here, even when excluded as objects of economic exchange, women and blacks are cataloged together and separated from Portuguese males. The English, in the midst of warfare with the Portuguese and Indians in Brazil, block off a harbor and capture all enemy goods that come in: "And this farther good chance or blessing of God we had to helpe us, that assoone as we had taken our cartes, the next morning came in a ship with some 60 Negros, 10 Portugall women and 40 Portugals: the women and the Negros we turned out of the towne, but the Portugals our Admirall kept to draw the carts when they were laden, which to us was a very great ease. For the countrey is very hote and ill for our nation to take any great travell in" (8:37). At this point in Lancaster's narrative, issues of numbering and cataloging seem to take precedence over narrative detail. Although we are told precisely how many people were on the ship by gender and race, we are not told who leads the invasion or, far more important, what exactly happens to the women

17. Bartels goes on to note that "it seems no coincidence that, when they [women] appear in Africa, they appear in Negro communities and serve to dehumanize the native population" ("Hakluyt" 526).

and Africans. In the exigencies of European contest and warfare, these marginal figures are excluded from civilization literally to disappear into oblivion.

Women can also function as positive signs of culture: in the Philippines, it is to the men's credit that while they go naked their women do not:

> Their beds is the ground with rushes strowed on it, and lying about the house, have the fire in the midst. The men go naked, the women take bulrushes, and kembe them after the manner of hempe, and thereof make their loose garments, which being knit about their middles, hang down about their hippes, having also about their shoulders a skinne of Deere, with the haire upon it. These women are very obedient and serviceable to their husbands. (8:63)

Containment of the female becomes the code—along with dress and eating habits—for judging alien cultures. Those cultures identified as "savage" are those whose habits are the farthest removed from the European—lack of clothing, wives in common, diverse religious practices and eating habits. Men who are continually identified as "comely" and "gentle" usually wear some sort of apparel and have "dutiful wives." Such cultures are also identified with their closeness to England, which Francis Drake indicates when he concludes the preceding narrative by noting that the general named the land Nova Albion because of its white cliffs and "because it might have some affinitie with our Countrey in name, which sometime was so called" (8:66).

Even animals are judged by their gender relationships. In describing the voyage of John Lok, for instance, George Barne includes an almost lyrical praise of elephants. In the course of his extremely anthropomorphic narrative, the animals become almost European:

> Of all beastes they are most gentle and tractable, for by many sundry wayes they are taught, and doe understand: insomuch that they learne to doe due honor to a king, and are of a quicke sense and sharpenesse of wit. . . . Plinie and Soline write, that they use none adulterie. If they happen to meete with a man in wildernesse being out of the way, gently they wil go before him, & bring him into the plaine way. . . . They have continual warre against Dragons, which desire their blood, because it is very cold. (4:55–56)

The praiseworthy traits of the elephants—their giving "due honor to a king," their near-Christianity (as they will bring a man "into the plaine way"), and, as Barne writes later, "their marveilous docilitie, . . . their generation and chastitie" (57)—were the attributes Europeans came to value in the perfect colonial subject.[18] Not only do elephants have the proper sense of obedience and social order, they endlessly produce commodities.[19] The narrative takes an even stranger turn when Barne goes on to describe the objects made from the elephant's ivory tusks:

> Josephus writeth, that one of the gates of Hierusalem was called Porta Ebur-nea, (that is) the Ivory gate. The whitenesse thereof was so much esteemed, that it was thought to represent the natural fairnesse of mans skinne: inso-much that such as went about to set foorth (or rather corrupt) naturall beau-tie with colours and painting, were reproved by this proverb, Ebur atramento candefacere, that is, To make ivory white with inke. The Poets also describing the faire necks of beautifull virgins, call them Eburnea colla, that is, Ivory necks. And to have said thus much of Elephants and Ivory, it may suffice. (4:57)[20]

In contrast to Hartwell, who speculates on the mysteries of blackness, and Leo, who finds nothing particularly humane about elephants, Barne is struck by the ability to find white beauty in the midst of African darkness. His overt discussion of "whiteness" works to establish whiteness as a cultural value through a series of displacements.

In his descriptions of the elephant world, "aesthetic" appreciations of color are inextricably intertwined with issues of race, gender, and, most obviously here, the true worth of a valuable commodity. Although he looks to the animal world to reify his own notion that white is the "natural" color of humans, the assertion of the naturalness of whiteness is immediately undermined by the possibility of "painting," suggesting a certain unease about the reliability of whiteness as a stable register of value. Such a movement is typical of the inscription of whiteness in Renaissance texts.

18. The elephant's alleged ability to recognize and understand authority—that is, the intuitive sense that Homi Bhabha mentions in his discussion of "the recognition of author-ity" ("Signs Taken for Wonders" 171–76) as both the sign of the colonial subject and an avenue of possible resistance (in the questioning and demand for proof of authority)—would seem to be its defining characteristic in such moments, one that is repeated over and over.

19. Barne goes on to catalog the many goods that can be manufactured from ivory: "[Pliny] also writeth in his twelft booke, that in olde time they made many goodly workes of ivory and Elephants teeth: as tables, tressels, postes of houses, railes, lattesses for windowes, images of their gods and divers other things of ivory, both coloured and uncoloured . . ."

20. The phrase Ebur atramento candefacere appears in a joking conversation about cosmetics from Plautus's Mosterellaria.

The posited ideal—the white, male, "classical" body—is the constant referent, enclosed (as the image of the gate suggests), "taken for granted," and always projected as beautiful.[21] Our attention is never allowed to remain focused on this ideal body for very long, however. The very creation of such a body in a description of Africa suggests a moment of cultural anxiety about standards of beauty that are culturally determined and therefore unstable. Barne moves from ivory like "the natural fairness of man's skinne" to another "undefiled" (but more suspect) body—the virgin—thus displacing the instability that surrounds whiteness onto the female body. In a brief moment, Barne eroticizes ivory (and elephants) as he directs the reader's attention to the beauty of whiteness with an evocation of the Song of Songs;[22] commodifies women in the conflation of ivory products and the feminine, and suggests the possibility of early miscegenative fear as he brings to mind not just a female but a virgin body, whose vulnerability must be protected from the encroachments of foreign others.

The purpose of this "white space" is revealed as we see that this passage provides a frame for the ensuing description of the Guinean people. Barne continues: "It is to be understood, that the people which now inhabit the regions of the coast of Guinea . . . were in the old times called Æthiopes and Nigritæ, which we now call Moores, Moorens, or Negroes, a people of beastly living, without a God, lawe, religion, or common wealth, and so scorched and vexed with the heat of the sunne, that in many places they curse it when it riseth" (4:57). Elephants, with their sense of gender and class hierarchies and "natural" submissiveness, are evoked as a normative model by which to judge Africans who are here summarily defined as the negative inverse of these European values.[23] By

21. I use the term "classical" body advisedly, although it does seem to me that the construction of African difference in travel literature is centered on the body—specifically, on an alleged elemental difference between white and black bodies. While not promoting the "disjointed" grotesque races of Mandeville, later narratives focus on nudity and the size and placement of primary and secondary sexual characteristics (penis, clitoris, breasts) as much as on the problem of skin itself. This certainly seems to be in opposition to a European body that is clothed and imaginatively projected as finished and enclosed. Actually, Stallybrass's and White's description of the "discursive classical body" sounds much like the use of the elephant's body in Barne (and indeed the project of the collected travel narrative): "In the classical discursive body were encoded those regulated systems which were closed, homogeneous, monumental, centred and symmetrical" (22).

22. See the Song of Songs: "Thy necke is like a towre of ivorie" (7.4).

23. The elephant/African dichotomy works along the same axis as the Manichaean allegory outlined by Abdul JanMohamed and similarly allows for the retention of superiority (although I would argue that in this instance the elephant allows the English man to exist outside of the Manichaean opposition and thus imaginatively to avoid the problematic involvement of self and other, the possibility of the self becoming a prisoner of the projected

metaphorically ending the first passage not with elephant's tusks but with the necks of white virgins, Barne locates racial/national fears in the female body in a way that tends to preserve the male body as pristine, white, and untouched.[24] The trajectory of the whole passage suggests that racial difference is worked out in the competition between white female and black bodies in the language of "fairness," which similarly encompasses ideals of aesthetic value, economics, and class and gender hierarchies.[25] That gender differentiation is key to maintaining whiteness may explain why it is that the gender of "blackamoor" is so often unspecified in descriptions of beauty. As I will demonstrate in the next chapter, whiteness as associated with the male is allowed to remain an ideal, because any complication or flaw (such as sunburn) is always discussed in terms of the female body. This image of white within dark, of discovering and merchandizing a precious whiteness from dark, foreign places, is the culmination of the separation of light from dark in Hakluyt's preface. Just as Hakluyt attempts to help create an English identity, such moments suggest that the search for foreign treasure is haunted by a search for the self, for a whiteness that is simultaneously priceless and valuable and that can become the defining, stable marker in a binarism that encodes difference.

Perhaps one reason for the obsessive insistence on order and control of foreign cultures in the collections and in the narratives themselves is that the perceived "barbarism" of these cultures reflects a sense of England's perilous proximity to that state of disorder. In *The Discription of Aphrique*, Prat gives a vision of early England that sounds not far removed from the unruliness of Africa given in *A Geographical Historie* and *The Principal Navigations*: "They became humayne, gentyl, and gracious, that at the laste they ruled themselves so [discreetly] that they themselves, banished all theur inhumanitte, and uncivilitie as to kill one an other, to

---

image). The elephant allows for the glorification of what JanMohamed calls the "overt aim" of colonialism, "civilizing the savage," while showing in relief the alleged bestial nature of the African, thereby allowing the infinite deferral of the overt aim that is a necessary strategy for continual occupation and exploitation.

24. My sense of this strategic directing of the reader's gaze is similar to the sense of distance and reference in Stallybrass's and White's discussion of the "distance" of the classical body: "The classical body, on the other hand keeps its distance. In a sense it is disembodied, for it appears indifferent to a body which is 'beautiful', but which is taken for granted" (22).

25. Although this narrative seems fairly straightforward in the uses of whiteness, it suggests a certain way of reading difference—we are encouraged to accept "white" as the aesthetic constant (which simultaneously embodies certain cultural/political values). Only then are we to focus our attention on the compelling "difference" of blackness.

eate the fleshe of men, and to occupye the company of the first they met without discrecion or regard of blud or kindred, with such like vices and unperfections" (22). Interestingly, a later pamphlet suggests that plantation may help eradicate those vices that Prat attributes to England's barbarous past. In his *Discourse of Western Planting*, written on behalf of Sir Walter Raleigh, the elder Richard Hakluyt warns Queen Elizabeth:

> But wee for all the Statutes that hitherto can be devised, and the sharpe execution of the same in poonishinge idle and lazye persons for wante of sufficient occasion of honest employmente cannot deliver our common wealthe from multitudes of loiterers and idle vagabondes . . . wee are growen more populous than ever heretofore: So that nowe there are of every arte and science so many, that they can hardly live one by another, nay rather they are readie to eat upp one another: yea many thousands of idle persons . . . be either mutinous and seeke alteration in the state, or at leaste very burdensome to the common wealthe, and often fall to pilferinge and thevinge and other lewdnes. (234)

This specter of idleness, civil unrest, and near-cannibalism among the unemployed and dangerously unruly lower classes is very close to the conditions travelers claimed to find abroad, leading one to suspect that the ideal of order in these narratives responds not so much to the external threat of a world of frightening "others" as to a sense of the erasure of the boundaries between those others and the newly expanding English nation. As Samuel Purchas later notes, colonial navigation "open[s] the Windowes of the World, to let it see it selfe" (2.8).

The conversion motive for colonization gives divine authority for England's imposition of order. Indeed, Sir Walter Raleigh finds the proper model for plantation in the aftermath of the flood:

> First, we are to consider that the world after the floud was not planted by imagination, neither had the children of *Noah* wings, to flie from *Shinaar* to the uttermost borders of *Europe*, *Africa*, and *Asia* in haste, but that these children were directed by a wise Father, who knew those parts of the world before the floud, to which he disposed his children after it, and sent them not as Discoverers, or at all-adventure, but assigned and allotted to every Sonne and their issues, their proper parts. (*History of the World* 131)

Raleigh's story of Noah reveals a vision of plantation as an orderly exercise of patriarchal authority in which Noah, the God-father, properly "disposes" his children and their lands. Echoing Hakluyt's emphasis on proper order and method, Raleigh's vision ironically reveals what both narratives conceal: the avarice and competition in European travel. Hakluyt's imperial project in some ways mystifies the all-too-disorderly fight between the colonial powers of Europe to appropriate land and wealth as his collection stakes a literal "claim" to the lands included therein. So, too, does Raleigh's vision of Noah efface the lust for money and power demonstrated in Noah's sons' struggle for inheritance after the flood. This is a crucial omission, because the story of Noah was a critical text for the explanation of racial difference.

Later narratives work in more obvious ways to license England's economic interests abroad. Samuel Purchas's *Hakluytus Posthumus, or Purchas His Pilgrimes,* the famous continuation of Richard Hakluyt's *Principal Navigations,* draws heavily on biblical models of travel to authorize England's national project. Richard Helgerson argues that the ethos of Hakluyt is primarily economic and that "conversion, if it is to happen at all, will follow and serve commerce rather than the other way around" (167). Purchas articulates a more complex relationship between conversion and commerce.[26] His title and preface announce his reliance on two traditions: that of the pilgrim-traveler, such as Mandeville, and the collector-editor, such as Hakluyt. Purchas foregrounds the economic underpinnings of his project, both for himself and for the reader, as he apologizes for not having included more voyages within Europe as promised:

> I confesse, I was too forward to promise, because others have beene so backward to assist: which I have in former Editions signified, but to blind Eyes and deafe Eares. Whose Library, whose Purse hath beene opened to me, let his mouth be opened against me also: Europe otherwise could not, nor now upon any price (it is too late) can be Purchased. . . . If I had not lived in great part upon Exhibition of charitable friends, and on extraordinary labours of Lecturing . . . then Pilgrime had beene a more agreeing name to me, then Purchas. (xli)

In noting the financial exigencies that prevented him from collecting European narratives, he declares that Europe can no longer be "Purchased" and punningly equates his own purchase of narratives with the economic

26. Loren Pennington makes the case that *Hakluytus Posthumus* is the outgrowth of Purchas's earlier works, which were meant to be histories of religion: "Through successive editions he expanded the scope of the *Pilgrimage* to the point where, though it retained its basic religious theme, it began to have a vague resemblance to the *Principal Navigations,* and, though rather incidentally, to become more and more promotional of English overseas trade and colonization. This change is particularly evident in regard to the East Indies" (6).

appropriation of land (perhaps also suggesting a certain inviolability on Europe's part).

This byplay between the religious and the economic interest in travel ("then Pilgrime had beene a more agreeing name to me, then Purchas") runs throughout Purchas's own preface and reveals some of the many ways in which conversion, one of the more persistently articulated motives for colonialism, works to support cultural hegemony and the economic imperatives of imperial trade. Michael Ragussis comments that the ideology of conversion is a cultural institution as well as a literary trope:

> Conversion, the master trope of this literary form [comedy], represents the institutionalization—that is, the legitimization—of one group's mastery and absorption of another group. The triumph of one group over another is marked by a festival of incipient conjugals in which propagation and propaganda become one. In other words, the end of the struggle between the groups is made complete when the audience is persuaded that the life sources of one group have been transferred to another. . . . This pattern takes the form of converting both the property and the identity of the marginal group—depleting its wealth, transferring its goods "legally" to members of the hegemonic group, and finally erasing its religious and legal identity through a set of procedures that the culture regulates under the aegis of the institution known as conversion. (135)

The transference of goods and the erasure of a cultural, if not legal, identity are an integral part of the conversion motive and remove the fears of cultural absorption by the other. That Purchas intends to restore the conversion motive may also be signaled by the reappearance of John Mandeville in his collection. Mandeville's text had been removed from the second and third editions of Hakluyt; but not only does Purchas restore the text, he places an engraving of Mandeville in his gallery of travelers on the frontispiece. Albeit discredited, Mandeville still serves a purpose; he is the "pilgrim" who precedes Purchas and whose image keeps alive the spirit of pilgrimage and conversion that Purchas wishes to sustain.

Purchas ends his prefatory material by equating navigation with Christian charity and envisioning a world converted to Protestantism:

> But the chiefest of these is Charitie, and the chiefest charitie is that which is most common; nor is there any more common then this of Navigation, where one man is not good to another man, but so many Nations as so many persons hold commerce and intercourse of amity withall; Salomon and Hiram together, and both with Ophir; the West with the East, and the remotest; parts

of the world are joined in one band of humanitie; and why not also of Christianitie? Sidon and Sion, Jew and Gentile, Christian and Ethnike, as in this typicall storie? that as there is one Lord, one Faith, one Baptisme, one Body, one Spirit, one Inheritance, one God and Father, so there may thus be one Church truly Catholike, one Pastor and one Sheepfold? (1:56)

Charity may not begin at home, but it certainly ends up there as the charitable cause of conversion redounds to the economic benefit of the English world. The initial ideal of "commerce and intercourse of amity" among many types of men is replaced by a vision of global unity that denies difference just as Purchas's own language does. (The singular construction ["one Lord, one Faith"] subsumes difference when it replaces the "and" that allows differences to exist simultaneously ["Jew and Gentile"].) English trade, rather than fostering a mixing of cultures, will eradicate religious as well as cultural and gender differences under one patriarchal God.

English travel and conversion become a corrective to the errors in previous attempts at conversion (both Christian and "heathen"). Purchas throughout excoriates the Spanish for inducting other cultures into the doctrinal errors of Catholicism, although he acknowledges that in the process they may have better prepared the natives for learning Protestantism. When he equates conversion with economic gain, even improper conversion becomes a model for the deserved gains of English travel:

> Spaine and Portugall, after a long servitude, fattened their Soile with the bloud of the Moores, and thence have growne by Divine Blessing not onely to free themselves of that Yoke, but with farre-spreading Boughes to overlooke and over-awe the remotest East and furthest West; paying themselves with the Drugges and Gemmes of Asia, the Gold and Slaves of Africa, the Silver and Possessions of America, as Wages for that Europæn slavery under the Mahumetans. (2.8).

In this rather strange history, the Iberian "escape" from Moorish control is rewarded with access to the world's wealth. Purchas's evocation of Moorish domination and "European slavery" makes Spanish (and by implication, English) imperial success and slavery mere reparation for previous servitude. In a similar passage, Purchas implicitly compares Protestant with Islamic travel: "And if the Devill hath sent the Moores with dammnable Mahumetisme in their merchandizing quite threorow the East, to pervert so many Nations with thraldom of their states and persons, out of the frying panne of Paynim Rites, into the fire of Mahumetrie: Shall not God be good to Israel, and gracious to the ends of the earth, so long given in inheritance to his Sonne?'' (1.14). In the equation of Islamic conversion with "merchandizing," Purchas simultaneously makes Christian conversion seem less economically motivated and proves that it will be at least as profitable. Purchas justifies such rhetorical sleights of hand through the notion of propriety: "But what shall we say of propriety? of propriety of Infidels? Christs Kingdome is not of this world, and properly neither gives nor takes away wordly proprieties, civill and politicall interests; but addes to his subjects in these things a more sanctified use, all things being pure to the pure, impure to the impure" (1.38). Here the notion of proper disposition of culture seen in other narratives gives England an economic advantage, for "propriety" and property are literally the same: mere possession by true Christians "converts" goods from "impure" material worth to "pure" Christian use.

Solomon becomes the chief biblical model for travel and conversion, not only in travel narratives but, as we shall see, in more literary texts as well. In his *History of the World*, Sir Walter Raleigh uses Solomon's fabled riches to argue, sotto voce, that England's fortune lay in the East Indies: "From this part of *Arabia* . . . did the Fleet passe on to the East *India*, which was not farre off, namely to *Ophir*, one of the Islands of the *Moluccas*, a place exceeding rich in gold: witnesse the *Spaniards*, who not-withstanding all the aboundance which they gather in *Peru*, doe yet plant in those Islands of the East at *Manilia*, and recover a great quantitie from thence, and with lesse labour than they doe in any one part of *Peru*, or new *Spaine*" (499). According to Purchas, "Solomon had a right not extraordinary as the Israelites to spoyle the Egyptians, by Divine especiall Precept" (1.9). This divine right "to spoyle" is typologically passed on to England when Purchas comments on the popular iconography of James I as Solomon:

> But blessed are we . . . that the God of peace hath with the Gospell of peace given us a Salomon, truest type of the Prince of peace, whose dayes are dayes of peace at home, whose treaties propound wayes of peace abroad, whose sun-like rayes have shined not only by bare discoveries, but by rich negotiations to this our Salomons Ophir in what part of the world soever the quarrelsome wits of men have placed it. If you looke neere hand, Scotland is added, and Ireland is now at last made English dispersing feares by English Cities, and plantations: If you look further, with those which seeke for Ophir in the West Indies, there you may see English Plantations and Colonies in Virginia. (1.35)

Solomon's fabled wealth and his travels become the literal "pre-texts" for English imperialism in *Purchas, His Pilgrimes*, as he becomes an "example [to] teach us the lawfulnesse of Navigation to remote Regions" (1.9).

Although attempts by authors of travel narratives to catalog, describe, and contain African difference may not at first glance seem to be overtly Western imperialist moves, such concerns do later come to influence the actual commodification of Africa. The inscriptions are of course complicated by the inconsistent nature of the travel narratives themselves. On the surface, these narratives are intended to be informative, to "shed light" on previously obscure material. They also have the secondary purpose of developing a sense of English identity: allowing English readers to know themselves by seeing others. Insofar as these narratives are also intended to bolster curiosity and future exploration and investment, they seduce the reader into imperialism. This type of textual erotics is a bit more pervasive than the "feminization of the land" that persistently occurs in new world narratives. The tension between the "informational" mode of the narrative and its very seductive purpose replicates the uneasy situation of the colonist—a condition Stephen Greenblatt has outlined in his *Renaissance Self-Fashioning*. As Greenblatt notes, the chief problem for the traveler—or colonial administrator—is exercising the requisite control over the culture without becoming seduced by or implicated in it.[27] This may seem an especially problematic program for the traveler-writer whose mission is, in essence, licensed voyeurism.

In fact, most of the travelers are at great pains to note the special delight or pleasure to be had in reading these narratives and in "seeing" the societies described. The very strangeness involved has a special pleasure in itself. Thus the close of *The Travels* apologizes for not giving more detail, appealing to the reader's appetite for novelty:

And also in the countries where I have been, be many more diversities of many wonderful things than I make mention of; for it were too long thing to devise you the manner. And therefore, that that I have devised you of certain countries, that I have spoken of before, I beseech your worthy and excellent noblesse, that it suffice to you at this time. For if that I devised you all that is beyond the sea, another man, peradventure, that would pain him and travail his body for to go into those marches for to ensearch those countries, might be blamed by my words in rehearsing many strange things; for he might not say nothing of new, in the which the hearers might have either solace, or disport, or lust, or liking in the hearing. For men say always, that new things and new tidings be pleasant to hear. (207)

27. See also Montrose's discussion of desire in Raleigh's *The Discoverie of the Large, Rich, and Beautiful Empire of Guiana* ("Work of Gender" esp. 10–12).

The narratives are continually seductive, not only in the mysteries and "strangeness" they describe but in the yet-untold wonders that they offer the future traveler. They often coyly claim that they could give more detail, but for lack of space, decorum, and so forth they cannot: "Many things more might be saide of the maners of the people, and of the wonders and monstrous things that are engendered in Africke. But it shall suffice to have saide thus much of such things as our men partly sawe, and partly brought with them" (Hakluyt 4:64). Such promises of more serve to stimulate future travel. William Prat goes as far as to say that he published only one part of his *The Discription of Aphrique* with a table and prologue, "to the ende that the reader shulde savour the residue . . . trustinge that he will covet the other two partes" (12–13). The objective, of course, is to know the particulars of these lands. John Bodin's praise of *A Geographical Historie* heightens the importance of the narrative by emphasizing the new knowledge it provides: "Certes of all others this is the onely man, by whom Africa, which for a thousand yeeres before had lien buried in the barbarous and grosse ignorance of our people, is now plainly discovered and laide open to the view of all beholders" (Leo Africanus 60). However, these writers use their sense of Africa's inexhaustible difference to defer continually the desired goal of a land "entirely known." In *The Discription of Aphrique*, Prat also apologizes for his text's incomplete status: "And be not offended with me (gentyll reader) for want of austeritie. In that I have not wholly satisfied thy appetite as peradventure thou desirest. I have done it rather to chalenge unto myselfe rebuke and shame, then praise" (35). Here the author goes farther than mere apology: he both extols the wonders of nature and admonishes the reader not to be too curious: "Howe can a man but wonder (thoughe that the giftes of God be not to be marveiled at)" (6).

The complex nature of the pleasure of seeing is common to all the travel narratives. The very act of looking at the sexual improprieties outlined in them provides its own illicit pleasure. As Foucault reminds us, "Different instances and stages in the transmission of power were caught up in the very pleasure of their exercise" (186); this is particularly true of surveillance, which carries within it its own type of voyeuristic pleasure. In her study of *The Rape of Lucrece*, Nancy Vickers demonstrates the close relationship in the Renaissance between the imperial gaze and the erotic gaze, particularly in virtuoso description: "Description, then, is a gesture of display, a separating off and a signaling of particulars destined to make visible that which is described. Its object or matter is thus submitted to a double power-relation inherent in the gesture itself: on the one hand, the describer controls, possesses, and uses that matter to his own ends; and, on the other, his reader/listener is extended the privilege or pleasure of 'seeing.' " (96). Even though Vickers here outlines the effect of a rhetorical description of the female body, the "body" of Africa, as we have seen, is displayed as a gendered object. This "signaling of particulars" is noteworthy in these texts which attempt to describe whole continents by "digesting" them in particular. Hence John Pory affixes to Leo's manuscript an addendum, because "it remaineth that we briefly describe in particular all the principall maine landes, and islands (undescribed by *John Leo*) which thereto belong, or adjoine" (8). Purchas, too, suggests that a whole map of Africa is insufficient: "Other Maps more particular we shall adde in their places" (5:303).

The very act of extending the pleasure of seeing, by putting these particulars in the public eye, teeters on the brink of danger, however. Just as Collatine's "publication" of Lucrece's beauty arouses Tarquin to the point of rape, the possibility of arousing the too-close involvement of the traveler is courted with the publication of the travel narrative. There is a critical conflict between the enticing promise of a trade in things yet unknown and the necessity of controlling the aroused desire of the future colonist. If the travel writers seem aware of the dangers of their own enterprise only in projecting it onto the natives themselves, they thereby attest to the doubleness of the seduction. Hartwell complains that the natives of the Congo are converted with Catholic pomp that "is able to allure any simple Man or Woman, even with the very sight thereof" (*4b).

The travel writers negotiate this problem in several ways. Hakluyt suggests that one find pleasure in the orderliness of the manuscript itself rather than in the things described therein; not surprisingly, he is "ravished" by his own order: "And such other rare and strange curiosities, which wise men take great pleasure to reade of, but much more contentment to see: herein I my selfe to my singuler delight have bene as it were ravished in beholding all the premisses gathered together with no small cost, and preserved with no litle diligence" (1:12). More often, however, these writers rely on encouraging travel for the more acceptable benefits of seeing Africa: "conversion and enterprise." Whatever the motivation, there is always a promise of "more to come"—a perpetuation of the endlessly deferred desire that fuels the hunger for colonial mastery.

CHAPTER TWO

Fair Texts/Dark Ladies:
Renaissance Lyric and the Poetics of Color

> Or would she her miraculous power show,
> That whereas blacke seemes Beautie's contrary,
> She even in blacke doth make all beauties flow.
> —Sir Philip Sidney, *Astrophel and Stella*

In William Basse's allegorical poem *Urania, or The Woman in the Moon* (c. 1612), Jove, angered by the degeneration of the earth, sends two messengers to "be as your Father's All beholding eyes" and to "let me know the whole world's general case" (1.2.6). Before reaching their final destination, the Americas, they stop in Ethiopia:

> For in the heate of the middle-aged yeare
> They chanc'd in Ethiopia to arrive
> Where double flames, of time & Climat, there
> Perswaded rest, in bathes of ease revive
>   Their toiled limmes: where they an object found
>   That their delay in double fetters bound.
>
>   (1.19)

Surveying Ethiopia becomes a dual threat when native heat and the time of year (midsummer) produce lethargy and heighten lust. Like Spenser's Guyon, they are forced to rest and are trapped by their own desire. The "object" that causes their delay and destroys their resolve not to "leave a Land unspied, / Empire unseene, or Island undescried" (1.14.5–6) is a white Ethiopian woman.[1]

---

1. Actually, their "delay" should perhaps be read as a "fortunate fall," since Basse, in verse oddly evocative of Hakluyt's legend that Africa blocked European access to America,

62

Basse explains the curious phenomenon of the white Ethiope with the story of Phaeton, who is a poet figure as well as the original cause of blackness:

> For ere Apollo's sonne his father's chayre,
> To leade the Light, on day did undertake,
> The Æthiopians then were white & fayre,
> Though by the worlds combustion since made black
> When wanton Phaeton overthrew the Sun,
> Which dredfull mischeife had not yet been done.
>
> (2.2)

This verse in some ways replicates a dynamic already seen in travel literature, most notably in Hakluyt. Lightness is associated with the order and control wrought by Apollo, whereas the blackness of the Ethiopians becomes a sign of chaos and transgression. The nymph here is not only one of these pre-Phaeton, "white & fayre" Ethiopians, she is in some ways a Phaeton figure herself, although in this case her transgressive nature is specifically linked to her femininity. Like Phaeton, she is a human who wants access to godlike powers, but her ambition (Basse tells us in the argument of the second canto, "Themselves her teach / Themselves to over-reach") is complicated by the fact that she is an unruly female. She tricks from the messengers the secret of flight and, once in Olympus, makes the gods worry, "Lest her loose tongue (that nothing holds) blab there / Amongst unworthy mortalls, mysteries / Peculier to immortall eares and eyes" (3.22.4–6).[2]

Basse's "allegory in four cantos" is a fascinating poetic response to the manifold fears of foreign entanglement and conversion seen in the travel narrative. Jove's "spies" are analogous to travelers for whom the pleasure of detached observation is stopped dead by the allure of the native female. In an interesting twist on the fear of foreign entrapment typical of colo-

---

claims that the spies' failure left the Americas for current discovery: "Wee only want some base Americans / that know not Jove, and Jove cares not to know, / Some barb'rous Gotes or salvage Indians, / No matter whether ever seene or no. / (And so rest undiscov'd to this day / The greater part of wilde America)." (2.15).

2. Samuel Purchas specifically uses Phaeton as a type of traveler, although he is compared unfavorably to the English travelers whom Purchas glorifies: "But these have attained what they sought, and what hee in his Vulcanian Chariot lost, these in Neptunian Chariots gained, and followed the Sunne round about the world. . . . Such were those which have passed the blacke Guineans, and doubled the Hopefull Promontory, from thence piercing into the Erythraean and Indian Seas, Lands, Islands, enriching our World, with a world of rarities for contemplation and use" (Purchas 2.286).

nialist discourses, she not only stops their project but appropriates their power. Basse defends his use of "amorous dieties" in the explanation of his allegory and introduces another ideal common to English poetry and travel— conversion:

> As Indian gold in Christian use we spend,
> So we vaine fictions use to vertuous end;
> And being not able heavenly workes t'expresse
> In their owne greatnes, strive in what is lesse.
> Through shadowes dim most shines a reall worth,
> As a dark foile best sets a diamond forth.
>
> (80–85)

In some ways Basse's simile particularizes crucial European anxieties over the proper use of new world wealth: his "Indian gold" spent in "Christian use" parallels travel narratives on the propriety of enriching the English/ Christian empire with "heathen goods."

More compelling for my purposes is Basse's equation of that process of material enrichment with his own literary project. His explanation converts "vaine fictions" of sexual intrigue and foreign entanglement into a "moralized" tale of the mind's search for knowledge. He is thus able to have it both ways: to appropriate the dangerous "matter" of the poem with its grounding in feminine unruliness, forbidden sexuality, and racial difference and, in naming the poem an "allegory," to keep the possibility of difference without the dangers of absorption. His attempt is doomed to failure, for, as Maureen Quilligan observes, allegory inscribes an "other" in its very name: "The 'other' named by the term *allos* in the word 'allegory' is not some other hovering above the words of the text, but the possibility of an otherness, a polysemy, inherent in the very words on the page" (*Language of Allegory* 26). It is the attraction to and fear of "the possibility of an otherness" and linguistic polysemy that underlie most of the tropes of blackness in Renaissance poetry, particularly in the black/light dichotomy of the English sonnet cycle. Basse's white Ethiope and the sonneteer's "dark lady" both represent attempts to negotiate involvements with the sexual, racial, and "linguistic" difference brought about by increased travel abroad.

I start with Basse because he foregrounds several little-discussed connections between English travel and trade and the seemingly "purely aesthetic" tropes of English poetry. My reading of the sonnets is based on the premise that "dark ladies" of the sonnets are at least in part the literary cousins of the foreign women encountered in travel narratives and that they share the same subject position. The sonnet form encodes not only erotic but political, economic, and literary desires as well. According to Nancy Vickers, Petrarch introduced to the Renaissance a power dynamic in which the poet achieves his desire—and power—through a process of poetically dismembering the female while remaining always at risk of destruction brought about by his own transgressive gaze. This dynamic of political/poetic competition and erotic danger is similar to that found in the travel narrative in which black women may represent the possibility of conquest and enrichment as well as the threat of potential destruction.

Drawing on Vickers's analysis of the gendered power dynamics of Petrarchism, Patricia Parker and Louis Montrose have convincingly demonstrated that the anatomizing and descriptive rhetoric of display were also prominent discursive practices in travel narratives. Little work, however, has been done on the colonial imperatives of lyric itself.[3] The supposedly insulated language of the love lyric is shot through with references to foreign difference and foreign wealth. More important, the connection between lyric and English discourses of travel and trade is not merely rhetorical. In his *Enterprise and Empire*, Theodore Rabb demonstrates that unlike that of the rest of Europe, the English aristocracy was deeply involved in English navigation and colonial trade.[4] Almost 80 percent of the members of the African companies were gentry, and that percentage was even higher for other colonial endeavors. The very class that formed its identity through the circulation of miniatures and sonnets (Fumerton 67–110) was also shoring up its economic position by not only investing in but in some cases actually controlling joint-stock companies (Rabb 28–31).[5]

Given the aristocratic interest in travel and lyric poetry, it is perhaps fitting that Sir Francis Wyatt, twice governor of Virginia, and great-grandson of one of England's first sonneteers, Thomas Wyatt, copies into his commonplace book a translation of a lyric poem, "La Bella Mora,"

3. This of course does not include Nancy Vickers's reading of the colonial language in Shakespeare's *The Rape of Lucrece.*

4. Holden Furber supports this view: "Because of the sharp social distinction in England between gentry and merchant, the presence of numbers of influential gentry, many of them members of Parliament, among the investors presented the directors of the English East India Company in its early years with problems their Dutch counterparts never had to face. Even the king wanted to be an investor, and it required a great deal of tact and diplomacy on the part of the directors to persuade James I to give up on the idea" (192). See also A. L. Rowse's discussion of English navigation in *The Expansion of Elizabethan England*, esp. 159–62.

5. T. S. Willan also gives evidence that Leicester took a very hands-on approach in running the Barbary Company (164–72).

described as "A Spaniard taking a Moore Prisoner, falls in love with her. Out of Spanish."[6] Much of the economic language of the lyric and its rejection of material gain in favor of spiritual love may then speak to the anxieties of this class, which is deeply involved in foreign trade and thus needs to distance itself from the merchant classes who were the primary force behind the trade (Helgerson 178). If, as Richard Helgerson points out, *The Principal Navigations* bridges the class differences within English trade by bringing "merchants into the nation and gentry into trade" (176), the gentry further mystify their role in previously looked-down-upon trade practices both by glorifying the trade as adventure (Rabb 38) and by writing lyric poems that seemingly refuse mercantilism.

In this chapter I sketch out the links between blackness and economics in the English sonnet, which, as I hope Basse's example demonstrates, is closely linked to the concerns of English travel. I will initially argue that much of the lyric is concerned with effacing the colonial economic practices of the English gentry. This effacement is linked to what I have called a poetics of color in which whiteness is established as a valued goal. Whiteness in this case is as much about a desire for a stable linguistic order as it is about physical beauty. As the most influential attempt to render the sonnet cycle in the vernacular (Marotti 397), *Astrophel and Stella* appropriately becomes the focal point for this chapter. Sir Philip Sidney's life is in some ways emblematic of the economic concerns of the aristocracy, and his sonnet cycle reveals sites of contestation between the old world and the new in the English language of praise. Each subsequent section of this chapter takes up a different troping of color and colonialism: white-washing, sunburn, and the Song of Songs. Finally, I discuss a subgenre of poems of blackness that inform the sonnet tradition even as they depart from it. As we shall see, the poetry of praise and the glorification of English women in the sonnet become part of England's nationalist project, a way for England to define itself politically, culturally, and racially and to establish itself as a dominant force on the world stage.

The sonneteer proves his poetic prowess by literally accomplishing the impossible, known in Renaissance proverb lore as "To wash an Ethiop/ blackamoor is to labor in vain" (Prager 257). Based on the line "Can the blacke More change his skin? or the leopard his spottes?" (Jeremiah 13.23 Geneva), this image is perhaps the dominant troping of blackness in the period. Although the proverbial whitewashed Ethiope and the emblems depicting him usually refer to males, the figurative representation

6. I thank my colleague Bruce Smith for bringing this poem to my attention and graciously transcribing it for me.

of this trope in poetry and drama is almost always gendered female (see figure 3).[7] The otherness of language is represented for the European by an extreme of otherness: the black female. Positing a mistress as dark allows the poet to turn her white, to refashion her into an acceptable object of Platonic love and admiration. The loveliness of these Petrarchan beauties, despite their color, represents not their seductive power but the poet's power in bringing them to light. Louis Montrose sees this dynamic in his reading of Spenser, where "the poet at once evokes and suppresses the darker aspect of the virtuous and beautiful lady, her vengeful power to deform or even destroy her devotees" ("Elizabethan Subject" 328).

Throughout *Astrophel and Stella*, Philip Sidney plays with the paradox of black beauty:

> So Tyran he no fitter place could spie,
> Nor so faire levell in so secret stay,
> As that sweete blacke which vailes the heav'nly eye:
> There himselfe with his shot he close doth lay.
>   Poore passenger, passe now thereby I did,
> And staid pleasd with the prospect of the place,
> While that blacke hue from me the bad guest hid:
> But straight I saw motions of lightning' grace,
>   And then descried the glistring of his dart:
>   But ere I could flie thence, it pierc'd my heart.
>
> $(20.5–14)$[8]

That "sweete blacke" (7) of Stella's eye, which seduces the "passenger" (9) or traveler into staying, becomes for Sidney no more than a removable veil; however, looking beyond the black veil is in itself dangerous. In this instance the "light[e]ning' grace" that reveals the essence of Stella also exposes the poet to the hidden Cupid's power. Throughout the cycle, Sidney develops his own lightening grace as he continually conjures up, in order to lighten, Stella's blackness. Shakespeare, too, reveals the com-

---

7. Carolyn Prager gives an excellent and thorough overview of the classical and biblical provenance of this proverb. She claims that before 1609 this proverb "refers seldom to dramatically realized Africans except in the most incidental fashion; however, after that date, at least for the drama, the proverb is applied primarily to and about Africans and pseudo-Africans whose poetic givens include elements of actual or fictive bondage" (258). See also Karen Newman's discussion of the significance of this trope in her reading of *Othello*, "'And wash the Ethiope white: Femininity and the Monstrous in *Othello*"; and Allison Blakeley, *Blacks in the Dutch World*, 92–95.

8. All *Astrophel and Stella* quotations are taken from *The Poems of Sir Philip Sidney*, ed. William A. Ringler. Subsequent references are to this edition and are noted in the text.

L EAVE of with paine, the blackamore to ſkowre,
With waſhinge ofte, and wipinge more then due:
For thou ſhalt finde, that Nature is of powre,
Doe what thou canſte, to keepe his former hue:
Thoughe with a forke, wee Nature thruſte awaie,
Shee turnes againe, if wee withdrawe our hande:
And thoughe, wee ofte to conquer her aſſaie,
Yet all in vaine, ſhee turnes if ſtill wee ſtande:
  Then euermore, in what thou doeſt aſſaie,
  Let reaſon rule, and doe the thinges thou maie.

Eraſmus ex Luciano.
Ablais Æthiopem fru-
ſtrà: quin deſinis artè?
Haud vnquā efficies
nox ſit vt atra, dies.
Horat.1. Epiſt.10.
Naturam expellas fur-
ca tamen vſque re-
curret.

———   ——— *equuſq̃*,
Nunquam ex degeneri fiet generoſus aſello,
Et nunquam ex ſtolido cordatus fiet ab arte.

Anulus in pict.
poëſi.

H   *Non*

Figure 3. This popular emblem was often used as a figure for the impossible. The motto, "Æthiopem lavare," draws on a verse in Jeremiah: "Can the blacke More change his skin? or the leopard his spottes?" (Geoffrey Whitney, *A Choice of Emblemes* [1586], by permission of the Folger Shakespeare Library.)

petitive dynamics of this rhetoric in *Love's Labour's Lost* when Berowne is forced to prove his "black as ebony" (4.3.243) Rosaline beautiful in the face of the company's barbs, declaring, "I'll prove her fair, or talk till doomsday here" (4.3.270).[9]

Sonneteers establish their power over female matter and their poetic prowess by drawing on the dismembering power of the blazon (Vickers, "Diana Described") and by grounding relations between the white European male and the foreign female through a metaphoric politics of color that permeates the sonnet cycle. Elizabethan "dark ladies" are a curious hybrid of the traditional opposition of black and white. Lauded for her "milk hands," "yellow hairs," "fair ivory brows," "ivory cheeks," and "snowy brows," this beauty is also continually associated with formulations of blackness as she is often "beamy black" or "black, but in blackness bright."

To understand this color complex, which is undergirded by a fundamental urge for whiteness, it is necessary first to reexamine the logic of the traditional dark/light opposition found in the sonnets. Christianity has long provided the Western world with a symbolic order in which good, purity, and Christianity itself are associated with light and whiteness, while evil, sexuality, and difference are linked with darkness.[10] Indeed, the imagery was so pervasive that it was a subject for humor even before the sonnet sequence fell out of vogue. The very ubiquity of the metaphoric system makes it difficult to assess what, if any, significance such metaphors may have had for the Renaissance reader. The task is complicated by literary criticism's traditional (and almost pathological) insistence that blackness means nothing beyond its antithesis to "whiteness"; that is, in the absolute insistence on a merely aesthetic basis for blackness in the Renaissance, a practice that extends even to reading direct references to Africa as mere signs of physical beauty. Even critics who purport to be open-minded in their interpretations of the sonnets become strangely recalcitrant when faced with the possibilities of racial difference in the "blackness" of the dark lady. Stephen Booth, who in his 1977 edition of the sonnets claims that "the notes in this edition are designed to admit that everything in a sonnet is there" (xiv) and that "some of the puns, allusions, suggestions, and implications [he] describe[s] are farfetched" (xi), becomes quite definitive when glossing the word "black" in the first

9. See Peter Erickson's reading of whiteness in Shakespeare's comedies ("Representing Blacks and Blackness" 519–20).

10. For further information, see Frantz Fanon, *Black Skin, White Masks*; Winthrop Jordan, *White over Black*; and Harry Levin, *The Power of Blackness: Melville and Hawthorne.*

of the dark lady sonnets: "*black*: The meaning of this word is established by its contrast to *fair*: (1) brunette; (2) ugly (Shakespeare and his contemporaries regularly use *black* as if it were a simple antonym for 'beautiful'" (434 n.1). Booth's gloss is typical of contemporary readings of the opposition of black and white: it reiterates an identification of difference by polarity, eliding the fact that this is part of a larger system of values (Belsey, "Disrupting" 178) that may inform a reading of the poem. The meaning of "black" is here only (and simply) established in an agonistic contest with the word "fair."

Such readings also tend to see these terms merely as aesthetic markers, ignoring the larger cultural values and gendered judgments that are at stake in this system.[11] Certainly in the Renaissance "light," "white" and "fair" were not merely descriptive terms used primarily for women but terms that, as I propose in the Introduction, carry specifically gendered judgments as well. William Basse's *Urania* contains a typical example:

> But I have heard how Nature did prepare
> Three Essences to make three women of,
> An amorous, a subtill, and a faire;
> Which Fortune seeing came & mix'd her stuffe
> All into one, that should have serv'd for three;
> And of that composition fram'd was shee.
>
> (2.6)

Here "faire" becomes more than an aesthetic or physically descriptive term; it has moral, sexual, and ethical implications that apply specifically to women. Furthermore, "faire" contains the possibility of economic involvement as well; when describing the spies' competition for the nymph, he remarks, "Diversitie of buyers raise the faire" (2.24.4). It seems that,

11. Janet Adelman's appendix "Cleopatra's Blackness" in *The Common Liar* works in approximately the same way. She is bothered by the lack of attention to Cleopatra's darkness, yet prefaces her discussion with a critique of Winthrop Jordan's insistence on reading most references to "black" as racially coded. In examining the references to blackness in *A Midsummer Night's Dream* and *Love's Labour's Lost*, she claims: "The point of the joke is of course lost if we assume that Shakespeare was thinking of any of these women as literally black, or even very dark. If Cleopatra is 'tawny' (1.1.6), so is Spain (*Love's Labour's Lost* 1.1.174): to the English, anyone darker than themselves is apt to be characterized as black. This point is worth making only because some recent literature on Elizabethan attitudes toward race has assumed that every time Shakespeare said black he meant black. . . . In fact, when Shakespeare wants us to consider race as an issue, he makes the point abundantly clear: there is no mistaking it in *Titus Andronicus* or *Othello.* Jordan's comments on *Othello* are extremely useful . . . , but these comments cannot be extended to include all of Shakespeare's dark ladies" (185).

in their caution to avoid an anachronism of race, most editors (and readers) are wary of admitting that terms such as "black" and "white" are more than, well, black and white.

Suggesting that there is an "unnamed, nontext of race" (Patricia Williams 117) in the lyric does not automatically mean that I wish to produce "anachronistic" readings. To insist on reading blackness solely as hair color equally ignores the fact that modern Western notions of race were developing at the very moment of the first contact between "white" European and his dark others.[12] In his *Shakespeare's Perjur'd Eye,* Joel Fineman offers the basis for a more complicated reading of blackness when he says that "paradoxical praise . . . turns its attention, by a kind of necessary logic, to issues and themes whose development establishes, stipulates, even exaggerates, the black and white, positive and negative polarities organizing strong cultural values" (34). The "dark lady" conceit organized certain cultural values regarding the proper "use" of foreign *materia,* both economic and discursive. In English sonnet cycles, "black," "dark," and "darkness" become the focal points for concerns over the economic and literary enrichment of empire as well as over fears of the colonial/imperial encounters with the twin otherness of culture and gender. Conversely, "whiteness" and "lightening" begin to function as a desire for a stable European linguistic order. The whitening of dark ladies reveals the contradictory impulses of a poetic that simultaneously wishes to "enrich" the language with new world matter and to deny excessive involvement in foreign difference. While creating an English language of praise, English poets revitalize a traditional opposition that works to control encroachments of cultural otherness and gender difference and that continues to inform subsequent English incursions onto the world stage.

One way of accounting for the compulsion to lighten the dark lady is to read it as a reflection of the poet's wish to master not only his own desire but language as well. Catherine Belsey notes:

12. Indeed, the American Black Power slogan of the 1960s, "Black Is Beautiful," speaks to the embedded politics of a purely aesthetic understanding of blackness. As the battle cry for a new aesthetic that would change the binary perceptions ingrained in Western thought, it aims to upset and conquer the system of power subtended by such perceptions. As Frantz Fanon argues, modern perceptions of race are linked to this early opposition with its negative associations with blackness and cannot be challenged successfully until we recognize this integral connection: "It would be astonishing, if the trouble were taken to bring them all together, to see the vast number of expressions that make the black man the equivalent of sin. In Europe, whether concretely or symbolically, the black man stands for the bad side of the character. As long as one cannot understand this fact, one is doomed to talk in circles about the "black problem." Blackness, darkness, shadow, shades, night, the labyrinths of the earth, abysmal depths, blacken someone's reputation; and, on the other side, the bright look of innocence, the white dove of peace, magical, heavenly light" (189).

Meaning depends on difference, and the fixing of meaning is the fixing of difference as opposition. It is precisely this identification of difference as polarity which Derrida defines as *metaphysical*. In conjunction with the common-sense belief that language is a nomenclature, a set of labels for what is irrevocably and inevitably there—whether in the world or in our heads— this process of fixing meaning provides us with a series of polarities which define what is. These definitions are also values. In the oppositions "I/you," "individual/society," "truth/fiction," "masculine/feminine," one term is always privileged, and one is always other, always what is *not* the thing itself. ("Disrupting Sexual Difference" 177)

The contest for meaning also takes its form in the "light/dark" oppositions common to the sonnet cycles, in which "light" (and the process of lightening) signals a wish for an ordered, stable language rather than the dark, unconquered territory of slippery linguistic "alienness." The contest may thus seem a never-ending play of contraries because, as Derrida demonstrates in his study of metaphor in philosophy, the ideal of univocity in language (that is, that language is intended specifically to "bring to knowledge the thing itself" [247]) is doomed to failure by its own refusal to acknowledge the problems of polysemy inherent in any use of language, metaphorical or otherwise.

Although Derrida points up the ultimate impossibility of fulfilling the dream of a stable language, his formulation may make the dominant term representing this wish seem more overpowering than is fitting. This linguistic struggle is most certainly not straightforward; it is only consistent in its infinite regress. The opposition is itself an encoding of power relations that tends to occur at the stress points in which issues of male, European control and cultural order are negotiated in hiding, as it were, beneath continual disruption and restructuring of the opposition. When thinking about the drive for univocity in the black/white language of sonnets, it is useful to keep in mind a Foucauldian notion that power, rather than being monolithic, is characterized by negotiation and disruption. As Foucault states:

Dispersed, heteromorphous, localised procedures of power are adapted, reinforced and transformed by these global strategies, all this being accompanied by numerous phenomena of inertia, displacement and resistance; hence one should not assume a massive and primal condition of domination, a binary structure with "dominators" on one side and "dominated" on the other, but rather a multiform production of relations of domination which are partially susceptible of integration into overall strategies. (142)

Foucault's proposal for "multiform production of relations of domination" is helpful, for Derrida's description of the desire for a "transparent" language may lead one to look at the black/white opposition solely as a struggle of opposites (Foucault 143), with "whiteness" always the privileged (if ultimately thwarted) term, rather than a more dynamic contest. Unraveling the "multiform production of relations of domination" in the sonnets means that I will not be producing a "reading" of a particular sonnet cycle that looks for the dominance of white over black; rather, in this chapter I will use Sidney and other poets to delineate several ways in which the English poetic project produced a politics of color that prepares generically, thematically, and economically a poetic for the "new world"—a world in which blackness is not a purely "aesthetic" indication of beauty standards but the site for the interplay of sexual politics and cultural and racial difference.

Astrophel and Stella: "New Found Tropes with Problemes Old"

Although he was not the first English sonneteer, Sir Philip Sidney is generally celebrated for his role in popularizing the sonnet sequence in England. The publication of his *Astrophel and Stella* in 1591 sparked a passion for sonnet cycles that established it as the model for the English subgenre. Sidney's own status as cultural hero makes his literary landmark an excellent place to begin a more specific discussion of the cultural pressures negotiated by the sonnet form. *Astrophel and Stella* reflects some of Sidney's concerns over issues of cultural hegemony as well as with the more immediate problems of court advancement and female favor. Sidney, the "English Petrarcke," and his circle all had investments in colonial trade. He and his sister, the noted literary patron Mary Herbert, invested in the Frobisher and Fenton voyages, and Sidney further invested in Gilbert's enterprises as well as in various privateering ventures. His father-in-law, Francis Walsingham; his friend, Fulke Greville; and his queen, Elizabeth, were all members of the Virginia Companies.

Sidney was vitally concerned with England's place in the ongoing encroachments into the "new world." Katherine Duncan-Jones's biography of Sidney indicates that he had an ongoing interest in colonial adventure, an interest stymied by his chronic lack of funds. She suggests that, in addition to his actual investment and "explosive" interest in Frobisher's first and second voyages (137–38), he may have desired to go to Meta Icognita (131). As Fulke Greville outlines in *The Life of Sir Philip Sidney,*

Sidney had a keen sense of the importance of England's role in this co-lonial expansion. Although Greville was most certainly using *The Life* for his own political purposes in a Jacobean court, his rendition of Sidney's imperial aspirations is not out of place with what is known about Sidney's political career. At the time he wrote *Astrophel and Stella*, Sidney apparently bought a patent that allowed him the right to "settle, cultivate and trade in three million acres" that were yet to be discovered by Gilbert (Duncan-Jones 230). However, Sidney's own desires for more immediate new world adventure were promptly squelched by Elizabeth, just as she denied his more local ambitions.[13] Chafing at Elizabeth's vacillations over using him for the political duties for which he was groomed, he arranged to join and finance Drake's voyage to the West Indies. While preparing to meet Drake under cover of performing a diplomatic mission, he was stopped by a messenger from Elizabeth, carrying "in the one hand grace, the other thunder" (Greville 88), who demanded his return to court.

Sidney's exploit presents a fascinating interchange of court and inter-national politics framed by frustrated personal ambition and a drive for new world enterprise. Although his attempt at finding adventure and glory in the new world was squelched, it forced Elizabeth to grant his original desire of going to war in the Netherlands. In a telling passage Greville describes the death of Sidney's colonial ambition: "Neverthelesse as the Limmes of *Venus* picture, how perfectly soever began, and left by *Apelles*, yet after his death proved impossible to finish: so that *Heroicall* design of invading, and possessing *America*, how exactly soever projected, and di-gested in every minute by Sir *Philip*, did yet prove impossible to be well acted by any other mans spirit than his own" (89–90). Greville's metaphor conflates the representation of love and beauty with plans for empire. He also adds a new dimension to the traditional associations of eroticism with heroic contest seen in such works as Shakespeare's *The Rape of Lucrece* and *Antony and Cleopatra* in his depiction of the imperial conqueror as artist; the passage thus makes the artistic reproduction of beauty analogous to the "Heroicall design" of empire. Although Sidney was kept from actively participating in new world exploration, he participated indirectly by cre-ating a sonnet cycle that, as we shall see, limned in little English trafficking in the new world.

Sidney perhaps began that unfinished project/picture with his *Astrophel and Stella*, which is characterized by a studied rejection of foreignness. The sequence opens with Astrophel searching for invention and new language

13. See Richard McCoy, *Sir Philip Sidney: Rebellion in Arcadia*, 1–35 and Maureen Quilligan, "Sidney and His Queen."

"to paint the blackest face of woe" (1.5), but with the caveat that this new language should not be tainted with "strangeness":

> I sought fit words to paint the blackest face of woe,
> Studying inventions fine, her wits to entertaine:
> Oft turning others' leaves, to see if thence would flow
> Some fresh and fruitfull showers upon my sunne-burn'd braine.
>   But words came halting forth, wanting Invention's stay,
> Invention, Nature's child, fled step-dame Studie's blowes,
> And others' feete still seem'd but strangers in my way.
> Thus great with child to speake, and helplesse in my throwes,
>   Biting my trewand pen, beating my selfe for spite,
>   "Foole," said my Muse to me, "looke in thy heart and write."
>
> (1.5–14)

As I will argue in more detail in a discussion of sunburn later in this chapter, it is significant that Sidney's anxieties about literary "production" are projected onto the dual differences of race and gender in his depiction of himself as pregnant female and sunburned poet.

The insistence on looking to the inward self is for Sidney linked with the rejection of all that is "strange." Sonnet 3 almost directly involves the sonneteering urge for linguistic purity in England's imperial project:

> Let daintie wits crie on the Sisters nine,
> That bravely maskt, their fancies may be told:
> Or, *Pindare's* Apes, flaunt they in phrases fine,
> Enam'ling with pied flowers their thoughts of gold:
>   Or else let them in statelier glorie shine,
> Ennobling new found Tropes with problemes old:
> Or with strange similies enrich each line,
> Of herbes or beastes, which *Inde* or *Afrike* hold.
>   For me in sooth, no Muse but one I know:
> Phrases and Problemes from my reach do grow,
> And strange things cost too deare for my poor sprites.
>   How then? even thus: in *Stella's* face I reed,
>   What Love and Beautie be, then all my deed
>   But Copying is, what in her Nature writes.

Sidney uses "strange" twice in this sonnet and, as G. K. Hunter notes, "strange" or "stranger" is a common synonym for "foreign."[14] The ad-

14. See G. K. Hunter, *Dramatic Identities and Cultural Tradition: Studies in Shakespeare and His Contemporaries*, 4, n. 13.

dition of newfound plants and animals from exotic places to England's consciousness is quickly associated with the strange "new found Tropes" that Sidney rejects although, like the new world commodities, they may prove a source of wealth. The speaker with an equally clear sense of superiority rejects the ridiculed literary techniques of "daintie wits" and "Pindare's Apes."

Unlike Basse, who is willing to appropriate strangeness under the guise of Christian conversion, Sidney castigates those who ennoble "new found Tropes." Implying that Africa and India are as rich with new linguistic matter as they are in material commodities, he refuses to enrich each line "with strange similies . . . / Of herbes or beastes, which *Inde* or *Afrike* hold" (3.7–8). The commodification implicit in this foreign "strangeness" is rejected as well. Rather than adopt such linguistic strangeness, he prefers to see himself as a mere imitator, "then all my deed / But Copying is, what in her Nature writes" (3.13–14). Like Lewis Carroll's Humpty-Dumpty Sidney battles language to prevent words from straying:

> And oft whole troupes of saddest words I staid,
>   Striving abroad a foraging to go,
>   Untill by your inspiring I might know,
> How their blacke banner might be best displaid.
>
> (55.5–9)

His words struggling toward foreign difference ("Striving abroad a foraging to go"), the poet resolves his linguistic dilemma through "naming," a rhetorical strategy more suited to warding off linguistic excess: "For let me but name her whom I do love, / So sweete sounds straight mine eare and heart do hit, / That I well find no eloquence like it" (55.12–14).

This rejection of strangeness and "foraging abroad" seems to be an integral part of Sidney's project for English poetry. In his *Apology for Poetry*, he often equates foreign strangeness with linguistic abuses: "So is that honny-flowing Matron Eloquence, apparelled, or rather disguised, in a Curtizan-like painted affectation: one time with so farre fette words, they may seem Monsters: but must seem straungers to any poore English man" (K4r). Once again, rhetorical excess is coded as both foreign and female. The "Matron Eloquence" is commodified, becoming merely "Curtizan-like." As I suggested in Chapter 1, female transgression is located in the space of the foreign or strange and is thus not recognizable by poor Englishmen. The evocation of the foreign becomes even more pronounced when he goes on to complain about ornate diction: "For nowe they cast Sugar and Spice, upon every dish that is served to the table; Like those Indians, not content to wear eare-rings at the fit & naturall place of the eares, but they will thrust Jewels through their nose, and lippes, because they will be sure to be fine" (K4v). In the *Apology*, Sidney collapses overly ornate language, female copia, cosmetics, and cultural difference. So too his rejection of foreign difference in the sonnets continually equates the acquisition of overseas commodities with excessive, insincere, and dysfunctional figurative language. He—and England—literally cannot afford such rhetorical excess. Such oddly evocative passages ultimately defeat the rejection of strangeness: each protest against foreign borrowing conjures up the very difference it purports to deny.

Sidney's xenophobic protests seem all the more strident when compared with Shakespeare's statements on invention:

> Why is my verse so barren of new pride,
> So far from variation or quick change?
> Why with the time do I not glance aside
> To new-found methods, and to compounds strange?
> Why write I still all one, ever the same,
> And keep invention in a noted weed,
> That every word doth almost tell my name,
> Showing their birth, and where they did proceed?
> O know, sweet love, I always write of you,
> And you and love are still my argument.
> So all my best is dressing old words new,
> Spending again what is already spent:
>> For as the sun is daily new and old,
>> So is my love still telling what it told.

(76)

Like Sidney, Shakespeare claims to use a familiar language. Unlike Sidney, he is so identified with his language that "every word doth almost tell my name / Showing their birth, and where they did proceed" (7–8); that is, his words are not of uncertain origin or "foreign" to him. Not only can he "name" his language, his words are almost literally his "name." In this sonnet, however, we see a vague dissatisfaction with a language that is recycled currency. When the poet spends "what is already spent," there is the unspoken wish to enrich his "barren" language with the linguistic and cultural *materia* from new worlds.

This grappling with the problems posed by foreign and familiar language is linked to an underlying nationalism that is one of the more curious features of the sonnet vogue. Many poets make broad claims for the "Englishness" of the sequences, even though many of the most notable tropes and conceits of the sequences were borrowed from continental poets.[15] The sense of international competition in the sonnet cycle is closely linked to the already-existing tensions between imitation and copying that we have seen both in Sidney and in European economic competition. This awareness of being engaged in a nationalist enterprise is quite acute. In the first commendatory sonnet to Spenser's *Amoretti*, G. W. senior begs Spenser to

> . . . hie thee home, that art our perfect guide,
> and with thy wit illustrate Englands fame,
> dawnting thereby our neighboures auncient pride,
> that do for poesie challendge cheefest name.
>
> (9–12)

Michael Drayton claims of his *Idea* that "my Muse is rightly of the English strain" (Lee 2:180) and queries, "Oh, why should nature niggardly restrain, / That foreign nations relish not our tongue?" (25.1–2). In his *Licia*, Giles Fletcher goes so far as to castigate continental borrowings by other poets:

> This age is learnedlie wise, and faultles in this kind of making their wittes knowne: thinking so baselie of our bare English (wherein thousandes have traveilled with such ill lucke) that they deeme themselves barbarous, and the Iland barren unlesse they have borrowed from *Italie, Spaine*, and *France* their best and choicest conceites; for my owne parte, I am of this mind that our nation is so exquisite (neither woulde I overweininglie seeme to flatter our home-spunne stuffe, or diminish the credite of our brave traveilers) that neither *Italie, Spaine,* nor *France* can go beyond us for exact invention; for if aniething be odious amongst us, it is the exile of our olde maners: and some base-born phrases stuft up with such newe termes as a man may sooner feele us to flatter by our incrouching eloquence than suspect it from the eare. (A4)

Even while understanding that demonstrating English virtuosity by writing in the vernacular is a nationalist act, we should still remember that gender is the primary sign of cultural disorder. Therefore, it is equally possible that the manipulation of gender and cultural difference that is integral to the sonnet also participates in the national project. In many ways, this literary competition, with its insistent control of foreign differ-

---

15. See Sidney Lee, *Elizabethan Sonnets*, xxxii–xxxix.

ence and gender, replicates Europe's international competition for expansion into the new world. Both are written as gendered acts, located in the feminization of the landscape found in the rhetoric of colonial expansion (Kolodny 10–25) as well as in the equation of the beloved with new world merchandise—a combination perhaps more easily recognizable in Donne's "To His Mistress Going to Bed":

> O my America! my new-found-land,
> My kingdom's safest, when with one man man'd,
> My Myne of precious stones: My Emperie,
> How am I blest in thus discovering thee?
>
> (27–30)

Donne continues with the master/mistress conceit: "To enter into these bonds, is to be free / Then where my hand is set, my seal shall be" (31–32). Like the other versions of the master/mistress relation that run throughout lyric poetry, Donne's verse rests on an underlying connection between sexual thralldom and economic possession and works to mystify—even as it exposes—slavery and bondage.

The strains of mercantilism in the sonnets are indirectly connected to competitive colonial trade. Sidney rejects the materialism of Stella's husband, Lord Rich:

> Rich fooles there be, whose base and filthy hart
> Lies hatching still the goods wherein they flow:
> And damning their owne selves to *Tantal's* smart,
> Wealth breeding want, more blist, more wretched grow.
>
> (*Astrophel and Stella* 24.1–4)

Sidney accuses Lord Rich of "commodifying" Stella, of counting her along with his other "riches" as a possession and consequently of missing her true value: "Let him, deprived of sweet but unfelt joyes, / (Exil'd for ay from those high treasures, which / He knowes not) grow in only follie rich" (12–14). Rich is not only a crass merchant but a bad one, because he withholds Stella's "wealth" from the marketplace. Sidney's comparison of Rich's commercialism and his own higher love resembles the conversion of value seen in the travel narratives when he claims that Rich is exiled "from those high treasures," whereas he, one of the lovers who "heav'n such wit doth impart" (5), sees "the richest gemme of Love" (10) set apart with "sacred things" (8). Rejecting foreign wealth, he claims in sonnet 32 that he is too poor to blazon Stella properly: "Phrases and Problemes from my reach do grow, / And strange things cost too deare for my poore sprites" (3:10–11). In a later sonnet, he accuses a rival of penury, using a mercantile figure—"Be your words made (good Sir) of Indian ware, / That you allow me them by so small rate?" (92:1–2)—which again connects descriptive display with foreign merchandising. Of course, as critics have often noted, Sidney's pure sense of Penelope Rich's worth is somewhat suspect in that she begins to represent his un-realized ambitions and missed chances for wealth (Marotti 400).[16]

Although his sonnets are informed by Sidney's very particular situation, these mercantile concerns are understandable within a larger context as well: English sonneteers are notoriously poor in these cycles; not able to buy or beg "credit," they create wealth from the mistress herself. In a culture and class in which women are literally connected to wealth through the exchange of dowry and portion, it is not surprising that the ultimately desirable sonnet mistress is directly associated with worlds of wealth, having ruby lips, pearly teeth, and eyes like diamonds. These jewels are an inevitable part of the "display" of the blazon in which literal wealth is rejected for the metaphoric wealth of the sonnet mistress. Linda Wood-bridge, in her anthropological reading of the sonnet mistress, sees in such wealth an indication that the sonnet mistress is drawn from the figure of the earth mother (254).[17] However, neither local domestic concerns over dowry nor more global anthropological explanations account for the cu-rious specificity of the sources of wealth. Why is the wealth associated with the sonnet mistress characterized not merely as jewels in general but as jewels from India? Donne's mistress, for example, is "both Indias of spice and Mine":

> If her eyes have not blinded thine,
> Look, and to morrow late, tell me,

16. Katherine Duncan-Jones finds Marotti's emphasis on Sidney's thwarted ambition more applicable to the *Old Arcadia* and warns that such a reading of *Astrophel and Stella* "underes-timates his deliberate artistry" (239). However, Duncan-Jones herself notes the intensity of Sidney's colonialist interests both before and after the writing of *Astrophel and Stella*, which leaves open the possibility that they informed his writing. The fact that, as I shall discuss later, many conceptions of "artistry" are in fact racialized conceits suggests that the artistry is inescapably linked to more overtly political concerns.

17. Woodbridge claims that the color symbolism of the sonnet is "part of a semiotic code visible throughout human history, worldwide, encoding seasonal fertility ritual and individual rites of passage" (247). This broad-based approach loses a certain historical and cultural specificity that does not reveal enough about the significance of the sonnet mistress for English culture; it also does not interrogate the possible ethnocentrism of its approach. For more anthropological approaches, see Don Cameron Allen, "Symbolic Color in the Litera-ture of the English Renaissance"; and Philip K. Bock, *Shakespeare and Elizabethan Culture*.

> Whether both th' India's, of spice and Mine,
> Be where thou left them, or lie here with me.
>
>   ("The Sun Rising" 15–18)

Although the plural here is somewhat ambiguous, this is not a generic reference to wealth.[18] It clearly evokes both the Indian subcontinent, which produced the fabled spices (pepper, cloves, mace, and nutmeg) of the East that brought in huge profits for English traders, and the new India (the Americas), from which the Spaniards exported gold mined by enslaved "Indians" and Africans.[19]

Spenser demonstrates a similar doubleness and specificity when he rejects any material wealth associated with the mistress:

> Ye tradefull Merchants that with weary toyle
> do seeke most pretious things to make your gaine:
> and both the Indias of their treasures spoile,
> what needeth you to seeke so farre in vaine?
>
>   (*Amoretti* 15.1–4)[20]

In praising his mistress, Spenser ironically denies the worldly wealth from India and the Americas that Europeans actively sought. Interestingly, Spenser then goes on to blazon his lady, creating from her body the very wealth he disdains:

> For loe my love doth in her selfe containe
>   all this worlds riches that may farre be found:
>   if Saphyres, loe her eies be Saphyres plaine,
>   if Rubies, loe hir lips be Rubies sound:
> If Pearles, hir teeth be pearles both pure and round;
>   if Yvorie, her forhead yvory weene;
>   if Gold, her locks are finest gold on ground;

---

18. In fact both Indias are loosely associated with spice and gold. The Indian subcontinent, particularly, was the source of much ornamental goldwork, and gold was traded for spice (a fact bitterly complained about by the English); whereas the Americas were the source for "raw" gold.

19. Spices from India represented enormous profit: "During the three years from 1616 to 1618, 1,432,186 lbs. of pepper bought at an average cost of 2 3/4d. were imported into England per annum and sold at an average price of 24 1/2 d. per pound" (Krishna 89). See also Niels Steensgaard, "Trade of England and the Dutch before 1750," who agrees that pepper was the single most important Asian commodity of the time (118).

20. Although Sir Sidney Lee points out in *Elizabethan Sonnets* that this trope originates with Ronsard, the frequency with which the English sonneteers pick up the trope suggests that it may have had some special resonance for the English.

if silver, her faire hands are silver sheene,
But that which fairest is, but few behold,
her mind adornd with vertues manifold.

(15.5–14)

These jewels are an inevitable part of the "display" of the blazon—literal wealth is rejected for the metaphoric wealth of the sonnet mistress.[21] Spenser's blazon clearly demonstrates the dismemberment and control of the female and also the competitive rhetoric of display that reveals—even as the poet denies—his economic motives. Patricia Parker notes that this rhetoric works to control and display the woman's body in a way that is specifically linked to "merchandising and to dominion, to conquest of a territory traditionally figured as female and controlled by its partition or division into parts" (132).

In his study of *Astrophel and Stella*, Arthur Marotti suggests that Sidney was the first Englishman to see the sonnet cycle "as a form of mediation between socioeconomic or sociopolitical desires and the constraints of the established order" (399). While Marrotti discusses Sidney's relation to the court and his strapped finances, it is also true that England itself was profoundly affected both economically and culturally by the influx of foreign wealth into Europe. Tzvetan Todorov maintains that the Spanish conquistador's plunder of gold and jewels in the Americas prefigured modern attitudes toward wealth: "The passion for gold has nothing specifically modern about it. What is new is the subordination of all other values to this one. The conquistador has not ceased to aspire to aristocratic values, to titles of nobility, to honors, and to esteem; but it has become quite clear to him that everything can be obtained by money, that money is not only the universal equivalent of all material values, but also the possibility of acquiring all spiritual values" (142–43).[22] The English rhetorically position themselves against such avarice. Sir Walter Raleigh, for example, decries the social disruption brought about by the foreign

21. For more on the ramifications of poetic display, see Nancy Vickers, " 'The blazon of sweet beauty's best,' " 96–97; and Parker, *Literary Fat Ladies*, 126–54.

22. See also Mary Douglas and Baron Isherwood (*The World of Goods*), who also see a new relation of the individual to wealth and adventurism, which reveals the effect of such competitiveness on the individual. They propose that the social environment promulgated by the precursors of individualist capitalism, the adventurers, is one of intense competition: "The individual is then drawn into a very difficult social environment, . . . where he must either compete or be despised as a deviant; and if he competes he must risk shame and seek honor, trust to luck, and create ever more uncertainty for all in his entourage. . . . That environment is a very harsh one to endure, and for that reason, individuals either opt out of it by seeking to hedge off a commune of like-minded souls, or they are forced out of it by being forced into a position of minimum choice and maximum isolation" (43).

wealth of Charles the Fifth ("who had the Maidenhead of Peru"): "it is his Indian Gold that indangereth and disturbeth all the nations of Europe, it purchaseth intelligence, creepeth into counsels, and setteth bound loyalty at libertie, in the greatest Monarchies of Europe" (Hakluyt, 7:279). However, even if forms such as the lyric and poets such as Raleigh demonstrate a rejection of wealth, mercantile desires often proved stronger. Frobisher, for example, was instructed by his aristocratic investors to give the search for gold precedence over the finding of the northwest passage.

Poetic complaints of poverty, aligned with evocations of Indian wealth, may mimic an actual trade dynamic. Immanuel Wallerstein notes the primacy of gold and luxury goods in European minds even though he minimizes their importance in bolstering Atlantic trade:

> At this epoch, the relationship of Europe and Asia might be summed up as the exchange of preciosities. The bullion flowed east to decorate the temples, palaces, and clothing of Asian aristocratic classes and the jewels and spices flowed west. The accidents of cultural history (perhaps nothing more than physical scarcity) determined these complementary preferences. Henri Pirenne, and later Paul Sweezy, give this demand for luxuries a place of honor in the expansion of European commerce. I am skeptical, however, that the exchange of preciosities, however large it loomed in the conscious thinking of the European upper classes, could have sustained so colossal an enterprise as the expansion of the Atlantic world, much less accounted for the creation of a European world-economy (Wallerstein 1:41–42).

Although Wallerstein doubts the economic force of this interest, he does hint at its conceptual importance; it can safely be said that the Euro-Indian exchange in precious metals loomed large in discussions of trade—particularly in England, where the ruling classes took a more active role. The West Indies, which produced mined gold, and India, which transformed gold into artifacts, were both sites of potential wealth.

A court as financially strapped as Elizabeth's could not avoid noticing the incredible riches brought into the Spanish court. Louis Montrose notes that Spain was England's "other" and that this relationship was in part shaped by Spain's colonial encounters and "the embarrassment of England's cultural and imperial *belatedness*" ("Work of Gender" 17). Even while in competition with Spain, the English looked with disapproval and envy at Spanish conquest and wealth: English travel writing was rife with assertions of Native American hatred for Spanish cruelty, assertions that implied that the "Indians" would therefore support and even welcome the benign exploitation of the English. One pamphlet ironically claims that the Irish hated the Spaniards for their "monsterous cruelties in the West Indies."[23] One wonders when the Irish, immersed in their own brutal colonial struggles, found the leisure to debate the relative cruelties of Spanish imperialism.

The much-noted English hatred of Spain was obviously connected to jealousy over Spanish wealth and exploration.[24] England felt itself in keen competition with Spain for the riches of the new world and glanced with envy at Spain's burgeoning empire and monopolies over foreign trade. The insistence on differentiating between "spiritual" rather than merely material wealth is written as the poet's desire for the wealth evoked by the descriptive display of the mistress. The desire for the mistress's golden hair over actual gold, then, masks a pan-European avarice that could quite literally have been first to overturn all social codes, as Todorov suggests. Thus Spenser's disdain of Indian jewels sounds much like Sidney's rejection of strange tropes: both mask the desire for foreign gold under an appreciation for the "home-grown" wealth of the sonnet mistress. In sonnet 32 Sidney claims that he is too poor to blazon Stella properly:

> Vouchsafe of all acquaintance this to tell,
> Whence hast thou Ivorie, Rubies, pearle and gold,
> To shew her skin, lips, teeth and head so well?
> "Foole," answers he, "no *Indes* such treasures hold,
>   But from thy heart, while my sire charmeth thee,
>   Sweet *Stella's* image I do steale to mee."
>
> (32:9–12)

Morpheus's reply eehoes the invocation of foreign wealth seen in other sonnets and participates in the exchange of women: it implies that he has opportunistically "stolen" Stella's image while Sidney is musing on the source of wealth.

In a 1594 sonnet, Henry Constable compares his love to the legendary gold-laden ships that sailed with increasing frequency through Elizabethan lore and hints at the dangers of such trade:

23. Robert Payne, *A Brief Description of Ireland: Made in this yeere. 1589*, quoted in Jordan, *White over Black*, 177.

24. For more on European views of Spanish avarice, see William S. Maltby, *The Black Legend in England: The Development of Anti-Spanish Sentiment, 1558–1660*; Bernadette Bucher, *Icon and Conquest: A Structural Analysis of DeBry's "Great Voyages"*; and Howard Mumford Jones, *O Strange New World: American Culture: The Formative Years*.

How can my hart so many loves then hold,
which yet (by heapes) increase from day to day?
but like a ship that's overcharg'd with gold,
must either sinke, or hurle the gold away.

(*Diana*, fourth decade, 32.9–12)

Constable's ship is reminiscent of the ships that contained Antonio's West Indian fortune in *The Merchant of Venice*, a play that rests on a nexus of connections between foreign trade, courtship, and cultural and racial difference. It may even help to contextualize the ships that are compared to Titania's pregnant Indian waiting maid in *A Midsummer Night's Dream*:

Which she, with pretty and with swimming gait,
Following (her womb then rich with my young squire)
Would imitate, and sail upon the land
To fetch me trifles, and return again,
As from a voyage, rich with merchandise.

(2.1.130–35)

This passage may similarly mystify Indian plunder and, possibly, slavery, in aligning the young squire with new world merchandise and hinting at the process of colonial trade in the pregnancy. Titania and Oberon's domestic quarrel is really a gendered contest over proper control of foreign merchandise. Titania becomes the intractable female who withholds merchandise and upsets the colonial project when she refuses to turn over the boy, claiming, "The fairy land buys not the child of me" (2.1.122).[25] This female refusal to trade also suggests that we should at that point place Titania in league with the unconquered Amazons (unlike Hyppolyta) who run throughout colonial tracts as obstacles to foreign conquest.

The Traffic in Fairness: Cosmetics and Blackness

The association of wealth with beauty demystifies "fairness" and reveals it as a commodity in the culture. The sonnet cycle *Zepheria* (1594) explic-

25. This reading turns on a crucial confusion of West Indian slavery with the East Indian spice trade. As I have suggested, the difference between African and Indian was often deliberately obscured: indeed, in Portugal, "India" also referred to parts of Africa. Peter Fryer records a similar conflation of black and Indian in his *Staying Power: A History of Blacks in Britain*. The libretto for an ironmongers' pageant by Thomas Dekker in 1629 calls for "an Indian boy, holding in one hand a long *Tobacco pipe*, in the other a dart." A contemporary sketch of this performance by a Dutch observer shows that this part was played by a black performer (27).

itly reveals fairness as a commodity, a connection given only obliquely in Sidney's "carelesse of the wealth because her own":

> Nature, I find, doth, once a year, hold market!
>   A gaudy fair of brooches and of babies;
>   And bounteously to all doth She impart it,
>   Yet chiefly to true Lovers, and fair Ladies.
> ....
>   The buyer pays no impost, nor no fees;
>   But rather to invite with wealthier pleasure,
>   She booths her fair with shade of broad-branched trees,
>   Wherein (good Queen!) her care doth match her treasure.
>   With wealth of more cost, Nature doth Thee beautify!
>
> (32.1–13)

Nature's "market" includes not only jewels but babies, the chief "production" of women. However, women's complexions are also marketable commodities, if not the market itself. Nature "booths" her fare/market but also the true "fair," the beloved's face, which is "wealth of more cost." Nonetheless, the autonomy of the female seller of the poem hints at another site of possible female resistance against an ideology of fairness.

Véronique Nahoum-Grappe suggests that beauty has a certain materiality as well as erotic force in European culture: "Beauty was a gift, an identifying characteristic as objective as wealth or education" (89). Although I am looking primarily at the colonialist discourse in these poems, it is perhaps worth remembering that these poems worked within a domestic "traffic in women"; the cementing of ties through marriage is linked to a dowry system in which women and money are literally exchanged. The attention paid to mistresses and to spiritual over material wealth posits an alternative to the more chiefly economic concerns of marriage.[26] Although it was one of women's main assets, "beauty was not as effective a determinant of good fortune as wealth. No aesthetic dowry could make up for the lack of an economic one" (Nahoum-Grappe 89). In a culture in which the link between economics and marriage is a given in a way that is resisted today, it is no surprise that the ideology of ro-

---

26. In her study of marriage and courtship in Shakespeare, Ann Jennalie Cook makes the point that "at those social levels where gentlemen did not work with their hands for a living, wealth in some form was necessary to continue living. Thus the arrangements for dowries and dowers, future inheritance and present income formed a critical part of courtship, for they determined one's standing in family and community" (149). Much of my discussion on dowry is indebted to her chapter "Dowries and Jointures."

mantic love that informs lyric is accompanied by a curious obsession with and mystification of economic concerns. The preceding poem suggests how these concerns are curiously linked on a domestic level: the woman's treasure, her "babies," and her "wealth of more cost," her fairness, must be protected. Courtship and colonialism may seem to be rather disparate arenas in this period, but they are often discursively conflated. For example, in *The Merchant of Venice*, the injunction on the lead casket, "Who chooseth me must give and hazard all he hath" (2.7.16), gives courtship the same aura of risk and adventure as Antonio's merchandising. If an effect of beauty is to "divert attention from one object to another" (Nahoum-Grappe 94), it may similarly function in discourse as a substitute for specific attention to other issues, both local and global.

The language of "painting" and cosmetics is the most widespread component of the rhetoric of women's fairness and value; it is also frequently linked to English discourses of blackness. The anticosmetic strain in lyric poetry speaks both to the search for a pure whiteness and to the larger movement against "foreign" and material wealth. Frances Dolan notes that "in the early modern period there was good reason for attacking the use of cosmetics: they were costly and imported (hence "foreign" and corrupting); they encouraged an emphasis on physical beauty at the expense of the soul, an objection constantly reiterated; and many were corrosive and thus actually damaging to women's beauty and health, as some contemporaries were aware" (229). The first two reasons Dolan outlines are integrally connected both to discourses of blackness and to the colonial anxieties of early modern lyric. At the end of this chapter, I will discuss the ways in which denigrations of face painting figure largely in the praise of blackness as that which is not "painted white" (and therefore is more true and valuable). Hints of the connection between cosmetics and foreign difference can be seen in Sidney's earlier rejection of a "Matron Eloquence" who is "disguised, in a Curtizan-like painted affectation," which demonstrates both the gendering of art and nature (Dolan 225) and the related disdain for the "foreign."

That the language of blackness and the language of cosmetic beauty are often mutually constitutive can be seen both rhetorically, in Thomas Browne's digression on beauty in his chapters "On the blackness of Negroes," and visually, in a curious engraving in John Bulwer's *Anthropometamorphosis* (figure 4), which shows a white woman with beauty spots and a black woman almost as her negative, with white beauty spots.[27] In keeping with his own condemnation of cosmetics, he inserts into Thomas

27. I am indebted to Fran Dolan for bringing Bulwer to my attention and giving me a photograph of this engraving.

Figure 4. An engraving from John Bulwer's *Anthropometamorphosis* (1658), which purports to survey beauty practices of different cultures. This particular engraving satirizes the wearing of beauty spots. Several poems such as Lovelace's "Another" make the link between the blackness of the patches and black skin: "But as a *Moor*, who to her Cheeks prefers / White Spots t'allure her black Idolaters." (By permission of the Folger Shakespeare Library.)

Browne's narrative his idiosyncratic theory that blackness began as a cosmetic practice, an "Artifice":

> that it may be the seed of *Adam* might first receive this tincture, and became black by an advenient and artificiall way of denigration, which at first was a meere affectation arising from some conceit they might have of the beauty of blacknesse, and an Apish desire which might move them to change the complexion of their bodies into a new and more fashionable hue, which will appear somewhat more probable by divers affectations of painting in other Nations, ... And so from this Artifice the *Moores* might possibly become *Negroes*.... For thus perhaps this which at the beginning of this Complexion was an artificiall device, and thence induced by imagination, having once impregnated the seed, found afterwards concurring productions, which were continued by Climes, whose constitution advantaged the artificiall into a natural impression. (468–69)

Bulwer's text suggests that there is a crucial distinction between "Moores" and "Negroes" that is rooted in their relationship to blackness. It also attributes blackness to yet another "transgression" (face-painting); in so doing, he implicitly warns against the powers of the imagination in the hands of women. This passage is particularly striking for the way in which the language of cosmetic/somatic blackness reverberates against literary language. His own "myth" evokes the dynamics of blackness in lyric poetry—as I will demonstrate at the end of this chapter, the "conceit" of the beauty of blackness is by Bulwer's time quite popular. Like the text, the engraving shows a powerful link between white women and black women in discourses of beauty. Both women are portrayed as "painted" and degenerate, but the black woman is positioned to be slightly lower and thus perhaps imitative of the white woman.

The admonitions against the "foreign" that Dolan notes in attacks on cosmetics may also undergird other lyric discourses: the objects used to describe women's beauty are often found in recipes for beautifying substances in domestic manuals. Bal Krishna argues that coral, a common "element" of lyric praise, was a source of contest between English and Indian traders. In a controversy over the moving of English trading headquarters in 1616, traders complained that the new location was not as "fit for the vent of three of our main commodities, which are coral, lead and teeth" (quoted in Krishna 112). These three commodities—coral, lead, and ivory—are also substances actually used in both cosmetics and paintings of women. Similarly, both coral and ivory appear frequently in evocations of Petrarchan beauty.

The painted woman often represents concerns over female unruliness, the power of whiteness, and the power of descriptive display. In an attack on face painting, Thomas Drayton declares that a painted women is "a false coiner, who on brazen face, / or coper nose can set a guilded grace" (Tuke B2).[28] As Joel Fineman has noted, cosmetics and the "painting" of women is a charged topic not only in misogynist and antimatrimonial tracts but in epideictic poetry as well: "The problem of female 'decoration' regularly evokes parallel concerns and ambivalences in speculation about what constitutes a decorous cosmology. So too this cosmeticized cosmology informs the language and metaphors with which rhetorical de-

28. Dolan discusses an interesting reversal of this imagery in a text that defends face painting, Thomas Jeamson's *Artificiall Embellishments*, which make plain women "counterfeit": "Those whose bodyes are dismist natures *presse* with some *errata's*, and have not the *royall stamp* of Beauty to make them *currant coyne* for humane society, make choice of obscurity; judging death lesse insufferable, then that ignominy which too often attends deformity" (quoted in Dolan 235).

corum, *exornatio*, will regularly be discussed. . . . The familiar question is always whether the ornamental, in woman or in language, is to be despised or prized, whether such an art adulterates or ekes out nature" (322–23, n. 8). Concerns about true and false "value"—both economic and social—underlie much of the debate over the ornamental in sonnets, as they do in much misogynist literature. Male writers continually accuse women of hiding their "blackness" under the fair disguise of cosmetics and worry that female vanity will feed the market for foreign ornaments.

The underlying misogyny of the praise of blackness is apparent in Edward Guilpin's epigrams on blackness, which play on the connections among cosmetics, portraiture, sunburn, and unregulated sexuality (see the Appendix). His "Of Nigrina. 61" suggests intricate and complex links between these discourses: "Painted *Nigrina* unmask'd comes ne're in sight, / Because light wenches care not for the light." His "Nigrina" is almost triply afflicted here because she is "painted," which paradoxically marks her as "light" or unchaste. He also reveals the negative side of the "sun-expelling" masks used by women; they can protect women from the sun, but they can also hide "painted" women from the eyes of men. His formulation again exposes both the precarious nature of fairness and the ways in which the rhetoric of fairness works against women. The white woman who protects her natural fairness by hiding it from the sun is then subject to the accusation that she is hiding her painted features from the light of day. The final pun on "light" similarly implies that the appearance of "light/white" purity can always hide an unruly female sexuality, which is connected with darkness.

The connection of fairness with the commodification of women and the competitive rhetoric of display is apparent in *Love's Labour's Lost*'s Berowne's diatribe on "painted rhetoric":

> O, but for my love, day would turn to night!
> Of all complexions the cull'd sovereignty
> Do meet as at a fair in her fair cheek,
> Where several worthies make one dignity,
> Where nothing wants that want itself doth seek.
> Lend me the flourish of all gentle tongues—
> Fie, painted rhetoric! O, she needs it not.
>
> (4.3.229–34)

Rosaline's fairness has a commercial value just as it does in the *Zepheria* poem seen earlier ("Do meet as at a fair in her fair cheek"). Although Berowne reveals that it is his linguistic power that makes Rosaline fair and

Fair Texts/Dark Ladies   91

thus valuable, he must distinguish between his praise and "painted rhetoric," which he associates with painted women: "O, if in black my lady's brows be deck'd, / It mourns that painting [and] usurping hair / Should ravish doters with a false aspect: / And therefore is she born to make black fair" (4.3.254–57). He again conflates the two in disparaging the company's mistresses: "Your mistresses dare never come in rain, / For fear their colors should be wash'd away" (4.3.266–67). His calling the women's hair "usurping" is key here, because it reveals a particularly gendered point of contest. One of the chief arguments against the use of cosmetics is that the "painted" woman usurps the prerogatives of God and nature by redoing nature's work. Women become false painters who, in a competitive appropriation of a male prerogative, obfuscate the search for a light, ordered language by disguising everything as white. The "painted" woman is threatening because her cosmetics reveal the "artifice" of the politics of color and thereby explode the contest of contraries set up by male discourse.

In lyric, the attempted effacement of the material, combined with the denial of the potential power and agency of women, works to subject the woman to the poet's will, although this dominion is always in struggle. Denied her own "art," a woman's natural beauty can fall prey to the vicissitudes of age:

> Though you be fair and beautiful withal;
> And I am black, for which you me despise:
> Know that your beauty subject is to fall
> Though you esteem it at so high a price.
>
> (Godolphin *Chloris* 26.1–4)

The poet here brings attention to the ephemeral nature of the mistress's fairness at the very moment he is most threatened—that is, when he is "black" and out of favor with her. Spenser rewrites the unequal relation between himself and his mistress in terms of color and light:

> Yee whose high worths surpassing paragon,
>> could not on earth have found one fit for mate,
>> ne but in heaven matchable to none,
>> why did ye stoup unto so lowly state.
> But ye thereby much greater glory gate,
>> then had ye sorted with a princes pere:
>> for now your light doth more it selfe dilate,
>> and in my darknesse greater doth appeare.

Yet since your light hath once enlumind me,
    with my reflex yours shall encreased be.

(*Amoretti* 66:5–14)

Typically, the poet here is able to turn his low estate into an advantage: his darkness can better set off her light. He can, in effect, make her white and enhance his status and poetic power in the process.

The poet is constrained, by the situation required of the sonnet form, to assume the stance of the black and unfavored suitor; nevertheless, his blackness is quite ephemeral and decreases in proportion to his control over the sonnet mistress and his own language. This equation of blackness with stature is most obvious in the first sonnet of *Astrophel and Stella,* in which the poet is black in several ways: he moves from wanting to paint or display his emotional "darkness" ("the blackest face of woe") to actually carrying the mark of darkness (in sunburn) because he is not favored by his lady and because he cannot write. Sidney sets his ostensible goal—Stella's favor—in the first stanza; he becomes almost immediately alienated from that goal, however, as he wants to be "lightened" of the heavy burden of black woe by gaining Stella's favor and by giving "birth" to the recalcitrant child or "matter" that burdens him. Darkness here is figured as too material and earthbound, preventing him from reaching the transcendent heights needed to express Stella's beauty properly.

Sunburn: Anxieties of Influence/Anxieties of Race

As I noted earlier, the struggle between dark and light does not operate purely as a contest of opposites; it is thus not surprising to find certain tropes operating on the edges of this division. The next two sections focus on two tropes—sunburn and whitewashing—that create liminal spaces that allow both for a very complex negotiation of difference and for a questioning, if not an overturning, of the logic of this binarism. Significantly, these tropes not only are key to racial discourses, they also are linked with issues of poetic authority. It is therefore worth returning to Sidney's first sonnet, which is based on a trope of sunburn. Sidney is first blackened when he proposes to paint himself as the woeful Petrarchan lover and student who scours others' verse for invention. This "oft turning others' leaves" (1.7) to find inspiration is a paradoxical and self-defeating enterprise that leads to his becoming, if possible, somewhat blacker as he hopes this will make "flow / Some fresh and fruitfull showers upon my sunne-burn'd braine" (1.7–8). In Sidney's use of the "sunburned" metaphor, not only does he show the impossibility of escaping imitation or poetic influence, his blackness provides a visual image of his estrangement from such influences. Paradoxically, it is inevitable and necessary that he insist on this estrangement, that "others' feete still seem'd but strangers in my way" (1.11), so that he can, as his Muse suggests, ignore his literary precursors and "looke in thy heart and write" (1.14).

With the childbirth metaphor in stanza 4, Sidney completes this alienation by becoming the dark, sunburned other. While this trope may simply be another version of the very traditional childbirth metaphors used by Renaissance poets, the darkness and delay that characterize this "pregnancy" seem to ally it with the figure Patricia Parker has labeled the "literary fat lady." Parker reads a number of subtexts that informed this Renaissance "topos of overcoming a female enchantress or obstacle en route to completion and ending" (11) and suggests that the dilated, "fat" bodies of these women may be fed by the Renaissance rejection of Ciceronian copia that was characterized as effeminate, fleshy, and Asiatic (14). Interestingly, Parker sees Sidney's pointed assertions of the "manliness" of poetry as part of the antifeminine tradition linked to the privileging of the Attic style over the Asiatic. The image of the pregnant Sidney, with its associations with blackness, and the link between the poetry of praise and the Song of Songs would seem to make him, at this moment, the "literary fat lady" filled with matter who dilates and defers the closure of a narrative.[29]

When Sidney speaks of his "sunne-burn'd braine" in the first sonnet of *Astrophel and Stella*, he taps into a web of associations that connect poetic imitation, racial difference, and female fairness. Twentieth-century medical views on sunburn may obscure for the modern reader the implications of reading sunburn as a significant and extremely ambivalent trope for discussions of racial difference. Sunburn suggests another concern about the difficulties of maintaining an unblemished fairness; like anticosmetic discourses, this troping of racial difference is also connected to the feminine in that sunburn is usually evoked as a threat specifically to female fairness. With the exploration of the Americas, literary, scientific, and popular discussions of sunburn become the conduit through which existing and comfortable oppositions—typically expressed through traditional black/white images—become questioned and altered as Europeans discovered a world of threatening difference. Just as the change to a

29. Parker also sees this verbal contest between the Asiatic and Attic styles underlying the contest between feminine Egypt and masculine Rome in *Antony and Cleopatra*. For the complete discussion, see *Literary Fat Ladies*, 8–35.

heliocentric astronomy brought a reconsideration of Western humanity's conceptions of self, so did comparison of the other's relation to the sun force early modern Europe to imagine and reimagine its own human identity. As I will discuss in more detail later, the "discovery" of dark inhabitants of the Americas with physical similarities to white Europeans upset traditional theories about African skin color. So, too, the darkening of their white skins from exposure to harsher tropical climes produced renegotiations of European constructions of racial difference through the use of sunburn as a literally tropical trope.

As in the contemporary world, the effects of sun on human skin were much debated in the later Renaissance: sun and skin tone were an important aspect of beauty culture. In the Elizabethan court, with its rage for fairness and whiteness, the sun was to be avoided at all costs, for the unwelcome effects of the sun interfered with courtship and desire. The earlier poem from *Zepheria* assumes that protection from the sun is crucial in preserving the value of fairness: "She booths her fair with shade of broad-branched trees / Wherein (good Queen!) her care doth match her treasure." Conversely, in *The Merchant of Venice*, the Prince of Morocco must draw attention away from his dark skin in order to be considered a suitor. He begs Portia:

> Mislike me not for my complexion,
> The shadowed livery of the burnish'd sun,
> To whom I am a neighbor and near bred.
> Bring me the fairest creature northward born,
> Where Phoebus' fire scarce thaws the icicles,
> And let us make incision for your love,
> To prove whose blood is reddest, his or mine.
>
> (2.1.1–7)

The Prince, "a tawny Moor," in making himself a Petrarchan suitor, shows an awareness of the cultural values surrounding skin color and also of the grounds for erotic competition. This passage specifically alludes to a commonly accepted Renaissance theory on skin color. The idea of sunburn becomes important not so much because it may have explained the origin of blackness but because it touches a crucial point of difference: skin color. Sunburn connects white European and black African; as such, the trope becomes an important way of negotiating difference through a shared sameness.

Many of the discussions of Africa and the Americas focused on the mystery of African blackness, a problem Sir Thomas Browne claimed had "no lesse of darknesse in the cause then in the effect" (508).[30] The causes of blackness were a great mystery that, although discussed by the ancients (Ptolemy, among others), seems not to have been of any real importance until the later fifteenth century and the opening of trade (Jordan 12). Not surprisingly, this interest springs up at about the time of the earliest European explorations.[31] The theory that black skin color was a direct result of overexposure to the sun was more or less discounted by later European travel. Journeying among South American natives many of whom lived just as close to the sun as Africans, Europeans "discovered" people who were not as dark as the "Negroes" in Africa but still had different skin color. The effect of sun on complexion remained a live concern—so much so that as late as 1646 Browne still felt compelled to refute the climatic theory in his *Pseudodoxia Epidemica.*[32]

The popularity of the idea that sun caused "black" skin color may have lasted because the very name "Aethiope" signified burnt or "torrid" skin, as many travelers intimated, or, more likely, because it provided an oblique way of addressing fears of miscegenation and the absorption of "white" European by the foreign other. Speculating on the sources of complexion (which is always written as a search for the origins of blackness) becomes an important mode for sorting out Western conceptions of humanity as well as for coping with religious difference. As I noted in Chapter 1, the biblical account of creation in Genesis, with its emphasis on separating light from darkness, becomes a critical subtext both for

30. John Bulwer also picks up on Browne's inquiries in a section of his *Anthropometamorphosis*, glossed in the marginalia as "Enquiry how so great a part of mankind became Black": "That Neither [the sun nor the curse of Ham] is the cause, the learned Enquirer into vulgar Errour's hath evinced, or at least made dubious; yet how and when this tincture began it was yet a riddle unto him, and positively to determine, it surpassed his presumption: seeing therefore, saith he, we cannot certainly discover what did effect it, it may afford some piece of satisfaction to know what might procure it." He then proposes his own hypothesis: "It may therefore be considered, whether the inward use of certaine waters, or fountaines of peculiar operations, might not at first produce the effect, since of the like we have records in History" (467).

31. Robert Boyle is a good example of this. In his *Experiments and Considerations Touching Colours*, he looks for the true origins of blackness and speaks specifically on the disjunction between travelers' accounts and theories of blackness: "Only as I shall freely Acknowledge, that to me the Enquiry seems more Abstruse than it does to many others, and that because consulting with Authors, and with Books of Voyages, and with Travellers, to satisfie my self in matters of Fact, I have met with some things among them, which seem not to agree very well with the Notions of the most Classick Authors concerning these things; for it being my Present Work to deliver rather matters Historical than Theorys, I shall Annex some few of my Collections, instead of a Solemn Disputation" (152).

32. For more discussion of this debate, see James Walvin, *The Black Presence: A Documentary History of the Negro in England*, 32–47; and Joseph E. Washington, *Anti-Blackness in English Religion: 1500–1700*, 70–101.

gathering materials in foreign lands and for the ideal of conversion. Despite the preoccupation with sunburn, there is a notable absence of apparent concern over whites turning black. This may be a subterranean fear that becomes important only once large colonies are established in the tropical regions. Obviously it was never far from the mind of the colonist, because one hundred years after Sir Thomas Browne there is record of a chronicler's insistence that colonial Europeans never turned black (Jordan 16). More immediately, Robert Boyle picks up Thomas Browne's concerns and testifies that "as on the other side, the White people removing into very Hot Climates, have their Skins by the Heat of the Sun scorch'd into Dark Colours; yet neither they, nor their Children have been observ'd, even in the Countreys of *Negroes*, to descend to a Colour amounting to that of the Natives" (161). George Herbert alludes to this concern and makes it the basis for a shared sameness in his "Aethiopissa ambit cestus": "You see a Trav'ller has a sunburnt face" (3).

Indeed, an inkling of how that fear haunted the English imagination throughout its growing empire is revealed in the "British empire" entry in the 1910 *Encyclopaedia Britannica*: "The effect of climate throughout the empire in modifying the type of the Anglo-Saxon race has as yet received only partial attention, and conclusions regarding it are of a somewhat empiric nature.... In the tropical possessions of the empire, where white settlement does not take place to any considerable extent, the individual alone is affected. The type undergoes no modification" (Kingsley 606). This entry demonstrates that climate is a pressing concern almost three centuries later and suggests that it is a primal component of Anglo-American racialism. The reassurance that "the type undergoes no modification" suggests a fear of the racial grouping's genetic mutation from something other than white as the result of the long-term exposure of the English to tropical climes.

The climatic theory of sunburn worked in tandem with a more literary theory that held that Africans were made black through the fall of Phaeton. Phaeton, the son of Phoebus Apollo, was an Ethiopian who sought out his father to prove his parentage: "and so with willing mind, / From Æthiop first his native home, and afterward through Inde / Set underneath the morning starre he went so long, till as / He found me where his fathers house and daily rising was" (Golding 16v). He begs his father to let him ride his sun chariot as proof of his heritage. Apollo reluctantly agrees, and Phaeton loses control of the chariot, goes off course, and flies too close to the earth: "The Aethiopians at that time (as men for truth uphold) / (By reason that their bloud was drawne foorth to the outward part, / And there bescortched) did become ay after blacke and swart"

(Golding 20v). Phaeton's loss of control causes cataclysmic upheaval and threatens earth and Olympus. Responding to the threat, Jove killed Phaeton with a thunderbolt, throwing his body from the chariot. He landed "almost in another world and from his countrie quite / The river Padus did receive and quench his burning head" (Golding 22). Other versions of the myth were amended in the Renaissance to suggest that Phaeton actually landed in Ethiopia and made the inhabitants black when the falling sun "scorched" them. This change becomes important in a literary context whenever the myth of Phaeton's causing blackness is connected to the use of Phaeton as a poet figure.

Many culturally different characters are sunburned. As we have seen, the Prince of Morocco wears "the shadowed livery of the burnish'd sun" (2.1.2). The Moorish Eleazar of *Lust's Dominion; or, the Lascivious Queen* (1600) declares his complexion is "ta'en from the kisses of the amorous sun" (3.4.14). Shakespeare's Cleopatra echoes the bride in the Song of Songs when she proclaims, "Think on me, / That am with Phoebus' amorous pinches black" (*Antony and Cleopatra* 1.5.27–28). Her formulation conjoins her erotic nature with her darkness and, indeed, almost implies that she is black because of her sensuality. For both Eleazar and Cleopatra sunburn is not only a mark of racial difference but also a mark of sensuality. In many ways the sunburned figure is the obverse of the white Ethiope who appears in William Basse's poem and who reverberates throughout Renaissance drama. Each use of the trope creates a space for articulating relations with an other and addressing the difficulties of economic and literary "appropriation" of foreign matter. The entanglements mandated by such appropriation are negotiated by the possibility for transgression inherent in each trope; sunburn allows movement between the strict dichotomies of black and white and so too between the racial absolutes mandated therein.

The differing cultural values associated with sunburn are most obvious in the attempts to explain the sunburned beloved in the Song of Songs. Sunburn can indicate cultural difference, but it can also be used to efface cultural difference, allowing one to be dark without being marked as culturally or racially different. In his commentary on the Song, Joseph Hall attempts to forestall any connection of blackness with cultural difference: "Looke not therefore disdainfully upon me, because I am blackish, & dark of hew: for, *this colour is not so much naturall to me;* as caused by that continuall heate of afflictions wherewith I have bene usually scorched" (5; emphasis added). Obviously, Hall is here concerned to remove any taint of "natural" blackness from the woman and to "Christianize" the verse, wholly effacing any hint of interracial eroticism. Just as the removal of the beloved's "blackness" in the Canticles demonstrates the power of Christian conversion, so does the removal of the sonnet mistress's darkness signal poetic and rhetorical might.

Sidney's sonnet 22 is a fascinating example of the trope of sunburn, which demonstrates how the dark lady's beauty and "fairness" exist at the will of the poet:

> In highest way of heav'n the Sunne did ride,
>   Progressing then from fair twinnes' gold'n place:
>   Having no scarfe of clowds before his face,
> But shining forth of heate in his chiefe pride;
> When some faire Ladies, by hard promise tied,
>   On horsebacke met him in his furious race,
>   Yet each prepar'd, with fanne's wel-shading grace,
> From that foe's wounds their tender skinnes to hide.
> *Stella* alone with face unarmed marcht,
>   Either to do like him, which open shone,
>   Or carelesse of the wealth because her owne:
> Yet were the hid and meaner beauties parcht,
>   Her daintiest bare went free; the cause was this,
>   The Sunne which others burn'd, did her but kisse.

This, another of Sidney's "court" sonnets, pictures the sun at its highest and most potent: "Having no scarfe of clowds before his face, / But shining forth of heate in his chiefe pride" (22.3–4). The "fair ladies," typical court beauties, are literally bound by language, "by hard promise tied," to go into the July sun. This excursion becomes a competition almost from the outset, as the ladies join the proud sun "in his furious race" (6). It is described as a battle, "yet each prepar'd with fanne's wel-shading grace, / From that foe's wounds their tender skinnes to hide" (7–8). Stella, however, "alone with face unarmed marcht" (9), is in a stronger position than the other ladies. She is almost an opposing sun herself, "to do like him, which open shone" (10). Here fairness and beauty are equated with wealth and, more important, with some sort of innate wealth: "Or carelesse of the wealth because her owne" (11).

The paradox and power associated with sunburn are apparent here when we see that the ladies who hid from the sun were still burned: "Yet were the hid and meaner beauties parcht / Her daintiest bare went free; the cause was this,/ The Sunne which others burn'd, did her but kisse" (12–14). The poet's linguistic prowess saves Stella from the darkness associated with the more common beauties. Placing Stella next to the "hid and meaner" beauties allows Sidney to show Stella's "difference," which comes not so much from her innate beauty as from his poetic license; his rhetorical skill suggests a higher poetic power that overcomes even the mysterious effects of the sun. As Ann Jones and Peter Stallybrass point out, the poet, no matter how seemingly submissive, always has the upper hand because "he controls the experience insofar as he articulates it" (54). Sidney's final couplet points to his own prowess when he turns the potential harmful effects of the sun to a mere kiss. His martial figures prepare the reader for contest; however, the battle posited between the women and the sun is overcome not with martial might but with erotic/ poetic force. The kiss abruptly changes the terms of the contest and makes it clear that the poet, like the sun, has been in control all along.

This competition between the poet and the sun is perhaps more obvious in *Zepheria*, where the poet claims that he has covered her whiteness with his praise/poetry: "How have I, jealous over Phœbus' rays, / Clouded thy Fair! Then, fearing he would guess it / By thy white brow, it have I cinct' with bays!" (30.10–12). Giles Fletcher, too, reworks Sidney's conceit in his *Licia* (1593):

> My love was maskt, and armed with a fanne,
> To see the Sunne so carelesse of his light,
> Which stood and gaz'd, and gazing, waxed wanne,
> To see a starre, himselfe that was more bright.
> Some did surmize, she hidde her from the sunne:
> Of whome, in pride, she scorn'd for to be kist:
> And fear'd the harme, by him to others done,
> But these the reason of this woonder mist,
> Nor durst the Sunne, if that her face were bare,
> In greatest pride, presume to take a kisse:
> But she more kinde, did shew she had more care,
> Than with her eyes, eclipse him of his blisse.
> > Unmaske you (sweet) and spare not, dimme the sunne:
> > Your light's enough, although that his were done.
>
> (23)

Fletcher's protection of the mistress in this sonnet is somewhat less dramatic and intrusive, if more common. He posits his mistress as yet another sun who carries the mask to protect the sun from her light. In closing the poem by urging her to unmask and eclipse the sun "of its bliss," he both displays and hides the mistress's potential might.

The juxtaposition of these two sonnets clearly reveals the gender politics of "fairness." Unlike Fletcher's Licia, Stella is compared with other women, and her fairness is accomplished, in part, by the denigration of other women. In its associations with agricultural labor, sunburn also becomes a way of articulating class distinctions. As I will discuss in more detail in Chapter 5, the effect of this competitive dynamic and its racial and class valences on women's relationships becomes very important for female writers. In many cases, women are only fair or black in comparison with one another. Beatrice in *Much Ado about Nothing* connects sunburn with darkness and lack of favor, exclaiming, "Good Lord, for alliance! Thus goes every one to the world but I, and I am sunburnt. I may sit in a corner and cry 'Heigh-ho for a husband!' " (2.1.318–20). In Elizabeth Cary's *The Tragedie of Mariam* (1613), Herod compares his sister, Salome, to his wife, Mariam: "Go your wayes / You are to her a sun-burnt black-amoor" (4.7.461–62).

Allied to the scientific/anthropological discussions of the causes of blackness is the idea of sunburn as a compelling, powerful trope for literary influence. The danger of this use may lie in the proverb "He that walks much in the sun will be tanned at last" (Tilley 640). In the *Epistle Dedicatory* to Spenser's *Shephearde's Calender*, E.K. suggests that "whenas this our Poet hath bene much traveiled and throughly redd, how could it be, . . . but that walking in the sonne although for other cause he walked, yet needes he mought be sunburnt" (32–37). Just as with E.K., for whom sunburn becomes a mark of inadvertent—and inescapable—poetic influence, and with Herbert, for whom sunburn marks the traveler's encounter with otherness, sunburn bespeaks for men an unavoidable power that captures the unwary traveler. In contrast, for women it represents the real danger of seduction, as when Hamlet tells Polonius to keep his daughter from the sun: "Let her not walk i' th' sun. Conception is a blessing, but as your daughter may conceive, friend, look to't" (2.2.184–86). In his *Arte of Rhetoric*, Thomas Wilson also uses sunburn as a metaphor for poetic influence: "He that goeth in the Sunne shall bee Sunne burnt, although he think not of it. So they that wil reade this or such like bookes, shall in the ende be as the bookes are" (A5v).

Sunburn seems to affect the male very differently from the female. Shortly after Stella escapes the perilous effects of the sun in sonnet 25, Astrophel is burned:

> The wisest scholar of the wight most wise
>   By *Phoebus'* doome, with sugred sentence sayes,
>   That Vertue, if it once met with our eyes,
>   Strange flames of *Love* it in our soules would raise;

But for that man with paine this truth descries,
While he each thing in sense's ballance wayes,
And so nor will, nor can, behold those skies
Which inward sunne to *Heroicke* minde displaies,
    Vertue of late, with vertuous care to ster
Love of her selfe, took *Stella's* shape, that she
To mortall eyes might sweetly shine in her.
It is most true, for since I her did see,
    Vertue's great beautie in that face I prove,
    And find th'effect, for I do burne in love.

He turns a commonplace heliotropic metaphor into one of sexual ambition and desire. Like many lyric poets, he burns in love. Curiously, these
men are rarely darkened by the sonnet mistress even when she is the sun:

Why should your fair eyes, with such sovereign grace,
Disperse their rays on every vulgar spirit,
Whilst I in darkness, in the self-same place,
Get not one glance to recompense my merit?

(Idea 43.1–4)

In Drayton's verse, the man, while "in darkness," is dark because of the
absence of the mistress, not because of the presence of her dispersed rays.
Sidney, too, is at his darkest in Stella's absence:

Now that of absence the most irksome night,
With darkest shade doth overcome my day;
Since *Stella's* eyes, wont to give me my day,
Leaving my Hemisphere, leave me in night.

(89.1–4)

Despite their sunlike and "sovereign" powers, the mistresses never recip-
rocate the darkening process; at most the poet will be "inward parched."
Hence, as I suggested in Chapter 1, not only does gender remain the
primary site for the production of blackness but female bodies serve as
the testing ground for the symbolic boundaries of culture and race.

The continual association of dark ladies with the sun poses a problem
for poets like Sidney who reject the "foreign" discourses linked with darkness. The heliotropic metaphor alternates between the poet's assuming a
stance of worshipful submission, where "*Stella's* eyes, [are] wont to give
me my day" (*Astrophel and Stella* 89.3), and his exercising his poetic

"light[e]ning grace" (*Astrophel and Stella* 20.12) as in Shakespeare's "For I have sworn thee fair, and thought thee bright" (147.13). Such attempts to contain the darkness of the sonnet mistresses are quite apparent when the poet paradoxically praises her "in blacknesse bright" (91.8), "beamie black" (7.3): a paradox that Shakespeare evokes in denial as he swears that his "mistress' eyes are nothing like the sun" (130.1).

In black/white dichotomies, white and lightness are traditionally favored at the expense of black and darkness. The sonneteer, wishing to bask in the light of his beloved, writes poetic favor as exposure to the sun/mistress. In claiming that "her heavenly face / Sent forth the beames, which made so faire my race" (41.13–14), Sidney wins not only the race that is the subject of the sonnet but also erotic favor. The poem punningly reveals the role of women in the project of colonial mastery in making them the vessels that make his bloodline "fair," because exposure to the sun can also be read as a form of eroticism. This pun can be seen as racialized even without reading the word "race" with its contemporary meanings;[33] the subterranean concern with fairness and its link to breeding is telling, especially when read against the first line of Shakespeare's sonnets, "From fairest creatures we desire increase." Typically, Sidney's bow to Stella is complicated by his assertion in the previous stanza that he is a superior horseman, because "of both sides I do take / My bloud from them, who did excell in this" (41.9–10). He also manages to have Stella make him the privileged "fair" suitor. However, the delicate balance of desire, alternating as it does between pure love and lust, keeps this privilege uncertain and the trope unstable. Stella's attentions may bring out his more impure desires, causing the poet to "burn" in love:

> But lo, while I do speake, it groweth noone with me,
> Her flamie glistring lights increase with time and place;
> My heart cries "ah," it burnes, mine eyes now dazled be:
>
> (76.9–11)

Caught up in his admiration of Stella's sunlike beauty, the poet is taken unawares and responds to this "burning" by lessening the light/power of the mistress: "Pray that my sun go down with meeker beames to bed" (76.12).

---

33. See the warnings against reading the word "race" with its modern applications in Kwame Anthony Appiah, "Race," 276–78; Lynda E. Boose, "The Getting of a Lawful Race," 35–38; and my discussion of her argument in the epilogue.

Not coincidentally, sonnet sequences are littered with allusions to actual sun worship. Shakespeare hints at foreign sun worship in sonnet 7:

> Lo, in the orient when the gracious light
> Lifts up his burning head, each under eye
> Doth homage to his new-appearing sight,
> Serving with looks his sacred majesty.
>
> (7.1–4)

Shakespeare eventually rejects the possibilities of difference suggested by the phrase "in the orient," through "converting" the trope, placing it in a more Christian context: "The eyes ('fore duteous) now converted are / From his low tract and look another way" (7.11–12).[34] Nevertheless, he specifically equates foreign religious difference with Petrarchan praise in *Love's Labour's Lost,* when Berowne begs his mistress, "Vouchsafe to show the sunshine of your face, / That we (like savages) may worship it" (5.2.201–2). The idolatry of the native supplicant parallels the poet's worship of the sonnet mistress, and it is in this absolute surrender to the sonnet mistress that we can see the hazards of the metaphor.

The link between paganism and darkness, carried over from English exploration in Africa, is practically inseparable from the construction of racial difference as an otherness (Jordan 24); this connection is in turn fed by the traditional Christian associations with white and black. The European tradition that claimed that "Mohammedans" and Muslims worshiped the sun (Chew 237) seems to have been transferred in the European mind to inhabitants of the new world. Certainly in the following passage, the phenomenon of sunburn is associated with both blackness and idolatry as it becomes a sign both of a predisposition to sin and of sin itself. Thus Thomas Herbert says of Africans that "the Devil . . . has infused prodigious Idolatry into their hearts, enough to rellish his pallat and aggrandize their tortures when he gets power to fry their souls, as the raging Sun has already scorcht their cole-black carcasses."[35]

---

34. See Booth, *Shakespeare's Sonnets,* 143–44. Booth glosses "orient" as meaning merely "East" and suggests that the poem's imagery gives it "vague, substantively unharnessed, but pervasive reference to the crucifixion and resurrection of Christ" (143, n. 5). Although I would agree with the latter assessment, this gloss of "orient" erases the multiple connections of foreign and religious difference with the orient (Said 73–78). Replacing the original associations of orient then throws "homage" into uncertainty. Compare the more famous sunrise of sonnet 33, which avoids any suggestion of even the "East."

35. Thomas Herbert, *Some Years Travels into Divers Parts of Africa, and Asia the Great Describing More Particularly the Empires of Persia and Industan,* 4th ed. (London, 1677; reprinted in Jordan 24).

In his *Diana* (1594) Henry Constable explicitly compares the futility of his love with the idolizing of Mohammed:

> Fools be they that inveigh gainst Mahomet,
>   who's but a morrall of love's Monarchie:
> by a dull Adamant, as straw by Jet,
>   he in an iron chest was drawne on hie.
> In midst of *Mecas* temple roofe, some say,
>   he now hangs, without touch or stay at all;
>   That Mahomet is she to whom I pray,
>   (may nere man pray so uneffectuall)
> Mine eyes, loves strange exhaling Adaments,
>   unwares to my harts temples height have raught
> The iron Idoll that compassion wants,
>   who my oft teares and travels sets at naught.
> Iron hath beene transformed to gold by arte,
> Her face, limmes, flesh, and all gold, save her hart.
>
> (Fourth decade 4.4)

This sonnet is typical in the poet's portrayal of himself as utterly abject to the mistress and consequently ineffectual in removing her resistance. The characterization of the mistress as Mohammed, like similar references to idolatrous sun worship, would seem to subvert the supposed value of his submission to the beloved. Naming his mistress, Mahomet, "the morrall of love's Monarchie," he implies that the godlike powers attributed to the sonnet mistresses in wooing belong more properly to pagan idolatry in foreign lands. We again see the poet attempting to transform the iron/ foreign Mahomet to a Petrarchan mistress ("to gold by arte") but failing to convert her heart, leaving her as "foreign" as before. This trope suggests that such wooing is foreign to the sensibilities of Englishmen and that female power can be granted only in a scene of foreign differences.

The connection between gender and religious difference becomes clearer in Shakespeare's rejection of the naming of his love "idolatry" in the young man sonnets:

> Let not my love be called idolatry,
> Nor my belovèd as an idol show,
> Since all alike my songs and praises be
> To one, of one, still such, and ever so.
> Kind is my love today, tomorrow kind,
> Still constant in a wondrous excellence;

Therefore my verse to constancy confined,
One thing expressing, leaves out difference,
Fair, kind, and true, is all my argument,
Fair, kind, and true, varying to other words;
And in this change is my invention spent—
Three themes in one, which wondrous scope affords.
   Fair, kind and true, have often lived alone,
   Which three, till now, never kept seat in one.

(105)

Joel Fineman argues that this sonnet, with its ideal consummation, is a commentary on desire that is "monotheistically, monogamously, monosyllabically, and monotonously 'to constancy confin'd'" (141). The poems written to the male express a "fair, kind, and true" love—as opposed to the idolatry of the traditional sonnet—precisely because they are about "kind" and omit difference. Like Samuel Purchas, who is able to envision a world where "wee may all be one, as he and the father are one" once differences in race, nationality, and religion are eradicated along with the unruliness of gender, Shakespeare is only able to write, "To one, of one, still such, and ever so" (4) in the young man sonnets, which do not have to cope with the intractability of the feminine.

The sunburned traveler, the sun-worshiping foreign native, and the dark European woman become the grounds where issues of poetic decorum, female power, and linguistic, cultural, and racial differences meet. The "sunburn" that these tropes have in common provides an interesting gloss for a much later sonnet written by Mary Wroth, Philip Sidney's niece and a performer in the *Masque of Blackness*.[36] Wroth also takes up the topic of blackness in her sonnet cycle and brings "to light" the strains of darkness and cultural difference in her uncle's sonnet cycle:

Like to the Indians, scorched with the sunne,
   The sunn which they doe as theyr God adore
   Soe ame I us'd by love, for ever more
   I worship him, less favors have I wunn,
Better are they who thus to blacknes runn,
   And soe can only whitenes want deplore
   Then I who pale, and white ame with griefs store,

36. Ann Rosalind Jones ("The Self as Spectacle in Mary Wroth and Veronica Franco" 144–47) and Nona Feinberg (187–88) discuss the possible impact of Wroth's performance in the *Masque of Blackness* on Wroth's use of blackness in general and on this sonnet in particular.

Nor can have hope, butt to see hopes undunn;
Beesids their sacrifices receavd's in sight
  Of their chose sainte: Mine hid as worthles rite;
  Grant mee to see wher I my offrings give,
Then lett mee weare the marke of Cupids might
  In hart as they in skin of Phoebus light
  Nott ceasing offrings to love while I Live.

                                  (*Poems* 22)

In this sonnet, she merges issues of foreign difference and poetic influence to write a female allegory of poetic influence. Wroth pointedly makes the sun-worshiping natives black "Indians" and ironically juxtaposes their cultural difference with her female difference and their abuse by the all-powerful sun with inaccessibility of females to male poetic power. Nona Feinberg shrewdly observes that "Wroth's intricate puns on her name, 'worth/wroth,' and on her writing, 'rite/write,' encode the intimate entanglement of the activity of writing and the creation of female subjectivity" (187–88).

For men, one of the few instances where sunburn is an acceptable (although not desirable) affliction is as a sign of poetic influence. While an anxiety of influence may make male poets shy away from their poetic past as a bar to invention, a female poet may have had cause to regret the lack of a female literary tradition. Cultural conditioning bars her from such a female tradition just as beauty culture bars her from actual exposure to the sun. In the first stanza, Wroth plays with sunburn as a male sign of poetic influence and a female sign of favor. Unlike her uncle, who consciously and theatrically stages his estrangement from his literary inheritance, Wroth has no need to create an artificial separation. In her fruitless search for poetic as well as erotic favor, she is both like "the Indians, scorched with the sunne" (1) and like the dark ladies I have shown who need male favor and poetic force to become white and beautiful. In a manner parallel to the fruitless search for erotic favor by idolatrous Petrarchan poets, Wroth searches for poetic favor: "for ever more / I worship him, less favors have I wunn" (3–4).

The second stanza would seem to be a continuation of Wroth's bemoaning of her grief over her unrequited love, signaled by her white skin: "Then I who pale, and white ame with griefs store." (This in itself seems another reversal, for such unacknowledged lovers are usually "black" and melancholic.) However, this writing of whiteness as a sign of grief is imbricated with her racialized judgments of the Indians: because their worship brings continual acknowledgment (by sunburn), their only problem from Wroth's perspective is that they cannot be white. Read within a Petrarchan tradition, however, this stanza also refers to Wroth's own poetics. Her extended conceit makes it apparent that it is the lack of a strong subject position that Wroth bemoans. In this reading, the sun-worshiping Indians can stand for male Petrarchan poets who also both "to blacknes runn" (in having "exposure" to a literary tradition) and "only whitenes want deplore" (whiteness being the blank slate of poetic invention). These poets can take for granted their immersion in a literary tradition in a way that Wroth cannot. Thus she is *too* white, lacking the "sunne-burnt conceits" (Markham, "To the Reader") of a Spenser or a Sidney. Her whiteness signifies a lack of a social "mooring" for her poetry much the same as the heroine, Urania, wanders in Wroth's prose romance, "not certaine of mine owne estate or birth."

Wroth's final two stanzas reinforce the equation of Petrarchan idolatry with savage worship and the disjunction between male public speaking/worship and her private art.[37] Poets are typically characterized as Apollo's sons. We have already seen the *Zepheria* poet use his own poetry to compete with Phoebus. In a dedicatory sonnet to the countess of Pembroke, Barnes names her a "Great Favourer of Phœbus' offspring" (Lee 1.315). In contrast, women who "publish" or circulate their writings break the codes for female behavior and put themselves at risk of public censure and ridicule. While male poets can speak publicly of their loves and circulate their "sacrifices" or poems received "in sight / Of their chose sainte" (read: beloved and Muse), her poetry must remain "hid as worthles rite." Male poets carry the mark of Phoebus's light (their "dark" exposure to a poetic past), while she must pledge to continue to write alone and without their recognition, "Nott ceasing offrings to love while I Live." Such a reading provides a very useful female gloss on the dark lady tradition. That is, the whitening of the dark lady, while a requisite exercise for male writers desiring to control female matter, serves to keep the female subjugated, without access to the copia necessary for invention.

Washing the Ethiope White: The Song of Songs

Issues of foreign difference, sunburn, lightening and gender difference coalesce in another text that may be the *Ur*-text for European renditions of blackness and that may also work to reconcile the conflict between Christian virtue and the desire for gold with which I began this chapter.

37. Jeff Masten compellingly argues that Wroth's sonnets "foreground a refusal to speak in the public, exhibitionist voice of traditional Petrarchan discourse; in the context of the published portion of *Urania* they articulate a woman's resolute constancy, self-sovereignty, and unwillingness to circulate among men" (69); although our readings might seem to

Although a critic such as Thomas Roche, Jr., can suggest that the dark/
light imagery in *Astrophel and Stella* and other sonnets springs from common Christian metaphor (193), it has also been noted that the Song of
Songs in particular provided a more specific and central formulation for
black beauty in the sonnets—" 'Nigra sum, sed formosa' ('I am black but
beautiful')" (Gilman 144). The poem also furnishes an earlier model for
a rhetoric of praise that dismembers women in poetic display. Moreover,
it may provide a literary link between sonnets and empire; the Song of
Songs is often tied to the figure of Solomon, whose story, as demonstrated
by Purchas, is an important subtext for English colonialism. Solomon's
fabled riches, particularly the gold and spices received through trade with
and tribute from the East, resonate powerfully for the early European
traveler. Richard Eden's preface to *The Decades of the Newe Worlde* uses Solomon's treasure to measure the mightier wealth of the Spanish: "And
although in the booke of kinges and Paralipomenon it bee hyperbolically
written that in the dayes of Salomon golde & silver were in Jerusalem in
maner as plentiful as stones, & that his servantes brought from Ophir
foure hundreth & fiftie talentes of gold, yet do we not reade that any of
his shippes were so laden with golde that they soonke, as did a shippe of
kinge Ferdinandos as you maye reade in the last booke of the firste Decade" (a4). Martyr's use of Solomon's wealth demonstrates how significant
a touchstone it is for colonialist discourse, although it is a bit different
from traditional English use. As I indicated in the previous chapter, the
English saw Solomon's wealth as an indicator of potential undiscovered
wealth, whereas here it becomes a measure of Spain's might. Like the
myth of Prester John, English versions of Solomon both hold out the
promise of untold wealth and resolve ideological tensions between spiritual striving and material gain.

Solomon's story and his song become a key part of the "typology of
colonialism," which came of age during these years of exploration. He is
both an exemplar of the sage colonial ruler and an example of the dangers of erotic entanglements with foreign women. The complementary
story of Sheba also works to resolve spiritual and material success: Solomon's wealth is a result of his God-given wisdom. Like the Song, Solomon's life is a map for viewing relations between Western males and
"other" females. The Bride of the Canticles is often seen as the typolog-
ical predecessor of the Queen of Sheba, commonly known as a queen of

---

diverge here they are not in conflict; this particular sonnet contains the withholding from
circulation among men while bemoaning the lack of a community of receptive, possibly
female, readers.

Ethiopia.[38] Her identification as an Ethiopian is important because the positive associations with her identity as the Bride spill back into the negative associations with Sheba's sensuality. She becomes an ambivalent figure whose story changes with the allegations of sexual involvement: male power and interracial desire are the pivotal points on which her stories turn. The association with Sheba is positive when Solomon has no erotic attachment to her; however, there is an alternative tradition that reads Sheba as a temptress and a precursor of the wives who fatally tempt him:[39] "Upon the queen as forerunner of the Gentiles on their way to Christ (the Magi now stood for them) was again superimposed the image of the temptress who put Solomon's virtue to the test" (Courtes 44).

The story of Solomon thus provides both a model, as in the collapsing of Sheba in the Bride, and a cautionary tale, as in Walter Raleigh's redaction:

> Now as hee had plentie of all other things, so had he no scarcitie of women. For besides his seven hundred Wives, hee kept three hundred Concubines, and (forgetting that God had commaunded that none of his people should accompanie the daughters of Idolators) hee took wives out of *Ægypt, Edom, Moab, Ammon, Zidon* and *Heth*: and when hee fell a doting, his Wives turned his heart after other Gods, as *Asteroth* of the *Zidonians, Milcom* or *Moloch* of *Ammonites*, and *Chemosh* of *Moab*. (*History of the World* 501)

Like the colonists we have seen, Solomon's downfall (according to Raleigh) results from his "doting" on foreign women. The Song plays an important role in English representation as well; royal consorts were commonly seen as types of the Bride, and the Spouse was an important part of royal iconography, appearing often in coronation ceremonies (King 37, 196). Elizabeth I, by virtue of her "two bodies," was seen alternately as both the wise male ruler, Solomon, and the female Bride of the Canticles (King 254–56).

Listed by Sidney in *The Apology for Poetry* as one of the chief poems "in

---

38. Sir Walter Raleigh disputes this tradition, claiming that Sheba was "Queen of Arabia, not of Aegypt and Ethiopia" (*History of the World* 501). Christopher Miller's discussion of the term "Ethiope" suggests that this association is particularly appropriate for the Bride: "From the moment 'Ethiopia' is spoken, darkness, and its cause, light, are posited together" (8).

39. For an outline of the debate over Sheba's blackness, which extends from Josephus to present-day Ethiopia and America, see Cain Hope Felder, *Troubling Biblical Waters: Race, Class, and Family*, 32–36; and Paul H. D. Kaplan, *The Rise of the Black Magus in Western Art*, 42. According to Kaplan, Mandeville implies that one of the three kings is black and links him with Sheba, based on their common origin in Saba of Ethiopia (41). See also *The Image of the Black in Western Art*, vol. 2, part 2, p. 18; and Erickson, "Representations."

antiquitie & excellencie" (C2v), Solomon's poem provides an obvious model in the poetry of praise for the subordination of the female to male power, the meeting and conversion of foreign female difference to Christian, male standards.[40] It is a guide for articulating the European's sense of what Edward Said has called Orientalism: "For Orientalism was ultimately a political vision of reality whose structure promoted the difference between the familiar (Europe, the West, 'us') and the strange (the Orient, the East, 'them')....A certain freedom of intercourse was always the Westerner's privilege; because his was the stronger culture, he could penetrate, he could wrestle with, he could give shape and meaning to the great Asiatic mystery, as Disraeli once called it" (43–44). The Song gives biblical authority for the political reality Said outlines, and provides for the reading of cultural difference through gender. Black becomes associated with the foreignness and difference of the female, and white with the orthodox (here Christian) homogeneity of the male.

The song articulates the central paradox of black beauty: "I am blacke, O daughters of Jerusalem, but comelie, as the frutes of Kedar, as the curtines of Salomon. Regarde ye me not because I am blacke: for the sunne hathe loked upon me. The sonnes of my mother were angrie against me: they made me the keper of the vines, but I kept not mine owne vine" (Geneva 1:4–5). The black but comely bride is a culturally different, dark other who is made the exemplar of Christian love of Christ: she becomes fair through God's favor. She is dark because of exposure to the sun, read variously as affliction, sin, adversity, persecution, and envy of the world (Van Noren 64). Her darkness, however, is to some degree subjective, addressed as it is to the daughters of Jerusalem (who are of ambiguous racial designation). Joseph Hall's explication of this verse makes it clear that here beauty is truly in the eye of the beholder: "For, whatsoever I seeme to you, I am yet inwardly wel-favoured in the eyes of him, whom I seeke to please; and tho I bee to you blacke like the tents of the Arabian shepherds; yet to him and in him, I am glorious and beautiful, like the curtains of Salomon" (4–5). The opinion of other women notwithstanding, it is the favor of Solomon that lightens the Bride's blackness and effaces her foreign difference: Hall signals this change in per-

---

40. I am not here making the anachronistic argument that Sidney was not swayed by the religious content of this verse (see Roche); in fact, his mixture of Protestant fervor and English nationalism is quite compatible with the power relations of the biblical text. I am suggesting that the dynamics of gender, power, and cultural difference inherent in the poem, as well as its evident obscurity to Renaissance (and modern) commentators made it an obvious originary text for an eroticized play of female containment and male Christian, European superiority.

ception in his change of metaphor from the foreign Arabian tents to the Western/Judeo-Christian curtains of Solomon.[41] Although earlier versions of the Song made the competition between the Bride and other women more explicit (Van Noren 47), it is apparent even here that Solomon's favor works against the common opinion, much as the sonneteers proclaim black beautiful in the face of contemporary standards of beauty.

Just as this text later comes to be seen in African-American tradition as representing the black woman in slavery ("they made me keeper of the vines . . ."), it seemed to the Renaissance central to the paradox of black beauty, a paradox that helped negotiate cultural as well as gender difference. Henry Ainsworth's 1623 annotations of the Song (which, interestingly, includes both the phrases "I am black, *and* comely" and "I am Black, *but* am pleasing-comly" [B1 emphasis mine]) suggest a known link between the Bride's darkness and Africa. He refers to a paraphrase of the verse that reads: "When the house of Israel made the Calfe . . . their faces were blacke, like the sonnes of Cush (the Ethiopians)" (C1v). Not only Renaissance biblical commentary but bibles themselves reminded readers of the cultural difference of the Bride. The Geneva Bible tells us that Kedar was Ishmael's son, originator of the "Arabians that dwelt in tents." Gervase Markham's version of the Song makes the sense of racial difference more apparent: "*Kedar* the large desent of *Ismaells* line, / From whom the tent-inclosed *Arabians* sprang" (First eclogue 6.1–2). More literal readings see her as "one of Solomon's exotic wives, an alien to Jerusalem" (Van Noren 55), whose conversion and marriage negate her original difference.[42]

That the Song was seen as an originary praise poem is obvious in its many commentaries and rehearsals. Markham rewrites the Song in eight eclogues (1596); in a sonnet dedicated to Elizabeth Sidney, he calls the canticle "The *Song of Songs*, that lent invention eies" (A6) and suggests that it is a possible model for married women, albeit a tricky one:

> Learne not but learne by this celestiall bride,
> To entertaine espoused happines,

41. Joseph Hall provides a more specific example of the easy slippage between the Christian language of sin and evil and racial blackness in his meditation "Upon the Sight of a Blackamoor," in which he proclaims: "The very Spouse of Christ can say, 'I am black but comely' [Cant. 1:5]. This is our color spiritually, yet the eye of our gracious God and Saviour can see that beauty in us wherewith He is delighted. The true Moses marries a blackamoor, Christ His Church" (143).

42. Sheba in Renaissance visual culture appears both as vaguely "dark" and foreign and as African. The Sodoma gallery has a fourteenth-century German tapestry that features a black Sheba.

Yet let thy Virgine-Taper ever bide
Like mid-day Sunne to light true holines

(9–12)

In suggesting that Elizabeth Sidney "Learne not but learne by" the Bride of the Songs, Markham may be alluding to the traditional unease with the Song's expressions of desire. Indeed, most commentaries on the Canticles seem to have the express purpose of removing the taint of desire from the text: "Besides all this, there are certaine places in this booke, whereby no otherwise then as it were by certaine beames and lights, this point is made so cleare and manifest, that we may very well say without any maner of doubt or wavering at all, that this Treatise is not carnally and literally, but spiritually and mystically to be understood" (Brucioli A2v). One wonders why, if the noncarnal nature of the Song is "so cleare and manifest," this author chose to spend a page insisting on its spirituality. His protest against "carnal" and "literal" readings does, however, tell us that this verse requires interpretive care. The wedding song was (and is) commonly seen as an allegory of Christ's love for the Church. The Bride has also been seen as Israel and thus Mary, as well as the Church, in relation to its soul and Bridegroom (Van Noren 48). Commentators seem to have accepted Origen's commentary that the Bride is a figure for the Church of the Gentiles,[43] a reading that reiterates the very traditional hierarchical structures of the Renaissance: man over woman, husband over wife, God over Church. In Protestant tradition, a literal reading guards against carnal readings in that it keeps potentially wanton words tied to their "proper" signification. However, the eroticism on the surface of the text forces an insistent appeal to a "mystical" reading. Thus the emphasis on the "beames" and "lights" necessary for a proper reading is linked to the effacement of desire and the fear of the otherness in the "dark allegories" of the Song.

This effacement of desire in commentary may be attributable as much to the poem's articulation of specifically female desire as to its clear statements of carnal desire. Ilana Pardes notes, "The Shulamite is the main vocalizer: it is primarily her yearnings and dreams that we follow throughout the Song" (119). Both the male and female voices of the Song focus on the body and equate individual parts of the body with ornamental and luxury goods, thus presaging the articulation and dismemberment of the female in Petrarchan lyric. In a section that the Ge-

43. See Jean Marie Courtes, 15; and Linda Van Noren and John Pollack, eds., *The Black Feet of the Peacock*, 45–66. See also Pardes' chapter on the canonization of the Song, 119–43.

neva Bible glosses, "She describeth Christ to be of perfite beautie, & comelines," the Bride praises her beloved in language that sounds much like later epideictic idolatry:

> His chekes *are* as a bed of spices, *and as* swete flowres, & his lippes *like* lilies dropping downe pure myrrhe. His hands *as* rings of golde set with the chrys- olite his bellie like white ivorie covered with saphirs. His legges *are as* pillers of marble, set upon sockets of fine golde: his counténace as Lebanon, excel- lent as the cedres. His mouth *is as* swete things, and he is wholy delectable: this is my welbeloved, & this is my lover, ô daughters of Jerusalem. (5:13–17 Geneva)

The male voice describes the beloved with similar particularity in a section that the Geneva Bible warns "is to be understand [*sic*] spiritually":

> . . . the jointes of thy thighs *are* like jewels: the worke of the hand of a cunning workeman. Thy navel *is as* a rounde cuppe that wanteth not lickour: thy belly *is as* an heape of wheat compassed about with lilies. Thy two breasts *are* as two yong roes that are twinnes. Thy necke *is* like a towre of ivorie. (7.1–4 Geneva)

The evocation of fairness for any gender in the Song is reliant on gestures of descriptive display. Although a sequence like *Astrophel and Stella* may incorporate some sense of female desire, we only need compare the elo- quent and forceful speaking of female desire in the biblical verse with Wroth's concerns over her public voice to see how the tradition later becomes more concerned with male power and desire.

The strategies of description in the Song link lyric praise and descrip- tion in travel through the image of Solomon as a proto-Christian colo- nizer. Textually, Solomon's Song is important not only because the Bride is sunburned and dark but because she is "whitened" by the love of the Bridegroom:

> My love, beholde, thou art faire: beholde, thou art faire: thine eyes *are like* the dooves. My welbeloved, beholde, thou art faire and pleasant: also our bed is greene. (1:14–15 Geneva)

As I suggested before, a necessary part of this fairness is the unfolding of beauty in the form of a blazon. Although power here is not as relentlessly masculine as in later lyric, the exercise of male, godlike power is revealed in the Song through the issue of color. The bride is turned white and beautiful by the Bridegroom through very much the same process found in the sonnets. Here we have the dual implications of "whitening" seen in lyric: whiteness as an effacement of cultural and racial difference and as a sign of the male exercise of power. The Bride becomes "above all comparisons glorious and faire." The change from black to white heralds a new beginning, a Second Coming. Although the Bride's whiteness is read as a conversion, it is important to note that her whiteness does not come from within. She can voice her comeliness only through the paradox of blackness. The actual whiteness is brought to her, or imposed on her, by the Bridegroom; thus her whiteness is as much (if not more) a sign of his power as of her acceptance of Christ. That her whiteness is taken as a sign of the Bridegroom's might is evident in Baldwin's 1549 versification of the Song:

> Loe thou my Love, art faier:
> Myselfe have made thee so,
> yea thou are faier in dede,
> Wherefore thou shalt not nede
> In beautie to dispaier:
> For I accept thee so
>   For faier.

(b.3v)

Although the Bride is "faier," the implication is that she is only so at the will of the Bridegroom, who has "made thee so."

The whitewashed Ethiopian is a ubiquitous image in Renaissance literature, appearing often in emblem books and proverbs as a figure of the impossible. Washing the Ethiope white is also, not paradoxically, a sign of a new beginning, or a Second Coming. In his "On the baptized Æthiopian," Richard Crashaw asserts a new era of power over blackness:

> Let it no longer be a forlorne hope
>   To wash an Æthiope:
> Hee's washt, his gloomy skin a peacefull shade
>   For his white soule is made;
> And now, I doubt not, the Eternall Dove,
>   A black-fac'd house will love.

(15)

Although Crashaw's poem has a specifically religious context, the sense of newness and difference is often associated with the white Ethiope in secular contexts as well. Crashaw's male Ethiope is exceptional in poetry; while emblematic representations of the whitewashed Moor are usually male, the poetic version of this image is almost exclusively gendered female, indicating that it may have come from another tradition, such as the Song of Songs, which, as we have seen, provides a model for effacing the threatening difference of foreign women.

These whitened Ethiopian females serve a dual function in that they allow poets to praise "fair" European women while simultaneously reminding their audience of the disguised, potentially unruly sexuality and destructiveness of these potentially "dark" women. Malcolm Evans sees a similar dichotomy in the Petrarchan conceits of *Love's Labour's Lost*: "In the letters, masks, rhetorical contrivance and 'penn'd speech' that insulate an essentially self-regarding love, which celebrates the transcendent Petrarchan lady as a bestower of superhuman powers while cowering in the shadow of the physical, mortal woman perceived as 'pitch that defiles' [IV.iii.3]" (78). The poet is left as the final arbiter of "fairness." His word, like that of the Bridegroom, confers fairness, constancy, and value. This poetic sleight-of-hand is staged in Ben Jonson's *Masque of Blackness*, where the audience is promised that the Ethiopian nymphs will be turned white; in the *Masque of Beauty* the play merges with the court, and the nymphs are revealed to be the court ladies they actually are. William Basse's *Urania* clearly displays the problematic position in which the "white Ethiope" figure places women when he makes her the original cause of female inconstancy. This Ethiope, "fair'st of all the land," is at first quickly divorced from English women:

> But for faire Womens sakes, I grieve to tell:
> But since th'unhappy Causer of such teares
>   They in our world of Brittaine did not finde,
>   Ladies untouch'd neede not to be unkinde.
>
> (1.18)

Basse here is at pains to make women in general guilty for this failure, while specifically absolving English women from blame. This move proves problematic and unconvincing when he later "moralizes" his poem. His story, he claims, lays blame on "faire" women (but not English women); Urania, however, is still the cause of all women's inconstancy, and so again becomes an indictment of a gender politics that does not discriminate between "dark" and "light" females.

The whitening of the dark lady becomes crucial for the exercise of male poetic power. In the first of Shakespeare's dark lady sonnets, we see:

In the old age black was not counted fair,
Or if it were it bore not beauty's name.
But now is black beauty's successive heir,
And beauty slandered with a bastard shame;
For since each hand hath put on nature's pow'r,
Fairing the foul with art's false borrowed face,
Sweet beauty hath no name, no holy bow'r,
But is profaned, if not lives in disgrace.
Therefore my mistress' eyes are raven black,
Her eyes so suited, and they mourners seem
At such who, not born fair, no beauty lack,
Sland'ring creation with a false esteem.
   Yet so they mourn, becoming of their woe,
   That every tongue says beauty should look so.

(127)

The first line of the sonnet evokes a sense of something new—if not a literal Second Coming, then certainly a new age of poetry: "But now is black beauty's successive heir" (3). Blackness seems to replace a degenerate old language/beauty, truer than "whiteness," which can be easily imitated with cosmetics: "For since each hand hath put on nature's pow'r, / Fairing the foul with art's false borrowed face, / Sweet beauty hath no name, no holy bow'r" (5–7). Moreover, we find the traces of the economics of the blazon: although black was not "counted" fair (it was neither named fair, nor had it the value of the traditional "fair"), it has now "inherited" beauty's name. The transition from "counting" to "inheritance" replicates an uneasy fluctuation between goods artificially created (or stolen) and "natural" wealth or value. As we have seen in many versions of the dark lady, her wealth is converted from something basely material to something of a more natural or spiritual value.

Aethiopissa and Her Sisters

Far from being an ephemeral "fad" emptied of significance and ripe for self-parody shortly after its inception, the rage for sonnet cycles at the end of the sixteenth century adopted an erotic/poetic dynamic that created a poetics for the "new world"—a world in which blackness is neither a purely aesthetic nor a moral category but the site for crucial negotiations of sexual politics and cultural and racial difference. The "dark ladies," who become the chief repository of these anxieties, acquire new life with explicitly racial valences in such later poems as "Aethiopissa," and "A Black-moor Maid wooing a Fair Boy," which have been prepared for and anticipated by the English sonnet. The poems sparked by Herbert's "Aethiopissa" are part of a constellation of poems (included in the Appendix of this book) that use Petrarchan praise for actual blackness rather than the imagined "darkness" of the sonnet mistress and retrospectively uncover the veiled possibilities of cultural difference in the sonnet. The poems themselves fall into three categories: interracial desire, conversion, and meditation on blackness. The tradition of the transcendent Petrarchan lady—and the parodies of that tradition—become intertwined with another strain of praise for the earthy, dark African woman. The language of blackness in such verse increasingly and self-consciously links the dark/light dichotomy to a system of somatic and cultural differences and to the commodification of Africa and African bodies.

The Latin poem that seems to have initiated this subgenre, translated as "Aethiopissa woos Cestus, A Man of a different colour," is noteworthy on several accounts: the "dark lady" is literally African;[44] it places the woman in the position of suitor; and, according to Robert Fleissner, "The very popularity of the poem is comparable with that of Sidney's sonnets" (459). The challenge of the sonnet is simultaneously to recognize and to control the dangers of darkness in praise of the mistress. In Herbert's poem, however, the higher challenge seems to be to praise not an elusively defined darkness but racial difference itself, and to change the traditional privileged position of the sonneteer. Herbert seems somewhat self-conscious of this difference (and of the binary logic of the sonnets) when he claims in a poem to Francis Bacon: "My inke was factious for that side." As I noted in connection with Shakespeare's sonnet 127, just as poets begin to depict Petrarchism as an empty and devalued currency, they turn to the language of blackness, which becomes an unexplored and endlessly fertile space for poetic invention.

Herbert's "Aethiopissa," like Sidney's *Astrophel and Stella*, seems to have initiated its own minor trend as responses to it began to be found in chapbooks: other poets adopted literary blackface, crossing gender and racial boundaries to assume the persona of an African female (Meyer; Tokson 21–27). As Grosart's translation of Herbert's title suggests, in

44. This argument was first made by Gerard Meyer, who was also the first to publish the poem in a group. He notes that it is the only amatory Latin poem extant as well as the progenitor of the other poems (370).

these poems black assumes the privileged position, and white becomes "different."[45] As in the sonnet, Aethiopissa associates her blackness with the less permanent darkness of the traveler: "You see a Trav'ller has a sunburnt face; / And I, who pine for thee, a long road trace" (3–4). As I demonstrated earlier, sunburn is used as a liminal space between black and white, and Aethiopissa uses it as such to overcome his resistance to her color by lessening the difference between her and her beloved. However, the attempt to efface the difference between the woman and the white, European beloved is negated by Henry King's response, "The Boyes answer to the Blackmoor," which insists on the absolute difference between black and white:

> Black Maid, complain not that I fly,
> When Fate commands Antipathy:
> Prodigious might that union prove,
> Where Night and Day together move,
> And the conjunction of our lips
> Not kisses make, but an Eclipse;
>
> (1–6)

Black and white in King's version must remain absolute opposites: they cannot inhabit the same space, "where Night and Day together move." The evocation of a primal state of chaos before the separation of day and night (a move reminiscent of Hakluyt's reading of Genesis) hints at a fear of dissolution of white by black, made stronger by the image of an eclipse. The submission of the white beloved to the desires of the black lover-poet is ultimately written as the annihilation and loss of white identity. King's poem concludes, "Else stay till death hath blinded mee, / And then I will bequeath my self to thee" (13–14). Even though they propose the overcoming of difference through the joining of black and white, these poems posit that joining as the loss of white identity and ultimately affirm the black/white binary.

If Petrarchan praise wishes away the white woman's whole body and therefore her sexual nature, the black women in these poems are praised (and praise their own blackness) in terms that continually evoke their materiality, thus making explicit the materiality of figures like Shakespeare's dark lady (Fleissner 465). Herbert's Aethiopissa reminds her be-

45. A more recent (and more lyrical) translation of "Aethiopissa ambit Cestum" by Mark McCloskey and Paul R. Murphy is available from Ohio University Press; however, I was not given permission to quote from it for this project.

loved of the connection of black with the earth: "If earth be black, who shall despise the ground?" She also suggests that she is black like his shadow: "A shadow-casting form you see." It is, however, difficult to make such generalizations about the characterization of blackness in these poems. Their general ethos seems to be not to find the words to explain or convey darkness but to play out (and exhaust) the traditional language of blackness. Every traditional association with darkness appears in these poems, often in the same poem. For example, Cleveland's "A Fair Nymph Scorning a Black Boy courting her" takes up, in order: smoke, night, eclipse, visors, checkers, ink, and mourning. More culturally specific tropes that I have discussed throughout this chapter make their appearance also—sunburn, masks, painting, whitewashing—and all are evoked either to surmount or to reinforce the difference of black and white.

The specificity and abundance of these tropes give a certain concreteness to blackness that is not found in the sonnet. This may, in fact, be the purpose of the poems—to remove the mystery of blackness by literalizing and exhausting its tropes. For example, whereas earlier sonnets seem more inclined to disdain material wealth in favor of the spiritual values represented by the sonnet mistress, these later poems focus more explicitly on riches and thereby heighten and make more material the evocations of riches in earlier lyric. This materiality is evident in the focus on concrete issues of labor and wealth. Eldred Revett's "The Aethiopian Baptized," while working with the same image of the baptized Ethiopian seen earlier in Crashaw, is much less about isolated spirituality:

> What *Stars* are those of *Orient* light
> Tremble on the *Brow* of *Night?*
> And their *daring* Beams display
> *Rival* Glories with the day?
> That baffle *Time, out-stare* the Sun,
> Scorn to wait *Succession;*
> No, 'tis an *Aethiop div'd* these streams
> Rich in *spoils* of *Ransack't* Gems,
> *New risen* from the *Chrystal Bed,*
> All in *Pearls aparalled;*
> What of *Night's* about his skin
> *Skreens*, like that too, Day within.

The change in the poem's tone ("No, 'tis an *Aethiop div'd* these streams"), which should in fact focus on the internal qualities and the spiritual state of the baptized African, is almost overpowered by the poem's very specific image of an Ethiopian diving for pearls. Conversion here is written as an act of acquisition—diving for pearls—which would be familiar to the readers of narratives of Africa and the West Indies.

While the poems on interracial desire seem to be concerned to a degree with divesting blackness of its mystery, other poems—such as Edward Herbert's "Sonnet of Black Beauty," "Another Sonnet to Black it self," and "The Sun-burn'd Exotique Beauty"; John Collop's "On an Ethiopian beauty," "Of the black Lady with grey eyes and white teeth"; and Eldred Revett's "One Enamour'd on a Black-moor"—revel in the mystery of blackness, often as it is found in black women. Unlike Sir Thomas Browne, Abraham Hartwell and other prose writers who are concerned with locating the origins (and thereby solving the mystery) of blackness, the writers posit blackness as a mystery to be celebrated (as well as a challenge to their poetic might).

George Herbert's brother, Edward, praises the heterogeneity of darkness and particularizes blackness in his poems. Herbert's rather philosophical poems on the nature of blackness consciously read themselves as new answers to the old conundrum of the power of blackness while simultaneously acknowledging—and even celebrating—the inability of poets to "write out" (or white out) its mystery:

> Black beauty, which above that common light,
>   Whose Power can no colours here renew
>   But those which darkness can again subdue,
> Do'st still remain unvary'd to the sight,
>
> And like an object equal to the view,
>   Art neither chang'd with day, not hid with night;
>   When all these colours which the world call bright,
> And which old Poetry doth so persue.
>
> ("Sonnet of Black Beauty" 1–8)

Herbert seems to suggest that the "old Poetry" glorified "brightness"— and the linguistic values inherent in that glorification—are doomed to oblivion; the new alternative seems to be to focus on darkness while recognizing that its heterogeneity puts it ultimately beyond poetic control.

In the poem that served as a prologue to his "Aethiopissa ambit Cestus," George Herbert claims to be reciprocating a poetic exchange, possibly with Francis Bacon: "A Diamond to mee you sent. / And I to you a Blackamoore present" (134). This evocation of the traditional exchange of poems written as an exchange of commodities—jewels and Africans—

again suggests the ways in which the sonnet form accommodates political issues such as cultural difference and global economics. As we shall see in the final chapter, the exchange of poems here may also be concurrent with the exchange of visual images of blacks in cameos and portraits. The new acceptance of blackness as appropriate "matter" for poetry coincides with an increased acquisition of slaves, jewels, and other foreign sources of income. The competition for jewels, spices, gold, and slaves only intensifies in the seventeenth century when England formed the East India Company and the Royal African Companies in addition to gaining West Indian islands. The appropriation of a black female subject position in these poems is thus concomitant with the increasing appropriation of black bodies in Atlantic trade. The first half of the seventeenth century saw the pieces being put into place for England's later competition for rights to the slave trade. For example, there were twenty-three Africans in the Virginia colony in 1623 but three hundred by 1640 (Giddings 36).[46] Whereas in 1585, the publication date for *Astrophel and Stella*, the number of African slaves was statistically insignificant, by 1640 England had established sugar plantations, which exponentially increased the demand for slaves (Craton 56). By the mid-seventeenth century, England had reconstituted the Guinea Company (1651) (Rawley 152); it also emerged as a serious competitor with the Dutch for access to the slave trade. By 1657, the publication date of Revett's poems, more than twenty thousand African slaves had been imported into English colonies (Curtin 119).[47]

George Herbert indicates that this "new" poetic is very consciously responding to the poetics of blackness in the sonnet. Apologizing for choosing a "blackamoore" as the subject of his poem, he entreats:

Onely, my noble Lord, shutt not the doore
Against this meane and humble blackamoore;

46. In the Virginia colonies, the period between the 1620s and the 1660s was one of increasing removal of African human rights in the service of slavery, including the first antimiscegenation laws (see Giddings 35–37).

47. It is difficult to find consistent and accurate numerical accountings of the slave trade in England before the very end of the seventeenth century; any attempt to estimate incremental growth is thus somewhat speculative. Michael Craton notes that the Guinea Company's interest began its upward movement in the 1640s; he estimates that by 1645, there were approximately one-quarter (6,400) as many slaves as whites in Barbados (44). Philip Curtin estimates a slave population of 20,000 in Barbados in 1655 and a population of 1,400 in Jamaica. This represents a possible growth of over 1,000 slaves per year by the time Richard Lovelace's poems were published (1658). I can only assume an accompanying percentage of growth in the English slave population, since a private profit was often made on individual voyages by selling a few of these slaves in England.

Perhaps some other subject I had tried,
But that my inke was factious for that side.

                                                    (10–12)

In asserting that his "inke was factious" for the side of the blackamoor, Herbert takes up the gauntlet of Petrarchan politics and energizes a poetics of color that informed expanding European contact abroad and subsequent English incursions onto the world stage as England went on to build the empire on which the everburning "sun never set."

CHAPTER THREE

"Commerce and Intercourse": Dramas of Alliance and Trade

Sir, you may thank yourself for this great loss,
That would not bless our Europe with your daughter,
But rather lose her to an African.

— *The Tempest*

I would like to begin this chapter by returning to my discussion of Samuel Purchas's *Purchas; His Pilgrimes* from Chapter 1. I suggested there that Purchas bases his vision of Britain's maritime growth on a faith in the easy combination of Christian conversion and mercantile trade, which the following passage illustrates:

> . . . and the chiefest charitie is that which is most common; nor is there any more common then this of Navigation, where one man is not good to another man, but so many Nations as so many persons hold commerce and inter-course of amity withall; . . . the West with the East, and the remotest; parts of the world are joined in one band of humanitie; and why not also of Chrisi-tianitie? Sidon and Sion, Jew and Gentile, Christian and Ethnike, as in this typical storie? that as there is one Lord, one Faith, one Baptisme, one Body, one Spirit, one Inheritance, one God and Father, so there may thus be one Church truly Catholike, one Pastor and one Sheepfold? (1:56)

In uniting economics and Christian values, Purchas highlights the fact that colonial trade involves not only economic transactions but cultural and political exchange as well. The anthropologist Gayle Rubin notes in her influential feminist critique of Lévi-Strauss, "Kinship and marriage are always parts of total social systems, and are always tied into economic and political arrangements" (207). Likewise, the exchange of goods (or even the circulation of money) across cultural borders always contains the pos-

123

sibility of other forms of exchange between different cultures. Purchas's glorified vision of the end of English colonization serves to efface the multivalent anxieties over cross-cultural interaction that permeate English fictions of international trade. Associations between marriage, kinship, property, and economics become increasingly anxiety-ridden as traditional social structures (such as marriage) are extended when England develops commercial ties across the globe. The multiple "joinings" (to use Purchas's term) mandated by imperialism coincide with the already-familiar notions of joining in marriage (see Parker 121–24). Extolling the homogenizing influence of trade suggests that English trade will turn a world of difference into a world of Protestant similitude. However, it leaves unspoken the more threatening possibility: that English identity will be subsumed under foreign difference.

This passage may be drawing on an ideology of union already current in the culture. When James I took England's throne, metaphors of marriage and union took on a different cast than they had under the virgin Elizabeth, not only because James was himself already married with a growing family but also because of the ideological work needed for the incorporation of England, Scotland, and Wales into one political entity. In making a plea for his pet project, the creation of "Great Britain," he described that union as a marriage. Both countries, he claimed, "shall ever acknowledge one church and one king; and be joined, in a perpetual marriage, for the peace and prosperity of both nations, and for the honour of their king" (G. Davies 8). His vision of a peaceful unification of two cultures who "live happily ever after" under "one church and king" suggests that the very act of union, coded as marriage, will efface an entire history of cultural and religious factionalism just as trade does for Purchas. Rather than read these seductively compelling visions as ideal humanistic unity, I would like to suggest that these imperial visions of "union" here articulated—one loosely domestic, one international in scope—are part of a larger vision of colonization and assimilation that underlies England's imperial ambitions. Ironically, these visions of union are undermined almost as soon as they are articulated; issues of union and trade, particularly within discourses of colonialism and imperialism, prove highly contested and fraught with anxieties over the ramifications of crossing borders as well as over the resiliency of internal boundaries.

It is the problem of "commerce and intercourse," of commercial interaction inevitably fostering social and sexual contact, that underlies representations of interracial desire in the early modern period.[1] In addition

---

1. Even though "intercourse" did not come to have its current sexual connotation until the eighteenth century, Purchas's sense of "commerce and intercourse of amity" resonates

to addressing domestic anxieties over the proper organization of male and female (particularly over the uncontrolled desires of women), the appearance of blackness in plays responds to growing concerns over English national identity and culture when England develops political and economic ties with foreign (and "racially" different) nations. Representations of women and uneasiness over changing gender roles are key in the working-out of these more overtly political issues, since women both "reproduce the boundaries of the symbolic identity of their group or that of their husbands" and act as "signifiers of ethnic/national differences" (Yuval-Davis and Anthias 9). Thus women's bodies become the site of struggle between, on the one hand, the need for both colonial trade and cultural assimilation through union and, on the other, the desire for well-recognized boundaries between self and other. Many Jacobean plays generally indict interracial or "racialized" couplings in ways that very often become a castigation of the female as well as an expression of attitudes about race.[2]

With the growing interest in blackness in the Jacobean court we see an increased depiction of couplings between white Europeans and cultural, racial, or religious "others." "Mixed" marriages (marriages or liaisons that feature ethnic, religious, or cultural difference) soon begin to be associated in some way with the signs of blackness, and such differences perpetuate and intensify already-existing anxieties over changing gender roles. As Catherine Belsey has suggested, marriage in the sixteenth and seventeenth centuries becomes the site of a struggle to create a private realm and at the same time to take control of it in the interests of the public good (*Identity and Difference* 130). The place of the family and the state is often challenged and questioned through tropes of blackness. For example, according to Holinshed's *Chronicles*, the infamous Alice Arden's choice of Mosby, "A black swarte man," represents the choice of lust over lawful wedded love (Belsey 131). His blackness indicts the female alone. Although he is, of course, culturally a white man, here Mosby's blackness becomes a sign of his low social status and her degeneration in marrying across class boundaries. After looking at ways in which tropes of race work to alleviate domestic anxieties over "union," I will focus, in this chapter, on two levels of interracial union. *The Tempest* (1611) and *Antony and Cleopatra* (1607) offer two versions of ruling women's roles in imperialism. Miranda embodies a cultural integrity that must be protected from en-

---

powerfully in this sense for a modern reader, and I would like to retain this anachronistic sense for the purposes of this chapter.

   2. I use "racialized" here to cover a wider array of possibilities. In some of these plays characters assume a racial disguise that brings a dynamic of race into play.

croachment by outsiders, while Cleopatra represents the twin fears of foreign difference and female sexuality that resists European patriarchal standards. Finally, *The Devil's Law-Case* (1619) and *The English Moore* (1637) feature women in blackface and suggest ways in which women are manipulated within categories of class and race in response to increasingly colonial economic systems.

Elizabethan England was extremely conscious of its developing power and identity. The cult of Elizabeth, while working to turn the potential liability of her gender into an asset, also fostered an identification of the queen's person with the English national identity (Stone 88). Under the rule of James I, however, internal and external factors made the threat to that precarious identity acute and pervasive. On one hand, James's assumption of the throne was greeted with some relief as it appeared to ward off the vexing problems of succession and threatening civil war (his growing family promised plenty of heirs to the throne). On the other, James's reign also gave rise to an intense nationalism that did not always operate to his advantage. James was still a foreign king bringing his broad Scots accent and Scottish cronies to court. His demeanor and his obvious dislike of the public ceremonies that had so endeared Elizabeth to the populace did nothing to lessen traditional English antipathy toward the Scots. Furthermore, growing reports of licentious and unruly behavior at court, as well as James's spending habits, gave rise to unfavorable comparisons with Elizabeth.[3]

James's foreign and domestic policies only fueled an already tense situation. The policies of the king whose motto was *rex pacificus,* "the royal peacemaker," of necessity conflicted with Elizabeth's inward vision symbolized by her motto, *semper eadem* (always one); Elizabethan insularity was seemingly abandoned in favor of forging alliances with foreign (and, often, enemy) powers. This is most apparent when James's policy of peace with Spain only served to estrange him further from his subjects. The country's feelings about Spain, a traditionally hated rival and enemy, were not as easily dispersed as James needed for success, and in some quarters his policies served only to feed suspicions that James had Catholic sympathies. His pet project of creating a united England and Scotland provoked, if anything, continuing anti-Scot sentiment and revealed the fragility of England's nascent national character, which the following passage from *Tom Tell-Troath* demonstrates in its mocking of James's ambi-

3. For more commentary on James's court, see Robert Ashton, "Jacobean Politics 1603–1625," in *Stuart England;* Lawrence Stone, *The Causes of the English Revolution, 1529–1642,* 89–90; and Derek Hirst, *Authority and Conflict: England, 1603–1658,* 54–59. On English nationalism, see Wallace Notestein, *The English People on the Eve of Colonization, 1603–1630,* 9–10.

tions: "Your word, Great Brittaine, and offer to prove that it is a great deal lesse then Little England was wont to be; lesse in reputation, lesse in strength, lesse in riches, lesse in all manner of virtue, and whatsoever else is required to make a state great and happy" (Ashton 218). Parliamentary opposition to James's proposal was vociferous and long-lasting. Much of the resistance was to all appearances based on economic and legal concerns: merchants claimed that Scottish competition would take trade, revenue, and jobs from Englishmen, and members of Parliament feared the strain on the economy from an influx of Scots as well as the usurpation of English law in the proposed assimilation of the two legal systems (Davies 9). This latter concern was addressed by the counterproposal that English law absolutely supercede Scottish law. The issues of birthright and power underlying the proposal were resolved in James's favor by the *post-nati* case. Known as Calvin's Case, this action found that the *post-nati* (subjects born in a territory with allegiance to the king) were natural-born citizens (Davies 10). The implications for England's future as a colonizing nation also informed such judicial and legislative wrangling: the future incorporation of territories such as those in the West Indies were at stake as well. Such debate clearly reveals the fear of cultural erasure that underlay the expansion of England's borders.[4]

The Jacobean court was a crucial site for England's development of its sense of national empire: the country earnestly stretched its imperial grasp, and England's poets began identifying it as "Great Britain" when James became king of Scotland, England, and Wales. As many critics have noted, perceptions of marriage and the family took on a different cast under James's rule. There was for the first time in nearly half a century a royal *family*, with children to marry off. Whereas the pursuit and avoidance of possible alliances through marriage had been the policy under Elizabeth, whose chastity eventually became the figure for the closing-off of England from foreign powers, for James marriage meant the creation of bonds with outsiders, a process he hoped would maintain his peaceful reign. Having children of marriageable age allowed James more chances to make alliances with neighboring countries; at times these arrangements—such as the match attempted between Prince Henry and the Spanish Infanta—created the enmity of his subjects. The movement from a fundamentally endogamous to a more exogamous policy on marriage was not without political fallout. These "mixed marriages" were fairly unpopular in England (Hirst 98).

Such political realities coincided with James's own penchant for the

4. For a provocative discussion of James's project for a Great Britain and Shakespeare, see the chapter on James in Leah Marcus, *Puzzling Shakespeare: Local Reading and Its Discontents.*

exotic or unusual. Representations of blacks, as well as actual black people, were an integral part of Scottish court entertainment during his reign as James IV. At his wedding to Anne, then princess of Denmark, James arranged an entertainment for his Oslo hosts: "By his orders four young Negroes danced naked in the snow in front of the royal carriage, but the cold was so intense that they died a little later of pneumonia" (Ethel Williams 21). This spectacle, the first entertainment by the royal couple, was followed by a wedding pageant featuring forty-two men dressed in white and silver and wearing gold chains and visors over blackened faces. One of the earliest-known European poems on a black woman, William Dunbar's "Ane Blak Moir" (see the Appendix) was written on the occasion of a "justing of the wild knycht for the blak lady" in Scotland in 1508 (Kinsley 308).[5] Blacks were a common feature in the Scottish court, kept there as dehumanized alien curiosities, on par with James's pet lion and his collection of exotic animals.

The *Masque of Blackness* and Jacobean Nationalism

When she commissioned Ben Jonson to write her first court masque, Queen Anne specifically asked for a performance in which she and her ladies would appear disguised as "Blackamoors." The result, the *Masque of Blackness* (1605), inaugurated a new era in the English court, which demonstrated a renewed fascination with racial and cultural difference and their entanglements with the evolving ideology of the state. The *Masque of Blackness* and its later counterpart, the *Masque of Beauty* (1608), became the catalyzing agents for a discursive network of "blackness," which participated in the process of identity and empire formation by dramatically reconfiguring issues of racial/cultural identity and gender difference.

Many critics who study the *Masque of Blackness* hasten to note that the conceit of blackness in a court masque was by no means a new invention. According to Enid Welsford, Jonson was influenced by the Florentine tournament that commemorated the marriage of Francesco de'Medici and Bianca Cappello (*The Court Masque* 170). Stephen Orgel reminds us that "Queen Anne's bright idea for a 'masque of blackness' was by 1605 a very old one" (*The Jonsonian Masque* 34); Anthony Barthelemy suggests that the request for blackness in the masque was "nothing extraordinary,"

---

5. Louise Fradenburg offers a compelling reading of the meanings of blackness in early Scottish court culture in *City, Marriage, Tournament*, 244–64.

given the history of black characters in court masques, although he does concede that the masque itself had a recognizable impact on its audience (20). Although it is very true that blackness was long a part of court tradition in Europe, critical attempts to discount the issue of racialized blackness in the interests of historical continuity or misogyny ignore the persistent presence of a discourse of blackness in James's court. The reactions of the audience to the masque and growth of actual contact with Africans, Native Americans, and other ethnically different foreigners (which went much beyond anything seen previously in England) indicate that a more disruptive reading of both the text and the performance may be useful.

In focusing merely on the chronological, such criticism works to preclude investigation of the issues of imperialism, race, and gender difference raised by the masque. The political import of Anne's request for a blackface disguise is often effaced by this insistence on locating the masque solely within a dramatic tradition. Interest in the importance of this first collaboration of Ben Jonson and Inigo Jones ignores the very central political question of why such a landmark production involves bringing "Africa" (albeit a European version) to the English court. Examining these masques in conjunction with other dramatic modes of court presentation, and within a more overtly political context of empire formation, demonstrates the centrality of racial difference in the Jacobean court as well as in the masques themselves. I further suggest that the "aesthetic" values of the audience, the playwright, and subsequent critics of the masque are actually political concerns that address crucial anxieties over gender and racial difference.

One example of the primacy of blackness and gender is found in the objection of Dudley Carleton, who, writing "to discerne the humor of the time," describes the *Masque of Blackness*: "At night was there a sumptuous shew represented by the Queen and some dozen Ladies all painted like Blackamores face and neck bare and for the rest strangely attired in Barbaresque mantells to the halfe legge" (Herford and Simpson 10:449). While this "humor of the time," was very likely the much-noted conspicuous consumption of the Jacobean court, it is equally likely that the reference is to the "Blackamore" disguise itself and the entire aura of strangeness and novelty that the masque strives to attain. Fascination with the culturally different and ongoing anxieties over gender coalesce in the unsettling vision of these English ladies posing as African nymphs.

The twin concerns of patriarchy and imperialism meet as Jonson's masque dramatizes the collision of the dark lady tradition with the actual African difference encountered in the quest for empire. This collision was not necessarily to the popular taste which Dudley Carleton's famous criticism in his letter to Ralph Winwood illustrates: "Their apparel was rich, but too light and Curtizan-like for such great ones. Instead of Vizzards, their Faces, and Arms up to the Elbows, were painted black, which was Disguise sufficient, for they were hard to be known; *but it became them nothing so well as their red and white, and you cannot imagine a more ugly Sight, then a Troop of lean-cheek'd Moors*" (Herford and Simpson 10:448). Although Carleton at times displays a Bottom-like need for verisimilitude in his criticisms of the masque (for example, when he describes "Images of Sea-Horses with other terrible fishes, which were ridden by Moors," he complains that "the Indecorum was, that there was all Fish and no water"), his descriptions of *Blackness* tell us a great deal about the compelling "difference" of the masque. Anne and her ladies painted themselves instead of using the visors courtiers usually wore to impersonate black characters, thus making it the first recorded use of blackface pageantry in an English masque.[6] This is a crucial change that Carleton notes again in a later letter to Chamberlain: "Their black faces, and hands which were painted and bare up to the elbowes, was a very lothsome sight, and I am sory that strangers should see owr court so strangely disguised" (Herford and Simpson 10:449). His connection of their face painting with their "Curtizan-like" apparel points to a time-honored association of blackness with lechery and supports the greater concern that the masque projects the wrong, "strange," image to outsiders, themselves strangers.

Carleton's first letter is telling in its comparison of the theatrical paint disguising the masquers with traditional cosmetics, "their red and white." In borrowing from the sonnet tradition's praise to evaluate this racial disguise, Carleton touches on a link between poetic discussions of blackness, racial difference, and beauty practices that recurs throughout English texts and that reveals one way in which the discourse of blackness is a gendered one. As I suggested in Chapter 2, praising blackness by denigrating face painting is fairly ubiquitous: *Love's Labour's Lost*'s Berowne claims that his "black" beauty, Rosaline, is pure and needs no "painted rhetoric" (4.3.253). The practice of painting is so pervasive that it taints (literally) all "native" beauties with the suspicion that they are painting. Berowne's praise, however, paints women into a box, as it were, by suggesting that these women are painting themselves black to avoid the imputation of cosmetic use. Such circular reasoning makes all women

---

6. For more on the costumes worn by "black" characters, see Anthony Gerard Barthelemy, *Black Face, Maligned Race*, 18–21.

dissemblers, because we cannot tell which women are truly "white" and which are not.[7] Jonson evokes this paradox in *Blackness*, when Niger speaks of his daughters' comparing themselves to "the painted beauties other empires sprung" (133). Similarly, Jonson corners the royal masquers: as African nymphs they are "painted" black and as representatives of England ("native blood") they are suspected of "red and white" painting.[8] This uncertainty is broken only by a powerful male, usually a poet (or a poet-king), who confers whiteness and "pure" beauty. Berowne's use of the proverbial "devil's soonest tempt," also dramatized in Webster's *The White Devil* and *The Devil's Law-Case*, draws upon this misogynistic tradition: devils appear disguised as white and beautiful women, thereby throwing all women's virtue into doubt.

At court, Jonson reenacts and complicates the dilemma of blackness in the sonnets, a process itself complicated by the conditions of performance. Although a troop of "lean-cheek'd Moors," the masquers are still aristocratic ladies who are part of the "golden world" of the court; this poses the problem for Jonson of presenting a spectacle of cultural difference without slighting the royalty and beauty of the participants. The conceit of *Blackness* is that twelve African nymphs, the daughters of the river Niger, discover that they are not beautiful but black, and are promised in a dream that if they find a country "whose termination . . . Sounds *-tania*" (lines 164–65) they will be turned white. In Niger's opening plea to the court, he laments his daughters' sense of inferiority. Alluding to the popular myth that the sun caused blackness, he declares that his daughters are beautiful as well as black:

> Who, though they were the first formed dames of earth,
> And in whose sparkling and refulgent eyes
> The glorious sun did still delight to rise;
> Though he—the best judge and most formal cause
> Of all dames' beauties—in their firm hues draws
> Signs of his fervent'st love, and thereby shows
> That in their black the perfect'st beauty grows,
> . . . .
> Since Death herself (herself being pale and blue)

7. For more on the traditional criticism of face painting, see Lisa Jardine, *Still Harping*, 93–95; and Annette Drew-Bear, "Face Painting in Renaissance Tragedy," 71–76.
8. In her "The Challenge of the Impossible: Ben Jonson's *Masque of Blackness*," Anne Cline Kelly glosses "painted" in this line as "superficial" or "inconstant." However, I think that at this moment, the masque literally refers to the paint of the participants.

Can never alter their most faithful hue;
All which are arguments to prove how far
Their beauties conquer in great beauty's war.

(Lines 113–27)[9]

However, Jonson opens *Blackness* with a hymn of praise to Niger's daughters that, in reminding us that the African nymphs are to be seen as beautiful in everything except their color, directly contradicts Niger's praise of blackness (Barthelemy 21). Here Jonson draws upon the "black but comely" formulation of the Song of Songs; like Solomon's Bride, Niger's daughters become the meeting ground between East and West, as the opening song announces:

> Sound, sound aloud
> The welcome of the orient flood
> Into the west;
> . . . .
> With all his beauteous race,
> Who, though but black in face,
> Yet are they bright,
> And full of life and light,
> To prove that beauty best
> Which not the color but the feature
> Assures unto the creature.
>
> (Lines 76–87)

The masque specifically warns the audience not to imagine these women as actual Africans ("not the color but the feature") by pointing out that these disguised nymphs still have the features of European women—a paradox that, ironically, occasions Carleton's disparaging "you cannot imagine a more ugly Sight, then a Troop of lean-cheek'd Moors."

The masque further reveals that these nymphs' dissatisfaction with their color springs from their contact with Western poets. Although Niger is here ostensibly to guide his daughters, he begins by taking up the Petrarchan gauntlet and proclaiming their beauty in a form that has embedded in it issues of race. The English poetry that celebrates bright/white beauty represents them as inferior:

---

9. All line references to Jonson's masques are from the Yale edition of *The Complete Masques of Ben Jonson*, ed. Stephen Orgel.

> Yet since the fabulous voices of some few
> Poor brainsick men, styled poets here with you,
> Have with such envy of their graces sung
> The painted beauties other empires sprung,
> Letting their loose and wingèd fictions fly
> To infect all climates, yea, our purity . . .
>
> (Lines 130–35)

Jonson here reveals the cultural imperialism rampant in European discussions of beauty. The assertion that poets, with "their loose and wingèd fictions," were the promoters of Eurocentric notions of beauty suggests that the early, cultural mavens such as Jonson well understood the damaging imposition of white standards of beauty, which the author Toni Morrison has called one of "the most destructive ideas in the history of human thought" (*The Bluest Eye* 97).[10]

Empire works with the same efficacy in delimiting an other. It is no accident that this first court masque is both an elucidation of the nature of blackness and a celebration of empire. *Blackness* was performed shortly after the coining of the term "Great Britain." Although it was not legally adopted until 1707, James I spent much of his energies trying to make the term official; consequently, it is the site of much discussion and debate over England's imperial growth and identity. *Blackness* is filled with references to the new status of England as the seat of a growing empire and the significance of its identity as Britannia:

> With that great name Britannia, this blessed isle
> Hath won her ancient dignity and style,
> *A World divided from the world,* and tried
> The abstract of it in his general pride.
> For were the world with all his wealth a ring,
> Britannia, whose new name makes all tongues sing,
> Might be a diamond worthy to enchase it.
>
> (Lines 216–22)

This pride in the revival of ancient Britain is continually yoked to the glorification of whiteness. In guiding his daughters to the promised land,

---

10. For more discussion on the lasting effects of Eurocentric beauty standards on black cultures, see Toni Cade, *The Black Woman*, 80–89 and 90–100; Audre Lorde, "Eye to Eye: Black Women: Hatred and Anger," in *Sister Outsider: Essays and Speeches by Audre Lorde,* and Jeanne Noble, "Bitches Brew," in *Beautiful, Also, Are the Souls of My Black Sisters: A History of Black Women in America,* 313–44; and Alice Walker, "If the Present Looks like the Past, What Does the Future Look Like?" in *In Search of Our Mother's Gardens,* 290–312.

Niger circles the globe, finding "Black Mauretania first, and secondly / Swarth Lusitania; next we did descry / Rich Aquitania" (173–75). Visiting these countries in an ascending (lightening) order of color (with Spain, interestingly, wealth replaces a color designation), Niger happens upon England, which is throughout associated with whiteness. Oceanus identifies England by its white cliffs: "This land that lifts into the temperate air / His snowy cliff is Albion the fair, / So called of Neptune's son, who ruleth here" (179–81). This primary name of England—Albion ("white land")—assumes great importance; its repetition throughout the masque stresses England's titular link with whiteness.

Although the *Masque of Blackness* does, as Barthelemy notes, deal with the fact of "blackness itself" (26), it cannot be made too obvious that such discussions of blackness are almost inevitably yoked to problems of gender difference. The cultural imperative of both masques is the turning of females white: none of the male "Blackamoors" seem to feel any such need. In general, little critical attention has been paid to the place of gender either in the masques or at court. Anne's role as Jonson's patron is not much discussed, perhaps because of the widespread opinion that Anne was an empty-headed spendthrift in endless pursuit of the unusual or the bizarre.[11] Although Jonson's claim that Anne specifically asked for "some dance, or show that might precede hers and have the place of a foil or false masque" (*Masque of Queens* lines 11–12) does not suggest that her creation of the antimasque is anything more than a continuing quest for novelty, it is also possible that her request reflects some awareness on the queen's part of her own female estrangement from James's court. Further, it plays up the possibly transgressive nature of both female "painting" and acting. The patriarchal structures that underlie many discussions of female beauty often create unstable subject positions for women. As women come to be judged solely by their adherence to male standards of desirability and decorum, they are often put into the position of competing for patriarchal approval.

Blackness, a culturally authorized trope for distinguishing between women, is rooted in just such competition. Blackness is often a mutable and relative quality; in early modern England, it is less a sign of complexion than one of status. As I will discuss in more detail later, women are

11. When she is even mentioned, Anne is roundly condemned by James's biographers and other students of the Jacobean court. Antonia Fraser (*King James* 53–55) comments on the way this phenomenon overlooks Anne's significance as a patron. William McElwee faults Anne's spending and her "placid stupidity" (*The Wisest Fool in Christendom* 122). Stephen Orgel, although somewhat less scathing, notes Jonson's "sensitivity to his audience" and proceeds to ignore or belittle Anne's place as patron, most obviously in his comment on Anne's "bright idea" for *Blackness* (*The Jonsonian Masque* 65).

only "black" or fair in competition with, or in relation to, each other. In this special sense of inequality, all women were "black" in King James's court. Female beauty was fairly powerless next to the "fair" men who enjoyed James's acutest attention. If, in the play world, James beneficently integrates these "dark" ladies into court, in the real world, his attentions to his favorites denied women the status that accrues from being sought-after prizes in erotic competition. Stephen Orgel suggests that *Blackness* and *Beauty* may work together as an antimasque and masque.[12] Jonson reports that the idea of the "foyle or false masque" was also Anne's, and it may be that her masque allowed her the creation of a strange other that worked to place her closer to the center of court, much in the way that *Blackness* prepares for and privileges *Beauty*.

The promise of *Blackness*—turning the nymphs white—is fulfilled two years later in the *Masque of Beauty*. The denigration of Anne's part in the creation of the masques may be sparked by the dynamic of the masques themselves. The blackness that originally marks her as different also marks her as inferior. For, in the execution of Anne's royal will, the masques concede power to the court males. Although Anne was the impetus for the performance of the masques, the actual power to do the impossible, to "wash the Ethiope white," is credited to Britain's chief poet and sun, James, "whose beams shine day and night, and are of force / To blanch an Ethiop, and revive a corse" (*Blackness* lines 224–25); the force behind the masque becomes the royal James, who watches a spectacle brought about by his kingly powers, "which now expect to see, great Neptune's son, / And love the miracle which thyself hast done" (*Beauty* lines 142–43). James's authority is called upon to break the deadlock of feminine beauty, to make the masquers, neither painted blacks nor painted white women but simply "beautiful." The whitening of the nymphs is presented in terms of conquest as the language of blackness surrenders to a more powerful heliocentric language:

> Yield, night, then, to the light,
> As blackness hath to beauty,
> Which was but the same duty.
> It is for beauty that the world was made,
> And where she reigns Love's lights admit no shade.
>
> (Lines 240–44)

Such a "surrender," even more than beautifying the nymphs, glorifies the king and his country: "And now by virtue of their light and grace, / The

---

12. *The Jonsonian Masque,* 119.

glorious isle wherein they rest takes place / Of all the earth for beauty"
(lines 109–10).[13]

The completion of the *Masque of Beauty* proclaims the triumph of Albion
and the return of proper, Platonic order to the world:[14]

> Now use your seat—that seat which was before
> Thought straying, uncertain, floating to each shore,
> And to whose having, every clime laid claim;
> Each land and nation urgèd as the aim
> Of their ambition beauty's perfect throne,
> Now made peculiar to this place alone,
> And that by impulsion of your destinies,
> And his attractive beams that lights these skies . . .
>
> (Lines 319–26)

As the verse suggests, James's England was beset by subterranean anxieties
of cultural impotence, which are offset by the cultural imperative, mandated by the demands of patriarchy and colonialism, of establishing the
primacy of whiteness/beauty. In asserting the power of Albion and of
James to convert African difference into European whiteness through the
return of the now-white nymphs to court, Jonson dramatizes a "positive"
model for the confrontation of cultures. This model explicitly reveals the
ways in which imperial contact is shaped by an organization of racial values
rooted in the control of gender mandated by patriarchy.

In her study of *Blackness*, Anne Cline Kelly notes that Anne would have
been visibly pregnant at the performance of this masque and suggests that
much of the water imagery highlights the "fruitfulness" signaled by Anne's potential delivery. One can only speculate that the fortuitously pregnant Anne acts as a dark, disruptive "fat lady" (Parker 20); nonetheless,
it is certainly true that children were a point of contention between James
and Anne. While the arrival of royal children after Elizabeth's childless
reign was no doubt a cause for celebration, the issue of royal progeny may
also have been another sign of female unruliness. Anne and James had
protracted disputes over her wish to raise the children, particularly Prince
Henry, herself; she made several unsuccessful attempts to regain custody
of the children (E. Williams 52–57). James preferred to follow the Scottish

13. Richard Peterson sees this as "the almost imperialistic conquest of night by day," but
insists that it does not "overcome the genuine strain of seductiveness in the masque" (190).

14. For a thorough discussion of the basis of the masque's symbolism in Renaissance
Platonism, see D. J. Gordon's "The Imagery of Ben Jonson's *The Masque of Blacknesse* and *The
Masque of Beautie*" and his expansion of that argument in *The Renaissance Imagination* (Orgel).

practice of having royal children raised away from court, and he commanded in writing that Prince Henry's guardian, the earl of Mar, was to deliver his son only on his orders and "in case God call me at any time see that neither for the Queen nor Estates, their pleasure, you deliver him till he be eighteen years of age, and that he command you himself" (quoted in Ethel Williams 55). The turning of Anne white may have represented the king's power over unruly females as well as the appropriation of African fertility and wealth. Ania Loomba forcefully contends that such a need to control female behavior is evidence of a fear that is more powerful than any actual threat: "Surely the paranoid and violent attempts to control female independence, property rights, movement and sexual autonomy indicate that the fears generated by the possibility of female transgression are *real* and *actual,* even where such subversion is only potential" (82).

The *Masque of Beauty* presents an idealized world in which normally intransigent blackness is subdued by a European order predicated on white, male privilege and power. In actuality, female unruliness was not so easily contained: the performance itself featured many women who resisted patriarchal standards of female decorum. Besides Sidney's own "dark lady," Penelope Rich, who was the mistress of Edward Blount and the mother of four illegitimate children, the play cast: Lady Arabella Stuart, who would later be sent to the Tower (again) for her secret marriage to Lord Seymour; Frances Howard, Lady Walsingham, who later became notorious for poisoning her husband in the "Overbury affair"; and Lady Mary Wroth, who had two illegitimate children by her first cousin and was sent down from court after the publication of her prose romance in 1621. From the first entrance of James into England, the court ladies are associated with lawless, transgressive behavior. In her diary, Lady Anne Clifford, the countess of Pembroke, comments on the reputation of the queen's ladies, connecting their scandalous behavior with the performance of masques: "Now there was much talk of a mask which the Queen had at Winchester, & how all the Ladies about the Court had gotten such ill names that it was grown a scandalous place, & the Queen herself was much fallen from her former greatness & reputation she had in the world" (16–17). In Clifford's report, masques seem less like peaceful celebrations of royal power and virtue than sites of female misrule.

The *Masque of Blackness* was not an isolated incident of "strangeness" but the best-known (and most visual) sign of a discourse of blackness emanating from the court. While the implication of blackness in the masque depends on the actual painting of these court beauties, Jonson provides many verbal "signs" of otherness in his printed text. As in Shakespeare's *Antony and Cleopatra,* the appearance of blackness itself does not constitute its sole presence in the play. The sight of blackness is invariably accompanied by a vocabulary similar to what Edward Said terms the representative figures or tropes of orientalist discourse (71). As Jonson himself notes in claiming that he chose hieroglyphics to signify the nymph's names, "as well as for strangeness as relishing of antiquity" (*Blackness* 239–40), these signs carry the religious and cultural associations of and assumptions about blackness. Jonson's textual emendations and stage descriptions contribute to the illusion of cultural difference even as they display his erudition; for example, he describes the nymphs as having ornaments of "the most choice and orient pearl" (*Blackness* 60) and hair "thick and curled upright in tresses, like pyramids" (*Blackness* 57).

By such specificity we see that blackness had, as early as the *Masque of Blackness,* become part of the linguistic currency of James's rule. Not only did James keep Africans at court as part of his passion for oddities, the actual excesses of the court seem to have been perceived as "oriental." Racial difference, particularly in descriptions of the perceived decadence of the court, was a privileged idiom for self-description and critique. Orientalism, another trope of difference with a broad arsenal of effects, opens up religion as a category of difference. For example, Sir John Harrington's description of the entertainments for King Christian of Denmark in 1606 links James's court with the alleged idolatry and licentiousness of Islam: "The sports began each day in such a manner and such sorte, as well nigh persuaded me of Mahomet's Paradise. We had women, and indeed wine too, of such plenty, as would have astonished each sober beholder. Our feasts were magnificent and the two Royal Guests did most lovingly entertain each other at table" (Nichols 72).[15] From the middle ages on, Mohammed and "Mohammedism" had been a sign for sexual and moral depravity (Said 62). Harrington's description of the court as Mohammed's paradise would seem to be less a way of bringing the East closer to the West than one of distancing the "private" indecorous behavior of these Western rulers from their royal function. Indeed, the entertainments Harrington describes sound much like the representations of James's public kingly persona. For example, a banquet designed for the same occasion used the common motif of James as Solomon:

15. Samuel C. Chew gives further examples of English allegations of carnality in "Mahomet's Paradise," in *The Crescent and the Rose: Islam and England during the Renaissance.* See also Donne's "To his Mistress going to bed": "Thou Angel bringst with thee / A heaven like Mahomets Paradice" (20–21).

One day a great feast was held; and, after dinner, the representation of Solomon his temple and the coming of the Queen of Sheba was made, or (as I may better say) was meant to have been made, before their Majesties, by Device of the Earl of Salisbury and others. . . . The Lady who did play the Queene's part, did carry most precious gifts to both their Majesties; but forgetting the stepps arising to the canopy, overset her caskets into his Danish Majestie's lap, and fell at his feet, though I rather think it was in his face. . . . His Majestie then got up, and would dance with the Queen of Sheba; but he fell down, and humbled himself before her, and was carried to an inner chamber and laid on a bed of state; which was not a little defiled with the presents of the Queen, which had been bestowed on his garments; such as wine, cream, jelly, beverage, cakes, spices and other good manners. (Nichols 2)

Harrington's rhetoric, echoing as it does the official descriptions of court entertainments, only throws into relief the burlesque nature of the masque.[16] The fascination with alien difference Scottish James brought to court becomes speakable as orientalism in Harrington's account.

Such a description of court debauchery takes on an added resonance when one remembers the appearance of Solomon in colonialist discourses and the popular representation of James as an English Solomon. The lengths to which the proponents of this analogy went can best be shown by Bishop Williams's funeral oration for James: "*Solomon* was of a Complexion White and Ruddy. . . . *Solomon* was a great maintainer of Shipping and Navigation . . . A most proper Attribute to King *James*. . . . Every man lived in Peace under his Vine and his Fig-tree in the days of *Solomon*. . . . And so they did in the blessed days of King *James*. And yet towards his end, King *Solomon* had secret *Enemies, Razan, Hadad*, and *Jeroboam*, and prepared for a War upon his going to his Grave" (Ashton 19–20). As we have seen, the story of Solomon is used to represent two sides of colonial encounters. In one version, the Song of Songs, the dominant white male refashions and whitens the foreign, dark female into an object of a transcendent wedded love; this "positive" aesthetic model reverberates through English sonnet cycles and the *Masque of Beauty*. This vision is

16. For more on the associations of masques and consumption of sweets, consult Patricia Fumerton who sees such ritual consumption of masques and void foods as key to Jacobean subjectivity: "What contemporaries viewed through the ornamental perspective scenery and (as we shall see) 'sweet' conceits of masques in the Banqueting House was an exposure of the King's privacy as an insubstantial fiction—as self made void—even while they saw, or hoped to see, bodily 'restoratives' " (136).

countered, however, with an image of a Solomon too much given to plea-
sures of the flesh, which are associated with the allures of a foreign female;
this negative model underlies most representation and works in dialectical
fashion to maintain proper boundaries between self and other within an
economy of desire.

Thus the entertainment for King Christian demonstrates how easily the
control exercised in the one model slips into the degeneration and excess
warned of by the second. The domination over (and eradication of) foreign difference seen in the *Masque of Beauty* is inverted into a carnivalesque
spectacle that shows the threatening nether side of cultural interaction
when the powerful Western ruler is seen to succumb to Eastern disorder
and riot. The king's drunken departure echoes the problematic side of
Solomon's womanizing, described as "defiling" the bed of state (albeit
with food and drink). Harrington also reads the scenes as a subversion of
gender roles when he describes James—with the aptly named King Christian—as "humbling himself" before Sheba.

Traditional notions of "Englishness" and the concomitant issues of social disorder were being interrogated and threatened on all sides by the
growing pains of imperialism. For, in addition to these internal court tensions, Englishmen were going abroad in increasing numbers, implement-
ing James's plantation policies, exploring "undiscovered" lands, and
seeking new economic opportunities abroad. Stephen Greenblatt's examination of these travels reveals an obsession with the potential disregard
of traditional social restraints and the subsequent loss of discipline inherent in the distancing of contact with the homeland (*Shakespearean Negotiations* 150–52). The fear underlying this obsession is of course one of loss
of identity: Englishmen were forced to grapple with the problem of maintaining their sense of "Englishness" in a strange land.[17]

Although it is difficult to estimate precisely how questions of birthright,
religious toleration, economic viability, and gender organization affected
the English sense of self and country, one measure may be the predominance of the trope of blackness in the drama of the period. As Sander
Gilman has noted, such an evocation of an other is not unusual in times
of stress: "A rich web of signs and references for the idea of difference
arises out of a society's communal sense of control over its world. No
matter how this sense of control is articulated, whether as political power,

17. Peter Hulme provocatively contends that one solution to the mystery of the lost
colony of Roanoke directly affects the sense of American/Western identity: "Historically this
seems in part to have *had* to remain a mystery because the obvious explanation, that the
settlers simply *became* Croatoans, is too uncomfortable to be seriously contemplated" (143).

social status, religious mission, or geographic or economic domination, it provides an appropriate vocabulary for the sense of difference" (20). With the loss of a "communal sense of control" at a moment of real historical change, blackness becomes a cultural idiom for interrogating issues of social order, particularly as they are related to problems of race, gender, and economics. Black figures—both "actual" and disguised—become the focal points for an extraordinarily dense system of signification that, unpacked, reveals layered and interconnected anxieties over difference. A study of the play of difference on the stage demonstrates early signs of the complicated interactions among many different systems of oppression and how inseparable they are in a later, more fully articulated, chauvinist culture: "But if we look closely at the portrait which the racist draws of a man or a woman of color, or that the anti-Semite draws of the Jew, or that the pornographer draws of a woman, we begin to see that these fantasized figures resemble one another. For they are the creations of one mind. This is the chauvinist mind, a mind which projects all its fears in itself onto another: a mind which defines itself by what it hates" (Griffin 299). Griffin goes on to suggest that as much as the chauvinist wishes to force the "other" away, in his ambivalence he surrounds himself with symbolic representations of the other (304). Sex and race, seen through violence and intimacy, become the primary foci of the exercise of social control.

Marriages of State:
The Tempest and *Antony and Cleopatra*

Colonialist readings of *The Tempest* have shown the text to be a fertile ground for exploring issues of race, cultural contest, and authority in English encounters in the "new world."[18] They have been less attentive to roles of women in colonial structures. The threat of interracial desire, although only one element in the myriad contests over social control in the play, is key to the establishment of an ideal of patriarchal authority.

18. For examples of what "new historicism" and cultural materialism have made of the colonial themes in this play, see Paul Brown, " 'This thing of darkness I acknowledge mine': *The Tempest* and the Discourse of Colonialism"; Stephen Greenblatt, *Shakespearean Negotiations: The Circulation of Social Energy in Renaissance England*; Peter Hulme, *Colonial Encounters: Europe and the Native Caribbean, 1492–1797*. For discussions of postcolonial issues see especially Thomas Cartelli, "Prospero in Africa: *The Tempest* as Colonial Text and Pre-Text"; Ania Loomba, *Gender, Race, Renaissance Drama*, 142–58; and Rob Nixon, "Caribbean and African Appropriations of *The Tempest*."

Perhaps because of his indeterminacy (to which I shall return later), Caliban has been read alternatively as black African, Afro-Caribbean, and Native American; however, in all these permutations, he embodies and resists ideologies of dark and light even as he is continually read as dark other.[19] Ania Loomba proposes that "explicitly social-Darwinist, racist and imperialist productions indicated Caliban's *political* colour as clearly *black*" (143). The text itself locates Caliban on one side of a binarism in Prospero's final pronouncement on Caliban, "this thing of darkness I / Acknowledge mine" (5.1.275–76), and in clearly marking him as a slave who is associated with darkness and dirt: "thou earth" (1.2.314; Vaughan and Vaughan 15).[20] Caliban functions as a "thing of darkness" against which a European social order is tested and proved. Conversely, Miranda is the emblem of purity and integrity whose person is the grounds of this struggle: the contest for access to her reveals a concern over the purity of the aristocratic female body that symbolically assures the integrity of aristocratic bloodlines ("fair issue" [4.1.24]) and an orderly disposition of property (Loomba 83). In addition to the connection between Caliban and Miranda, the play features a series of attempted joinings or unions that momentarily disrupt categories of race, class, and gender. These unions generally draw attention to the increased fluidity of these categories in new world enterprise and particularly question the future of dynastic alliance and succession in an Atlantic economy.

In the first scene Prospero charges Caliban with the attempted rape of Miranda: "I have used thee— / Filth as thou art—with humane care, and lodged thee / In mine own cell, till thou didst seek to violate / The honour of my child" (1.2.345–48). While Caliban's response indicates that he did indeed make advances to Miranda, modern minds conditioned by American racism are compelled to disrupt Prospero's fostering of Ferdinand's "seduction" in place of Caliban's "rape," for, as Susan Griffin reminds us, the rape threat is the prime image formed by the racist imagination:

> At the heart of the racist imagination we discover a pornographic fantasy: the specter of miscegenation. The image of a dark man raping a fair woman

19. Alden T. and Virginia Mason Vaughan's *Shakespeare's Caliban* offers a wide-ranging reception history of the play.

20. A. and V. Vaughan also explore the intriguing possibility that the name Caliban derives from the Romany word *Cauliban*, which meant " 'black' or things associated with blackness" (33–34). Line references to *The Tempest* are to the Oxford edition, ed. Stephen Orgel.

embodies all that the racist fears. The fantasy preoccupies his mind. A rational argument exists which argues that the racist simply uses pornographic images to manipulate the mind. But these images seem to belong to the racist. They are predictable in a way that suggests a more intrinsic part in the genesis of this ideology. (298)

Although it may seem anachronistic to impose such a race/sex dialectic on an early text, and possibly offensive to seem to "explain" Caliban's behavior, it is nonetheless true that interracial sex does become an issue in the Virginia colonies not twenty years after the first performance of *The Tempest.* In the first Virginia law case (*Re: Davis* 1630) involving race, a white, Hugh Davis, was publicly whipped for fornication with a black woman (Giddings 35–36).

Completely authorized by the play, Prospero's hostility toward Caliban is linked to his obsessive attempts to control his environment and his daughter's sexuality. Caliban's response, "O ho, O ho! Would't had been done! / Thou didst prevent me—I had peopled else / This isle with Calibans" (1.1.348–50), strikes at the heart of European fears of the putative desire of the native other for European women and thus functions to license Prospero's anxiety (Loomba 149). Caliban's threat "to people the isle" with his offspring clearly suggests that he would control the island by creating a new "mixed" race and rebuts Prospero on his own terms. Territorial claims are backed here by a need for patriarchal control over women.[21]

Miranda's response to Caliban is equally telling: the language lessons (which she implies brought about the attempted violation), rather than fostering communication, reveal an epistemic "difference" that serves only to heighten her sense of racial difference and her estrangement from Caliban:

> I pitied thee,
> Took pains to make thee speak, taught thee each hour
> One thing or other. When thou didst not, savage,
> Know thine own meaning, but wouldst gabble like
> A thing most brutish, I endowed thy purposes
> With words that made them known. But thy vile race—

21. Stephen Orgel argues that the competing claims of Caliban and Prospero for the island represent the available ways of understanding royal authority under James I's reign ("Prospero's Wife" 58).

Though thou didst learn—had that in't which good natures
Could not abide to be with . . .

(1.2.352–59)

Miranda's tirade against Caliban's alien "ingratitude" does seem out of
character for the dutiful daughter she is in the rest of the play.[22] Her
claim that Caliban does not "know thine own meaning" replicates the
play's central ethos, which cannot accept that his "gabbling" has value:
just as Prospero's power is located in his book, "true" meaning (and
power) lies in European, aristocratic language. Like many colonial travelers who denigrate the language of other cultures when confronted with
meanings they do not accept, Miranda reads Caliban's native tongue as a
nonlanguage and refuses to accept his use of her discourse on the grounds
that it is corrupted with "uncivil" meanings. Her lessons, rather than re-
forming and "civilizing" him, only let him express his "savage" impulses
in terms she cannot help but understand. He controls the language rather
than be controlled by it. Caliban's "sin," as it were, is both linguistic and
sexual; in saying, "My profit on't / Is I know how to curse," he subverts
the language just as he is said to attempt to corrupt Miranda.

Caliban's rejected sexual advances signal his position in the web of economics, hegemonic control, and linguistic exclusion that is common to
discourses of race. In arguing that race becomes the central trope for
forming differences between "cultures, linguistic groups, or adherents of
specific belief systems which—more often than not—also have fundamentally opposed economic interests" (5), Henry Louis Gates, Jr., also suggests that "literacy . . . is the emblem that links racial alienation and
economic alienation" (6). Caliban's "difference" is produced out of just
such a combination of linguistic exclusion and economic competition: his
reply ("my profit on't / Is I know how to curse") articulates both economic and linguistic/racial alienation. Although writing is not directly an
issue, access to a language of power is; curses (or spells), while seemingly
powerful weapons for Sycorax, have no efficacy for Caliban. In this new
linguistic economy, powerful curses and spells are located in Prospero's
book. This triangulated linguistic community, with Prospero at the apex,

22. For a discussion of the critical commentary on these lines and the theater's attempts
to resolve them, see Stephen Orgel's introduction to the Oxford edition of *The Tempest.* I
will add that violent rejections of the other's sexual advances only serve, rather than disrupt,
the interests of patriarchy. Although this may be a case of the "radically discontinuous"
speech attributed to women (Belsey, *Subject of Tragedy* 160), it also true that women bear the
responsibility of policing the borders of the state and rejecting differences that threaten
patriarchal structures and are licensed to speak out in that capacity.

serves to enforce both a racial hierarchy and patriarchal authority. Miranda, while teaching Caliban, performs the proper role of the woman within culture: she teaches a "mother language" to Caliban that is supposed to replace his original mother's tongue. However, neither Miranda's nor Caliban's relationship to language is powerful. Miranda's own mastery of language is still secondary to Prospero's: it is represented as purely oral, and she is frequently conjoined to silence in the beginning of the play. Juliet Fleming astutely notes that the vernacular and the oral are often associated with the feminine; more important, she contends that such mediated relationships to standardized languages are typical: "But while women (and foreigners) may be permitted to lend their assent to the new authoritative functions of English, they are not expected to use it authoritatively themselves; indeed the adequately 'ruled' English turns out to be the exclusive possession of men" (299).

So, too, the enforcing of a subject people's "assent" to a ruler's language is a key tool of colonial power. Caliban, typically, has been taught language as a tool of his own subordination; it is so tied into his labor as servant and guide that its use merely "profits" Prospero. We can see a similar ethos of language and national/ethnic competition in Spenser's *A View of the Present State of Ireland,* which is concerned in many ways with the legal, cultural, and economic ramifications of the union of cultures under imperialism. One of the fears that erupts from the discussion of the dubious lineage of Spaniards (seen as a mixed-race people) is the problematic purity of the Englishmen living in Ireland.[23] Miscegenation (which, like blackness in George Best, is dubbed an "infection" by Spenser) and assimilation show their first effect in language:

> Irenius: . . . and first I have to find fault with the abuse of language, that is, for the speaking of Irish amongst the English, which, as it is unnatural that any people should love another's language more than their own, so is it very

23. Spenser outlines one of the sources of this sense of Spain's mixed heritage when he suggests that Spain's current riches are the inheritance of a long history of invasion, particularly by Africans: "For the Spaniard that now is, is come from as rude and savage nations as they, there being as it may be gathered by course of ages and view of their own history (though they therein labour, much to ennoble themselves) scarce any drop of the old Spanish blood left in them: . . . And yet after all those the Moors and barbarians breaking over out of Africa, did finally possess all Spain, or the most part thereof, and tread down under their foul heathenish feet, whatever little they found there yet standing; the which though afterwards they were beaten out by *Ferdinand of Aragon* and Elizabeth his wife, yet they were not so cleansed, but that through the marriages which they had made, and mixture with the people of the land during their long continuance there, they had left no pure drop of Spanish blood; no, nor of Roman nor Scythian; so that of all nations under heaven I suppose the Spaniard is the most mingled, most uncertain and most bastardly" (43–44).

inconvenient and the cause of many other evils. Eudoxus: It seemeth strange to me that the English should take more delight to speak that langauge than their own, whereas they should (me thinks) rather take scorne to acquaint their tounges thereto, for it hath been ever the use of the conquerer to despise the language of the conquered, and to force him by all means to learn his. So did the Romans always use, insomuch that there is almost no nation in the world but is sprinkled with their language. (67)

The discussion here shows a crucial connection between inscriptions of racial difference and colonial control. Cultural and political differences between the English, the Scottish, and the Irish are distilled to problematic linguistic differences, the overcoming and assimilation of which is the first step in an imperialist project.[24] Irenius replies to Eudoxus's concerns that so few can be influenced linguistically by linking language acquisition to social formations, particularly to domestic practices:

I suppose that the chief cause of bringing in the Irish language, amongst them, was specially their fostering, and marrying with the Irishe, which are two most dangerous infections, for first the childe that sucketh the milke of the nurse must of necessity learn his first speech of her, the which being the first that is enured to his tongue is ever after most pleasing unto him, insomuch as though he afterwards be taught English, yet the smack of the first will always abide with him, and not only of the speech, but of the manners and conditions, . . . The next is the marrying with the Irish, which how dangerous a thing it is in all commonwealths, appeareth to every simplest sense, and though some great ones have used such matches with their vassals, . . . yet the example is so perilous as it is not to be adventured . . . (67, 68).

In this section of the *View*, fears of interracial alliance are very explicitly linked to fears of assimilation of the ruler by the ruled. This particular passage presents English fears of alternative social structures, such as Irish fosterage, and presents women as a chief danger. In some ways, fosterage is an even more powerful way of forming alliances between groups than marriage. Patricia Fumerton says of the Irish practice: "So strong was the bonding of fosterage that it cemented ties not only between the child and its foster parents but also between the foster parents and the natural par-

24. José Piedra analyzes the first grammar of a modern European language, Antonio de Nebrija's *Gramática de la lengua castellana*, as an arm of imperial rule: "Europe, Africa, and America became the grounds on which Spain planned to practice enslavement justified as a rhetorical brokerage of universal knowledge" (282). He further claims, "Nebrija provided the New World with the justification for a cohesive Hispanic Text; he unified 'otherness' under the grammatical self-righteousness of the colonial letter" (284).

ents" (46). This forming of bonds, which is not significantly different from Elizabethan practices of child exchange, is here a threat both because of the "unhealthy" mixture of Irish and English, and because of the ever-present danger of English assimilation. Women in this scenario become dangerous carriers of the infection of foreign difference, a danger so perilous that intermarriage needs to be avoided at all costs.

The connection between language and profit in Caliban's reply reverberates throughout *The Tempest.* The Europeans see Caliban as the conduit to the various means of new world wealth talked of in traveler's tales. Prospero makes Caliban a slave after he shows his knowledge of "every fertile inch o' th' island," taking the profit of both the island and Caliban's labor and leaving him with only the dubious gain of language ("my profit on't / Is I know how to curse"). Trinculo and Stephano immediately see the economic potential in Caliban. At first sight, Trinculo imagines putting Caliban on display: "Were I in England now, as once I was, and had but this fish painted, not a holiday-fool there but would give a piece of silver. There would this monster make a man—any strange beast there makes a man" (2.2.27–30). Trinculo's enterprise again demonstrates the ambiguous allure of economic involvement. In gaining wealth from possession of the native, the European is rhetorically made one with the other, just as the hunger for novelty allows a "monster" to "make a man." In Trinculo's formulation, he is created (made) by the native even as he makes him an object of exchange: "There would this monster make a man." Colonialism and class interact when Trinculo (who, unlike Ferdinand, is not "the best of them that speak this speech" [1.1.430]) unwittingly creates the very entanglement that imperialism dreads: "Any strange beast there makes a man. When they will not give a doit to relieve a lame beggar, they will lay out ten to see a dead Indian" (2.2.30–32).

This entanglement is itself ironically staged in the image of Trinculo and Caliban under the gabardine. Stephano associates the sight with foreign strangeness, crying, "Do you put tricks upon's with savages and men of Ind? Ha?" (2.2.56–57). Like Trinculo he instantly thinks of profit as well as of the monstrous mixture of Englishman and native: "This is some monster of the isle with four legs, who hath got, as I take it, an ague. Where the devil should he learn our language? I will give him some relief, if it be but for that. If I can recover him, and keep him tame, and get to Naples with him, he's a present for any emperor that ever trod on neat's-leather" (2.2.63–68). Significantly, Caliban's oddity or monstrosity is due in part to his ability to speak a master language, an ability that (at least in Trinculo's formulation) rewards him: "I will give him some relief." Trinculo sees yet another profit in Caliban, perhaps buying favor from an emperor in exchange for this new world oddity. The comic entanglement of the lower-class European and the native is reminiscent of colonial propaganda, which locates a dangerous blurring of the line between the civilized and the barbaric in the lower classes and which uses the threatening economic need of the lower classes as the impetus for colonial expansion.[25] Indeed, this coalition threatens Prospero's imperial project as much as the plot itself threatens his life. Prospero's much-noted hasty exit would then be read as a reaction to a class threat to aristocratic power. It also gestures toward an anxiety about class mobility enabled by colonial enterprise, an issue to which I will return at the end of this chapter.

Despite such class concerns, the proper disposition of both gender and race remains the central anxiety. Ferdinand's appearance on stage immediately after Prospero's dismissal of Caliban highlights interesting parallels between the noble European and the foreign "savage." Like Caliban, Ferdinand requires instruction from Miranda: "Vouchsafe my prayer / May know if you remain upon this island, / And that you will some good instruction give / How I may bear me here" (1.2.423–26). However, unlike Caliban, Ferdinand is "culturally sound" as well as of noble birth. His first thought upon seeing Miranda is that she "speaks his language": "My language! Heavens! / I am the best of them that speak this speech, / Were I but where 'tis spoken" (1.2.429–31). His characterization of his status as an epistemic connection rather than one of consanguinity signals an instant bond with Miranda. Linguistic compatibility, seen in other Shakespearean couples such as Romeo and Juliet and Beatrice and Benedick as a mere sign of sexual compatibility, takes on racial overtones in that racial and cultural difference are tied to rhetorical skill. The emphasis on linguistic prowess serves in some ways to efface crucial similarities between Ferdinand and Caliban. Prospero is, with good reason, equally concerned with regulating Miranda's courtship with Ferdinand, although his reaction to that courtship is qualitatively different from his reaction to Caliban. As Eric Sundelson points out, Ferdinand's reassuring reply to Prospero suggests both hidden rape fantasies and the possibility of abandonment (48), revealing a basic sexuality—common to both men—that must be contained by the father. These similarities in some ways suggest that the "real" difference between Caliban and Ferdinand is racial, not moral or sexual.

The pressures of imperialism insist on the control and regulation of female sexuality, particularly when concerns over paternity are complicated by the problems of racial and cultural purity. Prospero's manipu-

25. See Chapter 1, pp. 53–54.

lation of Ferdinand rewards him insofar as it creates a marriage of state that forms the basis for a new empire as well as a romantic attachment. Act 2 opens with a discussion of the marriage of Claribel, daughter of the king of Naples, in which Shakespeare provides an alternative glance at the way in which the traditional political marriage is endangered by European contact with less desirable others. The king of Naples arranges a political marriage between Claribel and the king of Tunis, a move he consequently regrets, because it has indirectly separated him from a daughter and a son. Once on the island, Alonso is roundly castigated by Sebastian for abusing his authority over his "fair daughter" (2.1.70) because he chose to "lose her to an African" (2.1.123):

> You were kneeled to and importuned otherwise
> By all of us, and the fair soul herself
> Weighed between loathness and obedience at
> Which end o' th' beam should bow. We have lost your son,
> I fear, for ever. Milan and Naples have
> More widows in them of this business' making
> Than we bring men to comfort them.
> The fault's your own.
>
> (2.1.126–33)

Sebastian's criticism, like Alonso's regret (Would I had never / Married my daughter there, for coming thence / My son is lost [2.1.105–7]), directly attributes Ferdinand's loss—and the loss of the royal bloodline—to the marriage. All sorts of privation are attributed to the wedding (in contrast to the bounty promised in Miranda's wedding masque): in Sebastian's condemnation, European families are ruptured and bloodlines broken because of this marriage. Prospero prospers not only because of his successful manipulation of the Ferdinand-Miranda alliance but also because of Alonso's disastrous decision to open up the sex/gender system to an African king. In refusing to open the sex/gender system to non-European outsiders, Prospero demonstrates his ability to preserve the integrity of the "fair" aristocratic body and, consequently, the state. Not only does he regain his kingdom, he becomes the father to a new dynasty.

The attention to paternal authority only throws into relief the very visible absence of mothers in the play. Typically, Prospero gives the maternal history of both Miranda and Caliban. Miranda's mother is mentioned in order to confirm the purity and insularity of Prospero's own bloodline:

Prospero: Twelve year since, Miranda, twelve year since,
           Thy father was the Duke of Milan, and
           A prince of power—
Miranda: Sir, are you not my father?
Prospero: Thy mother was a piece of virtue, and
           She said thou wast my daughter; and thy father
           Was Duke of Milan, and his only heir
           And princess no worse issued.

                                              (1.2.53–59)

Ironically, her presence is evoked by Miranda's unwitting, yet witty, denial of her father's royal power. Prospero's reply ("She said thou wast my daughter") reveals an anxiety over inheritance and the woman's role in reproduction, a factor that had a particularly strong resonance for James, whose own claim to England's throne was particularly vexed because, as Stephen Orgel notes, "His legitimacy, in both senses [as designated ruler and son], thus derived from two mothers, the chaste Elizabeth and the sensual Mary" ("Prospero's Wife" 59). Caliban counters Prospero's attacks with an equally strong claim to an "empire" through his African mother's bloodline:

> This island's mine by Sycorax my mother,
> Which thou tak'st from me. When thou cam'st first
> Thou strok'st me and made much of me; wouldst give me
> Water with berries in't, and teach me how
> To name the bigger light and how the less,
> That burn by day and night; and then I loved thee,
> And showed thee all the qualities o'th' isle,
> The fresh springs, brine pits, barren place and fertile—
> Cursed be I that did so! All the charms
> Of Sycorax, toads, beetles, bats light on you!
> For I am all the subjects that you have,
> Which first was mine own king, and here you sty me
> In this hard rock, whiles you do keep from me
> The rest o'th' island.

                                              (1.2.331–44)

It is in response to Caliban's claim of property rights that Prospero charges Caliban with rape, a rhetorical move that reinforces Valerie Smith's point that "instances of interracial rape constitute sites of struggle between black and white men that allow privileged white men to exercise their property rights over the bodies of white women" (158). Although Smith is referring here specifically to the view of white women as property, historically claims of rape have worked to mystify property interests.

Caliban poses the ultimate threat to such a quest for social and political integrity. Not only is he made into a sexual threat against an aristocratic body, his own unfixed and ambiguous origins make him an embodiment of the miscegenative threat. Caliban himself is that site of anxiety provoked by the expansion of England. Peter Hulme persuasively suggests that the play is situated within a fundamental dualism, represented both geographically in the island and physically in Caliban:

> The island is the meeting place of the play's topographical dualism, Mediterranean and Atlantic, ground of the mutually incompatible reference systems whose co-presence serves to frustrate any attempt to locate the island on a map. Caliban is similarly the ground of these two discourses. As "wild man" or "wodehouse", with an African mother whose pedigree leads back to the *Odyssey*, he is distinctly Mediterranean. And yet, at the same time, he is, as his name suggests, a "cannibal" as that figure had taken shape on colonial discourse: ugly, devilish, ignorant, gullible and treacherous—according to the Europeans' descriptions of him. (108)

As I argue in the Introduction, Africa is a foundational presence in new world discourses. Hulme's formulation provides a necessary corrective to many colonialist readings that look only to new world materials as influential on the play. Alden and Virginia Vaughan note the surprisingly infrequent attempts to link *The Tempest* to discourses of Africa (51). Although it is not my intent here to embark on that project, thinking along Hulme's lines opens up the possibility for Caliban to occupy multiple sites of difference and might counter some of the unease that critics have felt with the imprecision with which one can identify the play as "colonialist." Meredith Skura, for example, bases a large part of her critique of what she calls "revisionist" readings of the play on a survey of new world materials and a conclusion that there was no stable colonialist discourse that Shakespeare could be said to draw on.[26] As a useful counter

26. Skura's essay is itself quite fascinating in that it critiques attempts at historical specificity while at the same time insisting on ahistorical psychoanalytic paradigms (such as "man's timeless tendency to demonize 'strangers' "[45]) that re-inscribe the universality of Shakespeare. Ironically, the very materials she uses would seem to question the "timeless tendency to demonize strangers": although all colonial narratives are in some sense motivated fictions, the recurring trope of the friendly, welcoming native who suddenly turns hostile suggests that demonization is not the first response—unless one assumes that white Europeans are never strangers. So, too, Caliban's first response is not to demonize the "stranger" Prospero but to welcome him. Skura also claims that "Shakespeare was the first to show one of *us*

to Skura's argument, it would be helpful to combine Hulme's insight with Mary Louise Pratt's concept of the "contact zone," which is a colonial space "in which peoples geographically and historically separated come into contact with each other and establish ongoing relations, usually involving conditions of coercion, radical inequality, and intractable contact" (6). The island is a space of competing and conflicting discourses that are about the contact itself. There are any number of these "contact zones" in Renaissance travel literature, and it might be fruitful to think of those in relation to the play. For example, one might think about the infamous example of Sir Francis Drake, whose crew, on his third circumnavigation, impregnated a black woman named Maria and abandoned her on an island along with two black men.

Caliban embodies the contradiction and contest characteristic of border spaces, and in that position he contests Prospero's imperial visions. Just as Caliban verbally refuses Prospero's attempts to construct a seamless colonial narrative and critical attempts to construct a unified play of forgiveness and restoration, his "difference" itself is unsettled; it defies categories and is therefore, for the Europeans and contemporary critics, "unsettling." Even the seeming resolution seems to open up the issues of Caliban's birthright and inheritance once more:

> This misshapen knave,
> His mother was a witch, and one so strong
> That could control the moon, make flows and ebbs,
> And deal in her command without her power.
> These three have robbed me, and this demi-devil—
> For he's a bastard one—had plotted with them
> To take my life. Two of these fellows you

------

mistreating a native, the first to represent a native from the inside, the first to allow a native to complain onstage, and the first to make the New World encounter problematic enough to generate the current attention to the play" (58). This peroration contains a set of highly problematic and offensive assumptions that reveal the difficulties of her critical approach. Her references to the "universality of racial prejudice" (56) and "general psychological needs" (69) are specifically linked to her assertion that Shakespeare was the first to show one of *us* mistreating a native. These assertions, like her insistence on the universality (yet uniqueness) of Shakespeare, rely on the notion of a unified and universal white subject—in other words, herself. Who is included in the italicized "us" that we are shown in the play? Any reader of the play? Any literary critic? Any teacher? Am I, a black feminist critic of Shakespeare part of the "us" that Skura imagines? Like those who accept Prospero's narratives as the "truth," Skura assumes that all readers are potential Prosperos.

Must know and own; this thing of darkness I
Acknowledge mine.

(5.1.268–76)

The terms originally used to control and disinherit Caliban ("misshapen knave," "bastard," "demi-devil") are here reproduced along with a discourse of theft and illegitimacy, which are used to license Prospero's moves to create a political dynasty. Both moves publicly establish Prospero's ownership in a proprietorial sense, suggesting that any "acknowledgment" or bond with a dark other can be safely made only within a context of ownership and control.

The play opens up another perspective on interracial union through the perplexing "widow Dido" jesting that precedes the breast-beating over Claribel's marriage. It is now a commonplace that the *Aeneid* is a crucial subtext for issues of dynastic politics and royal authority in *The Tempest* (Orgel, *Tempest* 39). The story of Aeneas, the founder of imperial Rome, and Dido, the African queen, provides yet another cautionary tale of the threat of female sexuality to colonial expansion when Dido's passion is read as diverting Aeneas from the task of empire. The bantering over Dido's status as widow represents conflicting Renaissance readings of the Dido story (Orgel, *Tempest* 42), which speak to the issue of proper marriage. Gonzalo's insistence on Dido as widow authorizes her union as a marriage (since one must be a wife to be a widow) and thereby legitimizes the foreign female's part in the creation of empire. In contrast, Antonio's jesting reduces Dido's importance: she becomes a mere dalliance on Aeneas's part and no significant threat to Aeneas's imperial project.

Gonzalo, in changing the subject from the king's doomed children, turns to an imaginative politics that paradoxically creates a "new" commonwealth with existing political structures. The proximity of the description of his "socialist" state to the issues of dynastic succession suggestively links changes in the European social order to the threat of miscegenation. Issues of racial difference are consequently collapsed into problems of economics, politics, class, and gender. Like Shakespeare's Cleopatra, Gonzalo's Dido competes for title of widow and a legitimate place in the imperial text and provokes the possibility of alternative dynastic structures that are not purely European.

Shakespeare's *Antony and Cleopatra* is the play that perhaps is most closely concerned with the ways an African queen threatens empire. Cleopatra's darkness makes her the embodiment of an absolute correspondence between fears of racial and gender difference and the threat they pose to imperialism. As Ania Loomba states, "Dominant notions about female identity, gender relations and imperial power are unsettled through the disorderly non-European woman" (125). In his tirade on Antony's "dotage" in the opening scene, Philo comments on both Cleopatra's sexuality and her darkness, claiming that Antony's eyes "now bend, now turn / The office and devotion of their view / Upon a tawny front" (1.1.4–6) and calling him "the fan / To cool a gipsy's lust" (1.1.9–10).[27] His language, typical of orientalist discourse, makes it clear that Shakespeare is at pains to have us see a black Cleopatra. For Shakespeare, as Leonard Tennenhouse notes, "Cleopatra is Egypt. As such, however, she embodies everything that is not English according to the nationalism which developed under Elizabeth as well as to the British nationalism later fostered by James" (144).

Although there seems to be no male tradition in England of a swarthy Cleopatra, Samuel Daniel's Cleopatra (1594) may provide some clues to the darkness of Shakespeare's. While Cleopatra is never described as physically dark in *The Tragedie of Cleopatra*, her deeds are "black"; in many ways, she is an outsider even within her own country. The chorus's lament suggests that her unruly behavior is a danger to her own community and estranges her from the rest of Egypt:

> And likewise [she] makes us pay
> For her disordred lust,
> Th' int'rest of our blood:
> Or live a servile pray,
> Under a hand unjust,
> . . . .
> This have her riot wonne,
> And thus shee hath her state, her selfe and us undunne.
>
> (I6v)

In Daniel's version, Cleopatra is very much the unruly *female* whose sexuality destroys not only Antony but Egypt as well. Although it is apparent in Shakespeare's *Antony and Cleopatra* that Cleopatra has lost Egypt to the Romans, there is no Egyptian censure for this, whereas in Daniel's *Cleopatra* her servants, rather than Antony's, turn traitor and repent. One

27. Although "gypsy" is usually glossed as a shortened form of "Egyptian," it typically carries connotations of darkness as well as associations with lechery and deceit. Sir Thomas Browne calls gypsies "Counterfeit Negroes" in the section "Of Gypsies" in his *Pseudodoxia Epidemica*. See also Alden and Virginia Vaughan's discussion of gypsies in *Shakespeare's Caliban: A Cultural History*, 33–36.

reason for Cleopatra's lack of darkness may be that *The Tragedie of Cleopatra* begins after Antony's suicide, which tends to minimize the ominous specter of mixed-race children, a vision that would have been incompatible with the maternal role Daniel envisions for her.

As I shall point out in the next chapter, there seems to be an emerging female tradition of a dark Cleopatra. One most obvious reason for this phenomenon is that female writers in various ways identify with the Roman Octavia, an identification that makes Cleopatra a different threat than is found in the male tradition. In her *Salve Deus Rex Judaeorum*, Aemilia Lanyer makes Cleopatra black, but only in relation to the fair Octavia:

> Yea though thou wert as rich, as wise, as rare,
> As any Pen could write, or Wit devise;
> Yet with this Lady canst thou not compare,
> Whose inward virtues all thy worth denies:
>   Yet thou a blacke Egyptian do'st appeare;
>   Thou false, shee true; and to her Love more deere.
>
> (1427–32)

In describing Cleopatra, "as rich, as wise, as rare, / As any Pen could write," Lanyer zeroes in on the crucial matter of Cleopatra as text. Her literary appropriation is much like colonial appropriation in that she is the rich matter to be tamed and controlled for imperial growth. However, as Shakespeare's Octavius discovers, Cleopatra is a highly resistant text in her insistence on fashioning her own role in the empire. This resistance is perhaps due to her absolute identification with Egypt. Although her blackness and difference appear in proportion to her Dido-like threat to empire, the strong correlation between Cleopatra's sexual difference and her cultural difference makes it difficult to manipulate one against the other.

Egypt itself is a very malleable sign. Indeed, as with contemporary Eurocentric geography, many writers of the Renaissance did not locate Egypt on the African continent. Often in geographical and political discourses, Egypt is spoken of as though it is a separate continent, unconnected with Africa. Here Egypt is a focal point of East-West confrontation, claimed as African or "Asiatic" simultaneously, existing as a constantly claimed but ultimately unfixed signifier. Throughout Leo Africanus's *Geographical Historie*, for example, Egypt is alternately both an early cradle of Christianity and a bastion of "Mahommetism." With its mixture of religions and races, Egypt is itself like the threatening "infinite variety" attributed to Cleopatra. This absolute identification of Cleopatra with Egypt is most apparent in the association with the Nile. Her speech to Charmian is a case in point:

> "Where's my serpent of old Nile?"
> (For so he calls me). Now I feed myself
> With most delicious poison. Think on me,
> That am with Phoebus' amorous pinches black,
> And wrinkled deep in time?
>
> (1.5.25–29)

Here, we see three of the elements associated with the Nile: serpents, poison/pollution, and blackness. It has been suggested by many editors of the play that this link with the Nile is meant to suggest Cleopatra's fecundity and fertility; travel writings, however, offer a different, more negative understanding of the significance of the Nile. As I noted in Chapter 1, travelers' tales of Africa's rivers, which regularly overflow their boundaries, had become a source of fascination for the English, and the geographical fact of inundation is regularly conflated with the sense of darker-skinned Africans as people who resist boundaries and rule. In his description of the Nile, Leo Africanus demonstrates how depictions of the Nile become inextricably connected with assessments of Egypt's political order: "Creatures therein contained are exceeding strange, as namely sea-horses, sea-oxen, crocodiles, and other such monstrous and cruel beasts, (as we will afterward declare) which were not so hurtfull either in the ancient times of the Egyptians or of the Romaines, as they are at this present: but they became more dangerous ever since the Mahumetans were lords of Egypt" (335). The Nile and its inhabitants become more dangerous as they move farther from the "civilized" world. Depictions of the Nile invariably involve unspoken comparisons with English rivers, and the inundations conjure up the specter of Western impotence and stagnation in the face of Egypt's "fat prosperity" (Daniel, L3v).[28]

Similarly, the Nile runs throughout *Antony and Cleopatra* as a sign of

28. Ania Loomba suggests that the association of Cleopatra with eating also locates her as a racial other: "The recurrent food imagery reinforces her primitive appeal: she makes men hungry, she does not cloy their appetite (II. ii. 240–42); she is Antony's 'Egyptian dish' (II. vi. 122), she is 'salt Cleopatra' (II. i. 21). She is the supreme actress, artifice herself, and simultaneously primitive and uncultivated" (78). Cultural critic bell hooks sees the desire for the primitive in modern capitalist culture as rooted in an ethos of consumption: "When race and ethnicity become commodified as resources for pleasure, the culture of specific groups, as well as the bodies of individuals, can be seen as constituting an alternative playground where members of dominating races, genders, sexual practices affirm their power-over in intimate relations with the Other" (hooks, *Black Looks* 23).

overwhelming sexuality and social disorder and associates Cleopatra with the kind of overflow and excess characteristic of the female grotesque. Antony, like the Renaissance traveler, regales the drunken triumvirate with tales of Egypt and the "flow o' th' Nile" (2.7.17), while Enobarbus tells the attendants tales of Cleopatra's "infinite variety." The play opens with an evocation of the flooding of the Nile as Philo proclaims, "This dotage of our general's / O'erflows the measure" (1.1.1–2). Antony's and Cleopatra's assertions "Melt Egypt in Nile. . . . Let Rome in Tiber melt" (1.1.33) also link this powerful image of inundation with the struggles of empire. The dark/light binarism, here acted out as a division of Egypt and Rome, is continually on the verge of dissolution. More than a wishing-away of worldly cares or a sign of Egyptian dispersal of symbols of order and measurement, the metaphors of excess bespeak an anxiety striking directly at the heart of Europe's primal fear: loss of identity in measureless expansion. Antony's absorption with Cleopatra is only the romantically reversed reading of Rome's political absorption. Although it is true that "the luxury and feasting of the Egyptian court image a natural plenty which is curbed by no Roman temperance," this natural plenitude, so seductive to a modern audience, is precisely what would have been threatening to a Europe struggling to control its own countrymen loosed into a foreign world of plenty (Kermode 1345).

This combination of unlicensed sensuality and economic exchange is perhaps best symbolized by Antony's gift of an "orient pearl" (1.5.41):

> "Say the firm Roman to great Egypt sends
> This treasure of an oyster; at whose foot,
> To mend the petty present, I will piece
> Her opulent throne with kingdoms. All the East,
> Say thou, shall call her mistress."
>
> (1.5.43–49)

Like Emilia's admonition of husbands that "pour our treasures into foreign laps" (*Othello* 4.3.88), Alexas's message from Antony evokes both male submission and sensuality: Antony pictures himself placing kingdoms at the foot of Egypt's throne (rather than Rome's) and delivering the treasures of the Orient to Cleopatra. The image of his message is suggestive of the imperial image of Elizabeth in the Ditchley portrait, in which she literally has kingdoms at her foot.[29] Unlike Elizabeth's virgin pearl,

---

29. For discussions of this portrait see Roy Strong, *Gloriana: The Portraits of Queen Elizabeth I*, 135–41. See also Andrew and Catherine Belsey, "Icons of Divinity: Portraits of Elizabeth

however, this "treasure of an oyster" continues the conflation of sexual and material exchange: oysters were long thought to be an aphrodisiac.[30] Similarly, Cleopatra's wealth and the sexual threat represented by her children underlie her contest with Octavius when she counters his perhaps false offer of protection for her children with an inaccurate accounting of her "money, plate, and jewels" (5.2.138). The fertility associated with Cleopatra is a threat to the Roman world; in this scene her illegitimate children become the battleground on which she struggles to maintain her stake in the empire.

Antony's affair with Cleopatra is perhaps not as damaging as his "going native" and falling into the plenitude and excess of Egypt. Cleopatra's court is a place of sexual misrule, and in Rome Antony is continually censured for sexual freedom, which is taken for granted in Egypt. In Octavius's eyes, Antony is humbled and effeminized; he uses an image of cross-dressing to denigrate the relationship further: he "is not more manlike / Than Cleopatra; nor the queen of Ptolomy / More womanly than he" (1.4.5–7). The descriptions of the court feature all sorts of transgressive behavior, which includes neglecting class as well as racial and sexual boundaries:

> Let's grant it is not
> Amiss to tumble on the bed of Ptolomy,
> To give a kingdom for mirth, to sit
> And keep the turn of tippling with a slave,
> To reel the streets at noon, and stand the buffet
> With knaves that smells of sweat.
>
> (1.4.16–21)

In descriptions of Antony's "dereliction of duty" (some of which sound not very much different from Harrington's scenes of license in James's court), we see that the Romans blame Antony not so much for the affair as for the behavior it provokes: "Mark Antony / In Egypt sits at dinner, and will make / No wars without-doors" (2.1.11–13).

The closing scenes of *Antony and Cleopatra* turn upon the manipulation

---

I," 15–17. Ania Loomba draws a more sustained connection between the ways in which Elizabeth I and Cleopatra "evoked specifically Renaissance fears of female government" (76).

30. I thank Gwynne Kennedy, whose paper on the correspondence between Lady Mary Wroth and Lord Denny, "She 'thincks she daunces in a net': The Reception of Lady Mary Wroth's *Urania*," addresses the use of the oyster in the exchange of poems between Wroth and Denny.

of Cleopatra as an imperial text. Like "widow Dido" of *The Tempest,* she is subject to variant readings. Octavius wants finally to tame and display the previously unruly matter of Cleopatra:

> Know, sir, that I
> Will not wait pinion'd at your master's court,
> Nor once be chastis'd with the sober eye
> Of dull Octavia. Shall they hoist me up,
> And show me to the shouting varlotry
> Of censuring Rome?
>
> (5.2.52–57)

As her speech shows, Cleopatra proves well aware of Roman efforts to fix her position in the imperial picture. Octavius attempts to read her as the dangerous female subject, the strumpet who brought down Rome by causing Antony's downfall:

> Saucy lictors
> Will catch at us like strumpets, and scald rhymers
> Ballad's out a' tune. The quick comedians
> Extemporally will stage us, and present
> Our Alexandrian revels: Antony
> Shall be brought drunken forth, and I shall see
> Some squeaking Cleopatra boy my greatness
> I' th' posture of a whore.
>
> (5.2.214–21)

Cleopatra poses an alternative reading of her part in the imperial text. Refusing to be seen as a fatal dalliance, subject to conflicting interpretations, she inscribes herself as a wife. As in *The Tempest,* the issue of lawful marriage with the other is crucial. In chastizing Cleopatra, Antony bemoans the time diverted from creating legitimate children:

> Have I left my pillow unpress'd in Rome,
> Forborne the getting of a lawful race,
> And by a gem of women, to be abus'd
> By one that looks on feeders?
>
> (3.13.106–10)

Shakespeare here has Antony erroneously evoke the idea of a "lost" pure bloodline. Antony did produce children with Octavia, a fact obscured in

Shakespeare's text, which is a crucial indication of character in North's translation of Plutarch and, later, for Dryden's in *All for Love*.

Although, as Stanley Cavell notes, Antony deliberately distances himself from any possibility of marriage to Cleopatra (22–24), he dies thinking of himself as a bridegroom: "My queen and Eros / Have by their brave instruction got upon me / A nobleness in record; but I will be / A bridegroom in my death, and run into't / As to a lover's bed" (4.14.97–101). Cleopatra, in turn, stages her death as an imperial marriage: "Husband, I come! / Now to that name my courage prove my title! . . . Peace, peace! / Dost thou not see my baby at my breast, / That sucks the nurse asleep? (5.2.287–307). Her insistence on being seen as a legitimate wife threatens the closure of the imperial text. Reading these "other" mistresses as wives forces the acceptance of their mixed offspring and directly negates the Roman emphasis on noble deeds and pure bloodlines.

Egypt and Caliban's island are both liminal spaces in which the separations of dark and light, self and other, are momentarily broken down, and the anxieties over that collapse are displayed and explored. Both *Antony and Cleopatra* and *The Tempest* grapple with difficulties of maintaining cultural integrity and endogamous unions within imperial/colonial economies of desire. In doing so, the texts offer early hints at what will later become entrenched racial stereotypes. Rome is England's imagined forefather in empire, and *Antony and Cleopatra* provides an object lesson in imperial history; Antony becomes a warning against the dangers of overinvolvement with the reputed sexual excess of black women. *The Tempest*, looking forward to future colonization, offers the greater threat of the black man as rapist. Both images work less to control actual black sexuality than to shape an image of a white, male ruling class as rational, restrained, and powerful in the face of dangerous excess and unregulated sexuality. However, just as in the travel narrative, such warnings against the other have embedded in them a fascination with the other. Difference always escapes the desire for control. The model imperial powers, Octavius and Prospero, both fail in their attempts to control and order foreign others for their own use. Octavius is ultimately not able to restrain and display Cleopatra, and Prospero is forced to acknowledge his connection to a "thing of darkness."

Colonialism and the Economics of Marriage

In John Webster's last play, *The Devil's Law-Case; or, When Women go to Law, the Devil is full of Business* (1609–12), we see again the disruption of traditional patriarchal structures, caused this time by the new class mobility brought through new world wealth. The play opens on Romelio, "an East Indy merchant" with "the spice of pride" in him, confidently boasting of his unbounded fortune:

> My factors' wives
> Wear chaperons of velvet, and my scriveners,
> Merely through my employment, grow so rich
> They build their palaces and belvederes
> With musical water-works. Never in my life
> Had I a loss at sea.
>
> (1.1.7–11)

Romelio reveals that his foreign trade has created a new world in Spain where, as in Jacobean England, the signs of noble birth are bought and consequently devalued by the rising merchant class. Traditional social order is askew, and conspicuous consumption rules the day: scriveners build elaborate waterworks, and factors' wives wear velvet in clear violation of sumptuary law.[31] Romelio feels himself part of a new order that need no longer be sensitive to the nuances of class. His contempt for the gentry is undisguised: "What tell you me of gentry? 'Tis nought else / But a superstitious relic of time past; / And sift it to the true worth, it is nothing / But ancient riches" (1.1.38–41).

Much of Romelio's disdain for the aristocracy is brought to the surface because Contarino, a member of the landed gentry, wishes to marry his sister. Contarino, too, considers this courtship a capital venture: "I would not publish to the world, / Nor have it whispered scarce, what wealthy voyage / I went about, till I had got the mine / In mine own possession" (1.1.92–95). Jolenta metaphorically becomes the less than romantic Indian "mine" to be exploited for her riches when Romelio appropriates her in naming her "mine." He woos Jolenta under cover of selling family lands to Romelio, an act undermining his own class, which Jolenta's mother, Leonora, points out: "Next to their begging churchland, is a ruin / Worth all men's pity" (1.1.204–5). The search for capital and marriage, romanticized in *The Merchant of Venice*'s Belmont, is laid bare in Webster's Venice: traditional courtly modes are challenged by a brash new economic order.

The influence of wealth represented by the crass commercialism of Ro-

---

31. See Lisa Jardine, "Dress Codes, Sumptuary Law, and 'Natural Order,' " in *Still Harping*, 141–68.

melio makes the play world one of carnivalesque inversions. Characters masquerade as outsiders, disguising themselves as Jews and Moors; class, gender, and racial divisions go awry, all because of merchant wealth. The marriage that Contarino proposes underscores the danger of opening up social strata and destroying all decorum:

> I shall be proud
> To live to see my little nephews ride
> O'th' upper hand of their uncles; and the daughters
> Be rank'd by heralds at solemnities
> Before the mother: all this deriv'd
> From your nobility.
>
> (1.1.105–10)

These local disruptions are mirrored on a larger scale; we are told that Romelio has interfered with international trade:

> . . . the King of Spain
> Suspects that your Romelio here, the merchant,
> Has discover'd some gold mine to his own use,
> In the West Indies, and for that employs me
> To discover in what part of Christendom
> He vents this treasure; besides, he is informed
> What mad tricks has been play'd of late by ladies.
>
> (3.1.4–11)

Crispiano's description of his mission rhetorically links Romelio's withholding of income from the state with gender transgressions. These ladies' "tricks" consist of ruling over their husbands, fulfilling male fears by creating a society with women on top:

> Why, they use their lords as if they were their wards;
> And as your Dutchwomen in the Low Countries
> Take all and pay all, and do keep their husbands
> So silly all their lives of their own estates
> That, when they are sick and come to make their will,
> They know not precisely what to give away
> From their wives, because they know not what they are worth.
>
> (3.1.12–18)

The comparison to unruly Dutchwomen tells us that the local women constitute an economic threat: they take control of property and, like

Romelio, steal revenue from the commonwealth by hiding their resources from the proper authorities.

This gendered threat has also infiltrated Venice. Romelio's mother's unlawful lust for her daughter's suitor drives her to attempt to disinherit Romelio by legally declaring him a bastard. Her actions constitute some of the worst fears of an English audience. As Lisa Jardine informs us, "It is . . . a built-in feature of the European inheritance system that women are potentially powerful, albeit within a basically patrilinear system—they intrude and intervene where necessary to amend the simple law of male inheritance, either as subsidiary heirs, or in marriage settlements" (84–85). This threat of disinheritance by the mother's active sexuality seems to be a persistent presence on the stage. Given the tensions caused by James I's inheritance of the throne through his maternal ties and the allegations of illegitimacy with which James grappled throughout his reign, we can only assume that not only did the fear of disinheritance at the word of a mother have broad cultural resonance in the commonwealth, it had personal significance for the king. It is, however, quite apparent in these plays that the social havoc brought by these women springs from their unlawful desires.

The combination of her brother's crass mercantilism and her mother's lust licenses Jolenta to take on a black disguise to escape their manipulation of her marriage. Although Jolenta chooses Contarino as a suitor, her mother and Romelio insist on marrying her to Ercole, a candidate who is (even in Jolenta's eyes) as noble as Contarino. Her romantic attachment is validated when the play reveals her family's motives. Her mother desires Contarino for herself, and Romelio covets the land, which will revert to his family if Ercole does not survive his imminent expedition against the Turks (seen as a heroic enterprise in sharp contrast with Romelio's merchandizing abroad). Ercole's own disgust with Romelio's double-dealing goads him to perform a "manly" office: "I will leave you to the freedom of your own soul. / May it move whither heaven and you please" (1.2.101–2).

Ercole's defense of Jolenta's preference demonstrates the strong division between the landed gentry with their old world values and the cash economy represented by Romelio. Despite his monetary interest in Jolenta, Contarino is also firmly placed on the side of the honorable nobility. He refuses Jolenta's servant's suggestion to solidify his hold by consummating the marriage; so too, rather than enter into a legal battle against a worthy opponent, he opts to duel with Ercole for the right to her hand. In the absence of a suitor, Romelio proposes that Jolenta pretend to be pregnant and give birth to his own illegitimate child (expected any moment from a nun he has impregnated). The apparent deaths of the noble-born suitors remove all obstacles from Romelio's social-climbing avarice and introduce the specter of the dilution or dissolution of aristocratic bloodlines:

> That my fair Jolenta should be rumor'd
> To be with child by noble Ercole,
> Makes me expect to what a violent issue
> These passages will come. I hear her brother
> Is marrying the infant she goes with,
> 'Fore it be born; as, if it be a daughter,
> To the Duke of Austria's nephew; if a son,
> Into the noble ancient family
> Of the Palavasini.
>
> (4.2.15–23)

There is no indication that Romelio (a villain who, Iago-like, reveals all to his audience) intends anything other than covering up his own sin; Contarino's fear of his manipulation of the aristocratic sex/gender system seems to be an illusory projection of the anxieties of the vulnerable gentry in a time of economic strain.

Jolenta forestalls this apparent degeneration of the social order by assuming a blackface disguise. In doing so, she alienates herself from the social world of the play and protects her honor by distancing herself from her brother's "politic ends." Her disguise is not shown until the play's end, when she enters with Angiolella, the nun who is pregnant with her brother's child: "A couple of strange fowl, and I the falconer / That have sprung them. This is a white nun / Of the order of Saint Clare; and this a black one" (5.6.30–32). This staging of her entrance makes visible Jolenta's dilemma; the one woman in the play who is not "strange fowl" is the one whose sexuality is most impugned. The contrast between her and the white nun signals both her "difference" from the impure women in the play and the warped values of the play world in which virtue is maligned and sin covered up. The "discovery" of her whiteness rings familiar as she draws on the paradox of her disguise to restore an almost Platonic sense of value to the play:

> Hence, vain show! I only care
> To preserve my soul most fair;
> Never mind the outward skin,
> But the jewel that's within;

And though I want the crimson blood,
Angels boast my sisterhood.
Which of us now judge you whiter,
Her whose credit proves the lighter,
Or this black and ebon hue,
That, unstain'd, keeps fresh and true?
For I proclaim't without control
There's no true beauty but i' th' soul.

(5.6.38–49)

Whereas the Prince of Morocco in *The Merchant of Venice* tries to remove attention from his skin color by drawing attention to his equally red blood ("And let us make incision for your love, / To prove whose blood is reddest, his or mine" [2.1.6–7]), Jolenta insists that as a Moor, she "want[s] the crimson blood." In revealing her disguise, she defends blackness with a rhetoric that insists on its absolute difference and that suggests that this final "conversion" is not complete. After her defense, Crispiano, the judge whose return from the West Indies proves Leonora false and ends his son's profligate spending, metes out punishments. He forces Romelio to marry Angiolella and to restore the dowry taken from Ercole. He further commands Romelio, Contarino, and Ercole "for seven years [to] maintain against the Turk / Six galleys" (5.6.84–85) and forces Leonora, Jolenta, and Angiolella to build a monastery.

These gendered sentences respond directly to the threats posed to the state by the disorder of the Venetians. The punishments end the play with the sense of a land protected internally and externally from the presence of unruly others, an enclosure that mitigates the anxieties of a society that feels its cultural unity diminishing in direct proportion to imperial expansion. Instead of being disposed of by the "loose" will of a Romelio, the money is appropriated by the state for defense against the Turks. This defense against the outsider also restores the illusion of endogamous union and untainted bloodlines that the play disrupted. The women's punishment answers that same fear: in building another monastery, the women are made to use their resources to enforce the control of their own sexuality. They, like Miranda, act as agents of the state to guard against the threat of unbridled sexuality to patriarchal interests. Even though Jolenta—unlike the other characters who have all explicitly broken Spanish law (Ercole and Contarino duel)—has committed no visible crime, she is sentenced along with the other members of the play. The license she assumes in exercising her own will and protecting her own honor is not excused at its end. Her assertion of her own "difference" fails in that she is found guilty along with all other women, a fate that reveals the intransigent nature of patriarchal readings of racial and sexual difference.

It is in many ways most fitting to close this chapter with Richard Brome's *The English Moore; or, the Mock-Marriage* (1631), even though it is not a Jacobean play. It seems to draw specifically both upon the *Masque of Blackness* and *The Merchant of Venice* for its cultural stereotypes: the reputed lechery of the black woman; the association of blackness with religious difference; and blackness as a visible sign of marginality and alienation. Moreover, it carries hints of later, more entrenched, racial values. In both the *Masque of Blackness* and *The English Moore*, these ideas converge around women who are painted black only to demonstrate a male's power to display them as white and beautiful.

The English Moore features a mixed marriage between the young Christian, Millicent, and the old usurer, Quicksands. A Venetian Jew, this "bottomles devourer of young Gentlemen" (1.1.88) is resented for his economic power over the young bachelors who are indebted to him: "He that has / Undone by mortgages and Underbuyings, / Soe many Gentlemen that they all despair'd / Of meanes to be reveng'd" (1.1.90–93).[32] Gender becomes the ground for economic contest as the young men resolve to cuckold Quicksands in revenge:

> The case is ours: His wrongs are common to us;
> Soe shall his wife be, can we purchace her.
> To which we must take time for best advantage;
> And then our lotts, and turnes, & equall shares.
>
> (1.2.81–84)

Instead of a preoccupation with the proper containment and organization of female sexuality, we find Christian men exploiting fears of the sexually unruly woman as they make Millicent "common" to them in economic retaliation, dividing her into "lotts, and turnes, & equall shares" in place of the money Quicksands withholds.

Much of the sexual disorder in Brome's Venice is attributed to a lack of proper patriarchal control of sexuality. In *The Merchant of Venice* Portia bemoans being curbed by the "will" of a dead father; in this play, fathers have no such foresight. The rake Nathaniel notes, "For, to speake / Plaine truth, the losse of fathers are good findings, / As this age governes"

---

32. All line references to *The English Moore; or, The Mock-Marriage* are to the University of Missouri Press edition, ed. Sara Jayne Steen.

(1.2.102–4); the death of fathers means not only wealth for the younger generation (just as Crispiano's absence in *The Devil's Law-Case* allows his son to spend "loosely") but also the neglect of economic and sexual restrictions. This absence of paternal restraint brings a carnivalesque air to a play that is filled with masques and disguises. There is no hidden Prospero overseeing the proper disposition of sexuality in Venice: the play begins with the information that the fathers have disappeared in the midst of an argument, leaving one daughter to "fall" by the hand of the rake Nathaniel; while another is forced by her grasping uncle to forego her younger suitor for the elderly Quicksands; and a third assumes a transvestite disguise in order to avenge her father's death.

Millicent, who as a wife is the site of this homosocial contest, is forced to play radically different roles in a way that is an almost parodic reflection of the "discursive instability" Catherine Belsey identifies in utterances attributed to women (*Subject of Tragedy* 149) of the period. Millicent's uncle, Testy, sees in her silent acquiescence stubborn disobedience and demands that she show affection to her husband, only to repent when she acts the part of a lustful wife, alarming her husband with thoughts of the cuckoldry that proverbially accompanied May-December marriages:

> Let women Judge. Tis very possible
> That a young lusty wife may have six children
> By one at once in five yeares Sir and by
> One father too. I'll make him young enough
> To father mine.
>
> (1.3.82–86)

Millicent assumes a disguise of apparent sexual aggressiveness to avoid consummating the marriage, and Quicksands's fears of her desire are exacerbated when the town gallants announce their intentions by performing a wedding masque of cuckoldry. Her plan is successful, and Quicksands refuses to accept his wife's advances, accusing her of cuckoldry.

Millicent responds by claiming responsibility for her own honor, exempting herself from the sexual arena altogether:

> But since these men pretend; and you suppose'hem
> To be my friends, that carry this presumption
> Over my will, I'll take chardge of my selfe;
> And doe faire Justice both on them & you.

My honor is mine owne; and I am noe more
Yours yet (on whome mine Uncle has bestowed me)
Then all the worlds (the Ceremony off)
And will remaine soe, free from them & you,
. . . .
Till you recant your willfull Ignorance,
And they their petulant follies.

(2.2.41–52)

Her eloquent defense of her honor restores her reputation and forces both her uncle and Quicksands to give in to her will with the caveat that she agree to don a disguise of her husband's choosing. Ironically, once she has removed herself from the charge of cuckoldry, she is free to engage in ribald jesting with her uncle about her husband's age (2.2.93–100).

Quicksands chooses to disguise Millicent as a Moor, claiming that the disguise will destroy his as well as other men's lustful desires:

Now this shall both
Kill vaine attempts in me, and guard you safe
From all that seeke subversion of your honor.
. . . .
After this Tincture is laid upon thy face.
Twill cool their Kidneys, & lay down their heats.

(3.1.62–68)

Quicksands paints Millicent black (a ploy he claims to have learned from a Venetian merchant) to make her ugly and undesirable, forgetting that black women were also considered prone to venery. In convincing his wife to use this disguise, Quicksands takes on the rhetoric of the Petrarchan lover and sings the praises of blackness:

Why, thinckst thou, fearefull Beauty,
Has Heaven noe part in *Egypt?* Pray thee tell me
Is not an *Ethiops* face his workmanship
As well as the fairst Ladies? Nay more too
Then hers, that dawbes & makes adulterate beauty.

(3.1.72–76)

Quicksands here uses a typical Petrarchan defense of the black beauty, insisting that her beauty is better than that of possibly painted beauties; however, he is quickly caught in a rhetorical trap because Millicent's blackness is in fact painted on and thus also "blot[s] out Heavens Workmanship" (3.1.70–71).

He then defends painting, using Queen Anne's disguise in the *Masque of Blackness* as a precedent:

> Some can be pleas'd to lie in oyles & paste
> At Sinnes appointment, which is thrice more wicked.
> This (which is sacred) is for Sinnes prevention.
> Illustrious persons, nay even Queenes themselves
> Have, for the glory of a Nights presentment
> To grace the worke, suffer'd as much as this.
>
> (3.1.77–82)[33]

His eagerness for the disguise and Millicent's obvious reluctance only beg the question of why Quicksands chooses to change his wife black. This is an even more vexing problem, given that the more time-honored disguise, cross-dressing, is also included in the play. Quicksands obviously knows the tradition that black women were considered undesirable. It may be, however, that his motives are also informed by a knowledge of other alleged characteristics of black women. In Quicksands's eyes, Millicent is already blackened; that is, in playing the lewd, outspoken young wife, she appears already to possess the characteristics attributed to black women. His language after she expresses desire sounds much like the rhetoric used to speak of black women: "This Impudence / Has mortified my Concupiscence. / And dasht me out of Countenance. What a beast / Was I to marry?" (1.3.98–101).

Quicksands clearly sees his painting as an exercise of patriarchal privilege. Unlike another usurer, Shylock, who eschews masques ("What, are there masques?" [2.5.28]), Quicksands tries to beat the Christians at their own game. As part of the "unveiling," he stages a second masque that will nullify the effects of the first masque, establishing his authority over Millicent and ensuring her inaccessibility to the town gallants. Quicksands thinks to avenge himself by publicly displaying his power: he stages Millicent as the pliant Bride of the Canticles, complete to bedecking her with jewels:

---

33. In addition to being his apprentice at the time Jonson wrote the *Masque of Blackness*, Brome dedicated *The English Moore* to William Seymour, whose first wife, Arabella Stuart, was a performer in the *Masque of Beauty*. The editor of *The English Moore* suggests that Brome's knowledge of this is mere conjecture, but I suspect that Brome would have been familiar with *Blackness* and the stir it caused, as well as the notoriety surrounding Seymour's marriage to Stuart.

> . . . Use her Casket;
> And, with the sparckling of her Jewells, shine;
> Flame like a Midnight beacon, with that face;
> Or a pitcht ship on fire, the streamers glowing
> And the keele mourning. Get thee glorious
> Be like a running fire worke in my house.
>
> (4.3.95–100)

Just as the *Masque of Beauty* demonstrated James's sovereign power by turning the Ethiopian nymphs white, Quicksands stages the "whitening" of his wife as a show of his power. His anticipation at the moment of revelation demonstrates Nancy Vickers's insight that "within the economy of a competition, wealth is not wealth unless flaunted, unless inspiring envy, unless affirming superiority" ("Blazon of sweet beauty's best" 101):

> Helpe to beare up the Joy
> That I conceave in thy concealed beauty,
> Thy rich imprison'd beauty, whose infranchisement
> Is now at hand: When those illustrious Emblemes,
> That Red & White, those two united houses,
> (Whence Beauty takes her faire name & decent,)
> Shall (like my Gold and Jewells) be drawne againe
> Out of their Ebon Casket, and shine forth
> In their admired glory.
>
> (4.1.3–11)

Both the language of heraldry and that of beauty are here connected to the politics of the blazon (Vickers 95); Quicksands's appropriation of heraldic language thus represents his attempt to describe (and thus own) the now-hidden beauty of his wife. For both Quicksands and his rivals, jealousy and struggle over his literal wealth is displaced onto the body of Millicent, who can be both displayed and competed for rhetorically.

The language of enclosure and controlled display ("thy rich imprison'd beauty"; "be drawne againe / Out of their Ebon Casket") in the preceding passage also reveals Quicksands's own insecurity as an outsider. According to Peter Stallybrass, the surveillance of woman has a particular utility in times of increased social mobility:

Like the members of the male elite, the class aspirant has an interest in preserving social closure, since without it, there would be nothing to aspire *to*. But, at the same time, that closure must be sufficiently flexible to incorporate *him*. His conceptualization of woman will as a result be radically unstable: she will be perceived as oscillating between the enclosed body (the purity of the elite to which he aspires) and the open body (or else how could he attain her?), between being "too coy" and "too common." ("Patriarchal Territories" 134)

In a play that conflates class and Christianity, Quicksands becomes just such an aspirant. Millicent is his link to Christian society, but the very ability of the sex/gender system to incorporate him through marriage provokes his jealousy over his wife's access to other men. Throughout the play, Millicent is alternatively "too coy" and "too common," behaviors that in different ways reinforce his insecurity.

The rakes who attempted to use Millicent to avenge themselves on the usurer are retaliated against in kind; Quicksands reads his manipulation of Millicent as power over her admirers. His deflowering of her is not only an act of possession, but evidence of a power he sees as strong enough to kill his enemies:

> It shall be such a night!
> In which I meane thy Beauty shall breake forth
> And dazell with amazement, even to death
> Those my malicious enemies, that rejoyc'd
> In thy supposed escape & my vexation.
>
> (4.1.33–37)

Absent either rhetorical or social power, Quicksands relies on Millicent's beauty; her body becomes a weapon in a contest over assimilation and economics.

However, Quicksands's ploy is ineffective. An alien himself, the cultural privilege of "conversion" does not accrue to him. His own masque makes this clear when the player recounts the story of Chariclea, claiming, "If this damsell liv'd to married be / To a white Man, shee should be white as hee" (4.4.31–32). The use of the word "white" is remarkable here because it is a moment of attention to racialized whiteness, which is rare even in modern texts—a fact noted by Lisa Young: "Part of the success of 'Whiteness' is that most of the time it does not appear to exist at all" (194). The indeterminacy introduced by "if" may also withhold "whiteness" from Quicksand, thus reserving white as a category only for Christians. Whiteness in this play is particularly modern in that, as a category, it aligns power, wealth, and Christianity. All else becomes "other."

Unlike the *Masque of Blackness*, which worked to dispel anxieties over the differences of the Scottish court, Quicksands's countermasque, the story of Chariclea, the white Ethiope, only conjures up the cultural anxieties it was meant to dispel. It summons the threat of exogamous union in its focus on the "monstrous" progeny of Chariclea:

> The queene of *Ethiope* dreampt upon a night
> Her black wombe should bring forth a virgine white
> . . . .
> Till this white dreame filld their black heads with feares.
> For tis noe better then a Prodigee
> To have white Children in a black Contree.
> Soe twas decreed, that if the Child prov'd white
> It should be made away.
>
> (4.3.14–24)

The very plot, an inversion of Jonson's *Blackness* (a black queen expels a white daughter from the country), presages Quicksands's failure. The story of Chariclea fulfills the need for a strict binarism of black and white. Unlike Caliban, her child is not mixed but white, and thus represents the literal "impossibility" of mixture. Quicksands is not empowered by the masque. Nor is his male privilege established: instead of cooling male lust, the disguise only inflames the rake Nathaniel, who, in a Carleton-like projection, sees African features in addition to the dark skin: "How I am taken with the elevation of her Nosthrills!" (4.4.69).

Furthermore, the masque empowers women to enforce the status quo: Millicent herself escapes, is restored to her original suitor, and uses her disguise to force the rake Nathaniel to marry the fallen Phillis. Millicent's actions are validated after the fact by the providential return of the proper fathers, who discover that Quicksands has already had a "prodigee," an illegitimate, idiot son. She becomes the agent of proper marriage: although Nathaniel agrees to "justify" his act and marry a Moor, he discovers that the Moor is actually the Phillis he had already dishonored. His marriage both reveals her white skin and makes her metaphorically "white" by removing the taint of fornication.

Although the presence of blackness here is one that serves ultimately to stabilize, rather than disrupt, social order, there are other disguises that do prove much more disruptive. In a related subplot, the appropriately named Dionisia disguises herself as a man to avenge her father's death. Unlike Millicent's blackface, Dionisia's disguise is portrayed as a sin for which she must do penance:

> Sir take noe thought for me
> Till my strict life,
> In expiation of my late transgression
> Gainst Maiden modestie, shall render me
> Some way deserving th'honor of a husband.
>
> (5.3.203–7)

Her decision to expiate her sin provokes her father's approval—"Spoke like a good new woman" (5.3.208)—ironically echoing Testy's approval of Millicent's decision to uphold her honor: "Now shee speakes woman" (2.2.40).

When Dionisia first cross-dresses, her warriorlike stance causes her man-servant to claim:

> All the Viragos that are found in story
> *Penthesilea* and *Simiramis*
> Were noe such handy strikers as yourself.
> But they had another stroke, could you but find it;
> Then you were excellent. I could teach it you.
>
> (3.5.23–27)

As the servant's wordplay implies, the cross-dressed woman is connected with both uncontrolled sexuality and cultural difference. The sexual pun here, as Jean Howard has suggested of all cross-dressing, "strengthens notions of difference by stressing what the disguised woman *cannot* do" (439). The Amazonian threat is often encoded as an imagined cultural difference constituting an external danger to society. Indeed, the threat of cross-dressing is put on par with the domination of England by foreigners, a conflation Jean Howard notes in her discussion of *Hic-Mulier*:

> The very state is represented as threatened by her [the mannish-woman's] behavior. The author writes: "If this [cross-dressing] bee not barbarous, make the rude *Scithian*, the untamed *Moore*, the naked *Indian*, or the wilde *Irish*, Lords and Rulers of well governed Cities" (Bv). In a stunning revelation of a racial and national chauvinism, the aspiration of women beyond their place is associated with the monstrous notion of the black in rulership over the white, the Irish over the English. Such consequences—though imagined only—invite reprisal. (425)

Here gender unrest is quite explicitly linked with submerged fears of cultural domination.[34] Whereas both disguises in *The English Moore* are taken on to restore feminine "honor," the gender-crossing is written as an actual threat to the social order, while the racial crossing is not. This may be because, unlike the cross-dressing, the racial disguise is not a woman's attempt to usurp patriarchal privilege. The racial disguise is instead imposed by a man who is thought to be an outsider: in attempting to borrow and manipulate a discourse that is reserved for a cultural elite, the production of masques, he mangles that discourse and is mocked by his failure.[35]

Unlike its pre-text, the *Masque of Blackness*, Quicksands's device fails: Millicent, instead of being controlled—or even advertised as the obedient wife—subverts the masque and escapes her husband. His masque is false, as is his "Mock-Marriage." Just as Shylock loses his wealth as a result of his involvement with the Venetian legal system, Quicksands is forced to divorce Millicent and to part with his wealth:

> *Qui.* My chaines & Jewells, worth a thousand pounds
> I'll pay it for my folly.
> *Nat.* Twill be twise
> The price of my pawnd goods. I'll put the rest
> Up, for your Jieres, past on my frends & mee.
>
> (5.3.88–92)

The penalty for his "folly"—failure to master the "language" of the royal masque—is the loss of goods and the restoration of wealth to Christian males.

Blackness has been used in all the plays to comment on the moral state of the play world. The many versions of "washing the Ethiope white" that recur in these texts, rather than recognizing difference among females (as Jolenta hopes), only reinforce negative female stereotypes and establish European, patriarchal control over difference. The devil in *The devil's*

34. This may be with good reason. Economically, this fear of foreign takeover is also allied with sumptuary order. England's very reliance on foreign trade is what enables a woman to dress above her class. Although Jean Howard puts more stress on the link between class and gender in studies of cross-dressing, these economic concerns are precisely what increasingly links transgressions of class and gender with race throughout the seventeenth century.

35. In fact, this play so obviously imitates its predecessor (and Brome's mentor) that one wonders if Quicksands's failure is in some ways a sign of an anxiety of influence. Brome actually outdoes his master in dramatically resolving *Blackness*'s much-noted dramatic problem of removing the painted disguise. Nevertheless, the possibility of failure is brought forth in Quicksands, whose "failure" is Brome's triumph.

Law-Case is ostensibly Leonora, whose sexuality, like that of *The Tempest*'s Sycorax, threatens white male prerogatives; however, the devil's "case," a slang phrase for female genitalia (Parker 27–29), belongs to all women and evokes the threatening specter of female sexuality, which must be controlled and dispelled.

The mobility of such racially charged tropes threatens the boundaries between self and other that racial and sexual stereotypes help maintain: "They perpetuate a needed sense of difference between the 'self' and the 'object,' which becomes the 'Other.' Because there is no real line between self and the Other, an imaginary line must be drawn; and so that the illusion of an absolute difference between self and the Other is never troubled, this line is as dynamic in its ability to alter itself as is the self" (Gilman 18). The very dynamism of this boundary allows for a continual slippage of racial, cultural, and religious difference, all in the service of maintaining patriarchal prerogatives. Thus in Webster's *The White Devil*, sexual difference and racial difference are linked as the negative other in misogynist discourse. Indeed, in *The White Devil*, the male disguises himself as a Moor to redeem the chaos brought about by errant female sexuality; and the true Moor, Zanche, serves as scapegoat for the actual perpetrator of license, the pander, Flamineo:

> *Mont.* . . . here's your sentence: you are confin'd
>   Unto a house of convertites, and your bawd—
> *Flam.* [Aside].
>   Who, I?
> *Mont.* The Moor—
> *Flam.* [Aside]   Oh, I am a sound man again.
>
>   (3.2.263–265)

In sentencing Zanche instead of the actual bawd, Monticelso tries and sentences Zanche for her literal blackness just as he charges and tries Vittoria for her "black concatenation of mischief" (3.2.29) and "black lust" (3.1.7).

Ironically, Quicksands's failed masque in *The English Moore* may actually reveal the failure of the English cultural project as well. Attempts to use tropes of blackness to maintain cultural and racial boundaries ultimately undermine themselves as their appearance only continually suggests the lack of difference between self and other. If Christopher Miller is correct in asserting that in Africanist writing black and white cannot remain as meaningful opposites and that their use inevitably marks the "void" or absence inherent in both terms (30–31), then the troping of cultural difference through this binarism likewise reveals the absence at the heart of national/racial discourses. At first glance, Elizabeth's and James's responses to England's contacts with Africa seem divergent: Elizabeth twice attempts to expel "Blackamoores" from England while James and Anne bring Africans to the country and generate an Africanist discourse at the center of power. However, both gestures work to protect the fragile sense of group identity threatened by decreasing geographic isolation that Peter Fryer sees as a precondition for the development of race prejudice (133). Rhetorically and politically, the Jacobean fascination with otherness was the logical successor to Elizabethan insularity. Ultimately, this fascination only proved the futility of Elizabeth's legal attempts to enforce avoidance of the other: the attempted banishment of difference and the maintenance of England's borders through figurations of Elizabeth as the pure and fair national body only helped to produce a void of English whiteness that her successor, himself a foreign other, could not fill. English identity comes to rely on both the appropriation and the denial of differences troped through blackness in order to fill this void and preserve a sense of self.

The Daughters of Eve and the Children of Ham: Race and the English Woman Writer

Chams servile curse to all your sex was given,
Because in Paradise you did offend:

—The Tragedy of Mariam (1613)

W hile curiosity about the nature and meanings of blackness permeated English culture, the other side of the dark/light binarism—fairness—was also the site of crucial delineations of
cultural difference. As I suggested earlier, the language of fairness was
associated specifically with women and thus becomes a key factor in the
issues of sexuality and gender difference that also inform the development
of racial distinctions in this period. The bodies of white English women
become the map upon which imperial desire and national identity are
marked. Discourses of fairness work to control and shape women's sexuality and agency even as they speak to larger issues of group identity and
cohesion. Through their uses of the dark/light dichotomy, women writers
both speak to the gender politics of fairness and articulate their own relationship to the primarily male arena of travel and adventure. Women
writers provide ample evidence of the racialized nature of the language
of fairness and beauty as well as of the importance of the language of
fairness in constructions of female subjectivity. Even more important, they
reveal women's consciousness both of this racialization and of the competition that discourses of fairness introduce between women.

Lady Mary Wroth's *The Countess of Montgomerie's Urania* (1621) clearly
demonstrates how the racial aesthetic of fairness is continually gendered.
By the time of Wroth and Shakespeare, one can see a growing awareness
of how the nexus of female beauty and male power, contained within the

emerging language of race in early modern England, encompasses problems of public voice and literary authority. For a woman writer struggling
for a subject position from which to write, dark/light dichotomies become
a key point of contest. In this chapter I first examine the ways in which
tropes of blackness in descriptions of beauty function as markers of race
that work to differentiate between women. Using women's representations
of Cleopatra, I suggest that tropes of blackness reveal a female anxiety
about the eroticism of travel figured as desire for the foreign female. In
my ensuing reading of the *Urania* I propose that Wroth's use of the romance genre reveals a specifically female view on imperial/colonial travel.
Wroth and other women writers demonstrate a heightened awareness of
the cultural and racial politics of their own investment in the language of
racial difference; however, they seem to use the arbitrariness of this aesthetics of beauty to strengthen their own rhetorical and social positions
at the expense of more marginalized groups.[1]

The "Other" Woman:
Beauty, Women Writers, and Cleopatra

Mary Ellen Lamb argues that patriarchal texts deprive women of "a
primary source of the subjectivity necessary for them to construct themselves as authors" (*Gender and Authorship* 9). The intertwining of subjectivity and literary authority is central to tropes of blackness that are both
racial and literary topoi as well as products of patriarchal structures that
manipulate and may preclude female subjectivity. In female-authored
texts, the appearance of such tropes may represent women's attempts
(since gender is not a privileged category for writing) to borrow authority
from other categories reified by patriarchal structures: class, whiteness,
and "Englishness."

English women's resistance to the exclusivity and hegemony of a patriarchal tradition is itself fraught with difficulty: in attempting to expose
and escape destabilizing constructions of gender, these women position
themselves at the site of other differences that further complicate the
creation of "the" female subject. In her report on the 1982 National
Women's Studies Association Conference, Chela Sandoval contends that
white males achieve power by "othering" white women and people of
color. Within this stratagem, white women always inhabit secondary posi-

1. My deepest gratitude goes to Josephine Roberts for allowing me generous access to
the typescript of her forthcoming edition of the manuscript *Urania.*

tions in which they simultaneously experience oppression (in relation to white men) and a "will-to-power" (in relation to people of color):

> For while white women are "othered" by men and feel the pain of objecti-
> fication, within this secondary category they can only construct a solid sense
> of "self" through the objectification of people of color.... The final and
> fourth category belongs to women of color who become survivors in a dy-
> namic which places them as the final "other" in a complex of power moves.
> Social relations in the U.S. are overlaid by this dialectic of interlinking cate-
> gories, a pattern which relegates women of color to the crucial category
> against which all the other categories are provided their particular meanings
> and privileges. (64)[2]

The early modern period gives evidence of this paradigm forming in the constitution of a gendered subject position. Certain texts by women display in a like manner the simultaneous recognition of their own oppression and a will-to-power that helped shape women's experience.[3] These women writers employ what Ann Rosalind Jones terms a "negotiated viewer position" in relation to discourses of race and beauty. Adopting this term from feminist film criticism, Jones suggests that "a 'negotiated' viewer position is one that accepts the dominant ideology encoded into a text but particularizes and transforms it in the service of a different group" (4). From the moment of England's earliest colonial encounters, European women negotiate patriarchal discourses to construct a subject position for themselves, not only in relation to white patriarchal power but also in relation to the "foreign" women coded as a threat to an already insecure, secondary position.

Beauty, more than simply a matter of aesthetic pleasure, becomes a site of contest for women writers who represent their own oppression and will-to-power in the intersections of gender, race, and empire formed by the language of Petrarchan beauty. One manifestation of this language is the appearance of dark/light pairs of women in which one is "dark" and the other, golden blonde. From Pamela and Philoclea in *The Countess of*

2. See also Marilyn Frye ("On Being White: Toward a Feminist Understanding of Race and Race Supremacy," in *The Politics of Reality: Essays in Feminist Theory*, 110–27), who argues that whiteness is a male construct that offers the illusion of power to white women: "Since white women are *almost* white men, being white, at least, and sometimes more-or-less honorary men . . . we can cling to a hope of true membership in the dominant and powerful group, we can be stuck in our ignorance and theirs all our lives."

3. For what are probably the best-known expressions of resistance to this dynamic, see bell hooks, *Ain't I a Woman*; and Gloria T. Hull et al., *All the Women Are White, All the Men Are Black, But Some of Us Are Brave*.

Pembroke's Arcadia, to Lucy and Mina in *Dracula*, to Joan Collins and Linda Evans in *Dynasty*, such pairings are ubiquitous in Anglo-American culture. When women compete for the interest of a man, often one is made the black and demonized other. Of course, there are interesting reversals of this dynamic. However, even this demonization of the blonde is often predicated on an expectation of purity in much the same way as the figure of the "white devil" in the Renaissance; the fundamental desirability of blonde fairness is not disrupted.

The languages of beauty and colonialism intersect when the ubiquitous "darkness" in these pairings comes to include foreign women who are posed to compete with fair, European women for male attention. Consequently, the "darkness" of the foreign other implicates all women.[4] One can see how the competition for male favor intensifies and is accentuated in Shakespeare's *A Midsummer Night's Dream*, when Lysander rejects his "dark" lover, Hermia, with the epithets "Away, you Ethiop" and "Out, tawny Tartar." Here Lysander expresses his choice in terms of color and uses masculine "reason" (which in later racial discourses becomes an attribute of whiteness [Dyer 47–48]) to justify his completely arbitrary choice of Helena: "Who will not change a raven for a dove? . . . reason says you are the worthier maid" (2.2.113–15). In the forest of Athens, Hermia's physical "darkness," her brunette hair, is changed to a sign approximating that of a racial distinction when she and Helena are pitted against each other for the attentions of Demetrius and Lysander. Such confrontations, provoked by the arbitrariness of male favor and desire, push women into inconsistent and unstable positions. Indeed, Helena bitterly rejects the label "fair" in her realization that she is not desired:

Hermia: God speed fair Helena! whither away?
Helena: Call you me fair? That fair again unsay.
          Demetrius loves your fair, O happy fair!

                                                    (1.1.180–82)

Helena's somewhat overwrought punning reveals a very real problem for the would-be female subject. No two women who are the objects of one

---

4. See Catherine Belsey's deconstructive argument on binary oppositions, "Disrupting Sexual Difference: Meaning and Gender in the Comedies." Although Belsey does not include "dark/light" or "black/white" in her list of oppositions, it is obviously as fundamental as the others she does include; "white" is privileged and "black" is the term that is "always other, always what is *not* the thing itself" (177). In her discussion of stereotypes of black women, Patricia Hill Collins (*Black Feminist Thought: Knowledge, Consciousness, and the Politics of Empowerment* 68–70) identifies black/white as a fundamental dichotomy in the "process of oppositional difference" linked to the objectification of black women.

man's attention can be fair at the same time. When one is "fair" or desired, the other is almost as a matter of course "other" or dark. Even when desired by different men, women are then placed into competitive positions, for each man literally denigrates the other's mistress as "darker" or less beautiful than his own.

In *Two Gentlemen of Verona*, the disguised Julia reveals that the absence of male favor as well as neglect causes "blackness":

> She hath been fairer, madam, than she is:
> When she did think my master lov'd her well,
> She, in my judgment, was as fair as you;
> But since she did neglect her looking-glass
> And threw her sun-expelling mask away,
> The air hath starv'd the roses in her cheeks,
> And pinch'd the lily-tincture of her face,
> That now she is become as black as I.
>
>   (4.4.149–56)

As I noted in Chapter 2, exposure to the sun is a paradoxical sign of male favor. The male whose original rejection provoked the loss of "fairness" almost disappears from the text as the cross-dressed Julia's description shows how the discourses of beauty naturalize a male prerogative. Her "fairness" is replaced by the darkness of his disfavor, which in the course of these lines turns into darkness created by the elements—sun and air.

The language of beauty is one of the few ways in which men can make distinctions between women without compromising their own power. Fairness becomes a powerful, if relatively unexamined, way of creating distinctions within a category—gender—that has embedded in it the instability of women's subjectivity (Belsey, *Subject of Tragedy* 150). In this way it is radically distinct from other terms of difference, such as class. In his "Patriarchal Territories: The Body Enclosed," Peter Stallybrass outlines the contradictory formations of women within categories of gender and class: "To emphasize gender is to construct women-as-the-same: women are constituted as a single category, set over against the category of men. To emphasize class is to differentiate *between* women, *dividing them into distinct social groups . . . the differentiation of women simultaneously establishes or reinforces the differentiation of men*" (133; second emphasis added). When discussing *Othello*, Stallybrass returns to this formulation of relations between gender and class and suggestively refers to classification by race: "It is only if woman is differentiated by class (and race) that Othello's marriage to Desdemona is significant" (135). However, this parenthetical moment does not fully express the ways in which gender and race reconstitute each other when women are differentiated by color.

Race seems to be an even more powerful trope than class, because it allows men to differentiate among women without regard to the material conditions of social class and without the loss of material privileges that are the basis of class differentiation. If one reads "fairness" as a racialized category, Henry Louis Gates, Jr.'s assertion that race is a "dangerous trope" rather than an "objective term of classification" becomes particularly useful. Gates further notes that "we carelessly use language in such a way as to *will* this sense of *natural* difference into our formulations" (5). Differentiation by beauty shares its arbitrariness—and power—with differentiation by race, and both categories increasingly enable each other in Anglo-American discourses.[5] The emerging racialized language of beauty is one way in which the category of "race" is made to act as a "natural" difference. In a like manner, this "willed" sense of natural difference runs throughout the discourses of beauty in the early modern period when signs of racial difference are embedded in so-called aesthetic descriptions.[6]

Both economic and gender concerns are articulated through arbitrary distinctions in color. Racial otherness allows white men to lump all "others" (male and female) into another, less valued, group. In the devaluing of dark-haired women as "Ethiops" or "Tartars," all people of color are placed in secondary positions that reinforce European hegemony. Nevertheless, although the manipulation of gender inherent in formulations of beauty obviously puts women in very unstable positions, such a system does provide a basis for negotiation. Its hierarchical nature can be manipulated by a woman writer to negotiate a more powerful position for herself. Thus race, as much as class, becomes a crucial category used by women writers to differentiate between female characters.

The representation of Cleopatra in women's texts of the early modern period clearly displays the nexus of beauty, race, and empire in such differentiation between women. Cleopatra's sexual allure seems as problematic as her political/erotic power is compelling. Unlike most male writers, women writers continually remind their readers of Cleopatra's dark for-

5. For more on the racial valences of beauty culture and its role in white privilege, see Wendy Chapkis, 37–58.
6. Certainly the heated arguments against cosmetics in antifeminist and antitheatrical literature might suggest both the arbitrariness of the "beautiful" and a recognition that women's use of cosmetics simultaneously denies the existence of the "natural" beauty and usurps the male prerogative to create and manipulate the category.

eignness. According to Lucy Hughes-Hallett, "the European writers and artists who reimagined Cleopatra before 1800 were seldom preoccupied with her foreignness" (201). Her observation is clearly based on a survey of male writers and actually makes the English woman writer's insistence on Cleopatra's foreignness all the more striking.[7] Hughes-Hallett goes on to suggest that a foreign Cleopatra poses a conceptual difficulty for writers because "her reputation for beauty . . . was not consonant with the possibility of her being anything other than a light-skinned European lady" (202). However, it is precisely this disjunction between Cleopatra's reputation for beauty and her (dark) foreignness that would be intriguing to European women because it offers a space from which to negotiate an otherwise confining system of beauty.

More significant, the paradox of Cleopatra's dark beauty becomes the site for female inquiry into male fascination with the "foreign" other. Beauty and race become contested categories that English females use to reveal their investment in the masculine engagement with foreign, female difference in imperial travel. Women writers invariably comment on the fact that Cleopatra's affair with Antony takes place in the shadow of Octavia, an abandoned wife. In *Salve Deus Rex Judaeorum*, Aemilia Lanyer clearly identifies with the Roman Octavia, the wife abandoned through her husband's involvement with the other. Consequently, Lanyer emphasizes the blackness of the adulterous Cleopatra along with her beauty:

> Great *Cleopatra's* love to *Anthony*,
> Can no way be compared unto thine;
> . . . .
> No *Cleopatra*, though thou wert as faire
> As any Creature in *Antonius* eyes;
> Yea though thou wert as rich, as wise, as rare,
> As any Pen could write, or Wit devise;
> Yet with this Lady canst thou not compare,
> Whose inward virtues all thy worth denies:

7. While Hughes-Hallett is correct that male writers do not focus on her darkness, I do not agree with her ultimate conclusion that the fascination with Cleopatra's exoticism is a purely post-Romantic phenomenon: "Such Cleopatras are queens of Egypt, but their non-European home is not much remarked on. It does not make them so different from their Western creators as to be mysterious. It does not automatically endow them with the set of characteristics (cruelty, idleness, sexual voracity) typical of the Orientalist Cleopatras of the post-Romantic period" (203).

Yet thou a blacke Egyptian do'st appeare;
Thou false, shee true; and to her Love more deere.

(1409–10; 1425–32)

Although blackness here does refer to Cleopatra's moral state and thus may seem more part of an older Christian language, I would argue that her blackness is inextricably linked to her foreignness and that Lanyer resorts to Octavia's "inward virtues" merely to counteract Cleopatra's seductive power. While not denying Cleopatra beauty, Lanyer, "to take revenge for chast *Octavia's* wrongs" (1426), replaces Antony's right to make Cleopatra fair with her own judgment in favor of Octavia. So, too, in Mary Sidney's *Antonie* (c. 1590), a translation of Robert Garnier's *Marc Antoine*, Cleopatra's allure poses a problem when Sidney excises references to Cleopatra's beauty in an otherwise faithful translation. Alexander Witherspoon somewhat patronizingly notes one of the few changes in Mary Sidney's translation: "Virtuous lady as she was, she did not think it needful or edifying to dwell on the charms of Cleopatra, and where the Frenchman had written with some animation of '*la singulière beauté de Cléopatre, Roine d'Egypte, arrivée en Cilice en royale magnificence,*' she dismisses the fair Egyptian with a curt phrase, 'Cleopatra Queene of Ægypt' " (86). Sidney's reluctance to "dwell on the charms of Cleopatra" may be due more to a concern with the category of beauty (particularly as it applies to Cleopatra) than to Sidney's feminine modesty. Margaret Ferguson and Gary Weller note that the competition between Mariam and Cleopatra in *The Tragedy of Mariam* is linked to Plutarch's and Samuel Daniels's portraits of Octavia (58, n. 81).

Indeed, *The Tragedy of Mariam* is striking in this regard; in Herod's absence, women vie for power and position by reading religious/national differences within the black/white binarism. The invisible Cleopatra becomes Mariam's antagonist, evoked whenever Mariam's moral and physical "fairness" is at issue. Mariam's mother, Alexandra, describes Mariam as the victor in the pursuit of Antony's favor:

Then glanc'd his eye upon my Mariam's cheek:
And that without comparison did deem,
What was in either but he most did like.
And, thus distracted, either's beauty's might
Within the other's excellence was drown'd:
. . . .
Where if thy portraiture had only gone,
His life from Herod, Anthony had taken:

> He would have lovèd thee, and thee alone,
> And left the brown Egyptian clean forsaken,
> . . . .
> Then Mariam in a Roman's chariot set,
> In place of Cleopatra might have shown:
> A mart of beauties in her visage met,
> And part in this, that they were all her own.
>
> (1.2.180–98)

Writing the Cleopatra/Mariam battle as a standard betrothal complete with the exchange of portraits, Cary also evokes the merchandizing rhetoric of display when Alexandra describes the "mart of beauties [that] in her visage met" (1.2.197). Although Alexandra depicts this beauty contest as potentially immobilizing Antony, in the course of the play, it becomes obvious that Mariam's beauty—which should have been Cleopatra's undoing—is actually her own when Herod has Mariam killed in a fit of Petrarchan rage. Mariam too articulates a competitive relationship with Cleopatra, reminding herself that when Herod favored her he rejected "the brown Egyptian" Cleopatra:

> That face that did captive great Julius' fate,
> That very face that was Anthonius' bane,
> That face that to be Egypt's pride was born,
> That face that all the world esteem'd so rare:
> Did Herod hate, despise, neglect, and scorn,
> When with the same, he Mariam's did compare.
>
> (4.8.547–52)

In the somewhat obsessive anaphora, Mariam foregrounds the competition with Cleopatra implicit in rest of the text.[8] The use of complexion to accentuate status, cultural, and religious differences is quite striking in *Mariam* particularly in its connection to the combination of female competition and imperial politics that characterizes the text.

Although much has been said about the combination of desire and restraint that permeates European male engagement in travel, European women's perspectives on the erotics of travel remain in the realm of conjecture. For example, it is intriguing to speculate on Lady Raleigh's motivations for having herself painted as Cleopatra (figure 5) and to read the portrait as a response to the rhetoric of foreign travel as articulated

---

8. Ferguson and Weller note that the references to Cleopatra present her as a "sensual 'antitype' to Mariam" and thus closer to Shakespeare's Cleopatra (29–30).

Figure 5. Lady Raleigh as Cleopatra by an unknown artist. Lady Raleigh may have been the first woman in England to own an African slave. (By courtesy of the National Portrait Gallery, London.)

by her husband in passages like the following one from the *Discoverie of Guiana*: "But I protest before the Majestie of the living God, that I neither know nor beleeve, that any of our company one or other, by violence or otherwise, ever knew any of their women, and yet we saw many hundreds, and had many in our power, and of those very yong, and excellently favoured, which came among us without deceit, stark naked" (316). Although Raleigh continually protests that he does not fall for the allure of foreign women, his *Discoverie of Guiana* is full of praise of comely native women and the eroticized land. Here he insists on the restraint of English colonizers even as he emphasizes the ample opportunities for sexual pleasure that they have rejected. Of any woman in the early modern period, Lady Raleigh was well positioned to comment upon such imperial posturing. Her portrait seems to appreciate the ambivalence of Cleopatra as a model for women. In reenacting the moment of Cleopatra's suicide, Raleigh fashions herself both as object of desire *and* as loyal wife (in the poem that floats above her head).

Blackness and Status in the *Urania*

These issues of imperial travel, desire, and power are particularly resonant in Mary Wroth's works. *The Countess of Montgomerie's Urania* uncovers the ways in which "literary" tropes of blackness shaped and articulated issues of gender and class for members of James I's court. In Wroth's life and her works, we have a clear example of the objectified and fetishized woman straining for a stable subject position. An intimate member of Anne's circle, Wroth was deeply implicated in the Jacobean fascination with difference. She helped stage the mixture of transgressive sexuality and imperial desire in Ben Jonson's *Masque of Blackness* and thus was present at a defining moment of the British empire that used blackness to privilege white beauty. While sent down from court, Wroth penned her own sonnet sequence, which both demonstrates the problematic and powerful control that tropes of blackness give the poet over the poetic subject and uses those tropes to refigure her own estrangement. The collision of the language of beauty with cultural difference in the *Urania* reveals Wroth's own complex—and often contradictory—engagement in the systems of power inherent in literary representations of blackness. Her awareness of the positioning of foreign women vis-à-vis the European woman is also intricately connected to a demonstration of how patriarchal systems work to objectify women, denying their subjectivity in delineating relationships between women.[9]

Wroth's *Urania* opens with the shepherdess Urania, a woman not "certaine of [her] owne estate or birth" (1), who has just been told by her country parents that she is a foundling. The wandering Urania meets the lovelorn knight Parselius, and they, with other adventurers, sail to Naples to meet the famous knight Amphilanthus. This band of travelers is almost immediately blown off course to Venus's Isle (Cyprus), where they suffer their first trial by the House of Love. After drinking from a magic fountain, each character experiences an "enchantment" that creates illusions that propel the women into the House of Love. Notable among the illusions is the one suffered by Urania's maidservant, who sees her beloved, Allimarlus, embracing a black woman: "*Urania's* maide beheld *as she beleev'd Allimarlus* in the second Towre, kissing and embracing a Blackmoore; which so farre inraged her, being passionatly in love with him, as she must goe to revenge her selfe of that injurie" (emphasis added).[10] For a moment the reader sees what the maid fantasizes, a white man embracing a black woman. While this is an unusual (although not unprecedented) act in the literature of the period, its rarity begs the question of why the first dark other in the text is conjured up by this silent and almost forgotten character. This black figure, a vision entirely the product of the maid's imagination, is the locus of the varying concerns over status, beauty, race, and empire typical of the consistent use of tropes of blackness by England's earliest women writers.[11]

During the seventeenth century there is an emerging tradition of black maids that begins, most likely, with Zanthia in John Marston's *The Wonder of Women; or, The Tragedy of Sophonisba* (1606). These women commonly serve twin functions: a legitimate function as a maid and an illegitimate one as a bawd or whore (Barthelemy 123). Frequently, the two functions are often assumed, if not actual. In *The White Devil*, Vittoria's maid, Zan-

9. I propose for a slightly more complex version of identity formation than that offered by Naomi J. Miller, who asserts "that Wroth's women more consistently realize their identities through affirmations of their relatedness than through assertions of difference" ("Nott much to be marked" 126). Although Wroth's primary emphasis is on connections between women, that very emphasis seems to provoke a set of tensions about difference.

10. Mary Wroth, *The Countess of Montgomerie's Urania*, 40. All references to the *Urania* are hereafter cited in the text.

11. In her discussion of this figure, Josephine Roberts reads the figure as a dream symbol that "serve[s] physically as a double for the maid, allowing her to view her subservience from the outside and eventually to become conscious of her own self-abnegation" (188). Roberts makes the maid and the "black-moore" part of a shared sameness, whereas my argument is to highlight blackness as a difference that helps constitute whiteness as a value.

che, is assumed to be her pander as well and is punished for the misdeeds of Flamineo, the actual pander. According to Anthony Barthelemy, in each appearance, the black woman "stands as a symbol of everything evil and low" (123) and often serves as a metaphor for sexual evil. As he notes in his discussion of *Sophonisba*, these women are often embraced by a white, male character: at such times the black female serves as "a symbol of lust and sin" and as an external representation of the spiritual state of the man who embraces her (126). This dynamic works even when the women are not African characters. In Richard Brome's *The English Moore*, the villain, Nathaniel, rather than being repelled by the black painted Millicent, is attracted to her—an attraction that becomes further proof of his villainy. The dramatic and metaphoric implications Barthelemy outlines are undeniably true in the drama; however, the similarities of this moment only highlight the differences of the *Urania*.

In a larger sense, Allimarlus's embrace of the black woman represents female fears of the foreign difference that heroes—and travelers—encounter on these romantic adventures. The House of Love episode foregrounds a gendered difference key to romance: men desire conquest, whereas women desire men. The men abandon the women, fleeing the House of Love in the hot pursuit of adventure and glory. When Wroth conflates erotic passions and the passion for adventure in this embrace, the resulting jealousy the black woman evokes may be as much jealousy over male adventurism as jealousy over another woman. Wroth demystifies a tradition of European male refusal to acknowledge that the seduction of conquest and exploration and the seductiveness of native women are often the same. European women thus are always in subtle competition with the glory of travel and adventure that is the essence of male romance.

Wroth begins the episode by "estranging" Love from the courtly world of the pastoral. The House of Love is not in some pastoral retreat but in a dangerous, strange, and, most important, un-Christian land. While waiting to land in Naples, the company is caught in a tempest that blows them across the Mediterranean and hurls them to Cyprus:

> None being able to expresse the desperateness of this storme, but by saying, it was the picture of the last day for violence, but like the world for strangenes and uncertainty.... When heaven did think this storme had lasted long enough crosse to those, though crost, yet still most loving lovers, it commanded the seas to be at quiet, which being perform'd, the Pilot againe began to use his skil, which first had meanes to let him know, that so farre they were from the place resolv'd on, as in stead of the coast of *Italy*, they were within sight of the Island of *Ciprus*: this not onely amazed them, but

much troubled them, considering the barbarousness of the people who there inhabited, and their extremity such, as of necessity they must land to replenish their wants, caused by the rigor of the tempest. . . . (38)

Cyprus, a typical stop for pilgrims on their way to the holy land as well as a center for international trade, was known as the seat of Venus.[12] In typical romance fashion, Wroth's storm removes her adventurers from the gloss of courtly civilization to (perhaps not coincidentally) the site of *Othello*'s interracial tragedy.[13]

More important, the storm begins the dissolution of the band of travelers. Oaths taken in "civilization" are deliberately put into doubt: "This storme had lasted long enough crosse to those, though crost, yet still most loving lovers" (38). During this tempest, the author is at great pains to remind us that the adventurers hold fast to the oaths and promises made to one another: "Thus, all for others grieved, pitty extended so, as all were carefull, but of themselves most carelesse: yet their mutuall care, made them all cared for" (39). As we shall see, such reminders only serve to emphasize the eventual fragmentation of the group. Their care for others makes them investigate a fire, which leads them to their own destruction:

> Wherfore passing on they landed in the Island, which no sooner was done, but their former wonder was encreased, by the sudden falling a fire of their own Ship, which had but delivered herself of them, and then as a Martyr suffer'd for the paine they had in her endur'd. But this past, admiration brought new sorrow to them, considering they were in a strange Country, among barbarous people, depriv'd of all hope to get thence any more, but there to continue at the mercy of unchristened creatures. (38)

The narrator implies that it is the travelers' "admiration" of this magical event that exacerbates their troubles. Indeed, "admiration" later becomes a vexed term throughout the romance, as Wroth uses it not only to refer to a character's wonder at the foreign and magical happenings in the world of the *Urania* but also to describe male admiration of female beauty, a conflation much like Ferdinand's view of "Admired Miranda" in Shakespeare's *The Tempest*.

12. See the 1611 letter of Master William Biddulph from Aleppo: "In this Ile Venus was greatly honoured. There is still a Citie therein called Paphia, built by Paphus, who dedicated it to Venus," in *Purchas; His Pilgrimes*, vol. 8, 249.
13. For a more complete discussion of possible correspondences with *Othello* in Wroth, see Naomi Miller, "Women's Voices," 162–67.

The barbarous nature of this land proves peculiarly appropriate, for Christian virtue throughout the *Urania* (as in *Pamphilia to Amphilanthus*) is allied with constant love: inconstant lovers are often described as heretical. We see this most clearly when Parselius falls in love with Dalinea and forgets his protestations of love to Urania:

> All this *Parselius* beheld, but most the Princesse, who he so much admir'd, as admiration wrought so farre, as to permit him to thinke that she equal'd *Urania*; this was a sudden stepp from so entire a Love, as but now hee vowed to his Shepherdesse, being an Heresie, as he protested, for any man to thinke there liv'd a creature like his Love. But into this hee is now falne, and will lead the faction against her. Uncertaine Tyrant Love, that never brings thy Favourits to the topp of affection, but turnes againe to a new choice; Who would have thought any but *Urania's* beauty could have invited *Parselius* to love? (102)

His "Heresie" is the forgetting of faith, the breaking of his vows to Urania in his "admiration" of Dalinea. "Admiration" is a peculiarly appropriate characterization of Parselius's response to his first vision of Dalinea and suggests that his marveling at her beauty is not far from the transitory admiration of foreign wonders felt by the travelers in Cyprus. In the same theological trope, after discovering his lover is herself unfaithful, another lover wishes to be rid of his love for her, declaring that "I cried out against my birth, mine eyes, mine owne life, my judgement, my beliefe, wishd I had bin borne an Heritick to love" (468) and declares that "my Youth in travell led me to such folly" (469). Significantly, the House of Love episode concludes not with the freeing of the lovers but with the conversion of the natives of Cyprus:

> Thus to *Pamphilia's* tent they came, where most sumptuously shee entertain'd them: then did all the great Princes feast each other, the last being made by the King of *Ciprus*, who out of love to the Christian Faith, which before he contemned, seeing such excellent, and happy Princes professors of it, desired to receive it, which *Amphilanthus* infinitly rejoicing at, and all the rest, Christ-ned him with his wife, excellently faire daughter, and *Polarchus* his valiant Sonne, and so became the whole Island Christians. (142)

The spell of the House of Love broken, the barbarous and "unfaithful" land, previously the site of unbridled desire, is now "converted" under the auspices of Pamphilia to a Christian (and, we presume, constant) kingdom.

While this foreign setting is most appropriate for the exploration of female desire, the travelers' recognition of their insecure and tenuous position in a foreign land seems somewhat misplaced, since their own psyches lead them astray. Although the reader is continually reminded of the traveler's fear of the Cypriot natives, ultimately they are trapped by their own desire or "fault." While explaining the "triall of false or faith-full lovers," the aged man they meet warns that "therein once inclosed, they endure torments fit for such a fault" (40). Unlike the enchanted inland sea Guyon encounters in *The Faerie Queene,* the enchanted stream in Cyprus does not provoke lustful sloth; rather, it incites them to passionate action. The land may be frightening, not so much because of the barbarity of the native inhabitants as because in their "amazement"—and desire—the travelers gradually lose their sense of proper order and restraint.

Love in the romance is insistently and intricately interwoven with empire. In her "confession," Urania describes her affair with Steriamus:

> I entertaind his sute, which was his kingdome wonne in sweet delight; then was that as an Empire to my gaine, when I first saw him rudely, yet innocently clad, like a Lamb in wool for colour and softnesse to the eye, or touch his face blushing like modesty, after his arme had showed manly power, his delicacie asking pitie, but his commanding absolutenes, disdaining it as much, as the bright Moone, if we should say wee were sorry in a frostie night, to see her face in the water, least she might bee cold: rather might I say, I feard the Sunne would burne him, when hee enamourd of his dainty skinne, did but incloase him with his power from other harme, touching him not to hurt, but to make difference twixt his favours, shind, and shielded him, while others she did burne, kinde in embracements, and soft in his force. (276)

His control, "his kingdome wonne in sweet delight," which ordinarily might be read as an extension of male power gained in the achievement of the mistress's favor, here becomes subsumed under her allowance of the favor, "that was as an Empire to my gaine." Her gain of "Empire" (which shows an interesting instance of the female blazoning gaze) ends, however, with his "commanding absolutenes." The oscillation of power between the (female) lover and the (male) beloved, written out in political terms, runs throughout Wroth's text. Wroth's use of the "loving Sun" trope recasts an earlier use of the trope by her uncle in *Astrophel and Stella*'s sonnet 22: "Her daintiest bare went free; the cause was this, / The Sunne which others burn'd, did her but kisse" (13–14). As we saw in Chapter 2, this trope in Sidney's poem works to prove Astrophel's poetic prowess.

Here the sun in a somewhat homoerotic fashion makes "difference twixt his favours" and protects Steriamus while burning others.

Combining as it does adventure and "love," the romance is the perfect form for problematizing Elizabethan and Jacobean exploration and adventurism. It is even possible that encroachments on foreign territory in travel and discovery may have become more charged in later romances because of the increased interest in actual quests for new world adventure. Stephen Greenblatt's reading of book 2 of *The Faerie Queene* demonstrates how Spenser's experience with colonial administration in Ireland influenced his portrayal of difference and, as we have seen, the Jacobean court was beset with a fascination with foreign and culturally different "others" that tended to work to exclude European women from power. Such "foreign affairs" simply beg an observer to question the implications of the male pursuit of adventure for European women. Wroth herself may have had intimate experience with such questions since her uncle, Philip Sidney, died in an action worthy of his own romance heroes, leaving his family insolvent.

Wroth's romance is particularly concerned with the vexed relationship of women to adventure and travel. As Paul Salzman notes, "*Urania* has its valiant heroes, but the reader's attention is directed to the women who are left behind by the questing men, or whose paths cross the heroes' with invariably miserable results" (141). As I suggested earlier, what seems to be jealousy over another woman could also be read as anger over this type of abandonment. It is in Cyprus that Urania and the other women are deserted by the males in hot pursuit of adventure. The company is parted strictly along gender lines; the men's desires are all for personal glory, conquest, and war: "*Parselius* forgot all, but his promise to the dead King of *Albania*, for the setling his Sonnes in that Kingdome. *Leandrus* afflicted with the lossse of *Antissia*, must straight into *Morea* to finde her, and take her from *Amphilanthus*; *Steriamus* and *Selarinus* would not be refused the honour of Knight-hood, *Mars* having so possessed them with his warlike disposition, as worlds to their imaginations were too little to conquer, therefore *Albania* was already wonne" (40). Even Leandrus, who is "afflicted with the loss of *Antissia*" and therefore motivated by lost love, is characterized as an adventurer; his desire for her seems subsumed under the challenge to Amphilanthus. Nona Feinberg implicitly suggests that, unlike in the sonnets, there is in the romance a certain "pull of adventure towards public life" (180–81). This is certainly supported by Antissia, who in the manuscript says that the end of her "adventure" "was pleasant beecause freedome with libertie came alonge with itt" (2, fol.

17). Although the troping of adventure does allow for a degree of pub-
licness and movement for women, the "pull of adventure" is more possible than real for women in the *Urania*—they still wind up in interior
spaces and absent from the action as indicated by Pamphilia's imprison-
ment in the House of Love.

There is an apparent hierarchy of passions from adventure to "love"
with adventure made antithetical to love. Urania, in a move contrasting
Leandrus's, is the only woman who wants to "adventure," but even then
only in the cause of love: "*Urania,* whose heart before was onely fed by
the sweet lookes, and pleasing conversation of *Parselius,* loves him now so
much, as she imagines, she must try the adventure, to let him see her
loyalty is such, as for his love, and by it she would end the Inchantment"
(40). The narrator continues: "These distractions carried them all, as
their passions guided them. *Parselius* having knighted the two Princes,
tooke their way to the next Port: *Urania* now not seene or thought on"
(40). Although Urania blames herself for being parted from Parselius—
"When as thus much sense came to her, as to know she had left *Parselius,*
which strak her into a mourning passion, confessing that, an unpardon-
able fault, and what he in justice could not excuse" (41)—Wroth syntac-
tically connects Parselius's chivalric desires with his abandonment of
Urania. Recovering from the spell, Parselius remembers his desertion of
Urania not as his betrayal but as hers: "Who had (as hee dreamed) forsaken him, and left him sleeping, while shee went with another" (41).
His memory provides an interesting gloss on the male chivalric/romance
tradition that automatically reads woman as unfaithful, especially since
Parselius is persuaded to leave the island with the promise of another
adventure, the killing of his imagined rival: "Then he might recover her,
and kill his enemie" (41).

Gary Waller notes that "adventure" is a recurring word throughout the
romance (41), which would not be unusual for the genre; Wroth, however, makes quite explicit an ambivalence about this aspect of the genre
that is rooted in gender concerns. In male descriptions of travel, the European women left home are often neglected in favor of describing the
seductiveness of native women. We see throughout the *Urania* that travel
was often a source of tension between men and women. Often it is the
call to duty and adventure that separates lovers—sometimes fortuitously,
as when Steriamus takes leave of his beloved Pamphilia: "Besought her,
she would honour me but so much, as I might kisse her hands before my
departure, which was forc'd by an adventure, calling me away: she nobly
granted that, and said, she wisht me good fortune" (57). Unlike Steriamus, many men in the *Urania* view adventure as a welcome escape from

women, or at least preferable to them. Selencius tells us that his nephew, Antissius, is interrupted from his search for his sister, Antissia, by his father's demand that he get married: "His obedience having mastred his affection, which rather was to follow Armes, then fall into the armes of *Love*" (42). Interestingly, the terms here seem to be reversed, for we see that the young man's true "affections" are for adventure, not love.

Even in the House of Love, war takes precedence. Our narrator tells us that the House of Love is covered with a pantheon of gods, appearing "their proportions such as their powers, and qualities are described" (39). Given this comment, it is perhaps significant that Mars is the only god described fully: "As *Mars* in Armes, weapons of Warre about him, Trophies of his Victories, and many demonstrations of his Warre-like Godhead. *Apollo* with Musicke, *Mercurie*, *Saturne*, and the rest in their kind" (39). Of course it is not unusual that Mars should be the most powerful; after all, he did win Venus's love; however, his prevalence (in description at least) is interesting given the movement of the men away from "love" to war after the enchanted stream heightens their desires.

Indeed, it is often the case in misogynist discourses that travel becomes a more than acceptable reason for avoiding women, particularly unmanageable women. In Fletcher's *Rule a Wife and Have a Wife* (1624), Leon declares, "I'd rather guide a ship Imperial, / Alone, and in a storme, then rule one woman" (57). In *Much Ado about Nothing*, Benedick, complaining of Beatrice's caustic wit, begs Don Pedro to sent him abroad: "Will your Grace command me any service to the world's end? I will go on the slightest arrand now to the Antipodes that you can devise to send me on; I will fetch you a toothpicker now from the furthest inch of Asia, bring you a length of Prester John's foot, fetch you a hair off the great Cham's beard, do you any embassage to the Pigmies, rather than hold three words' conference with this harpy" (2.1.263–71). Benedick's incredible catalog evokes nearly every trope associated with mercantile adventure and discovery while it also pushes Beatrice into the realm of the foreign impediment to empire when he makes her a "harpy."

Although the *Urania* comments critically on the ways in which male travel leaves women behind, what remains largely unspoken is a positive space for female adventure in the text. While the women in the *Urania* do a great deal of traveling, adventure is often readily acknowledged to be a usurpation of a male prerogative. In discussing the absence of Parselius, Urania reads adventure as an "offense." "I thought rather (said she) he had been offended with us for adventuring; which well he might, considering by that folly we lost him" (147). At the opening of book 2 Urania is reluctant to engage the next trial because of her previous negative experience of "adventuring." In the manuscript continuation of the *Urania*, Pamphilia proclaims, "Itt is not in a woeman to adventure" (1:50). Her feeling has already been made less explicitly, though with more force in book 2, when Pamphilia scornfully berates her rival, Nereana, for being a female "Knight": "And in truth I am sorry, that such a Lady should take so great and painefull a voyage, to so fond an end, being the first that ever I heard of, who took so Knight-like a search in hand; men being us'd to follow scornefull Ladies, but you to wander after a passionate, or disdainefull Prince, it is great pitie for you" (163). Later, Nereana castigates herself for her transgression:

> As she wandred in amaze, and at last quite lost in her selfe, straying up and downe, now exercising the part of an adventurous lover, as *Pamphilia* in jest had call'd her, a thousand thoughts at this time possessing her, and yet all those as on a wheele turnd, came to the same place of her desperate estate. One while she curs'd her love, then dislike of her folly, for adventuring, and rashly leaving her Country: she raild at the uncarefull people who permitted her to have her fond desires without limiting her power, but that she check'd againe, for said she, rather would I be thus miserable, then not absolute. (165)

Interestingly, Nereana realizes both that she has taken on a male "role," and refuses to abandon it, and that the adoption of male prerogative makes her "absolute."

The narrator of the House of Love episode tells us that the blackmoor is the maid's "affliction," a projection of the self onto the other. Although Fredric Jameson sees such projection as central to romance, Wroth's subsequent unraveling of the servant's tale and her use of the black/white dichotomy demonstrates one of the difficulties of what Jameson has called the genre's central "ideologeme"—the opposition between good and evil: "What is really meant by 'the good' is simply my own position as an unassailable power center, in terms of which the position of the Other, or of the weak, is repudiated and marginalized in practices which are then ultimately themselves formalized in the concept of evil" (117). However, Jameson's own critique of Nietzsche's analysis—that it does not address the problem of the protagonist's identification with the enemy he designates as evil—ignores the very real problem of gender.[14] The insistence on an identification of self and other proves intractably problematic for Wroth's heroines, for whom, as we are told from the first lines of the

---

14. For further discussion of Jameson's analysis see Maureen Quilligan, "Lady Mary Wroth and Family Romance."

romance, "my own position" is anything but simple. Wroth shows that the black/white opposition, the time-honored representation of the good/evil dichotomy drawn on in romance, is in "aesthetic" terms one that absolutely denies women "an unassailable power center."

Before reaching the enchanted fountain, the company is told by Venus's priest that lovers caught in the House of Love "suffer unexpressable tortures, in severall kindes as their affections are most incident to; as Jelousie, Despaire, Feare, Hope, Longings, and such like" (40). In other words, these visions in some way represent the innermost fears and desires of the lovers. Interestingly, this is the only fantasy that seems to block the desires of the lover and to repel rather than seduce or attract her. Outraged at the sight, she rushes into the Tower of Desire intending to revenge herself against her rival. The narrator tells us that this vision represents the "affliction" of the maid, jealousy, encouraging us to see the episode as an almost iconographic representation of jealousy. This is not an actual embrace but the waiting maid's fantasy, and the embrace involves not a villain but the truly (and tediously) heroic Allimarlus. As I suggested earlier, the introduction of racial difference serves to distinguish between types of women without affecting the status of men. Absolutely no blame falls on Allimarlus himself, "being the onely sensible man left" (41); in fact he is the only one of the company who does not drink from the enchanted fountain that diverts them from their intended journey. The narrative thus makes it quite clear that the Moor both represents and kindles the maid's rage. The maid's vision is not only a projection of jealousy but also a desire: in fantasizing an African "other," this shepherdess/servant creates a privileged position for herself that does not affect the reader's view of Allimarlus. Thus blackness exists only to make white that much more beautiful and acceptable, and the maid's class difference from Allimarlus is effaced under the more obvious racial difference of the "Moor."

The use of darkness to reify whiteness is not uncommon in the *Urania* and, as Ann Jones reveals, is particularly notable in the sonnet cycle *Pamphilia to Amphilanthus* (Jones 144–46). For example, in praising Pamphilia's verses, Amphilanthus claims that they only show Pamphilia through contrast, their "darkness" revealing her actual fairness all the more: "That for any other, they might speake for their excellencies, yet in comparison of her excelling vertues, they were but shadowes to set the others forth withall" (266). In these verses, Wroth evokes the arbitrary power of such binary thinking even as she rejects the problematic subject position that it creates for women. Throughout the sequence Pamphilia sees such divisions as dark and light, night and day, as subject to the vagaries of "favor" and leading to uncertainty. In a sonnet on "suspicion," she shows how love is subject to change: "Noe little signe of favor can I prove / Butt must bee way'de, and turnd to wronging love, / And with each humor must my state begin" (66.12–14).[15] Her demonstrations of favor are shaped by *his* humor and define her state. In a verse oddly evocative of both Dolorinda's judgment and the maid's view of the Moor, Wroth shows how love's trials force an identification of black and white: "Heere are affections, tri'de by loves just might / As gold by fire, and black deserned by white, / Error by truthe, and darknes knowne by light, / When faith is vallued for love to requite" (79.5–8). Although the black/white binarism would seem to separate the two, there is also a process of identification present in the interdependence of the two categories.[16] In the next sonnet, Pamphilia wishes to escape the trap of such oppositions: "Never to slack till earth noe stars can see, / Till Sunn, and Moone doe leave us to dark night, / And Second Chaose once again doe free / Us, and the world from all devisions spite" (80.5–9). As we shall see, Pamphilia reiterates this longing (albeit in a less apocalyptic vein) for the absolute destruction of these damaging encodings of women throughout the *Urania*.

Beauty is one such value that Wroth simultaneously reasserts and deconstructs. According to Carolyn Ruth Swift Wroth uses stereotypes of feminine charm "to reject masculine standards of female beauty and virtue. . . . Heroines in *Urania* are beautiful because Wroth finds in women a wit, courage, and spirit that create beauty" (333). Swift's reading suggests that the *Urania* is an apolitical female world where women are defined solely by virtue; but as an examination of Wroth's use of blackness reveals, this world is not quite as "pure" as Swift's reading implies. Although Wroth seems acutely aware of such tropes as signs of often arbitrary male favor, she nonetheless does collude with masculinist scripts when she finds differences in women according to their rank and uses the language of beauty to reinforce distinctions in class. Thus we find racial difference often subtends Wroth's emphasis on class differentiation as it does in the maid's fantasy. While Swift is correct in her assertion that Wroth's depiction of women is never as devastating as her uncle's depiction of the lower-class Mopsa in *The Countess of Pembroke's Arcadia*, both

15. Mary Wroth, *The Poems of Lady Mary Wroth*, ed. Josephine Roberts. All references to Wroth's poems are to this edition and are hereafter cited in the text.
16. In his *Discerning the Subject*, Paul Smith notes the dual nature of the verb "to cern": "For Marx subjects/individuals are *cerned*. That is to say, and punning on the words 'to cern' and 'to cerne,' they must: first, accept a given inheritance or patrimony (the legacy of their class provenance and of its economic determinations); and, second, be encircled or surrounded, in a synecdochal figure or by the definition of the whole in and through which they accede to 'real' existence" (5). This second definition in particular suggests the dual sense of identification and difference in Wroth's use of "discern" in the *Urania*.

Sidneys' evaluations of women are inextricably tied to their sense of class or rank.

Consequently, rank and beauty both read very much the same throughout the romance. For example, when Wroth describes Lisia—"The Lady was great, and therefore faire, full of spirit, and intising, pleasing and richly shee was attired, and bravely serv'd, an excellent hors-woman, and hunts-woman she was" (470)—she implies (albeit ironically) that for Lisia, as "great, and *therefore* faire," fairness is dependent on her rank. In an earlier moment, the duke Severus recognizes royalty by its complexion: "The Duke all Supper time, curiously beholding the Knights, especially *Ollorandus*, who, he imagined by his complexion, and the favour of his face, to be the King, though it was long since he had seene him; but the ground he had in malice made him discerne that, which otherwise had laine hidden (envy having sharpnesse in discovering)" (224). Elsewhere, the shepherdess Allarina describes a May Day contest won by a woman who is beautiful almost in spite of her rank:

> The rarest, and the choicest beauties came, among the rest one, who in truth I must confesse, was faire above the common beauties in our time, but of the meanest parentage and ranke, being a servant to a Shepherdesse, who was of greatest place, for there is difference, and distinction made of their degrees, (though all below your sight) as well as in the great ones, and as much curious choice, and shame to match below their owne degrees, as among Princes, whose great bloods are toucht, if staind with basenesse in the match they make. (184)

In a passage fascinating for its display of the niceties of rank, Allarina slights the beauty of a rival not because of her virtue (or lack of it) but because of her rank. The shepherdess, while making the argument that her rival is "meaner" than she and showing that shepherds are as sensitive to the nuances of rank and birth as lords, never loses sight of her audience, the queen, who is really beyond such pastoral bickering. In parenthetically noting Pamphilia's alleged disinterest, Allarina forces a closer connection between herself and the queen based on their distance from the status competition she outlines.

The only lover who does not seem to foster such competitiveness is one best described by Donne as "The Indifferent": "I can love both fair and brown, / Her whom aboundance melts, and her whom want betrayes. . . . Some two or three / Poore Heretiques in love there be, / Which think to stablish dangerous constancy."[17] In the shared language of Donne

17. John Donne, *Poems, & c., by John Donne.* London, 1669.

and Wroth, we see both men and women are "indifferent."[18] Not constant in their attachments (or in Donne's case, not passionate), they make no real distinctions between their loves. At one point, a shepherdess is unable to choose between a "fair" hunter and a "brown" shepherd:

> My Lord said she, you heare by these two the story related of my love. I cannot but confesse it is true, onely I beseech you not to thinke any lightnesse was more in these affections then in the indifference of my choice, I loved this faire man I confesse first, I had not then seene the other, but when I perceived his lovelines, beauty me thought was more ordinary, and therefore I prized him dearer, but when the faire youth came againe, brownnes appeared nothing so pleasing, both together mee thought they were both fit to be beloved, and the rather both, because different complexions would hold one still to love one of them; when affection to sweetenesse and delicatenesse possessed me I looked on him, when love to fairnes, and whitenes claimed place, I turned to the other, thus mee thinkes I loved equally, and so it was but one love being still to one end, content and to be contented with those had made themselves one in all things, even love to me. (385–86)

However, the indifference of this shepherdess uncovers the lack of power that women have in exploiting such patriarchal signs. Unlike the dark and fair women we have seen who are made "fit" or "unfit" under even the most arbitrary choices of the male, the shepherdess's fickleness does not translate into inequalities for the beloved men. As she turns from one man to the other, she notes that "both together mee thought they were both fit to be beloved." Not only are the men themselves not devalued as the result of her inconstancy but, acutely conscious of her inability to wield the power of choice, she fears that her freedom will lower her in a man's estimation: "It is most true, I am now brought to choose one, for my father will have me marry, I cannot find in my heart to refuse either, or have power to choose whether, I hope this freedome which hath continued with us will not be a cause now to make me lesse esteemed, my love is the same it was, and therefore Sir, which you will allot me to I must take" (386). Essentially, she initially wishes to restore that power to the king. In what may be an interesting twist on the choice presented in Philip Sidney's "The Lady of May," the lady here is told to choose blindly, and ends by rejecting both the men. Similarly, the prince of Jambolly is a type of indifferent love who, if anything, is judged more harshly than the shep-

---

18. However, Wroth pointedly reads constancy as the "religion" of love and inconstancy as the "heresy."

herdess: "And of any this Prince was one that least troubled himselfe with constancy, all women were pleasing to him, after a tall woman, a little one was most pleasing, after faire, browne, white, blacke, all came to his staid-nesse welcomly, and varietie he had sufficient, for many refused not, nor was he nice to demand of more, so as he had plenty, and was plentifull in love to them" (463). Wroth here makes a pointed, gendered distinc-tion. Unlike the shepherdess, who wishes to be constant, but cannot choose an object for her attentions, the prince, by virtue (or privilege) of rank and gender, does not have to choose, because he has the power to sample all.

This description of the prince of Jambolly's arbitrariness demonstrates clearly that beauty is the site for status competition for women. However, status competition for men is more often located in knightly display, and Wroth's portrayal of the chivalric code so integral to romance reveals most clearly the racial and patriarchal privileges generated by black/white op-positions. If typically in this genre the unidentified enemy, the unknown "other," is the black knight, the *Urania* demonstrates that this chivalric system, naturalized in romance, is in fact a highly artificial and male sys-tem of signification. Knights wear certain armors and emblems as signs of their status in erotic competition, but this status is always defined by a knight, not imposed by a lady (although it is always ostensibly assumed *for* a lady). Whereas in male-authored romances, knights convey status through the use of emblems and mottos, in the *Urania*, knights often signal their romantic status through the use of colors in armor. This "dressing for success" occurs throughout the *Urania*. When Nereana, the "lady knight," signals her competition with Pamphilia by her attire, "for the kings being set, there entred a Lady of some beauty, attended on by ten knights, all in Tawny, her selfe likewise apparreld in that colour; her Pages, and the rest of her servants having that liverie" (162), it is entirely possible that she has appropriated a system of signification seemingly open only to knights/males.

Unlike women, for whom color and complexion are constructed as "natural" effects rather than as subject positions assigned by men, men display for themselves their sense of being favored or disfavored through their chivalric garb, which can be removed at will. When planning their self presentation, Steriamus and Amphilanthus disguise themselves in col-ored armor: "*Steriamus* desiring, that because his name was not yet knowne by desert, it might be still kept secret; and most he desired it, by reason of his vow. They agreed to it, and he was only call'd, The true despis'd, which was all the device in his shield. *Amphilanthus* did desire to be held unknowne too: but his reason was, that it was not so safe for so

famous a man to be commonly knowne, in so great & imminent dangers"
(61). Just as the two disguise themselves together, their disguises work as
paired opposites: the unfavored one, Steriamius, is tawny and black and
Amphilanthus, appropriately as the "never enough admired," wears red
and white: "But then came the honour of his sexe, never enough admired, and belov'd *Amphilanthus*, his Armour was white, fillited with Rubies; his furniture to his Horse Crimson, embroidred with Pearle; his
Shield with the same device, from which hee took his name. *Steriamus*
according to his fortune was in Tawny, wrought all over with blacke" (62).
These passages visually re-create the red-white-black triad common to Petrarchan discourse. Nonetheless, these colors are not imposed upon the
men; they are adopted in a manner as artificial as their armor.
Furthermore, these "disguises" seem never to conceal an identity for very
long, and the men are never placed in the precarious subject positions of
the women. Indeed, Amphilanthus's disguise is not a disguise at all, for a
gentleman approaches him, claiming, "My Lord, your worth cannot bee
hid, though you have obscured your name" (62).

This obvious use of armor as a system of self-signification in the pursuit
of "amour" suggests an interesting gloss on a sudden tournament that
begins a new adventure. After Pamphilia assures her friend and rival, Antissia, that she has no romantic interest in Amphilanthus, they are greeted
with a strange spectacle:

> Tenne Knights comming in russet Armours, their Beaners up, their Swords
> in their hands; who comming more then halfe way to the State, making low
> reverence, stood still, parting themselves to either side of the Chamber, to
> let the followers better be discerned. Then came tenne more, but in blacke
> Armours, chain'd together, without Helmets or Swords. After them came sixe
> armed like the first, three carrying Speares of infinite bignesse; one, the
> Sheild, and the other two the Sword and Helmet of a Knight, who for coun-
> tenance seem'd no lover; his colour like a Moore; his fashion rude and proud,
> following after these sixe, who, as the first, divided themselves. (79)

Coming so immediately after this picture of (albeit friendly) female rivalry, this alternating procession of red and black provides a visual analogue to the Pamphilia-Amphilanthus-Antissia triangle as well as an
indication of Pamphilia's own ambivalence in her relation to Antissia. It
also presents a powerful convergence of jealousy, beauty, chivalric disguise, and race as the knights in "blacke Armours" are suggestively connected with a visual pun to the knight who "seem'd no lover" because
he has "colour like a Moore." Louise Fradenberg suggests that such ra-

cialization is nothing new; she outlines a similar conflation of racial disguising with actual black people in early Scottish court tournaments. She notes that in such disguising, "the figure of the Moor would serve a variety of talismanic functions, providing protection from danger and preventing protection from becoming dangerously safe" (251). Although she focuses on female "Moors," the black knights "chain'd together" in the preceding passage belie the orderliness of the display and suggest a similar wavering between safety and danger.[19]

The rivalry between Antissia and Pamphilia provokes yet another extreme of color and, with the link between beauty and jealousy (which is so key to the earlier vision of the Moor), underscores the competition between women that is at the heart of discourses of beauty. In an almost parodic glance at the artificiality of the trope, Wroth shows us Pamphilia's jealous reaction to Amphilanthus's praise of Antissia:

> But one day as they were alone together, some discourse falling out of the beautie of Ladies, *Amphilanthus* gave so much commendations of *Antissia*, as she betweene dislike, and a modest affection, answered, hee had spoke sufficiently in her praise: for truly my Lord, said she, me thinkes there is not that beautie in her as you speake of, but that I have seene, as faire and delicate as shee; yet in truth shee's very white, but that extreame whitenesse I like not so well, as where that (though not in that fulnesse) is mix'd with sweete lovelinesse; yet I cannot blame you to thinke her peerelesse, who viewes her but with the eyes of affection. *Amphilanthus* gave this reply; That hee till then had never seene so much Womanish disposition in her, as to have so much prettie envie in her, yet in his opinion (except her selfe) he had not seene any fairer, *Antissia* with that came to them, which brought them into other discourses, til they were forced to part. (50–51)

In her friendliness to Antissia, Pamphilia is not able to contradict Amphilanthus's judgment and make Antissia black to her "fair." Instead, she opposes his masculine word with her sight, thereby making the issue his authority in granting "whiteness" rather than her actual beauty. Thus the "extreame whitenesse [she likes] not so well" is not so much Antissia's white complexion as it Amphilanthus's admiration of her. Of course, Am-

---

19. Wroth, of course, has earlier literary models for such use of race in chilvalric display. Philip Sidney gives a description of a procession that incorporates blacks in the display in his *Countess of Pembroke's Arcadia*: "And so, getting on their horses, they travelled but a little way when, in the opening of the mouth of the valley into a fair field, they met with a coach drawn with four milk-white horses furnished all in black, with a black-a-moor boy upon every horse, they all apparelled in white, the coach itself very richly furnished in black and white" (119).

philanthus's very nature (as the lover of many) makes it easy to see how unstable and arbitrary such male designations of fairness are. Part of Pamphilia's "womanish disposition" is not only her jealousy but her exposure of Amphilanthus's masculine right to make women fair or black as he desires and her anticipation of Amphilanthus's inconstant reminder that both Antissia and Pamphilia are fair in his eyes.

In Pamphilia, Wroth locates resistance to the hegemony of male favor and color. After the conversation with Amphilanthus, Pamphilia expresses her sense of being stuck in this system of signification as she talks to the inconstant moon:

> Looking out beheld the Moone, who was then faire and bright in her selfe, being almost at the full, but rounded about with blacke, and broken clouds. Ah *Diana* (said she) how doe my fortunes resemble thee? my love and heart as cleare, and bright in faith, as thou art in thy face, and the fulnesse of my sorrowes in the same substance: and as thy wane must bee, so is my wane of hopes in my love; affections in him, being as cold to me, as thou art in comparison of the Sunnes heate: broken joyes, blacke despaires, incirkling me, as those dissevered clouds do strive to shadow by straight compassing thy best light. (51)

Here we see Pamphilia again recognizing that fairness is imposed, "affections in him, being as cold to me, as thou art in comparison of the Sunnes heate"; refusing to submit to Amphilanthus's inconstancy and thereby read herself as black/unfavored, she is only surrounded by blackness, "blacke despaires, incirkling me, as those dissevered clouds do strive to shadow by straight compassing thy best light." It is at this moment, when she is least favored and, like the moon, not in the light of the sun, that the reader first sees her write.[20]

Of all the female characters, Pamphilia is the only one who continually wishes to be beyond such binary systems. Although it may be that her doubly secure rank as queen of Pamphilia allows her this privilege, the wish is certainly in keeping with her constancy, as well as with her literary heritage: the reconciliation of the opposing virtues of the *Arcadia*'s Philoclea and Pamela (Beilin 215). Pamphilia's wish is, above all, to resist male inscriptions that may deny her subjectivity with their fickle incon-

20. Ann Rosalind Jones suggests that in *Pamphilia to Amphilanthus*, Wroth finds much of her authority in her identification with Night: "Many of the most forceful poems in the sequence establish Night as a feminine figure with whom Pamphilia identifies and through whom she can prove her merit" (146).

stancy. At one such moment of resistance, she projects herself as a "Black-moore":

> Torture me not with sorrowes, I will truly and religiously confesse, I am not worthy of you; but it is not my fault, I wish I were so fit, as you might ever love, and such an one as all the world might thinke fit for you, then I know you would be just: nor wish I this for any benefit, but for your love; for else in the comparison of other gaine unto my selfe, or any other then your loved selfe, I rather would wish to be a Black-moore, or any thing more dreadfull, then allure affection to me, if not from you; thus would I be to merit your loved favour, the other to show my selfe purer, then either purest White or Black: but faith will not prevaile, I am forsaken and despised, why dye I not? it is not fit, no, tis not fit, I still must live, and feele more cause of woe, or better to say, to see my cause of woe. (396)

This complex passage conflates many of the disparate and contradictory strands of the discourse of blackness seen throughout early modern England. First, in wishing "to be a Black-moore, or any thing more dreadfull" rather than attract another's desire, Pamphilia draws on an increasingly common sense that black women are undesireable. Even in the House of Love, the maid projects the undercurrent of that belief in seeing Allimarlus embracing a black woman. Paradoxically, this assumption almost never turns out as anticipated, and men end up in the arms of black women in these texts, perhaps revealing that the male construction of black, female difference is a manifestation of desire complicated by a fear of difference. Hence, the dread inspired by the maid's "Black-moore" is merely an inversion of the desire evoked by a black Cleopatra. However, the wish and the punning desire to "dye" or change color (the latter a form of escape performed by Wroth in the *Masque of Blackness*) is a form of identification as Pamphilia implies that there is a strength in the outsider status of the black female; that is, to not have one's subject position circumscribed by disabling tenets of female beauty (although black women are of course circumscribed by them in other ways).

In Pamphilia's wish to be simultaneously "black" and beloved by Amphilanthus, Wroth draws on the topos of impossibility and highlights the lack of subject position offered by the language of beauty, which does not allow a woman the possibility of being both "black" and favored. Pamphilia's subsequent claim recognizes the implications of her desire. In saying, "Thus would I be to merit your loved favour, the other to show my selfe purer, then either purest White or Black," she again wishes to have a stable—or "pure"—subject position beyond the objectification that accrues from being the focus of (inconstant) male desire. Like the author of her story, she readily acknowledges—and resists—her own subjection to the vagaries of male favor exhibited in the binarism of black and white.

Although I have insisted that the language of beauty and favor that is troped through the dark/light binary works primarily to define females, the manuscript continuation of the *Urania* suggests that Wroth finds this visual schema useful in articulating the romantic status of male characters. In the manuscript continuation Pamphilia marries Rodomandro, the king of Tartaria, who comes from a "sunn-burnt" people (2, fol. 21v) and is described as "an exquisitt man in all things and a Christian" (1, fol. 14v). This knight operates within a color/race schema that from the beginning marks him as unfavored and in some ways peripheral even though he wins Pamphilia's hand. Interestingly, the text never overtly questions this union or marks it as illegitimate because of race (although we might ask whether it makes a difference that this particular union takes place in her kingdom, which seems to be on the borders of Asia); nonetheless, Rodomandro's status as Pamphilia's husband/lover is always contingent, always qualified by Pamphilia's and the reader's knowledge that Amphilanthus is her destined mate. His blackness thereby marks that secondary status as if to assure the reader that the marriage is only temporary. In a quite complicated way, Rodomandro's blackness identifies the alliance as impossible in much the same way that the poetry discussed earlier confirms the impossibility of interracial union even as it toys with it as a possibility.

In many subtle ways, the narrative "others" Rodomandro while never overtly calling into question his desirability. In wooing Pamphilia, Rodomandro tells her that his people (the Tartarians) are "noe Orators," perhaps echoing Othello's self-assessment, "Haply, for I am black, / And have not those soft parts of conversation / That chamberers have" (3.3.263–65). Pamphilia herself marks this "most undesired wedding" (2, fol. 22v) with blackness; she wears black, ostensibly because she is in mourning for her brother when in truth she is mourning the loss of Amphilanthus. Although the marriage is approved by her father, Pamphilia's ambivalent agreement is clearly signaled by her dress and the narrator, who tells us that Pamphilia "had said 'aye,' though nott in soule contented" (2, fol. 22).

Like many of the men in Wroth's work, Rodomandro is described in Petrarchan terms: "His eyes darts shuting sparckling affection in black, butt brightest shining, like tow pointed diamonds sett in black foiles, for indeed most excellent eyes hee had" (2, fol. 21v). Her language describes his blackness in ways that echo descriptions of darkness and sunburn such as I discuss in Chapter 2. He has a face "of curious and exact features. Butt for the couler of itt, itt plainely shewed the sunn had either liked itt to much, and soe had too hard kissed itt, ore in fury of his delicasy had made his beames to strongly to burne him, yett cowld nott take away the perfect sweetnes of his lovliness" (1, fol. 13v). Again, the language of blackness is a language of contradiction. Like the Bride of the Song of Songs, Rodomandro is black *but* handsome: "For *though* black, yett hee had the true parfection of lovliness, and in loveliness the purest beauty" (1, fol. 13v; emphasis mine).

Although the language of disfavor does not operate as overtly as in previous passages, it still underlies the representation of the king of Tartaria. Like the Prince of Morocco in *The Merchant of Venice*, Rodomandro begins his quest for Pamphilia's hand with the assumption that his darkness presents an obstacle to his wooing: "Prowde indeed wee ar, butt onely of Ladys favours, knowing our sunn-burnt faces can butt rarely attain to faire ladys likings" (2, fol. 21v). The marriage is approved by her father, and the text gives no hint that Rodomandro is anything but the perfect lover; nevertheless, his blackness marks him as not a true mate for Pamphilia. Rodomandro's color thus functions much as blackness does for women in other texts, such as *A Midsummer Night's Dream*, to denote one who is out of favor (or at least not truly loved). Unlike Steriamus who, as I have demonstrated, shows his disfavor by temporarily assuming dark armor, Rodomandro's darkness becomes a mark of permanent disfavor, a visual cue that he will never win Pamphilia's love or desire as it is valued in the romance. He is almost literally "the tawny Tartar," who is black and out of favor.

Interestingly, Rodomandro's arrival at court is the occasion of yet another highly (if obscurely) symbolic narrative moment. Rodomandro arrives at court and meets Pamphilia's father while she and Amphilanthus are hunting:

All this while the most rare pieces of admiration were nott yett seene, for Pamphilia and Amphilanthus were rid abroad to hunt a stag, which newes was brought to them of, beeing for couler and greatnes strange, the stag beeing cole blacke, hornes and all, and as big as tow ordinary ones were, onely one white spott on the left side in shape of an arrowe. This beast they went forthe to slay and sawe him and pursued him hottly and fiercly, yett cowld nott kill him, for when they had him (as they thought) att ther bay, as att their dogs, the Queene shuting att him, hee vanisht. Her Arrow flying and lighting, as Cupids owne many times doe, fruictlessly and to little purpose shott only against a shadow, yett this moved them to admirasion, and soe they returned. When beeing arived, they found this brave Tartarian, black as the stag and as humble, giving such testimony of that rather hee wowld seeme to vanish to, then to give the least disrespect to any of that Court. (1, fol. 14)

The stag may in some way represent jealousy, which is a problem that plagues the relationship. Indeed, it is out of jealousy of the Tartarian that Amphilanthus marries in the first place. More important, as the narrator makes clear, the stag also represents Rodomandro ("black as the stag and as humble") and Pamphilia's futile shooting of Cupid's arrow symbolizes their loveless marriage. So too, the stag's vanishing comments obliquely on Rodomandro's place in the manuscript. He is equally ephemeral in the Pamphilia story: their marraige only temporarily impedes the desires of Amphilanthus and Pamphilia. Their son dies shortly after Rodomandro (although, as Lamb points out, he mysteriously reappears later [*Gender and Authorship* 235]), leaving no material trace of the marriage and no bloodline to carry on. Ultimately, the sense of Rodomandro's "difference" and the possible exclusion that appears only faintly in the main narrative seems to become more overt in this scene.

Like Rodomandro, the stag is marked with whiteness; it has "one white spott on the left side," while the dark Rodomandro has "hands soe white as wowld have beecome a great Lady" (1, Fol. 13v). As I will discuss presently, white hands are not uncommon in the *Urania*; nevertheless, in this case, a black figure with white hands bears some further thought. Hands are so richly symbolic that it is difficult to say exactly what Wroth means by including this detail, and I can only gesture toward its many possible meanings. That the stag's white spot is in the shape of an arrow suggests a potential for alliance that a strict black/white binarism might disallow. Rodomandro's white hands would then be the visible sign of the possibility of entrance into a sex/gender system that is particularly sensitive to categories of class and race.

Wroth includes another character with a similar physiology earlier in the manuscript. The choleric Follietto blames his lack of favor in love on his darkness: "One may see . . . what feminine fairnes doth among ladys. My tanned, scorched face cowld gaine noe thing" (1, Fol. 19). The narrator continues:

Wee must goe with Follietto in such rage and distraction for having his hand-somnes disgraced, which hee held most deere and more then in truth de-served, yett hee was, to speake truthe, tollerable and soe enough to bee commended for a very hansom black man, well-shaped for strength, well-featurd of face, butt ill-complexioned, yett had hee exceeding white hands, and they showed a hope his skinn was answerable. For the rest, his minde was only to haughty; els indeed, hee was a gallant man. (1, fol. 19v)

Drawing as it does on the "black but comely" formulation from the Song of Songs, the narrator's description operates much in the same way as Rodomandro's. Given, however, that Follietto's behavior is so linked to his "complexion," Follietto's hands might also be read as a comment on class. In one sense, the "hope his skinn was answerable" may mean that his entire body has the capacity for a more appealing whiteness and is thus black only because of his choler; in another, she might also be suggesting that the signs of whiteness make him answerable or accountable to a code of gentility that he is clearly breaking.

Whiteness (and white hands) are very often a sign of class, and the language of whiteness and fairness thus simultaneously articulates ideologies of race, class, and gender. In Wroth's manuscript, class and race seem to inform the appearance of white hands as much as gender does. The folio describes Celina's hands "said by their unmatched whitenesse, that they were to be adored, not put to use unlessc to cherish hearts, their softnesse knowing no hard worke, could not be cruell, but gentle to wounds, by themselves especially given" (541). Her hands are the sign of membership of (or aspiration to) a leisured, aristocratic class in which bodies are purest white because they can escape signs of labor such as exposure to the sun. In this case, Celina's hands are white because they are "not put to use." So, too, the Forester, Mirasindo, has hands "most excellently faire" (2, fol. 42v) that mark his class heritage—he is the third son of Rosindy and Meriana. As we shall see in the next chapter, hands also become significant in aristocratic portraiture.

Although Follietto rather spitefully alludes to "feminine fairnes" and its attractiveness to ladies, white hands seem to be equally meaningful for men and women. Peter Erickson has pointed out that white hands are significant in courtly love tradition (Erickson, "Representations" 521). We might also remember that in *A Midsummer Night's Dream*, the now-desired Helena's hand becomes whiter than white: "That pure congealed white, high Tarus' snow, / Fann'd with the eastern wind, turns to a crow / When thou holds't up thy hand. O, let me kiss / This princess of pure white, this seal of bliss!" (3.2.141–44). Indeed, Wroth often uses such rhetoric to describe males, and hands become a salient feature. Pamphilia in one instance is able to recognize Amphilanthus by his hands: "His hands bare, she was soone assured who itt was. For though the strongest and bravest man breathing, yett hee had hands of that delicasie for pure whitenes, delicate shape, and softnes as noe lady could compare with

them" (2, fol. 2). Naomi J. Miller notes that this moment marks Amphilanthus as more feminine and suggests that this type of description "parallel[s] his increased capacity for friendship and mutual bonding"
("Engendering Discourse" 167). This reading of Amphilanthus implies
that Wroth marks such qualities as already existing in Rodomandro who,
as Mary Ellen Lamb has noted, is exceptionally chivalrous and, more significantly, responsive to Pamphilia's need to be an independent subject
("Women Readers" 220).

Rodomandro's whiteness may also work to negotiate his entrance into
the text's sex/gender system. It is conceivable that his hands function as
a sign of rank, which then mitigates his race/color status. The joining of
hands is often symbolic of the marriage bond. For example, when Othello,
after suspecting Desdemona, claims, "The hearts of old gave hands; / But
our new heraldry is hands, not hearts" (3.4.46–47), he hints at his suspected loss of Desdemona's love by suggesting that their marriage bond
(signaled by the joining of hands) is now purely legal and ceremonial
rather than affective. The language also suggests a class alliance that is
the basis for many marriages by alluding to the practice of combining the
arms of the new couple. So too, Rodomandro's white hands suggest the
possibility of his alliance with Pamphilia even as his "sunn-burnt" body
marks the couple as mismatched in some way. Rather than by an image
of combined difference—"To checker Limbs with black and white"—to
use John Cleveland's phrase, this marriage would be symbolized by the
joining of white hand to white hand. However, if hands can be symbolic
of a legal rather than an affective union, one might also conclude that
the hands simultaneously disavow this as a true marriage because it is
based on a ceremony, not on feeling.

Paradoxically, Wroth's negotiation of Rodomandro's blackness reveals
just how powerfully the language of beauty and favor seems to shape female subjectivity as well as how that language is shaped by race. We see
her play race and class against each other to negotiate differences within
the world of the romance. However, unlike the black women Wroth
evokes in the printed text, Rodomandro is allowed to be both black and
beautiful (if not favored). The language of blackness indicates Rodomandro's status as a suitor by insisting on his ultimate desirabilty. In this
sense, he is more like the disfavored European males discussed earlier in
the chapter whose darkness never touches their character. The inclusion
of a figure such as Rodomandro, who has to be made to fit into the culture
through strategies of color, clearly demonstrates how a social order seemingly based solely on class is profoundly—if invisibly—racialized.

"An Object in the Midst of Other Objects":
Race, Gender, Material Culture

I came into the world imbued with the will to find
a meaning in things, my spirit filled with the desire
to attain to the source of the world, and then I found
that I was an object in the midst of other objects.
            —Frantz Fanon, "The Fact of Blackness"

Fanon's haunting articulation of colonized black male subjectivity in his *Black Skin, White Masks* has a disturbing resonance when one thinks of the status of blacks in early modern England. A young African, usually male, would have been brought to a world new to him, renamed, and kept as a slave in his younger years. Once in his new "home," he would have found himself in the midst of the objects with African figures that circulated with increasing frequency throughout sixteenth- and seventeenth-century Europe. Before he reached puberty, he might have been made to sit with his master or mistress for a double portrait that would demonstrate his European master's wealth or status, a status largely derived from his own subjugation. The "black skin" of both male and female attendants becomes a key signifier in such portraits: associated with wealth and luxury, it is the necessary element for the fetishization of white skin, the "white mask" of aristocratic identity.

The evidence of visual representation of blacks in this period suggests that long before England gained a foothold in the Atlantic slave trade, blacks played an important role in the symbolic economy of elite culture. Black people were brought to England not only as slaves with the absolute objectification of that state but also as curiosities who represented the riches that could be obtained by European travelers, traders,

212 2 1 2   Things of Darkness

and collectors in Atlantic enterprise.[1] Yi-Fu Tuan insightfully notes that their visibility made these domestics all the more valuable: "Slaves who performed the necessary tasks soon became invisible, but slaves who served luxury needs and prestige retained the visibility of all prized objects" (137–38). The placement of black faces on furniture, flasks, signs, lights, and other artifacts indicates that dark-skinned Africans were objects of symbolic importance and cultural exchange long before they became a numerically significant group in the English population. Later, the appearance of actual black attendants in English portraiture is associated with the increase in consumer goods in the seventeenth century.

In his landmark study of early modern materialism, Chandra Mukerji reminds readers that "the growth of the trading system depended on cultural innovation: the development of social meanings for the new consumer goods" and maintains that a "level of social strain and conceptual discomfort . . . accompanied changes in the meanings of goods. . . . The proliferation of goods and their exchange in the early modern period was an important source of cultural confusion and innovation" (13). Representations of black Africans play a key role in this period of cultural confusion and burgeoning trade: black servants become meta-objects, symbols for the accumulation of profitable foreign goods during this era. The objectification of black people in material culture signifies both the rarity of foreign luxury goods and the subjectivity and value of white owners.[2] In any form, the use of a black figure as a focus of an artist's skill in England was increasingly linked to the use of black people as household slaves and as colonial labor. Unlike any other form of human labor, black African slaves became commodities both literally and symbolically, a difference that also distinguishes the triangular trade from indentured

1. *The Diary of Samuel Pepys* records a clear, if disturbing, use of a black servant as both labor and object of display when he visits the curiosity cabinet of Sir Robert Viner, 7 September 1665: "The window-cases, door-cases, and Chimnys of all the house are Marble. He showed me a black boy that he had that died of a consumption; and being dead, he caused him to be dried in a Oven, and there lies entire in a box" (6:215). In what may be another interesting juxtaposition of black and white, Pepys's entry demonstrates the boy's status as an object/curiosity. The owner's preservation of the male's black body and the way Pepys includes him in the "inventory" with other expensive items (albeit more unusual than the others) suggests a fetishization of the skin that has little to do with labor, although one might consider this continuation of a state of display and servitude an instance of "surplus value."
2. I borrow Arjun Appadurai's definition of luxury goods as "goods whose principal use is *rhetorical* and *social,* goods that are simply *incarnated signs.* The necessity to which *they* respond is fundamentally political" (38). Thus the use of the black servant as a status symbol in England and the continent is in contrast to the use of Africans as slaves on sugar and tobacco plantations.

servitude and previous systems of forced labor.[3] Anthropologist Igor Kopytoff asserts that slavery is a process of commodification: "Effectively, the slave was unambiguously a commodity only during the relatively short period between capture or first sale and the acquisition of the new social identity; and the slave becomes less of a commodity and more of a singular individual in the process of gradual incorporation into the host society" (65). While Kopytoff's general argument does obtain in a few instances in the early modern period, it really applies more to indentured servitude than to the status of most Africans in the period. Portraits work to preserve and display moments that demonstrate the power and superiority of white masters. Thus even if the possibility of freedom existed, the portrayal of black slaves with white masters in effect visually imprisoned black Africans in Kopytoff's first stage in which they were "unambiguously" commodities.

This chapter first examines the circulation of court jewels as racially coded signifiers of aristocratic identity in the late sixteenth century and then turns to the "black servant" portrait that becomes fashionable in England in the mid-seventeenth century, reaching its apex just as England charters its first Royal African Companies, but continuing in popularity well into the eighteenth century. Miniature jewels and portraits were the more prominent site for the display of black images in English visual culture and, not coincidentally, were forms more directly linked with the presentation of European aristocratic identity than any other artifacts. Art historians connect the increase in portraiture to the rise of individualism in the Renaissance, and the circulation of jewels also played a smaller role in the formation of aristocratic identity. Furthermore, jewels are connected not only to the miniature portrait but also to the circulation of sonnets, which, as I argued in Chapter 2, are the site of England's earliest colonialist discourses.

More important, it is in the language of visual culture that the racial valences of the dark/light dichotomy can be seen most clearly. The art historian Albert Boime suggests that racial signifiers are deeply embedded in the very language of art:

Negro is the Spanish and Portuguese word for the color *black*. Black is a pigment indispensable to artistic practice. Once the color black was applied to an ethnic group then peoples were differentiated like the colors arrayed on a palette, with *negro* at one end of the scale and *blanco* (*branco* in Portuguese)

---

3. For a discussion of the difference in black servitude in colonial America, see Basil Davidson, *The African Slave Trade.*

at the other. . . . The confusion of formalistic categories with ideological bi-
ases is a singular phenomenon in the history of art that has been sorely
neglected. The racial opposition of black and white derives from the color
scale; the famous *chiaroscuro,* or light and dark polarity, is intimately associated
with the religious dualism of Good and Evil; and the compositional isolation
of figures or inanimate motifs that is so central to the semiotics of Western
art becomes decoded as exclusionary in the political sense. (1–2)[4]

As Boime so cogently describes, the very language of color in art encodes
racial, political ideologies; the inclusion of Africans in Western art in many
cases merely serves to demonstrate their exclusion from Western culture.
Black Africans are thus not included in the "process of gradual incorporation into the host society" (Kopytoff 65) and, in representation, rarely
reach a state of "de-commoditization."[5] Given the international circulation of both portraits and portrait painters, I would hesitate to characterize the black servant portrait as an English phenomenon. Such portraits
appear in most European countries; however, the historian Allison Blakeley points out that England is second only to the Lowlands in the circulation of such images (105). This is not surprising given the early links
between England and the Netherlands. More important, it suggests that
England likewise had a special interest in creating public displays of whiteness.

At the end of Chapter 2, I suggested that the poetic exchange between
Sir Francis Bacon and George Herbert beginning with Herbert's couplet
"My Lord, a Diamond to mee you sent, / And I to you a Blackamoore
present" (Grosart 2:164), evoked an early trade of diamonds and black
Africans. However, there is possibly another level of exchange operating
here as well. Just as Herbert's poetic gift exchange allows for a wavering
between a black person and the poem and the diamond and poem, it also
suggests the exchange of jewels. His metonymic formulation offers multiple possibilities of exchange and representation within a language of
blackness. One might as easily imagine an exchange of a "blackmoor"
cameo from Italy with "moor's head" diamond earrings such as those
owned by Queen Anne (Scarisbruck 229), which similarly confirms a re-

4. Boime continues, "The predominance of black bile gave the skin a 'swarthy' appearance. Hence 'emotional expressiveness' in art took the form of skin coloration in the early
history of Western art, as well as of the grotesque and caricatured physiognomies that dehumanized various ethnic and social groups in the service of oppression" (5).

5. I do not include in this category the stunning portraits done by Eeckhout, Rembrandt,
and Rubens, among others, but these pieces are far outnumbered by the master/slave portraits that, I would argue, are more indicative of a cultural milieu, for they are generated to
a greater degree by the desires of the consuming public.

lationship between European subjects and establishes their dominance over the foreign others that are the object of exchange.

The circulation of jewels, as much as poems, was an integral part of court culture (Fumerton 69). More jewelry was worn in the sixteenth century than before or since, much of it inspired by European involvement in travel and trade (Cocks 16).[6] Pendants and brooches were made in the shapes of ships, elephants, and the various sea monsters that were the stuff of travel lore. According to Patricia Fumerton, both jewels and poems were seen as "ornamental" and both worked to establish subjectivity in much the same way. The incessant exchange of ornaments among aristocrats marked the boundaries of aristocratic identity, continually asserting a "private" self in an atmosphere of public display and exchange (68–70). This somewhat paradoxical mode of marking aristocratic identity with the display and exchange of objects becomes in fact the creation of a "white mask" of English identity when the objects kept for display are adorned with representations of black Africans.

The wearing of black cameos became a fad in European courts; these cameos were mass-produced in Italian workshops during the last quarter of the sixteenth century (*Princely Magnificence* 70).[7] Joan Evans quotes part of a 1576 inventory list from the goldsmith John Mabbe that includes "a brouche of gold like a Mores-head, the ground being Mother of pearl . . . a broache with a very fair Agott like a Blackamore enamelled all white about the said agott . . . a jewell with an Agott having a woman cut on it like a More" (98). The increased circulation of these gems was also part of the Renaissance's renewed interest in and emulation of classical antiquity (Cocks 15). Many pieces were restorations of antique classical gems, as in the antique pendant shown in figure 6, which has been re-made and surrounded with modern additions—black figurines and scarabs. These additions make the pendant a peculiarly Renaissance piece with its combination of classical past and increased interest in the newly discovered variety in foreign cultures. Still other jewels were simply given a classical "air" with the inclusion of classical garb, as in the double "Moor and emperor" cameo in figure 7 and the single cameo of a black male in figure 8. Later in England the association of Africans with classical

6. This was also the first era in which princes "made a formal association between certain specific jewels and their own dynasty, declaring them to be inalienable heirlooms" (*Princely Magnificence* 3).

7. Patricia Fumerton and Roy Strong ascribe this to an increased supply of black onyx in the period, but there are such cameos made of white sardonyx as well as artifacts made of other materials. It may be that more black onyx is used and that these cameos are in part sparked by the importance of blackness in the sonnet as well.

Figure 6. Gem with scarabs. Jewels were frequently remade from older pieces. The middle scene is evidently Roman. The scarabs and outer figures are sixteenth-century additions. (Royal Collection of Her Majesty Queen Elizabeth II.)

Figure 7. A double-sided cameo. Other Moor and emperor cameos feature a white man and a black man. Such cameos would have been exchanged as gifts and kept in curiosity cabinets as well as worn by the owner. (Kunsthistorisches Museum.)

antiquity is realized in the practice of giving servants classical-sounding names such as Pompey or Scipio (Fryer 24; Tuan 146), which, with its supposedly comic juxtaposition of high and low culture, mimics a larger pattern of African degeneration and Greco-Roman ascendancy.[8] It also suggests another way in which England linked its classical past with its current pursuit of empire. The humanist project of restoring the glories of classical antiquity also helped England find an imperial model to imitate in the expansion of its own borders. This blend of Africa and Rome is especially intriguing in the Diana cameos (see figure 9). The quiver of arrows and the crescent moon headpiece, which mark this as a Diana figure, are also the symbols used to connect Elizabeth to Diana (Strong, *Miniature* 85). There is no tradition of a black Diana in European art; however, Diana was traditionally the protector of slaves. Furthermore, her temple at Ephesus was said to have been built by Amazons and, as we saw in Chapter 1, Amazons quickly become linked with African and Asian women in early colonialist discourses.

More specific examples of jewel exchanges confirm the relationship be-

8. I owe this point to John Michael Archer's paper " 'False Soul of Egypt': Antiquity and Degeneration in *Antony and Cleopatra*," circulated at the Shakespeare Association of America panel, "Race, Ethnicity and Power in Shakespeare and His Contemporaries" (April, 1993).

Figure 8. These "Moor's head" cameos were mass-produced in Italian workshops and sold throughout Europe during the last quarter of the sixteenth century. Each took approximately three months to complete. (Kunsthistorisches Museum.)

tween developing white English subjectivity and self-representation and the use of blacks as decorative signifiers. The well-known Gresley jewel features a black woman surrounded by Cupids (figure 10). The jewel covers the miniature portraits of Catherine Walsingham and Sir Thomas Gresley (figure 11) and commemorates the couple's marriage. Fumerton suggests that such covers serve to protect and hide the private self even as they structurally reveal the private inside of the pendants (74). Additionally, the cover may actually create the "outer" self in that the black outside cover must be opened to reveal the white skins within. As I maintained in Chapter 1, the image of a white embedded in darkness, of discovering and merchandising a precious whiteness from "dark" continents is a typical colonialist gesture in Elizabethan England that works to define and preserve the value of whiteness. More significant, the black cameo is on the obverse side of Catherine Walsingham's miniature, which implies a special connection between white femininity and blackness which I shall return to later in this chapter.

Figure 9. The quiver of arrows and the crescent moon headpiece identify this cameo as a representation of Diana. As in the later portraits, most of the black figures in cameos wear pearl earrings. (Kunsthistorisches Museum.)

Elaborating on the paradox of public/private within Elizabethan gift culture, Fumerton further asserts: "On the one hand, the public self faced outward upon gift culture: it 'gave' of itself selflessly for the increase of the commonality (or put less idealistically, for a particular regime of commonality). On the other hand, the private self faced inward toward secrecy: it *withheld* itself from the cultural whole" (69). This jewel embodies both gestures: the enclosing of the portrait within the case of blackness hides the self just as the opening of the case reveals the aristocratic bodies within. However, this particular jewel also celebrates a public event—the marriage of Walsingham and Gresley—and thus represents another type of "increase" as well. If it "tells little of the couple's love," as Fumerton notes (74), it speaks volumes about the social function of marriage: the duplication/replication of the self through procreation and the continuation of aristocratic bloodlines. Such a commemorative jewel speaks to this "increase of the commonality" and lends added resonance to the declaration that opens Shakespeare's sonnets: "From *fairest* creatures we desire increase" (1.1; emphasis added). Both the jewel and Shakespeare's

Figure 10. The Gresley jewel, purportedly given by Elizabeth I to Sir Thomas Gresley and his wife, Catherine Walsingham, to commemorate their marriage. Much jewelry of the time featured mermaids and other fanciful sea creatures. (The Pennington-Mellor-Munthe Trust; photograph, Courtauld Institute of Art.)

Figure 11. An inside view of the Gresley jewel. The miniatures of Gresley (1522–1610) and Walsingham (1559–1585) are by Nicholas Hilliard. (The Pennington-Mellor-Munthe Trust; photograph, Courtauld Institute of Art.)

sonnet rely on the association of aristocratic identity with the Elizabethan cult of fairness.

Perhaps the best known of these black cameos is the Drake pendant (figure 12), given to Sir Francis Drake by Queen Elizabeth during the winter of 1586–87. According to Roy Strong, this jewel is notable because "it pinpoints exactly the moment when this act became an acknowledged sign of regal favour" (*English Renaissance Miniature* 85). From the moment of this gift, the queen's miniature portrait (figure 13) became a popular and coveted personal adornment, and the mass production of her legendary "fairness" began in earnest. Not much is known about the occasion for Drake's receipt of the portrait.[9] In 1586 Drake, authorized to raid the Spanish West Indies, returned from this first voyage as a naval commander. Although the voyage was not a financial success, his capture of Santo Domingo and Cartegna (and the destruction of a Spanish fort in Florida) did substantially raise English morale (Hampden 248). The jewel itself has a black African profile superimposed on a white European profile; it may be yet another version of a "Moor and emperor" cameo. It is, however, tempting to speculate that this is a reference of sorts to Drake's success over the Spanish. Anti-Spanish rhetoric in England often made note of Spain's ill-defined—and therefore dubious—racial origins: these twin heads may be a sign of that mixture.[10] More concretely, enclosing this representation of the queen's fairness within a black jewel again makes material the creation of "fairness" as a particular quality of Englishness.

Significantly, this jewel is featured in a Gheeraerts portrait of Drake done in 1594 (figure 14). One hand rests on a globe that is turned to display the continent of Africa. This gesture may be a reminder of his famous circumnavigation, which would also involve, as I suggested in the Introduction, a conquering of Africa. It might also visually represent English desires for "possession" of Africa, made possible by breaking Spanish control over that trade. The pendant itself is visually linked to the globe. The objects are parallel to each other, and both contain the only bright color in the portrait: the rubies of the pendant are linked to the red lines indicating the Tropics of Cancer and Capricorn above and below the continent. As a closed locket, the jewel covers the portrait of Elizabeth

9. The correct date was only comparatively recently changed from 1574 to 1586.

10. This would be a highly ironic gesture as well, given Camden's recording of the earlier controversy over Drake's "most inhumanely exposed in an island that negro or blackamore maid who had been gotten with child in his ship" (reprinted in Hampden, *Francis Drake, Privateer* 244). As I noted in the Introduction, Drake was involved in England's entrance into the slave trade on other levels as well.

Figure 12. The Drake jewel, presented to Sir Francis Drake by Elizabeth I in the winter of 1586–87. The cover has a black male head superimposed on a white female head. Note again the pearl earring. (Reproduced by kind permission of Sir George Meyrick, Bt.)

Figure 13. Inside view of the Drake jewel. The phoenix, emblem of Elizabeth I, appears on the inside cover, which opens to reveal a miniature portrait of Elizabeth by Nicholas Hilliard. This jewel contains the first miniature portrait given as a sign of Elizabeth's favor. (Reproduced by kind permission of Sir George Meyrick, Bt.)

Figure 14. Sir Francis Drake (1540?–1596), by Gheeraerts the Younger. Drake is wearing the jewel given to him by Elizabeth I. The rubies in the jewel visually connect it to the globe, which shows a view of Africa. (National Maritime Museum.)

inside, hinting at a private relationship with the queen while publicly advertising Drake's status as adventurer-gentleman. The positioning of the pendant near his genitals links Drake's imperial and navigational prowess with his masculinity. Louis Montrose's persuasive readings of the psychology of the male subject and female queen in court culture provides for a reading of Drake's representation of imperial/masculine prowess against the overwhelming fact of Elizabeth's power: "Within legal and fiscal limits, she held the power of life and death over every Englishman, the power to advance or frustrate the worldly desires of all her subjects. Her personality and personal symbolism helped to mold English culture and the consciousness of Englishmen for several generations" (Montrose, "Shaping Fantasies" 77). If Montrose is correct, then the placement of this gift, hinting at a certain intimacy between ruler and subject, might in this portrait paradoxically reflect Drake's imperial and masculine pride as well as a certain unease in relation to a powerful female ruler.

Male Portraits, Property, and Colonial Might

Drake's portrait is in some ways a harbinger of a later trend in portraiture. Wearing black cameos seemed to occur in inverse proportion to commissioning portraits with black slaves. Although this could be due in part to the increased slave trade in England, it is nonetheless true that shortly after the vogue for Mannerist jewelry of that sort tapered off, English men and women increasingly included black attendants in their portraits. Instead of wearing static images of Africans, colonizers in the mid-seventeenth century heightened the juxtaposition of black and white in the cameo by representing themselves with African children. Male portraits such as Drake's help link colonial practice and masculinity, while the more numerous female portraits realize the already existing ideologies of fairness and femininity found in lyric poetry within a context of consumerism and acquisition.

In less complex ways than the cameo and portrait miniature, the portrait also served to create aristocratic identity. Richard Brilliant compellingly demonstrates that portraiture is "a particular phenomenon of representation in Western art that is especially sensitive to changes in the perceived nature of the individual in Western society" (8). In the case of early modern England, portraiture provides fascinating clues to other areas of social change, such as England's increasing involvement in Atlantic trade, and to the ways in which those changes help shape English identity. Throughout Europe the aristocracy kept black slaves and dwarfs as evidence of social rank and privilege (Campbell 134).[11] Commenting on this phenomenon, the art historian Lorne Campbell articulates another use for such figures when he quotes Brantôme, who "could envisage a situation in which 'an excellent painter . . . , having executed the portrait of a very beautiful and pleasant-looking lady, places next to her an old hag, a moorish slave or a hideous dwarf, so that their ugliness and blackness may give greater lustre and brilliance to her beauty and fairness'" (quoted in Campbell 134). Portraits with black slaves, in addition to being more popular than portraits with dwarves or crones, are specifically shaped by the contrast between dark and light skins, which links the representation of black and white to the organization of property and gender that I have outlined in previous chapters. Portraits in particular chart the ongoing commodification of black bodies as England becomes more dependent on an involvement with Africa for economic expansion and symbolic definition. The early portrait of Peregrine Bertie, Lord Willoughby d'Eresby (figure 1), that I mentioned in the Introduction is interesting in that it marks some transitional moments between the Christian iconography of blackness and the actual appearance of black Africans in English art and literature. Here, as in most portraits, the black attendant is a liminal figure who inhabits edges, corners, and shadows and thus never fully "participates" in the painting. In this case he appears to have barely made it into the portrait. His posture suggests submission to both rider and horse and, by contrast, associates whiteness with power and dominance. It is also typical in that the black attendant is often a type of groom who may also reflect a social practice; black Africans seemed to have first been utilized as grooms or personal valets. I would argue that these attendants always work as figures for the exotic or foreign and are therefore associated with travel in a general sense; however, here the portrait seems to play with the name "Peregrine" in its depiction of Bertie on what is assumed to be his "final" journey. More important, the attendant carries a *memento mori,* marking this portrait as posthumous, and locating his black skin within traditional Christian associations of the color black with death and melancholy. Finally, the darkness of his skin and the icon are in startling contrast to the whiteness of the horse and rider, illustrating the use of blackness in art to render whiteness visible and, in this case, overpowering.

There is a clear difference in both the number and the manner of portrayals of white men and women; such gendered distinctions suggest

11. For more on the practice of keeping dwarves, see Erica Tietze-Conrat, *Dwarfs and Jesters in Art.* Peter Fryer documents the keeping of black servants as pets and entertainers, as do Nigel File and Chris Powers in *Black Settlers in Britain, 1555–1958.*

that black bodies served different needs for white, English men and women. Portraits of men tend to focus solely on rendering visible the power of the sitter, whereas portraits of women suggest subtle links between the status of women and slaves within the dominance of white over black.

Although vastly outnumbered by the women, several prominent male English colonizers had paintings of themselves done with their black servants. Prince Rupert, son of Elizabeth of Bohemia and cousin to Charles II, was a largely successful naval officer for the Royalist forces, whose career was interspersed with attempts at plantation in Africa, the West Indies, and the Americas. Rupert was intended to be governor of Madagascar under the failed settlement scheme proposed by Lord Arundel. His most recent biographer credits him with popularizing the practice of keeping black servants (Morrah 280). Significantly, Rupert was also a founding shareholder of the reorganized Company of Royal Adventurers Trading into Africa in 1663 and led England's attempt to break the Dutch stranglehold on African trade, enabling the English to establish a significant foothold in the transatlantic slave trade (Galenson 13; Hutton 219). He and his men pirated ships around Guinea and the Gambia, where he was wounded by Gambian natives. This particular child was evidently acquired in a New Year's Day battle in which one of Rupert's men shot a camel on which a man was escaping with his family: "But the rider soon remounted another, that sav'd himself and his wife, but for hast left a Male child behind them, which by Providence was guided to his H, as a New Yeares gift" (quoted in Morrah 264).[12]

Both the aggression recounted in the narrative and the mystification of the child's capture as a "gift from God" are duplicated in the Mytens portrait of Rupert (figure 15). The painting offers a standard colonial dynamic of dominant, powerful white with the submissive, even adoring, subaltern. Not mere marginalization and exclusion in Boime's sense but the visible exercise of power is a crucial element of the male portrait. While portraits of both sexes depend on the gaze of the black servant to direct the spectator's gaze and to promote the superiority of the sitter, the male portraits operate on the specific exercise of militaristic/phallic power. In his discussion of the Manichean aesthetic in colonial literature

12. A transcription of the original papers describing Rupert's sea voyages can also be found in Warburton, who is the primary resource for Rupert's popular biographers; however, his accuracy has been cast into doubt, and I thus have used Morrah's transcription. Although Morrah does not connect the captured child with the figure in the portrait, another biographer, Maurice Ashley, includes an engraving of this portrait and claims that it is the same child (144).

Figure 15. Prince Rupert, count Palatine (1619–1682), by Daniel Mytens. Born in Prague, Rupert was a popular cousin of Charles II and a commander of the king's forces during the Civil War. He was a founding member of the Company of the Royal Adventurers of England Trading into Africa as well as of its successor, the Royal African Company. (Collection of the Duke of Brunswick-Lunebourg [1952]; photograph, Courtauld Institute of Art.)

Abdul JanMohamed points out that the desire to be recognized by the other is a fundamental desire ideally fulfilled in colonialism. The exercise of military force is used to create the fantasy of loving recognition: "By thus subjugating the native, the European settler is able to compel the Other's recognition of him and, in the process, allow his own identity to become deeply dependent on his position as master" (85). The most obvious function of black attendants is to provide this "loving recognition" within subjugation: they are always positioned so as to look up (often from behind) at the sitter. Although the child is marginalized within the space of the portrait, Rupert's identity as sitter depends on just such simultaneous gestures of power (the firmly clenched baton) and benevolence (the hand that rests lightly and patronizingly on the head) suggested by JanMohamed.[13] Consequently, Rupert here is identified as both white and powerful. Just as the gazes never meet, the touching is never reciprocal. Many of the portraits prefigure a later capitalist dynamic articulated by bell hooks: "When bodies contact one another, touch, it [is] almost always a white hand doing the touching, white hands that rest on the bodies of colored people, unless the Other is a child" (*Black Looks* 29).

Although the servant is not African, an earlier Van Dyck portrait of the earl of Denbigh evokes a similar dynamic of might and recognition (figure 16). In Denbigh's portrait, the flintlock is juxtaposed with the benevolently opened hand. This portrait may commemorate his trip to India in 1631 and suggests that England's colonial impulses are not realized solely by African slaves, although the prevalence of black Africans in such portraits suggests not only a more widespread slavery but also that the skin color has an additional cultural resonance.[14] The Indian here is used not so much to juxtapose dark and light skin as to heighten the exoticism of the landscape. He appears to be made part of the cultural "scene" in a way in which the black attendants (such as the man in Peregrine Bertie's portrait with its bleak landscape) are not. Like the Indian boy in *A Mid-*

13. Even if this is not the same child captured in the Gambia, as Maurice Ashley contends, Rupert's history with the child offers an interesting study of an actual social practice and of the ways in which the racist practices of historical figures are duplicated by modern interpreters. Rupert evidently gave this boy to his cousin, Frederick William of Brandenberg, who had him baptized and educated. We can only presume that he was given a name as well. Ashley further denies him human status, commenting that the boy "was subsequently to figure as 'the little nigger' in Rupert's life story as much as his dog Boye had done in his younger days" (147). No source is given for the "little nigger" quotation, and the reader is thus left with no way to determine whether this is a term from an original account, or Ashley's own language.

14. Peoples from India and Africa are often conflated in representation under the rubric of blackness. Anthony Barthelemy documents such semantic confusion in his *Black Face, Maligned Race*.

Figure 16. William Fielding, first earl of Denbigh (d. 1643), by Sir Anthony Van Dyck. Denbigh evidently commissioned this portrait after his trip to India in 1631. Although he had little military experience, he was given several important commands. (The trustees of the National Gallery.)

summer Night's Dream, this servant/guide is subtly associated with exotic foreign commodities. The painting is almost split in half, with Denbigh on the left with a more English-looking landscape and the boy on the right side of the painting with the valuable objects—parrots and coconuts—associated with India and, later, Africa. Jan Huygen van Linschoten, in his observations of the East Indies, declares that the coconut tree is "the most profitable tree of all India" as he catalogs the many commodities it can produce (Purchas 10.298). So, too, parrots are associated with riches and profit almost with the first stirrings of colonial travel. Todorov recounts a 1495 letter to Columbus that reads, "The great part of valuable things come from very hot regions, of which the inhabitants are black, or parrots" (21).[15] This association of blackness and valuable goods underlies most visual representation, and parrots often appear in European iconography of Africa and America. In his ignored beckoning, the boy also evokes another colonialist trope. Descriptions of commodities—indeed,travel literature itself—are always suffused with the promise of more. India and Africa, in particular, are associated with profitable and endless fecundity; in paintings, the servants are always offering something—usually jewels or flowers. Here, in particular, the boy stands at the site of riches and seems to offer more.

The connections of the black servant portrait with colonial expansion are even more pronounced in the Soest portrait of Cecil Calvert, the second baron of Baltimore (figure 17). In his discussion of the Lord Baltimore portraits, Ellis Waterhouse notes the Soest painting's distinctive difference from the earlier, more austere, Mytens portrait of the father, George Calvert (figure 18): "But this imposed austerity is compensated for by a luxury of incidental detail, which makes it one of the most fascinating portraits painted in England in the seventeenth century" (102). Rather than read these objects as "incidental detail," we might view them as examples of the "trivial" objects that Fumerton sees as so important to the constitution of the English subject. Calvert's portrait clearly evokes his father's stance—he stands next to the table that holds the "domestic" hat—and thus is meant to comment upon the earlier portrait. Here again, the black attendant is included on the periphery of the portrait with other expensive acquisitions; however, the gaze of the attendant focuses the viewer's eye to the center of the portrait, to Baltimore's statement of dynastic progression and colonial possession indicated by the centrally lo-

15. LeCourbeiller also notes the appearance of parrots in association with "America" in representations of the four continents (211).

Figure 17. This portrait of Cecil Calvert, second baron of Baltimore (1606–1675), by Gerard Soest is interesting for its luxurious trappings. The child holding the map with him has not been satisfactorily identified except as a close family member. The black attendant directs the observer's gaze to the map of the Calvert holdings in Maryland embellished with the family coat of arms. (Courtesy Enoch Pratt Free Library, Baltimore, © EPFL.)

Figure 18. The austerity of this Daniel Mytens portrait of George Calvert, the first baron of Baltimore (1580?–1632), contrasts strikingly with the later portrait of his son Cecil. Calvert was the secretary of state under James I. (Courtesy Enoch Pratt Free Library, Baltimore, © EPFL.)

cated map. Those "incidental" details are key to the second Lord Baltimore's presentation of dynastic and colonial success.

The first baron of Baltimore, after spending the earlier part of his life more directly involved in affairs of state as secretary of state under James I, dedicated himself to the plantation movement that was increasingly gathering steam. After attempting settlements first in Newfoundland (which his Catholicism and the climate made difficult) and later in Virginia, Calvert requested a royal patent for the regions north and south of the Potomac but died two months before the patent was sealed in June 1632. The charter of Maryland was obtained by his son, Cecil Calvert. Cecil sent a group of colonists to be governed by his brother, Leonard, while he remained in England to secure the patent, which was continually under attack. Cecil Calvert, despite his intentions, never set foot in his colony; however, his Soest portrait clearly attempts to efface the many difficulties of possession and ownership that thwarted his colonial aspirations. The elder Calvert and the younger hold between them a map of Maryland with the family coat of arms, suggesting a peaceful, orderly inheritance and transfer of property. The black attendant, his gaze on the child, focuses the spectator's gaze on the future of Maryland rather than on its beleaguered present. In giving such prominence to the family seal, Soest not only draws on a distinctly English custom of placing family markers on luxurious acquisitions but also establishes the prominence of the family name and ownership in competition with the original naming of the land "Mary-land" after Henrietta Maria.

Along with the specific negotiation of land ownership, the painting also makes a larger comment on the increase in the fortunes of the Calvert family. The painting of grandfather and grandson, with its evocation of the first baron of Baltimore, denotes a world of increasing luxury and ownership. The original table and hat are now overshadowed by sumptuous printed fabrics in brilliant colors—particularly evident in the carpet and the "Persian vest" worn by Calvert. The oriental carpet, according to Brian Spooner, represents "the epitome of Western concern with alien things—especially utilitarian alien things" (195). The "Persian vest," a fashion introduced by Charles II in 1666, was a deliberate attempt to distance English dress from its traditional imitation of French fashion. George Savile suggests national pride as an impetus for the innovation: "About that time a general humour in opposition to France had made us throw off their fashion and put on vests, that we might look more like a distinct people, and not be under the servility of imitation" (quoted in DeBeer 111). Paradoxically, the vest undermined the very ideals it was meant to embody: national distinction and thrift. The vests evidently were

Figure 19. Dressed in an animal skin, the attendant in this Daniel Mytens portrait of Charles I (1600–1649) and Henrietta Maria (1609–1669) seems to be deliberately exoticized; it was more common for such grooms to wear the family livery. The monkey and dog in the foreground mimic the stance of the groom and the horse and thus may evoke a connection between apes and blacks which became more common later. (Serlby Hall [1971]; photograph, Courtauld Institute of Art.)

no less expensive than any other garment, and many noblemen appeared on the scene with richly embroidered vests. Certainly the emphasis was taken away from French fashion, only to associate the court with Eastern, "oriental" nations. This pairing of portraits demonstrates the almost inescapable link between blackness and aristocratic consumption.

Another family group, the Mytens portrait of Charles I and Henrietta Maria (figure 19), uses almost all the popular tropes outlined earlier by Brantôme, including the black attendant, the dwarves, dogs, and monkeys that also became popular in portraiture. In many cases these figures represent a faithful servitude or marginal humanity that only reinforces the supposed humanity and dominance of the sitter. According to Jonathan Goldberg this particular portrait celebrates a new Stuart ideology of domestic married love, with the couple united "in their pleasure and vir-

Figure 20. A Diepenbeck engraving of a Turkish horse and groom from the 1657 book *Methode et invention nouvelle de dresser les chevaux* (A New Method and Invention to Dress Horses), by William Cavendish, first duke of Newcastle. There are five such engravings; each seemingly uses the national dress and the color of the grooms to identify the horse's breed. (By permission of the Folger Shakespeare Library.)

tue" (15). Perhaps this ideology also includes the domestication of difference, with the exoticized black groom enclosed within the cultivated landscape. He wears not a standard livery that we see on other grooms, as in the Diepenbeck engraving (figure 20), but a leopard skin, and his horse wears an oriental carpet, which calls attention to luxury consumption. The figure thus has the dual symbolic and economic function noted by Alain Locke: the black page "though grounded in slavery, still preserved something of the exotic" (139).

Indeed there is something of the "ceaseless overrunning and excess" of the carnivalesque (Stallybrass and White 8) in the portrait: the monkey in the lower left corner seems to be parodying the groom and the horse specifically and the human domestication of the horse in general. The juxtaposition of these figures with the black groom is all the more compelling, given European assertions of the alleged affinity of Africans, apes, and monkeys evoked in later travel literature (Jordan 29, 228). However, as Goldberg notes, this excess is represented within an atmosphere of restraint, evoked most obviously by Jeffrey Hudson's holding of the dogs at bay and the stasis of the royal couple in comparison with the almost frenetic activity around them. Not coincidentally, the "accessories" in this portrait are also the attractions in carnival. There is, however, always the element of moderation and control, a class difference much like that between Prospero's control and use of Caliban as a personal slave and Trinculo's projected use of him as a carnival attraction. Equally significantly, the black figure in these paintings is almost always made to offer something to the white sitter (if nothing but looks of adoration), a gesture that makes the sitter recipient of goods and perpetuates the ownership of the slave.

As the herald of a new ideology, this portrait may also be a negative comment on the van Somer portrait of Queen Anne (figure 21), who is also about to go hunting. She stands directly in front of a black groom who is her size, with her favorite castle, Oatlands, in the background. Charles I and Henrietta Maria's reign was characterized by a sense of temperance and domestic devotion in comparison with the excess and incompatibility of James and Anne. In a similar manner, the restraint that Goldberg sees in the Mytens is in subtle distinction from the sensuality of Anne's stance. Instead of being spread throughout the portrait, here the "company" surrounds Anne, almost enclosing her: the dog pawing at her dress (Hudson pulls the dog back in the Mytens) and the groom with the horse behind her, almost overtaking her. While this portrait is atypical in its inclusion of an adult black male, it is typical in its relegation of that male to the shadowy background of the portrait. In many such portraits black people literally become shadow, the key effect in chiaroscuro.[16]

16. Allison Blakeley contends that this invisibility is also a compelling feature of Dutch painting—"They seem often to go unnoticed, at least by the conscious eye" (115)—and shrewdly notes that art historians frequently ignore these servants as well. In England, many of these portraits are cataloged as having one sitter. Penshurst has a striking double portrait that features a full-length view of either Rupert or his brother, Frederick, and a black attendant who is both the same size as the European sitter and in full view.

Figure 21. The black groom who stands between Anne of Denmark (1574–1619) and her horse is barely visible in this Paul van Somer painting. Both Anne and James I clearly had a penchant for the unusual and exotic. Anne asked to appear in blackface at one of her earliest English court entertainments, Ben Jonson's *Masque of Blackness.* (Royal Collection of Her Majesty Queen Elizabeth II.)

Beauty, Colonialism, and the Female Subject

> She hath always two necessary Implements about her, a *Blackamoor*, and a
> little *Dog*, for without these, she would be neither *Fair* nor *Sweet*.

In this passage from the 1676 treatise *The Character of a Town Misse*, the
writer's description reflects an actual social practice that in this case connects the commodification of white women in prostitution and blacks in
slavery. Such a social practice demonstrates "the ways in which whiteness is
related to blackness, materially and emotionally dependent on it yet still
holding sway over it" (Dyer 54) and had far-reaching consequences. Edward Scobie notes that such slaves "belonged to the first sizeable colored
community in Britain" (9). Although this practice seems to have begun in
the latter half of the seventeenth century, it was prepared for by the black/
white binarism which ultimately suggests that white femininity and beauty
truly exist only when posed next to blackness. This passage gives evidence of
an early way in which the black servant might become a figure for illicit sexuality; a practice that becomes extremely popular in later centuries (Gilman
79); however, in this period the evocation of sexuality seems to take place
within a dynamic of fairness that is not as thoroughly sexualized.[17]

Certainly any discussion of beauty must begin with the Petrarchan rhetoric that "informed the Renaissance norm of a beautiful woman" (Vickers, "Diana Described" 95). As I argued in Chapter 2, the paradox of
black beauty creates women who are "beamy black," with "golden hair,"
"coral lips," and "ivory brows"—curious hybrids of black and white, flesh
and jewel. In visual representation, the "black *but* comely" formulation
that begins the Song of Songs fractures into opposition of African and
European women in later portraits in which English women construct
white beauty by juxtaposing themselves with African servants. The control
of women in Petrarchan rhetoric and the subsequent use of that rhetoric
in travel literature is, as Nancy Vickers points out, "a legacy shaped predominately by the male imagination for the male imagination; it is, in
large part, the product of men talking to men about women" (Vickers,
"Blazon" 96). Nevertheless, it is no less true that women also actively

---

17. Sander Gilman notes that "one of the central functions of the black servant in the
visual arts of the eighteenth and nineteenth centuries was as a maker of the sexualization of
the society in which he or she was found" (79). Although he is quite correct that "the
association of the black with concupiscence reaches back into the Middle Ages" (79), and
many of these portraits are of mistresses, there still seem to me to be other social pressures
to which the presence of the black servant responds.

participated in the rhetoric of fairness and that black/white dichotomies become key to their attempts to acquire subjectivity and literary authority. An ambivalent sense of identification and difference permeates early modern artistic and social practices as well. In either case, we see white women exercising dominion over blacks as a way of controlling, if not countering, the manipulative rhetoric of beauty.

David Dabydeen begins his study of black figures in Hogarth with a discussion of the widespread presence of black boys in Renaissance portraits of women. He asks: "Why were white women, from the evidence of Portrait Painting, and from social records, so fond of possessing little black boys—what psychological and sexual politics and neuroses were at play in the English boudoir or bedroom?" (39). Dabydeen seems to imply here that the overwhelming prevalence of these portraits of women over those of men represents some pathology of white women. Although Dabydeen does qualify this sentiment with the recognition that, in general, boy slaves were traded more often than girls, I would suggest that many of these servants seem to be somewhat androgynous in portraits. Certainly the fact that prepubescent children were preferred indicates that, at the very least, a more ambiguous eroticism may be at work. The androgyny of many of these children allows for the solidification of gender identity and contributes to the naturalization of whiteness; in other words, the child can then represent "race" in a seemingly ungendered way that leaves the sitters free to construct masculinity and femininity. In this dynamic, blackness paradoxically deflects attention from whiteness as a racial construct while at the same time making it highly visible. Instead of understanding this undeniable phenomenon with a rather dubious psychologizing, I would suggest that the practices of ownership and representation are in particular a response to the sexual politics of beauty and are informed not by some female pathology but by a tradition of representation that already associates white women and Africans.[18]

In her essay on Renaissance women's portraiture, Elizabeth Cropper alerts us to the ways in which women's portraits become part of the mascu-

18. This is not to deny that there was a psychological and sexual component to the phenomenon. Certainly, as Yi-Fu Tuan points out, these boys had access to arenas that would have been denied to adult or white servants: "Young black boys occupied a special position as exotic ornaments and pets. They were the favorite attendants of noble ladies and rich courtesans, and in that capacity gained entry into drawing rooms, bedchambers, and theater boxes and enjoyed an intimacy with their mistresses that could not be countenanced for other male servants" (141–42). However, it seems to me equally likely that the boys played a role in status competition, as I argue in this chapter; furthermore, given that these were some of the few males over which women had absolute control, they provide these women with an avenue for the exercise of power.

line contest over representing (and, I would suggest, buying and possessing) the perfect beauty. She claims that portraits of Renaissance women
become less portraits of individual women than resemblances of an ideal
beauty. Consequently, the woman loses her identity in the artist's pursuit of
the abstract ideal. Because the production of a portrait is so heavily rooted
in complex commercial interactions among painter, sitter, and patron, it is
indeed well advised to heed Cropper's implicit warning against attributing
agency to the women thus represented. There is, however, ample evidence
that women both owned slaves and had active roles in the commissioning of
portraits. Peter Mark records the efforts in 1491 of Isabella Gonzanga, a six-
teen-year-old girl, to obtain a replacement for a black serving-girl who died.
She was very much concerned about the complexion of the replacement.[19]
Lady Raleigh was one of the first women in England to own an African slave.
One of Charles II's mistresses, Hortense Mazarin, had a much-commented-
on black page, Mustapha. While separated from her husband (the famous
collector George Arundel), Lady Arundel bought a black servant, who may
have posed for the Van Dyck portrait of *George Gage and Servants*. She also
commissioned portraits of herself by Veronese and Rubens (Howarth 167).
In addition, historian Lorna Weatherill's research indicates that in certain
regions seventeenth-century women owned portraits in significantly larger
numbers than men (144). I am not making large claims for the subjectivity
of women as represented in portraits (and I certainly would not want to imply that they experience the same control over representation as the woman
writer who creates a female character and publishes her own work). I do,
however, see a similar will-to-power mediated by colonial trade and gender
difference.

The anonymous portrait by Constantyn Netscher is very typical of wom-
en's portraits (figure 22). As I noted earlier, the black attendant is always offering something to the primary sitter; for women, the objects offered are
usually nautilus shells, flowers, pearls, and other jewelry—the expensive trifles of foreign trade (and curiosity cabinets), which also happen to be the
stuff of Petrarchan lyric. Flowers, in particular, enjoyed a resurgence in
popularity (in part due to increased eastern trade) and are associated with
a culture of consumerism (Goody 183, 201). Less substantial (although
equally important) is the offering of an adoring gaze. The jewelry typically
offered in these portraits also provides biblical authority for the dual representation of beauty and servitude. Many of the portraits feature a black attendant tying a bracelet on the arm of the woman; this is one of the rare

19. See Peter Mark, *Africa though European Eyes*, 62; and Peter Erickson's useful critique
of Mark's historical approach ("Representations" 501–2).

Figure 22. *Woman in an Arched Stone Aperture,* anonymous portrait by Constantyn Netscher. Tying a bracelet onto a woman is one of the only ways that a black attendant can touch the primary sitter. As in other portraits, the gazes of the two figures never meet. (Christie's Images.)

moments in which an attendant can be seen "in intimate contact with the principal figure" (Blakeley 105). The rarity of this contact suggests that this gesture has a larger significance: it may deliberately evoke the story of Rebecca at the well from Genesis. As the mother of Jacob and Esau, Rebecca has an additional resonance, because that story can also be read as a narrative of racial difference and servitude. Abraham commissioned his chief servant to find a bride of his people for his son Isaac. Through prayer, the servant locates Rebecca, who fulfills the sign by offering water to the servant and his camels: "And when the camels had left drinking, the man toke a golden abillement of halfe a *shekel* weight, & two bracelettes for her hands, of ten shekels weight of golde" (Genesis 24.22 Geneva). The biblical narrative, which is one of recognition of hospitality, becomes in these portraits a monetary affirmation of beauty and nonforeign status. Here, as in most of these portraits, the reciprocal sense of the gift is lost. Although the attendant is always depicted as giving, the fact that the primary sitter is never portrayed as acknowledging the gift or the gaze means that the exchange has the impersonality of commodity exchange rather than the connectedness of gift exchange (Hyde 10).

In these portraits, the issues of dominance and identity become more complicated than in the male portraits because the European woman and her attendant are always connected in subtle ways, usually through the very objects on display. Often they wear similar jewelry—pearl earrings or pearl necklaces, as in the Gignes portrait (figure 23). This juxtaposition allows for a biased comparison of the attendant's black skin with the white skin of the woman. Here, the woman and attendant are subtly connected through their stance and their jewelry. Hers, of course, is closer to the desired color of pearl. They may also be linked by the parrot that sits between them. Not only are parrots associated with profit, as we have seen, but the parrot, along with the ape, figures prominently in discussions of racial difference as Englishmen try to tease out the difference between African and Englishman.[20] However, the parrot figures in misogynist treatises as well, in which women are said to be incapable of autonomous speech, able only to mimic the language of *man*kind. The association of woman and slave through object speaks to the problematic status of transplanted Africans. European women and African slaves are both objectified, but the slave becomes a sign of profitable difference and the promise of continually multiplying wealth and novelty that will fill her desires and complement her beauty.

20. Winthrop Jordan reports that William Petty, one of the founders of the Royal Society, decided that the parrot resembled man most in voice. He also insists that "Guiny Negroes" differ from "Middle Europeans" "as much as white differs from black, but also in their Haire . . . [and] in the shape of their Noses, Lipps and cheek bones, . . . They differ also in their Naturall Manners, and in the internall Qualities of their Minds" (*White over Black* 225).

Figure 23. It is quite common to find the attendant in the margins of a painting as in this anonymous portrait by Gignes (*Lady with a Negro Servant*). The chain holding the parrot between the black and the woman also suggests the attendant's slavery. Gold collars with the family seal or name were often riveted to the necks of these young boys. (Christie's Images.)

Figure 24. Barbara Villiers Palmer, countess of Castlemaine and duchess of Cleveland (1641–1709) by Sir Peter Lely. She became the first of Charles's powerful mistresses sometime before 1660–61, but her influence was supplanted by the duchess of Portsmouth. There are numerous portraits of her either by Lely or in the manner of Lely. Note the gold collar worn by the attendant. (Kedleston Hall [The National Trust]; photograph, Courtauld Institute of Art.)

If *The Character of a Town Misse* points out the use of a black servant and a dog as high-class accoutrements, the Lely portrait of the duchess of Cleveland (figure 24) suggests her status as a powerful mistress of Charles II. She holds at her left a fawning dog, and on the right an adoring servant who offers her the nautilus shell filled with flowers. If the servant and the dog fulfill similar symbolic functions, they are not equal. Blakeley points out that this grouping is yet another denial of black humanity: "The age-old positive image of the dog as man's loyal friend in this instance further lowers the worth of the Negro" (113). I would argue, however, that the attendant's position is slightly more complicated: he is connected to the woman through their neckwear.[21] Edward Scobie notes that gold and silver collars became a significant part of the servant's dress: "Silver or copper collars were riveted round the necks of these black boys and in the reign of Queen Anne it was the custom for ladies and gentlemen to inscribe their coats of arms and ciphers on these collars and to give the blacka-moors the same fancy names that they gave their lap dogs" (9). In this portrait, the servant's collar that signifies his slave status mimics the pearl choker that signifies the mistress's status as court beauty. As with the other portraits (particularly the van Somer of Anne of Denmark), the luster and brilliance of white skin is emphasized in a way that is similar to the pro-motion of whiteness that Richard Dyer sees in "glamour lighting" codes in film, which "were developed in relation to white women, to endow them with a glow and radiance that has correspondences with the tran-scendental rhetoric of popular Christianity" (63).

Black skin may have similarly served to create the "glow and radiance" of whiteness. The various aesthetic possibilities of the juxtaposition of black and white seem to be the chief feature of a Wissing portrait, reportedly of Louise Renée de Kéroüalle, the duchess of Portsmouth (figure 25).[22] In-

21. Yi-Fu Tuan sees the dog as connected to a materialist culture as well, noting that dogs were not "pets" in the modern sense: "From the Renaissance period onward, portraits of notables often show a dog or two, sometimes prominently placed in the center foreground, along with other precious possessions—rich fabrics, furnishings and glimpses of landscape and landed property—all drawn with attention to detail so as to suggest their material sub-stance and tangibility. The dogs in such a world were certainly valued, but did they, individ-ually, capture the affection of their master or mistress? Were they, for example, given personal names? In general, probably not" (110–11).

22. The National Portrait Gallery archives in London designates this a portrait of Ports-mouth with some doubt; it does not much resemble her other portraits. She may be Hortense Mancini, the duchess Mazarin, who was briefly Charles II's mistress, arriving in England with a black servant who provoked a good deal of comment, ribald and otherwise. "Rochester's Farewell" contains the reference "And having all her lewdnesses outran / Takst up with devil, having tir'd out man; / For what is else that loathsome filthy black / Which thou and Sussex in your arms did take?" (155–56; Mengel 2:225). See also Mengel 2:173, n. 73; and Noel H. Williams 177.

deed, the painting works in almost Petrarchan fashion; each feature of the
servant and sitter is carefully juxtaposed. The heads are almost aligned, and
the hands form a circle around the grapes, showing the skill of the painter
(hands being the most challenging part of the portrait).[23] As I mentioned in
the previous chapter, the emphasis on hands in many of these portraits may
foreground class status in that it echoes the emphasis on fair hands in
courtly love tradition (Erickson, "Representations" 521); for example, in
an excess of praise, Troilus says of Cressida, "O, that her hand, / In whose
comparison all whites are ink" (1.1.55–56). The symmetry of the poses and
dress again suggests a subtle identification of white woman with black slave.
This juxtaposition, however, is clearly not an innocent move. The attendant's skin is used here to demonstrate the whiteness of each of the woman's features. In Ben Jonson's words, it is the "dark foyle that best sets a
diamond forth." The whiteness of the skin is emphasized in portraits of
women to a degree not seen in male portraits. The duke of Denbigh appears positively ruddy in his portrait, whereas all these women appear to be
suffused with light. Prince Rupert's hand touches the hair of the boy, but it
is not carefully arranged so that white skin faces dark skin, as in the Wissing
portrait. The poses, however, are not exactly symmetrical: the servant here
seems to be attempting to escape with a stolen grape.

There are four or five such portraits of the duchess of Portsmouth, and
four of the duchess of Cleveland—more than I have been able to find of
any other women. All are in different poses, and all (as far as I can tell)
are with different servants. The number of these portraits hints at a more
historically specific use of the black servant. Both of these women were
longtime mistresses of Charles II, who from birth had a much-commented-
upon dark complexion and who was throughout his reign called "The
Black Boy" in popular and satirical writings.[24] The explosion of inns
named "The Black Boy" is evidently due to Charles's restoration. The
proliferation of such portraits of his mistresses may have been some sort
of inside joke at court—a way of signifying their erotic power over Charles
as well as identifying themselves as aristocratic beauties. This reading
might also explain the curious Jacques D'Agar portrait of the duchess of
Portsmouth (figure 26). She sits draped in ermine while being offered a
crown by a black page. A drape of fleurs-de-lis hangs in the background,

23. According to Campbell, "After the face, the hands are the most interesting and important areas of a portrait, but are so difficult to draw that some artists have contrived at
least partially to hide one or both of them" (95–96).
24. See Antonia Fraser, *Royal Charles*, 9–12. Agnes Strickland includes a letter by Henrietta
Maria commenting on the infant Charles's looks: "I will send you his portrait as soon as he
is a little fairer, for at present he is so dark that I am ashamed of him" (9:258).

Figure 25. This Wissing portrait may be of the duchess of Portsmouth; however, it lacks Kéroüalle's distinctive eyes (Charles II called her "Squintabella"). It is more likely to be Hortense Mancini de la Porte, duchess of Mazarin (1646–1699), a French woman who momentarily threatened the ascendancy of the duchess of Portsmouth when she became the mistress of Charles II in 1675. (Christie's Images.)

Figure 26. Louise Renée de Kéroüalle, duchess of Portsmouth and Aubigny (1649–1734), by Jacques D'Agar. This Breton maid of honor became the mistress of Charles II in 1671. The portraits include two views of the same attendant who appears to be an adult. The crown suggests that they may represent Charles II, who was known as "the black boy." (Det Nationalhistoriske Museum på Frederiksborg, Hillerød.)

reminding the viewer of her French origins, and she sits *dishabille,* demonstrating the sexual nature of her political power. Portsmouth had hopes
that Catherine of Branzaga would die during one of her frequent bouts
of illness and that Charles would marry her, a hope she evidently nursed
throughout her ascendancy as mistress.[25] Her commission of the portrait
may be an expression of wish fulfillment, of a hope that "the Black Boy,"
submitting to her erotic power, would offer her a crown.[26] The black
pages, who appear to be the same boy/dwarf, seem to represent two facets
of Charles: the one at the top left may suggest Charles in his private
capacity as lover, whereas the one who kneels and wears a crown represents Charles in his royal capacity.

Elaborating on the work of Lévi-Strauss, John Berger argues that the
introduction of oil painting brought with it a new mercantile aesthetic: it
"celebrated a new kind of wealth—which was dynamic and which found
its only sanction in the supreme buying power of money. Thus painting
itself had to be able to demonstrate the desirability of what money could
buy. And the visual desirability of what can be bought lies in its tangibility"
(90). Such a celebration of wealth—and whiteness—characterizes the
Mignard portrait of the duchess of Portsmouth (figure 27).The tangibility
Berger notes also seems present here in the painting's realization of the
tropes of Petrarchan beauty. The valuable things that make up beauty in
verse are presented here as objects that can be bought for display. Indeed,
this portrait could actually be given a title drawn from the Song of Songs—
not "I am black but beautiful," but rather "I am beautiful because she is
black." When this black girl is posed to offer lovingly the valuable objects
that constitute white female beauty in traditional representation—the
coral (associated with Africa) that creates coral lips, and the pearls that

25. Henri Forneron and Charles Carlton both make this argument. Noel H. Williams
records a French ambassador's comment: "He admits his apprehension that Mlle. de Kéroualle 'may easily become the dupe of all these parties, and all the more so, because she
does not know how to conduct herself in her good fortune, having got the idea in her head
that she may become Queen of England. She talks from morning till night about the ailments
of the Queen, just as though they were mortal' " (133).

26. Black servants seemed to play a significant role in everyday court "performance." In
addition to the dinner party recorded by Evelyn, which I discuss in the Introduction, Henri
Forneron in *Louise de Kéroüalle, Duchess of Portsmouth, 1649–1734,* records several instances of
black servants being used in court intrigue. For example, he claims: "Two young courtiers,
Jarret and Dunqout, set her little blackamoor drunk, and gave him money to tell them things
derogatory to the ladies, and in particular to the one most honoured by the attentions
of the King of England. When the slanderous tittle-tattle which they based on what they
heard from the blackamoor came to the king's ears, he forbade them to appear at Court"
(227–28).

Figure 27. Louise Renée de Kéroüalle, by Pierre Mignard. Although she was al-most universally unpopular because she was French and a Catholic, she remained influential with Charles II until his death. (By courtesy of the National Portrait Gallery, London.)

show the beauty of white skin—she hints at the increasingly complicated nature of "fairness" and its links to race, gender, and colonial trade.[27]

In using the servant's skin to accentuate her status, Portsmouth reinserts herself into a political economy of beauty. Dabydeen astutely notes that the poses of the white woman and smaller attendant are often evocative of Madonna portraits: "Finally the *aesthetic* image of Madonna and Child mirrors the *political*, imperial notion of Mother Country and Child Colony: a political statement, however unintentional, is being transmitted via art" (32). The binarism of white and black that informs representations of beauty here then operates within a more specifically historical context of colonial domination and acquisition.

In offering Portsmouth the objects that create beauty in metaphor, the black attendant offers the spectator an affirmation of an English ideal. However, as the pose of the child suggests, that English ideal of the fair woman is generated and maintained by the accumulation of foreign goods. Coral and pearl are not just metaphors. They appear prominently in both domestic manuals and art treatises: the acquisition of these items at times figured prominently in English trade practices. Often the very materials that made women "fair" (in both art and cosmetics), like the perfumes that made them sweet, are the fuel for colonial trade. Thus the painting reveals the anxieties of whiteness even as it celebrates white beauty—whiteness is not only constructed by but dependent on an involvement with Africans that is the inevitable product of England's ongoing colonial expansion.

27. In his *Africa*, John Ogilby marvels over the appearance of red coral: "In some places of the Red-Sea, unpassable for its shallowness, they gather up a finer sort of Corral than the common; especially useful to be set in deep Caves and Grotts, because it represents perfectly the shapes of little Trees, with great delight to the Eyes of curious beholders. In these Vegetables many times, by varying colours, or transparency, Nature plays and sports it self with great curiosity" (631). Clare Le Corbeiller notes that the association of Africa with coral begins in the Renaissance: "Deposited all along her Mediterranean coast, its magical attributes made it much sought after for jewelry" (218).

On "Race," Black Feminism, and White Supremacy

> I am also black and female, a status that one of my former employers described as being "at oxymoronic odds" with that of commercial lawyer.
>
> —Patricia Williams, *The Alchemy of Race and Rights*

L ike "black female/commercial lawyer," "black feminist/Renaissance critic" is in certain ways oxymoronic. My teaching and writing join together, often with ragged edges, fields that are, for the most part, invisible in relation to each other. They are usually not mutually engaged in conferences, classrooms, or most scholarly books. Despite Renaissance scholars' embrace of a wide range of theoretical models, with the exception of a few feminist critics who are beginning to study race, Renaissance studies has largely ignored the contributions made by black feminists.[1] Of course, this is not true only of Renaissance studies; this absence is part of a larger "invisibility of black feminist interpretation in the realm of the dominant discourse" (Wallace 61). Conversely (and more understandably, given the recovery work that remains to be done and the ongoing struggle for legitimacy in that field), the energies of the more prominent black feminist theorists are focused on black women's texts, histories, and popular culture. In writing a book that focuses on texts by white males in which black women are a barely visible presence, I run the risk of being identified as a feminist who is "riveted on male thinkers, preferably dead or European" (Christian 50).

The almost mutual exclusion of Renaissance studies and black feminist

---

1. This may in fact be why Renaissance studies has only recently come to explore blackness. This discussion of my own position vis-à-vis black feminism might be read profitably with Peter Erickson's discussion of identity politics, particularly his thoughts on a similar homology between critic and author in *Rewriting Shakespeare, Rewriting Ourselves*.

criticism also makes it difficult to generate a political and historical discussion of race in conferences and in the classroom. Most of the authoritative work on race and ethnicity begins with the insistence that race is always a construction (see Appiah, "The Uncompleted Argument"; Fields; Higginbotham), and much of it attempts to reveal the constructedness of the category by putting the term in scare quotes. For example, Henry Louis Gates, Jr.'s now famous observation that race "is a dangerous trope" (5) is accompanied by an imperative always to dislodge the tenacity of the term, "to deconstruct, if you will, the ideas of difference inscribed in the trope of race, to explicate discourse itself in order to reveal the hidden relations of power and knowledge inherent in popular and academic usages of 'race' " (6). Unfortunately, this semiotic point seems to have the effect of silencing racial politics in Renaissance criticism and makes it difficult to develop an antiracist pedagogy and criticism of early English texts. The correct insistence on race as a construction seems at times to be used as a shield against talking about racism, which is no less painfully real just because it is based in a fiction. This difficulty is compounded by the fact that the very word "race" has acquired a powerful and particular history in the United States, which has produced much of the scholarship on race.

I am increasingly concerned that much of the seeming anxiety over the propriety of the use of the term "race" in the Renaissance works to exclude an antiracist politics. Dismissing the term "race" altogether or imposing absolute historical boundaries between early modern and contemporary constructions may allow us not to think about race either in Renaissance texts or in our classrooms. More specifically, it serves to maintain white privilege in Renaissance studies, the luxury of *not* thinking about race—hence duplicating racism in writing and professional relations. Particularly in this current moment, when even to mention the word "racism" is, as Gloria Anzaldúa puts it, "to let loose a stink bomb" (xix), I worry that our developing work on race might become merely another new frontier for literary criticism, yet another way to reanimate Renaissance studies rather than to produce antiracist criticism and politically forceful pedagogy. Black feminist bell hooks suggests that this has been the direction of studies of race and ethnicity: the "passionate focus on race" becomes "neatly divorced from a recognition of racism, of the continuing domination of blacks by whites, and (to use some of those out-of-date, uncool terms) of the continued suffering and pain in black life" ("critical interrogation" 53).

Although this book is intended as a contribution to Renaissance studies, it is crucially informed by my advocacy of black feminism, and it is that position which prompts my concerns. Black feminist criticism insists upon an ongoing connection between the lived experiences of black women and critical practice (Brewer 15; Collins 13–16). Understanding the power and politics of race has been an essential survival skill for most African-Americans, especially in the academy. This premise allows me to bring to early modern texts the reading strategies learned as a black woman in a twentieth-century white supremacist culture and thus to overcome some of the inhibitions imposed on students and critics in the name of "propriety" or "historical accuracy."[2]

I realize that I am moving dangerously close to an essentialist identity criticism that has been critiqued ably by many in the field of black feminism. However, drawing from experience for critical insight need not automatically suggest a naive or essentialist use of experience. In her critique of the use of experience as evidence, historian Joan W. Scott reminds us that to be useful, experience must be recognized as "at once always already an interpretation *and* something that needs to be interpreted" (412). It is precisely this sense of experience as interpretation that I wish to retain. I am not arguing that my being black automatically results in critical consciousness and gives immediate insight into the workings of race. Rather, I am supporting the idea that critical consciousness is often developed in black communities in order to survive racism. For example, the black nationalist feminist Pearl Cleage explains that her understanding of herself as an oppressed African-American developed in relation to white racism in her everyday life:

> I understood that white people had been raised by their culture to be racist in order to maintain status and control and I was encouraged to question everything they did or said since it was never going to be in my best interest to believe them without checking some reliable black source first, preferably my family since they had a vested interest in my not acting a fool.
>
> All this critical information and racial analysis was presented to me as an integral part of my daily life, not a special ceremony during Black History Month. These African American survival lessons were part of the fabric of family; expected, accepted and continuous. (30)

While this view from the margins—what bell hooks has called "an oppositional world view" (*Feminist Theory* i)—may not be part of every Afri-

---

2. Erickson speaks quite forcefully on the problem of historicity in discussions of blackness from a different perspective—"No one wants to be accused of being ahistorical but we must not allow the specter of historicity so to frighten us that the very topic of race in the Renaissance becomes unthinkable and inquiry thereby prematurely closed off" (501)—and astutely argues that the problem may be with a certain unitary conception of history itself.

can-American's life and is shaped by differences in color, class, sexuality, and region, it often does inspire a profound skepticism about the presentation of power and a certain understanding of the ways whiteness masks itself.[3] Despite bias against it in the academy, this type of everyday analysis of the workings of race has shaped me as professional reader of literary texts as well: without the help of much Renaissance criticism, I found myself drawing more and more on remembered conversations with my family, my readings of black feminist work, and my own experiences of racism, sexism, and white supremacy to understand the workings of race and gender in these texts.

The very desire to write about the dark/fair binary comes out of my experience as a subject "interpellated" by the language of that binary. Henry Louis Gates, Jr., eloquently speaks to the problem of black subjectivity in English: "We are justified, however, in wondering aloud if the sort of subjectivity which these writers seek through the act of writing can be realized through a process which is so very ironic from the outset: how can the black subject posit a full and sufficient self in a language in which blackness is a sign of absence?" ("Writing 'Race' " 12). The language of blackness, however, is much more than an absence; it is an infinitely malleable presence that has been used, mostly negatively, to define white subjectivity. To discuss blackness in the Renaissance is for me to inhabit an uneasy and undetermined position in relation to my subject and my audience.

Since black feminists seek "to develop methods of analysis for interpreting the ways in which race and gender are inscribed in cultural productions" (Valerie Smith, "Split Affinities" 155), a black feminist methodology is uniquely positioned to reveal the dynamics of shifting racial ideologies and the "racial unconscious" (Lott) of the Renaissance. A criticism that understands the "multiplicative nature" of oppression offers the best way to de- or reconstruct the languages of race in Renaissance

---

3. See, for example, bell hooks: "I did not feel sympathetic to white peers who maintained that I could not expect them to have knowledge of or understand the life experiences of black women. Despite my background (living in racially segregated communities) I knew about the lives of white women, and certainly no white women lived in our neighborhood, attended our schools, or worked in our homes" (*Feminist Theory* 11). Ann duCille, who has vigorously critiqued essentialism in black feminist studies, refers to a similar knowledge and impatience, although from a different position: "I know my bad attitude comes from what in this instance might be called the arrogance of 'black privilege': after all, I—whose earliest childhood memories include finding a snake in our mailbox shortly after we moved into an all-white neighborhood and being called 'nigger' on my first day at an all-white elementary school—did not learn my racial consciousness from reading Richard Wright's 'Big Boy Leaves Home' as an adult" (617).

texts (Brewer 16). Rather than create "totalizing formulations of race on one hand, gender on the other" (Valerie Smith, "Split Affinities" 155), black feminist criticism reads race as a dynamic category that can be understood only in its contact with a number of other categories, such as gender, class, and sexuality. Legal theorist Kimberlé Crenshaw points out that this methodology uncovers the hidden mechanisms through which these categories function: "A framework of intersection will facilitate a merging of race and gender discourses to uncover what is hidden between them" (114).

Valerie Smith has argued that black feminist literary criticism intervenes in Afro-Americanist criticism and Anglo-American feminism, both of which have depended on totalizing formations of race and gender ("Black Feminist Theory" 44). Consequently, it has been at the forefront of offering models of race and gender to replace "additive" or "analogous" approaches to race (in which race is either tacked on as heightening another category, such as gender, or operating in the same way as gender [Brewer 16]). Not only are these categories mutually constitutive, they are historically contingent; that is, they are always determined by the values and images attributed to those categories at that period—and thus not easily explained by master narratives or "a theory" of race and gender. Deborah King points out that "in the interactive model, the relative significance of race, sex, or class in determining the conditions of black women's lives is neither fixed nor absolute but, rather, is dependent on the socio-historical context and the social phenomenon under consideration" (49). These factors of multiplicity and historical contingency make it doubly difficult to offer blueprints or models for reading "race," particularly in Renaissance texts, which usually elude such scrutiny. These factors make black feminist criticism particularly well equipped to intervene in Renaissance studies: the contingency of the interactive model is crucially important for reading race in early modern England, because the political and historical forces shaping the category (such as England's contact and trade with non-European cultures) were changing rapidly and somewhat chaotically. Thus while I have suggested some correspondences between seventeenth-century England and current Anglo-American racial discourses—and I continue to see disturbing similarities between the two—I do not therefore presume that the categories are the same. Like Crenshaw, I see the techniques of examining intersectionality provisional until we develop the language for a more complex understanding of multiplicity (114).

Recent published work on race in the period as well as discussions of race on the conference circuit frequently begin by decrying the difficulty of analyzing race when there is no consistent discourse of race in the early modern period. Take, for example, a recent essay by the feminist Lynda Boose that appears in *Women, "Race," and Writing* (1993), the first anthology on race and gender in early modern England. Boose opens her impressively wide-ranging essay on the "unrepresentable black woman" with a strongly worded statement on both the instability of the category and the need to divest it of modern meanings: "If ever a topic needed to be waylaid, queried and 'debrided' of its acquired meanings before discussion of its origin might fairly begin, surely it is a discourse of race. For while the twentieth century has generally presumed that skin color is the determining factor, what actually complicates any analysis of racial discourse is, to begin with, the pervasive ambiguity—in the late sixteenth or late twentieth century—surrounding the term 'race' itself" (35). I certainly concur with the need to "waylay" and "query" the term "race," and under no circumstances do I advocate abandoning historical context. However, in the expressed need to divest race of its "acquired" meanings, Boose's statement seems to move beyond interrogating the category to proposing that we seek a "pure" category of race: to say that the category must be "debrided" before we can start the discussion is in a sense to say that we must erase the very history that brought scholarship on race to the academy. I am not sure why, in a field so influenced by feminism and the new historicism—both of which insist on a recognition that we as critics are embedded in our own historical moment and therefore do not have access to a pure history—we call for such purity when it comes to race.[4] Rather than engaging with the ramifications of this "pervasive ambiguity," Boose undermines the politics of her project by collapsing a gesture toward ontological purity into her legitimate concern for historical accuracy.

Without calling into question Boose's motives or undervaluing Boose's project in putting the subject on the table, I want to play out the logical consequences of this position. In a note, Boose says that she finds the term "debriding," which she borrows from Susan Jeffords, particularly appropriate: "Given White Racism's fantasy of 'washing the Ethiop clean,'—'debriding'—a medical term for controlling infection and removing 'foreign matter' by scrubbing away the upper layers of skin— seemed especially appropriate for an essay on race/gender" (Boose n. 1). Apart from the historical echo, I am not sure why Boose finds this an appropriate term; as a black scholar, I find it especially inappropriate (and

4. For an excellent discussion of the relationship between new historicism and feminism and the politics of location in both, see Peter Erickson, *Rewriting Shakespeare*, 1–3.

somewhat painful) for a politicized discussion of race in the Renaissance precisely because of the evocation of that racial fantasy. The medicalized discourse suggested by "debriding" (like George Best's insistence that blackness itself is an "infection") brings to bear notions of purity and contamination that are often linked to blackness (Gilman 30–31). The version of the adage "washing the Ethiop clean," not to mention the metaphor implicit in the phrase "might fairly begin," duplicates the racial dynamic that this book seeks to critique. They both suggest that the category must be "whitewashed" or made "pure" before one can even think about it and disallow the category for a large number of readers, particularly students. The demand for debriding in many ways opposes a black feminist critical practice that insists on race as an interactive category. Even if I abandon my personal feelings of erasure, her connection of "debriding" with "washing the Ethiop white" deconstructs Boose's argument for purity: as I discuss in Chapter 2, "washing the Ethiop white" is a trope for an impossible or futile endeavor. The desire to access a "pure" past devoid of the baggage of race is likewise a fantasy.[5] At this juncture it is useful to see Margaret Ferguson make the case against such a move in her essay "Juggling the Categories of Race, Class, and Gender": "To stop the search for significant traces of such inequities is to accept an academic argument for hermeneutic 'purity' that is arguably an ideological defense against seeing systemic injustices in past societies— including those partly shaped and largely represented by European intellectuals—and in our own" (212).

I would suggest that from a black feminist standpoint, such purity is not only undesirable, it is in fact impossible. Seeing race and gender as dynamic and contingent categories that interrogate each other makes the instability of race much more amenable to critique and understanding, particularly for seventeenth-century England, which witnessed an explosion of contact with previously unknown cultures. A black feminist approach allows us to see the black/white dichotomy as powerful and compelling even as it competes with other discourses of race in the period. From my position as a black feminist, the better part of valor would be

---

5. The problem of racial politics may explain in part the curious absence of discussions of English interaction with Africa in new historicist work. It may in fact be easier to deal with past representations of American Indians who are currently made invisible to dominant culture except in times of stress. The success of England's colonial project was such that academics are not liable to be held accountable for their positions by American Indian colleagues and students, even to the minor degree that they may be by African-American students and colleagues. Reading blackness in a Renaissance text and actually abiding by the tenets of new historicism would involve thinking about one's own racial consciousness involving African-Americans, a project many might find too disturbing or revealing.

not to "debride" the category but to develop strategies for analyzing this ambiguity and holding on to an understanding of what such representations might mean in the present. I might call such a practice strategically anachronistic; that is, it demonstrates the historical construction of a category while providing an oppositional viewpoint rooted in the present.[6] This strategy does, however, pose certain challenges to clarity and strength of argument. My choice to bring to the forefront one dominant strand of racial thought springs not only from my sense of its importance for black people but also from a need to limit my focus so that I could play out the possibilities of multiplicity.

The contingency of race also suggests that critics and teachers of Renaissance texts need to be much more flexible and subtle in their identification of language and images as "racialized" or "race-neutral." Although I have been able to make visible only the contours of an exciting amount of material and the blueprint of a methodology, I hope this book demonstrates that the absence of a term for race in the Renaissance and of a distinct and coherent racial ideology does not make early modern English culture (or Shakespeare) race-neutral. I cannot argue that all dark/fair oppositions in the Renaissance are racially charged, but I do nevertheless argue strongly that this language is racialized to a much greater degree than critics have been willing to allow. At the very least I hope to have offered enough evidence to suggest that one cannot make easy distinctions between racialized and race-neutral texts. The language of fairness and darkness is always *potentially* racialized, and it does an injustice to the richness of the language to insist out of fear or ignorance that texts exist as "pure," above ideologies of race.

As I have indicated, it is more difficult to claim a place in black feminist literary criticism for a book that focuses on quite dead white males and that tries to move beyond the mere identification of negative or positive images of blacks in canonical texts. Although the boundaries of black feminist theory are expanding, much of it still presumes a homology between text and critic. This homology is of course not peculiar to black feminism: Peter Erickson, for example, has argued against a similarly disabling homology between white male critic and author (*Rewriting Shakespeare* 168–71). The key difference is that the black feminist is expected to bring a reading practice or epistemology derived from personal expe-

6. This view, if more overtly political, is similar to Jeffrey Weeks's instructive assessment of Foucault and his school of thought: "Foucault stresses that his work is basically aimed at constructing a 'genealogy,' the locating of the 'traces' of the present rather than reconstructing the past. It is basically 'a history of the present,' a concept which poses problems of its own" (5).

rience and historical knowledge to the texts and lives of black women. This stance is most obvious in Barbara Smith's ground-breaking and frequently anthologized essay "Toward a Black Feminist Criticism," which calls for "a viable, autonomous Black feminist movement" (169) that will develop the theoretical framework for reading black women's texts. What such a presumed homology between critic and subject ultimately does (in addition to excluding nonblack women as critical readers of black female texts) is to suggest that black feminist epistemology has currency in only one project—the recovery and analysis of writings by black women. Other black feminists have been troubled by this issue. Sherley Anne Williams adopts the term "womanist theory" and argues that black feminists need not only to focus on ourselves but to examine images of masculinity in black male texts in order to avoid the traps of "narcissism, isolation, inarticulation and obscurity" (74). However, while suggesting wider gender concerns, she still assumes criticism based on racial communities.

Deborah McDowell was one of the earliest and remains one of the most prominent voices against an isolationist black feminism. Responding to Barbara Smith in "New Directions for Black Feminist Criticism," she attempts to broaden the scope of black feminism by redefining the term "Black feminist criticism," which still primarily refers to "Black female critics who analyze the works of Black female writers from a feminist or political perspective." Her secondary definition bravely attempts to enlarge the vision of black feminist criticism, but her very syntax demonstrates the difficulties of the enterprise: "But the term can also apply to any criticism written by a Black woman regardless of her subject or perspective—a book written by a male from a feminist or political perspective, a book written by a Black woman or about Black women authors in general, or any writings by women" (191). In its very inclusiveness, this definition demonstrates the problem of reenvisioning black feminist criticism. As Williams points out, McDowell still implies that black feminists can profitably read only works by women or images of women (70). Although I should find this attempt at inclusion legitimizing for my own work, instead I find it deeply troubling. While this passage is certainly a welcoming gesture for those of us who are not in African-American studies, it suggests that a black woman's politics are immaterial to her production of black feminist criticism. In attempting to escape the homology of critic and text, McDowell falls into a disturbing essentialism. Can any black woman really produce black feminist criticism "regardless of her subject or perspective?"

I suspect that McDowell's difficulty in articulating a coherent definition or description comes not from a repressed essentialism or carelessness but from the anxiety many black feminists feel about the very problematic position of black feminist work in the academy. Ironically, this position is even more fraught than when McDowell first published her essay, because the burgeoning interest in black women's work has greatly outstripped the black female presence in the academy. And, as Hazel Carby has pointed out, in some cases the inclusion of black women's texts in the curriculum has become a substitute for the hiring and promotion of black women in the academy. Black women and black women's texts become interchangeable commodities, with the texts less threatening and seemingly equally useful in giving an appearance of inclusiveness. To define black feminist criticism and methodology is to engage very concrete economic and political issues in the academy and to face our own fears of co-optation and exclusion. Ann duCille reveals in her brilliantly honest essay "The Occult of True Black Womanhood" that "questions of turf and territoriality, appropriation and co-optation persist within my own black feminist consciousness, despite my best efforts to intellectualize them away" (597). With this concern over the position of black women's expressivity, it is no surprise that black feminists writing on black feminism as a discipline still focus more on the black women's texts rather than on the types of texts one might read using black feminist methodologies.

If black feminist criticism is a methodology rather than a performance of blackness, then it is in fact essential that I be able to claim a place for a black feminist book on Renaissance texts without ignoring the professional standards of black feminism as a field and without making myself the native informant on race in the Renaissance. I see this book as aligned with work by women of color such as Toni Morrison, Gayatri Spivak, and Ania Loomba, who have expanded black feminism and postcolonial studies by demonstrating how these approaches can reshape both the canon and the ways we read canonical texts. Cheryl Wall's introduction to *Changing Our Own Words* proposes a focus on canonical texts as a possibility for black feminist criticism: "In a complementary move, we may begin to ask the same questions about race, gender, and class of 'canonical' texts (and 'noncanonical' texts by white men, black men, white women, men and women of color, everybody) that we ask of those by black women" (9). Given Wall's generous vision, it seems only proper for me to help fill it out by suggesting the grounds on which such work might be evaluated. Rereading canonical texts and asking the questions Wall alludes to must be accompanied by the recovery work that has characterized much black feminist activity.

Apart from the suspicion of dominant narratives and an awareness of whiteness as an invisible yet powerful presence, I identify my project as black feminist literary criticism because it explores the interactions of race and gender in a specific cultural context, because it comes to the academy out of an oppositional consciousness, and, most important, because it is antiracist in its attempts to analyze traditional discourses and cultural assumptions that have been damaging to people of African descent. Michelle Wallace has argued that binary oppositions, particularly those of dark and light, have been destructive for people of color generally and for black women specifically: "There is no question in my mind that the unrelenting logic of dualism, or polar oppositions—such as black and white, good and evil, male and female—is basic to the discourse of the dominant culture and tends to automatically erase black female subjectivity" (Wallace 60). The opposition of dark and light has materially affected black women's lives, destroying our self-image and disfiguring our bodies. One specific manifestation of the ideology of fairness (which had its strongest articulations in the Renaissance) is a Eurocentric beauty culture that privileges one skin color over another. Black feminist writers and artists have relentlessly worked to show how Western beauty culture has helped destroy black communities and black women in particular.[7] A broad understanding of race as a factor in beauty culture, however, remains to be incorporated into white feminism. So too we need an historicizing of the ideology of beauty from a black feminist perspective. Exposing the logic of the dark/fair opposition should be fundamental to both these projects.

The impact of ideologies of fairness may be one reason why black women have been vocal advocates of a study of whiteness. The current interest in "difference" by white scholars, as bell hooks points out, may in fact merely perpetuate racism without a sustained study of whiteness: "Yet only a persistent, rigorous, and informed critique of whiteness could really determine what forces of denial, fear, and competition are responsible for creating fundamental gaps between professed political commitment to eradicating racism and the participation in the construction of a discourse on race that perpetuates racial domination" ("critical interrogation" 54). In *Playing in the Dark*, Toni Morrison makes the strongest case for a focus on "literary whiteness" in American studies.[8] According to Morrison, the field of American studies operates on the assumption "that traditional canonical American literature is free of, uninformed, and unshaped by the four-hundred-year-old presence of, first, Africans and then

7. See, for example, Mae Henderson's discussion of *Sula* in "Speaking in Tongues" (127; 141, n. 28).

8. See Erickson's discussion of *Playing* in "Profiles in Whiteness" and "Representations of Blacks."

African-Americans in the U.S.'' (4–5). Morrison here elucidates a double bind in contemporary critical practice: to isolate African-American texts as the site of discussions of "race" (and as the sole focus of African-American analysis) is to perpetuate a "whitewashed" literature that can deny its own concerns with blackness. More important, this ghettoization of African-American texts also leaves the gendered and racial politics of whiteness unexamined and undertheorized. Morrison's assessment hints at the separatism of black studies, which, if focused solely on black texts, can abandon a crucial part of our history to scholars who are neither by training nor by inclination prepared to examine the importance of an African presence in dominant literatures. As a black feminist teacher of Shakespeare, I cannot help but wonder why in the "culture wars" of the 1980s and 1990s we have not addressed the way we teach the classic texts of Eurocentric America. Opening the canon and recovering texts by people of color must happen concurrently with new readings of canonical texts. What damage do we do to students and history when we ignore the vital language of blackness that shaped the English as social subjects and that currently shapes our social relations today? If "the contemplation of this black presence is central to any understanding of our national literature" (Morrison, *Playing in the Dark* 5), then it is equally essential to the study of early modern English culture, which was the birthplace of current racial ideologies and that, while differently constituted, still shares our cultural, economic and legal history.

That the language of blackness has been a shaping force in black lives has been testified to from all quarters of black life. Over twenty years ago, actor and playwright Ossie Davis named sixty synonyms for blackness (apart from overt racial terminology like "Negro," "nigger," etc.) in his essay "The English Language Is My Enemy" and forcefully articulated the almost inescapable conflict these negative terms create for the black user of the English language. He speaks particularly to the effect of this language in the classroom, asking his reader to remember "the enormous heritage of racial prejudgment that lies in wait for any child born into the English language. Any teacher good or bad, white or black, Jew or Gentile, who uses the English Language as a medium of communication is forced, willy-nilly, to teach the Negro child 60 ways to despise himself, and the white child 60 ways to aid and abet him in the crime" (Davis 3). The term "white supremacy," bell hooks has suggested, is a more useful term than "racism" in that it identifies pervasive ideology and behavior that exists even as one moves beyond "overtly racist discrimination, exploitation, and oppression of black people" ("overcoming white supremacy"

113). It seems to me that Davis's scenario imagines the indoctrination of white supremacy through language itself. Thus although we may argue about the efficacy and historical accuracy of the term "race," that we literally speak a language of white supremacy may be a more obvious (though less palatable) point. Although feminists have made some inroads in raising cultural consciousness about the damaging effects of gender bias in language and the success of the civil rights movement in the United States has taught people to recognize and avoid the most obvious derogatory images and language about black people in this country, there is almost no discussion of the ways in which a language based on a hierarchy of black and white perpetuates racism. The language of dark and light is part of a white supremacist ideology and persists as a common way of marking peoples of the African diaspora as inferior.

Davis's formulation is particularly resonant for those of us who are educators. By using this language unconsciously or denying its racial effects, we support a system of thought that is terrifying in its complacency. Significantly, Davis puts the issue beyond racial guilt and demonstrates Patricia Williams's larger point that "we are all inheritors of that legacy, whether new to this world, or new to this country, for it survives as powerful and invisibly reinforcing structures of thought, language, and law" (Williams 60–61). Unlike Davis, I do not believe that we as teachers are "forced" to inflict on our students the psychic damage he identifies—the education of black students in their inferiority and white students in white supremacy. I am not claiming that "removing the words 'black' and 'white' from our vocabulary would render the world, in a miraculous flash, free of all division" (P. Williams 83). I am suggesting instead that acknowledging the power of that language and its material effects is a good place to address issues of race and to do antiracist work.

Although this book is almost deliberately not about "Shakespeare," it seems appropriate to speak of the field of Shakespeare studies, given its prominence in the academy and subterranean anxieties about the place of Shakespeare in Anglo-American culture at large.[9] Teaching Shakespeare is a good place to begin disrupting the language of white supremacy, both because Shakespeare figures so prominently in high school and college curricula and because questions of race are so easily raised—and so easily dismissed—in connection with Shakespeare's language, particularly in the sonnets.

Let's imagine that we are in the classroom evoked by Davis, and we ask

9. See, for example, the collection *Shakespeare Left and Right*, ed. Ivo Kamps, which grew out of an MLA session on the role of ideology in Shakespeare.

the students to read sonnet 138, "My mistress' eyes are nothing like the sun." A student who is immersed in the negative language of blackness and has been reared with an oppositional consciousness asks, "Is he talking about a black woman?" Do we ignore that student's experience as a racialized subject and silence her or him by responding that the woman is just a brunette? Do we then add insult to injury by insisting that the positive references to blackness be read only as a joke? Instead of seeing this student's comments as an interruption of our creation of Shakespeare as a mark of high culture and our examination of so-called universal themes, we might use that moment to make whiteness and its power visible or to discuss the politics of beauty standards and their negotiation in the sonnets. In treating Shakespeare "as if 'Shakespeare' were some fixed object, some physically determinate piece of marble, as if I could discount all my own interpretative power and responsibility over what I render from it" (P. Williams 84), we similarly discount the interpretative abilities of all students and deny black students in particular their experiences as subjects constituted by a highly racialized language.

Bringing these issues into the classroom will not be easy; it requires a subtlety and dialogic engagement with students that hour-long classes do not foster. In addition, the pattern of other modes of criticism does not offer much hope: they have revolutionized scholarship but have not had a similarly seismic impact on actual pedagogy (Howard and O'Connor 5–7). Even the most enthusiastic scholars and teachers can be hampered by lack of access to pertinent materials. Just as relying on the same critical models does not change critical practice, relying on standard anthologies does not change pedagogy (although I hope I have demonstrated that we can read those materials in new ways). We need new anthologies, not just of English literature but of English culture as well. We also need accessible editions of other primary texts. It may also mean changing the organization of knowledge in the academy by reconfiguring temporal and disciplinary boundaries; for example, instead of divorcing the *Masque of Blackness* from contemporary racial politics, we might teach it along with American blackface performances in a course on race and performance. So too, we can juxtapose the portraits I include in Chapter 5 with Beah Richards's *A Black Woman Speaks* and examples of whiteness in advertising in a course on the construction of beauty.

In my own Renaissance classes, I experiment with different texts and strategies and ask students to read the work of black feminist and postcolonial critics and the more accessible historical materials in addition to the "primary" texts. We also talk about how knowledge is organized in the academy and what it means to study the "Renaissance." Most recently

I gave students studying sonnet 138 copies of both the satiric engraving of the Petrarchan mistress from *The Extravagant Shepherd,* which is at times included in editions of the sonnets, and the Mignard portrait of the duchess of Portsmouth; we talked about how these images and the textual glosses might shape their readings of the text. Our scholarship on race should be accompanied with a discussion of new teaching strategies and pedagogical issues such as: how in class do we stop regarding only people of color as racial subjects? how do we generate discussions that are intellectually rigorous, historically sensitive, and meaningful to the students' own lives? Regardless of our critical positions or pedagogy, the ethnic composition of the United States and its classrooms is changing. This means that scholar-teachers can either reexamine our scholarship and teaching or continue to play the role of Prospero-teacher to passive students. We can create a cultural narrative for the white student based on a family tale of glorious origins and lost (but soon to be regained) power and make the student of color a Caliban, fit only to serve the psychic and social needs of those in power. Or, we can acknowledge the ongoing legacy of "this thing of darkness" and use that knowledge to create new ways of thinking about difference that let students approach the texts of Western culture as equals. If we are successful, we can give students the critical tools for a more meaningful and complex dialogue on race, one that comprehends the intersection of categories without disregarding our differences and that moves beyond racial guilt—but not beyond justice.

Poems of Blackness

T he following poems all draw on the different tropes of blackness discussed earlier. They deserve much more sustained attention both individually and as a group than I have been able to offer in this book, although I hope I have laid a foundation for further study. The inclusion of these poems in this book is in the tradition of Elliot Tokson's *The Popular Image of the Black Man in English Drama, 1550–1688,* which remains the basic text in the field. In his first chapter, Tokson introduces the Herbert-Cleveland-King topos and reprints the poems "Aethiopissa ambit Cestum," "A Fair Nymph Scorning a Black Boy courting her," "A Black-moor Maid wooing a fair Boy," and "The Boyes answer to the Black-moor." Although these poems are available in Tokson, the rest are not, and the poems as a group remain generally inaccessible.

I have arranged the poems roughly chronologically, beginning with William Dunbar's "Ane Blak Moir." Although some of them are clearly "individual" conceits, many of them respond to the sequence initiated by "Aethiopissa" and "A Black-moor Maid Wooing a fair Boy." Most are part of a larger genre of satiric verse and paradoxical praise. Variations on "A Black-moor Maid" and its responses can be found in numerous commonplace books from the 1630s through the 1660s. Beal's *Index of English Literary Manuscripts* lists seventy appearances of this topos, including two versions with musical settings. Most of these poems appear to have circulated privately, and many were not printed until the latter part of the seventeenth century.[1]

---

1. Unfortunately, I did not receive permission in time to include "On a fair Gentlewoman married to a black man likend to night and day" and "Of the same," which are in a manuscript in the Rosenbach collection in Philadelphia.

CONTENTS

William Dunbar	Ane Blak Moir	271
Edward Guilpin	Of Nigrina	271
John Weever	In Byrrham	272
George Herbert	To the Right Hon. the Lo. Chancellor	273
	Aethiopissa ambit Cestum diversi coloris Virum	273
	A Negress courts Cestus, a Man of a different colour	274
John Cleveland	A Fair Nymph Scorning a Black Boy courting her	274
Henry Rainolds	A Black-moor Maid wooing a fair Boy	275
Henry King	The Boyes answer to the Blackmoor	276
Edward Herbert	Sonnet of Black Beauty	276
	Another Sonnet to Black it self	277
	The Brown Beauty	277
	To her Hair	278
John Collop	On an Ethiopian beauty, M.S.	279
	Of the black Lady with grey eyes and white teeth	279
[*Abraham Wright*]	To a black Gentlewoman: Mistresse A. H.	280
[*Walton Poole*]	On a black Gentlewoman	280
Richard Lovelace	[A Black Patch on Lucasta's Face] Another	282
	Ode	283
Eldred Revett	The Aethiopian Baptized	284
Richard Crashaw	On the baptized Æthiopian	285
	Upon the faire Ethiopian sent to a Gentlewoman	285
Eldred Revett	The fair Nymph scorning a black Boy courting her	285
	The Inversion	286
	A black Nymph scorning a fair Boy Courting her	287
	One Enamour'd on a Black-moor	288

William Dunbar

ANE BLAK MOIR

Lang heff I maed of ladyes quhytt;
Nou of ane blak I will indytt
   That landet furth of the last schippis;
Quhou fain wald I descryve perfytt
   My ladye with the mekle lippis:

Quhou schou is tute mowitt lyk ane aep
And lyk a gangarall onto graep,
   And quhou hir schort catt nois up skippis,
And quhou schou schynes lyk ony saep,
   My ladye with the mekle lippis.

Quhen schou is claid in reche apparrall
Schou blinkis als brycht as ane tar barrell;
   Quhen schou was born the son tholit clippis,
The nycht be fain faucht in hir querrell—
   My ladye with the mekle lippis.

Quhai for hir saek with speir and scheld
Preiffis maest mychttelye in the feld
   Sall kis and withe hir go in grippis,
And fra thyne furth hir luff sall weld—
   My ladye with the mekle lippis.

And quhai in felde receaves schaem
And tynis thair his knychtlie naem
   Sall cum behind and kis hir hippis
And nevir to uther confort claem:
   My ladye with the mekle lippis.

The Poems of William Dunbar, ed. James Kingsley (Oxford: Clarendon, 1979), 106; by permission of Oxford University Press.

Edward Guilpin

OF NIGRINA

Of Nigrina. 57.
Why should *Nigrina* weare her mask so much?

Her skins lawn's not so fine, so soone to staine,
Her tendrest poultry may endure the touch,
Her face, face and out-face the wind againe:
   The cherry of her lip's a winter Cherry,
   Then weather-proof, & needs no masks
defence:
   Her cheeks best fruit's a black, no Mulberry,
   But fearelesse of sharp gustes impouerishments:
And to be briefe, she being all plaine *Ione,*
Why is she mask'd to keepe that where is none?
   O sir, she's painted, and you know the guise,
   Pictures are curtaind from the vulgar eyes.

Of Nigrina. 61.

Painted *Nigrina* unmask'd comes ne're in sight,
Because light wenches care not for the light.

Of the same. 62.

Painted Nigrina with the picture face,
Hauing no maske thinks she's without grace,
So with one case she doth another case,
Doth not her maske become her then apace?

Of Nigrina. 65.

Because Nigrina hath a painted face,
Many suspect her to be light and base:
I see no reason to repute her such,
For out of doubt she will abide the tuch.

Edward Guilpin, *Skialetheia: Or A shadow of Truth in certaine Epigrams and Satyres* (London, 1598), B5r–v.

John Weever

IN BYRRHAM

Is *Byrrha* browne? who doth the question aske?
Her face is pure as Ebonie jeat blacke,
It's hard to know her face from her faire maske,

Beautie in her seemes beautie still to lacke.
Nay, shee's snow-white, but for that russet skin,
Which like a vaile doth keep her whitenes in.

John Weever, *Epigrammes in the oldest cut, and newest fashion* (London, 1599), D4v.

George Herbert

To the Right Hon. the Lo. Chancellor

My Lord, a Diamond to mee you sent,
And I to you a Blackamoore present.
Gifts speake the givers, for as those refractions,
Shining and sharpe, poynt out your rare perfections;
So by the other you may read in mee,
Whome Scholler's habite and obscurity
Hath soyl'd with black, the color of my state
Till your bright gift my darknes did abate:
Onely, my noble Lord, shutt not the doore
Agaynst this meane and humble blackamoore;
Perhaps some other subject I had tryed,
But that my inke was factious for that side.

Aethiopissa ambit Cestum diversi coloris Virum

Quid mihi si facies nigra est? hoc, Ceste, colore
   Sunt etiam tenebrae, quas tamen optat amor.
Cernis ut exusta semper sit fronte viator;
   Ah longum, quae te deperit, errat iter.
Si nigro sit terra solo, quis despicit arvum?
   Claude oculos, et erunt omnia nigra tibi:
Aut aperi, et cernes corpus quas projicit umbras;
   Hoc saltem officio fungar amore tui.
Cum mihi sit facies fumus, quas pectore flammas
   Jamdudum tacite delituisse putes?
Dure, negas? O fata mihi praesaga doloris,
   Quae mihi lugubres contribuere genas!

A NEGRESS COURTS CESTUS, A MAN OF A DIFFERENT COLOUR

What if my face be black? O Cestus, hear!
Such colour Night brings, which yet Love holds dear.
You see a Trav'ller has a sunburnt face;
And I, who pine for thee, a long road trace.
If earth be black, who shall despise the ground?
Shut now your eyes, and, lo, all black is found;
Or ope, a shadow-casting form you see;
This be my loving post to fill for thee.
Seeing my face is smoke, what fire has burn'd
Within my silent bosom, by thee spurn'd!
Hard-hearted man, dost still my love refuse?
Lo, Grief's prophetic hue my cheek imbues!

The Complete Works in Verse and Prose of George Herbert, ed. Alexander Grosart, 3 vols. (London, 1874), 2: 164–65.

John Cleveland

A FAIR NYMPH SCORNING A BLACK BOY COURTING HER

Nymph	Stand off, and let me take the Air,
	Why should the smoke pursue the fair?
Boy	My Face is smoke, thence may be guest
	What Flames within have scorch'd my breast.
Nymph	Thy flaming Love I cannot view,
	For the dark Lanthorn of thy Hue.
Boy	And yet this Lanthorn keeps Love's Taper
	Surer than your's that's of white Paper.
	What ever Midnight can be here,
	The Moon-shine of your Face will clear.
Nymph	My Moon of an Eclipse is 'fraid;
	If thou should'st interpose thy Shade.
Boy	Yet one thing, Sweet-heart, I will ask,
	Take me for a new fashion'd Mask.
Nymph	Done: but my Bargain shall be this,
	I'll throw my Mask off when I kiss.

Boy   Our curl'd Embraces shall delight
To checker Limbs with black and white.

Nymph   Thy ink, my Paper, make me guess
Our Nuptial-bed will prove a Press;
And in our Sports, if any come,
They'l read a wanton Epigram.

Boy   Why should my Black thy Love impair?
Let the dark Shop commend the Ware;
Or if thy Love from black forbears,
I'll strive to wash it off with Tears.

Nymph   Spare fruitless Tears, since thou must needs
Still wear about thy mourning Weeds.
Tears can no more affection win,
Than wash thy *Æthiopian* Skin.

The Works of John Cleveland (London, 1687), 16–17.

Henry Rainolds

A BLACK-MOOR MAID WOOING A FAIR BOY:
sent to the Author by Mr. Hen. Rainolds

Stay lovely Boy, why fly'st thou mee
That languish in these flames for thee?
I'm black 'tis true: why so is Night,
And Love doth in dark Shades delight.
The whole World, do but close thine eye,
Will seem to thee as black as I;
Or op't, and see what a black shade
Is by thine own fair body made,
That follows thee where e're thou go;
(O who allow'd would not do so?)
   Let me for ever dwell so nigh,
And thou shalt need no other shade than I.

The English Poems of Henry King, D.D., ed. Laurence Mason (New Haven: Yale University Press, 1914), 16.

Henry King

The Boyes answer to the Blackmoor

Black Maid, complain not that I fly,
When Fate commands Antipathy:
Prodigious might that union prove,
Where Night and Day together move,
And the conjunction of our lips
Not kisses make, but an Eclipse;
In which the mixed black and white
Portends more terrour than delight.
Yet if my shadow thou wilt be,
Enjoy thy dearest wish: But see
Thou take my shadowes property,
That hastes away when I come nigh:
    Else stay till death hath blinded mee,
And then I will bequeath my self to thee.

The English Poems of Henry King, D.D., ed. Laurence Mason (New Haven: Yale University Press, 1914), 17.

Edward Herbert

Sonnet of Black Beauty

Black beauty, which above that common light,
    Whose Power can no colours here renew
    But those which darkness can again subdue,
Do'st still remain unvary'd to the sight,

And like an object equal to the view,
    Art neither chang'd with day, nor hid with night;
    When all these colours which the world call bright,
And which old Poetry doth so persue,

Are with the night so perished and gone,
    That of their being there remains no mark,
Thou still abidest so intirely one,
    That we may know thy blackness is a spark
Of light inaccessible, and alone
    Our darkness which can make us think it dark.

ANOTHER SONNET TO BLACK IT SELF

Thou Black, wherein all colours are compos'd,
   And unto which they all at last return,
   Thou colour of the Sun where it doth burn,
And shadow, where it cools, in thee is clos'd
Whatever nature can, or hath dispos'd
   In any other Hue: from thee do rise
Those tempers and complexions, which disclos'd,
   As parts of thee, do work as mysteries,
Of that thy hidden power; when thou dost reign
   The characters of fate shine in the Skies,
And tell us what the Heavens do ordain,
   But when Earth's common light shines to our eys,
Thou so retir'st thy self, that thy disdain
   All revelation unto Man denys.

THE BROWN BEAUTY

1.

While the two contraries of Black and White,
In the Brown *Phaie* are so well unite,
That they no longer now seem opposite,
   Who doubts but love, hath this his colour chose,
   Since he therein doth both th' extremes compose,
   And as within their proper Centre close?

2.

Therefore as it presents not to the view
That whitely raw and unconcocted hiew,
Which Beauty Northern Nations think the true;
   So neither hath it that adust aspect,
   The *Moor* and *Indian* so much affect,
   That for it they all other do reject.

3.

Thus while the White well shadow'd doth appear,
And black doth through his lustre grow so clear,
That each in other equal part doth bear;
   All in so rare proportion is combin'd,

That the fair temper, which adorns her mind,
Is even to her outward form confin'd.

4.

Phaie, your Sexes honour, then so live,
That when the World shall with contention strive
To whom they would a chief perfection give,
    They might the controversie so decide,
    As quitting all extreams on either side,
You more then any may be dignify'd.

To her Hair

Black beamy hairs, which so seem to arise
        From the extraction of those eyes,
That into you she destin-like doth spin
The beams she spares, what time her soul retires,
        And by those hallow'd fires,
        Keeps house all night within.

Since from within her awful front you shine,
        As threads of life which she doth twine,
And thence ascending with your fatal rays,
Do crown those temples, where Love's wonders wrought
        We afterwards see brought
        To vulgar light and praise.

Lighten through all your regions, till we find
        The causes why we are grown blind,
That when we should your Glories comprehend
Our sight recoils, and turneth back again,
        And doth, as 'twere in vain,
        It self to you extend.

Is it, because past black, there is not found
        A fix'd or horizontal bound?
And so, as it doth terminate the white,
It may be said all colours to infold,
        And in that kind to hold
        Somewhat of infinite?

Or is it, that the centre of our sight
        Being vailed in its proper night
Discerns your blackness by some other sense,

Then that by which it doth py'd colours see,
    Which only therefore be
    Known by their difference?

Tell us, when on her front in curls you lye
    So diapred from that black eye,
That your reflected forms may make us know
That shining light in darkness all would find,
    Were they not upward blind
    With the Sun beams below.

The Poems of Lord Herbert of Cherbury (Oxford: Clarendon, 1923), 37–39, 60.

John Collop

ON AN ETHIOPIAN BEAUTY, M.S.

Black specks for beauty spots white faces need:
How fair are you whose face is black indeed?
See how in hoods and masks some faces hide,
As if asham'd the white should be espi'd.
View how a blacker veil o'respreads the skies,
And a black scarf on earth's rich bosome lies.
When worth is dead, all do their blacks put on,
As if they would revive the worth that's gone.
Surely in black Divinity doth dwell;
By th' black garb onely we Divines can tell.
Devils ne're take this shape, but shapes of light;
Devils which mankind hurt, appear in white,
When Natures riches in one masse was hurl'd,
Thus black was th' face of all the infant world.
What th'world calls fair is foolish, 'tis allow'd,
That you who are so black, be justly proud.

OF THE BLACK LADY WITH GREY EYES AND WHITE TEETH

Like to the grey-ey'd Morn, your sparkling eyes
Dart lustre, while a sable clothes the skies.
And your white teeth resemble th' milky way,
The glory of the night, and th' shame of day,

Complain not then *Nigrina* of thy white,
Since stars shine brightest in the blackest night.

The Poems of John Collop, ed. Conrad Hilberry (Madison: University of Wisconsin Press, 1962), 116.

[*Abraham Wright*]

To a black Gentlewoman: Mistresse A. H.

Grieve not (faire maid) cause you are black; so's she
Thats spouse to him who died upon the tree:
And so is every thing. For to your thought,
If you but wink, the worlds as dark as nought.
Or doe but look abroad and you shall meet
In every hallowed Church, in every street,
The fairest still in this; who think they lack
Of their perfections if not all in black:
Their gowns, their veiles are so, nay more their necks,
Their very beauties are foild off with specks
Of the dark colour. Whilst thus to her mate
Each seems more faire. Now they but personate
What you are really. Your fairest haire
Shadows the Picture of your face more faire:
Your two black sphears are like two Globes beset
With Ebony, or ring'd about with Jet.
O how I now desire ene to depart
From all the rest, and study the Black art:
But since thats not alowed me, I will see
How I may truely, fairest, study thee.

Abraham Wright, *Parnassus Biceps; or Severall Choice Pieces of Poetry* . . . (London, 1656), 128.

[*Walton Poole*]

On a black Gentlewoman

If shadowes be a Pictures excellence
And make it seem more glorious to the sence:

If stars in brightest day are lost for sight
And seem more glorious in the mask of night.
Why should you think fair creature that you lack
Perfection cause your eyes and haire are black.
Or that your beauty, which so far exceeds
The new-sprung Lillies in their maidenheads,
The rosie colour of your cheeks and lips
Should by that darknesse suffer an ecclipse.
Rich Diamonds are fairer being set
And compassed within a foile of jet.
Nor can it be dame nature should have made
So bright a Sun to shine without a shade.
It seems that nature when she first did fancy
Your rare composure studied Negromancy:
And when to you these gifts she did impart
She used altogether the Black Art.
She framed the Magick circle of your eyes,
And made those hairs the chains wherein she ties
Rebellious hearts, those vaines, which doe appear
Twined in Meanders about every sphear,
Mysterious figures are, and when you list
Your voice commandeth like an exorcist.
Now if in Magick you have skill so far
Vouchsafe to make me your familiar.
Nor hath kind nature her black art reveald
By outward parts alone, some are conceald.
As by the spring head men may easily know
The nature of the streams that run below.
So your black eyes and haire doe give direction,
That all the rest are of the like complexion.
The rest where all rest lies that blesseth man,
That *Indian* mine, that streight of Magellan.
The worlds dividing gulph, through which who venters
With hoised sailes and ravished sences enters
To a new world of blisse. Pardon I pray
If my rude muse presumes for to display
Secrets forbid, or hath her bounds surpast
In praising sweetnesse which she nere did tast:
Starv'd men may talk of meat, and blind men may
(Though hid from light) yet know there is a day.
A rover in the mark his arrow sticks
Sometimes as well as he that shoots at pricks.

And if I might direct my shaft aright,
The black mark would I hit, and not the white.

Abraham Wright, *Parnassus Biceps; or Severall Choice Pieces of Poetry* . . . (London, 1656), 75–76.

Richard Lovelace

[A Black Patch on Lucasta's Face] Another

1.
As I beheld a Winters Evening Air,
Curl'd in her court false locks of living hair,
Butter'd with Jessamine the Sun left there,

2.
Galliard and clinquant she appear'd to give,
A Serenade or Ball to us that grieve,
And teach us *A la mode* more gently live.

3.
But as a *Moor*, who to her Cheeks prefers
White Spots t'allure her black Idolaters,
Me thought she look'd all ore bepatch'd with Stars;

4.
Like the dark front of some *Ethiopian* Queen,
Vailed all ore with Gems of Red, Blew, Green;
Whose ugly Night seem'd masked with days Skreen;

5.
Whilst the fond people offer'd Sacrifice
To Saphirs 'stead of Veins and Arteries,
And bow'd unto the Diamonds, not her Eyes.

6.
Behold *Lucasta*'s Face, how't glows like Noon!
A Sun intire is her complexion,
And form'd of one whole Constellation.

7.

So gently shining, so serene, so cleer,
Her look doth Universal Nature cheer;
Only a cloud or two hangs here and there.

ODE

1.

You are deceiv'd; I sooner may dull fair,
Seat a dark *Moor* in *Cassiopea's* chair,
  Or on the Glow-worms uselesse Light
  Bestow the watching flames of Night,
    Or give the Roses breath
    To executed Death,
      Ere the bright hiew
      Of Verse to you;
It is just Heaven on Beauty stamps a fame,
And we alass! its Triumphs but proclaim.

2.

What chains but are too light for me, should I
Say that *Lucasta*, in strange Arms could lie;
  Or, that *Castara* were impure,
  Or *Saccarisa's* faith unsure;
    That *Chloris* Love as hair,
    Embrac'd each En'mies air:
      That all their good
      Ran in their blood;
'Tis the same wrong th'unworthy to inthrone,
As from her proper sphere t'have vertue thrown.

3.

That strange force on the ignoble hath renown,
As *Aurum Fulminans*, it blows Vice down;
  'Twere better (heavy one) to crawl
  Forgot, then raised, trod on fall;
    All your defections now
    Are not writ on your brow.
      Odes to faults give
      A shame, must live.

When a fat mist we view, we coughing run;
But that once Meteor drawn, all cry, undone.

4.

How bright the fair *Paulina* did appear,
When hid in Jewels she did seem a Star:
  But who could soberly behold
  A wicked Owl in Cloath of Gold?
    Or the ridiculous *Ape,*
    In sacred *Vesta's* shape?
      So doth agree
      Just Praise with thee;
For since thy birth gave thee no beauty, know
No Poets pencil must or can do so.

The Poems of Richard Lovelace, ed. C. H. Wilkinson (Oxford: Clarendon, 1930), 121;139–40; by permission of Oxford University Press.

Eldred Revett

THE AETHIOPIAN BAPTIZED

WHAT *Stars* are those of *Orient* light
  Tremble on the *Brow* of *Night?*
And their *daring* Beams display
  Rival Glories with the day?
That baffle *Time, out-stare* the *Sun,*
  Scorn to wait *Succession;*
No, 'tis an *Aethiop div'd* these streams
  Rich in *spoils* of *Ransack't* Gems;
New-risen from the *Chrystal Bed,*
  All in *Pearls aparalled;*
What of *Night's* about his skin,
  Skreens, like that too, *Day within.*

Eldred Revett, *Selected Poems: Humane and Divine,* ed. Donald M. Friedman (Liverpool: Liverpool University Press, 1966), 50.

Richard Crashaw

ON THE BAPTIZED ÆTHIOPIAN

Let it no longer be a forlorne hope
        To wash an Æthiope:
Hee's washt, his gloomy skin a peacefull shade
        For his white soule is made;
And now, I doubt not, the Eternall Dove,
        A black-fac'd house will love.

Richard Crashaw, *Steps to the Temple* (London, 1648), 15.

UPON THE FAIRE ETHIOPIAN SENT TO A GENTLEWOMAN

Lo here the faire *Chariclia!* in whom strove
  so false a Fortune, and so true a Love.
Now after all her toiles by Sea and Land,
  O may she but arrive at your white hand,
Her hopes are crown'd, onely she feares that than,
  She shall appeare true Ethiopian.

Richard Crashaw, *The Delights of the Muses; or, Other Poems Written on Severall Occassions* (London, 1648), 29.

Eldred Revett

THE FAIR NYMPH SCORNING A BLACK BOY COURTING HER

Nymph
STAND off, and let me take the Aire,
Why should the smoke pursue the faire.
Boy
My face is smoke, thence may be guest
What flames within have scorch'd my breast.
Nymph
The flames of love I cannot view,
For the dark Lanthorn of thy hew.

Boy

And yet this Lanthorn keeps loves Taper,
Surer than yours that's of white paper,
Whatever mid-night hath been here
The Moon-shine of your light can clear.

Nymph

My Moon of an Eclipse is 'fraide,
If you should interpose your shade.

Boy

Our curl'd embraces shall delight,
To chequer Limbes with black and white.

Nymph

Thy ink, my paper, make me guess,
Our Nuptial bed would make a press;
And in our sports if any came,
They'd read a wanton Epigram.

Boy

Yet one thing sweet-heart let me aske,
Buy me for a new-false-mask.

Nymph

Yes, but my bargain must be this,
I'l throw my Mask off, when I kiss.

Boy

Why should my hew thy love impair?
Let the dark shop commend the ware,
Or if thy Love from black forbears,
I'l strive to wash [it] off with tears.

Nymph

Spare fruitless tears, since thou must needs
Still wear about thee mourning weeds,
Tears can no more affection win
Than wash thy Aethipoian skin.

THE INVERSION

Nymph

STAND off fair Boy, thou wilt affright
My solitude with sudden light.

Boy

My face is light, thence may be guest
The truth of my transparent brest.

Nymph
The truth of Love I cannot view,
For the full lustre of thy hew.
Boy
The lustre's sooner pervious made
Then your impenitrable shade;
What-ever Noon, my day doth trim,
Your thick how-ever Mist may dim.
Nymph
My Mist would fear to break away,
If you should intermix your ray.
Boy
Our curled embraces shall delight
With Limbs to shuffle day and night:
Nymph
Thy light my darkness make me fear
Our bed a *Chaos* would appear;
And in our sports did any pass,
They'd see the indigested Mass.
Boy
Yet one thing sweet-heart let me crave,
Me for a new-false mirror have;
Nymph
Yes, but my bargain must request,
I throw my glass by, when undrest:
Boy
Why should my hue thee less delight,
Let the Star-foiles set of the night:
Or if thy love from light forbeares,
I'le strive to put it out with teares.
Nymph
Spare fruitless teares, since thou must needs
Still have on thy Transfigur'd weeds,
Teares can no more affection win,
Then over-cast thy Angell skin.

A BLACK NYMPH SCORNING A FAIR BOY COURTING HER

Nymph
Fond Boy, thy vain pursuit give o're,
Since I thy shadow go before.

Boy

Ah fly not Nymph! we may pursue,
And shadowes overtake like you.

Nymph

I pass howe're in course away
The night to thy succeeding day.

Boy

If night thou art, oh! be not gone,
Till thou have stood a triple one:
Though Jove I fear, would then invade,
Not his *Alcmena*, but the shade.

Nymph

So should the thunderer embrace,
A cloud in his own goddess place.

Boy

So let us but commixt a while.
Distinguish one anothers foil;
That to advantage we may tell,
How either beauty doth excell.

Nymph

I need not thy betraying light,
To shew how far I am from white;
And to the piece that nature made,
I dare be no improving shade.

Boy

Then my dark Angell, I can charm
Thee (circled) in mine either arm.

Nymph

See! from thy slight embraces broke
Secure I vanish in my smoke.

ONE ENAMOUR'D ON A BLACK-MOOR

What a strange love doth me invade,
Whose fires must *cool* in that *dark shade!*
Round her such *solitudes* are seen
As she were all *Retir'd within*,
And did in hush't up silence lie   [5]
(*Though single*) a *Conspiracy*.
How did my passion find her out,
That is with *Curtains drawn about?*
(And though her eyes do *cent'nell keep*)

She is all over else asleep;   [10]
And I expect when she my sight,
Should strike with universal light.
A scarce seen thing she glides, were gon
If touch'd, *an Apparition*,
To immortality that dip't   [15]
Hath *newly* from her *Lethe slip't.*
No feature here we can define
By this, or that illustrious line,
Such curiosity is not
Found in an *un-distinguisht blot.*   [20]
This beauty puts us from the part
We all have tamely *got by hart,*
Of Roses here there Lillies grow,
Of Saphire, Corall, Hills of snow:
These Rivulets are *all ingrost*   [25]
And all in on *Black Ocean lost.*
The treasures *lock't up* we would get
Within the *Ebon Cabinet,*
And he that *Ravishes must pick*
Open the quaint *Italian Trick.*   [30]
She is her *own close mourning in*
[(]At Natures Charge) a *Cypress skin.*
Our common Parent else to blot
A moal, on the white mold, a spot.
Dropt it with her own *Statute Ink,*   [35]
And the *new temper'd Clay* did *sink:*
So the fair figure doth remain,
Her ever since *Record in grain.*
Ixion's sometime armfull might
Swell with, perhaps, a *fleece more bright,*   [40]
But she as *soft* might be allow'd,
The *goddesse's deputed cloud,*
Though sure from our distinct embrace,
Centaurs had been a *dapple Race.*
Thou pretious *Night-piece* that art made,   [45]
More valuable in thy *shade.*
From which when the weak tribe depart,
The skilful *Master* hugs his art.
Thou dost not to our dear surprise
Thine own *white marble* statue rise;   [50]
And yet no more a price dost lack,

Clean built up of the *polish't black.*
Thou like no *Pelops* hast supply
Of *an one joint* by *Ivory.*
But art miraculously set,   [55]
Together *totally* with *Jet.*
Nor can I count that bosome cheap,
That lies not a cold winter heap:
Where pillow yet I warmly can,
In *down* of the *contrary swan;*   [60]
Let who will wilde enjoyments dream,
And tipple from another stream;
Since he with equall pleasure dwells,
That lies at these dark fontinells:
These fair, Round, *sphears* contemplate on   [65]
So just in the proportion.
And the *lines* of either breast,
Find the rich *countries of the East.*
They not as in the *milkie* hue,
Are *broke* into *Raw streaks* of *blew.*   [70]
But have in the *more-lived* stains,
The *very Violets* of Veins,
They rise the *Double-headed* Hill,
Whose tops *shade one another still,*
Between them lies that *spicy Nest,*   [75]
That the *last Phoenix scorch'd,* and *blest.*
What fall's from her is rather made
Her own (just) picture, than her shade:
And where she walks the Sun doth hold
Her pourtrai'd in a frame of gold.   [80]

Eldred Revett, *Selected Poems: Humane and Divine,* ed. Donald M. Friedman (Liverpool: Liverpool University Press, 1966), 21–40; reprinted by permission.

Works Cited

Adams, Thomas. "The White Devil." In *The English Sermon: 1550–1650*, ed. Martin Seymour Smith. Cheadle, Cheshire: Carcanet, 1976.

Adelman, Janet. *The Common Liar: An Essay on "Antony and Cleopatra."* New Haven: Yale University Press, 1973.

Ainsworth, Henry. *Solomons Song of Songs in English Metre. . . .* London, 1623.

Allen, Don Cameron. "Symbolic Color in the Literature of the English Renaissance." *Philological Quarterly* 25 (1993): 248–57.

Andrews, Kenneth R. *English Privateering Voyages to the West Indies, 1588–1595*. Cambridge: Hakluyt Society at Cambridge University Press, 1959.

Anzaldúa, Gloria, ed. *Making Face/Making Soul= Haciendo Caras: Creative and Critical Perspectives by Women of Color*. San Francisco: Aunt Lute Foundation Books, 1990.

Appadurai, Arjun, ed. *The Social Life of Things: Commodities in Cultural Perspective*. New York: Cambridge University Press, 1990.

Appiah, Kwame Anthony. "Race." In *Critical Terms for Literary Study*, ed. Frank Lentricchia and Thomas McLaughlin, 274–87. Chicago: University of Chicago Press, 1990.

——. "The Uncompleted Argument: DuBois and the Illusion of Race." In *"Race," Writing, and Difference*, ed. Henry Louis Gates, Jr., 21–37. Chicago: University of Chicago Press, 1986.

Archer, John Michael. " 'False Soul of Egypt': Antiquity and Degeneration in *Antony and Cleopatra*." Paper presented at the annual meeting of the Shakespeare Association of America, Atlanta, April 1993.

Ashley, Maurice. *Rupert of the Rhine*. London: Hart-Davis, 1976.

Ashton, Robert. "Jacobean Politics 1603–1625." In *Stuart England*, ed. Blair Worden, 49–70. Oxford: Phaidon, 1986.

——, ed. *James I by His Contemporaries: An Account of His Career and Character as Seen by Some of His Contemporaries*. London: Hutchinson, 1969.

Bakhtin, Mikhail. *Rabelais and His World*. Trans. Hélène Iswolsky. Bloomington: Indiana University Press, 1984.

Baldwin, Thomas Whitfield. *On the Literary Genetics of Shakespeare's Poems and Sonnets.* Urbana: University of Illinois Press, 1950.

Baldwin, William. *The canticles or balades of Salomon, phraselyke declared in English Metres.* London, 1549.

Balibar, Etienne. "The Nation Form: History and Ideology." In *Race, Nation, Class: Ambiguous Identities,* ed. Etienne Balibar and Immanuel Wallerstein, 87–106. New York: Verso, 1991.

———. "Racism and Nationalism." In *Race, Nation, Class: Ambiguous Identities,* ed. Etienne Balibar and Immanuel Wallerstein, 37–67. New York: Verso, 1991.

Barthelemy, Anthony Gerard. *Black Face, Maligned Race: The Representation of Blacks in English Drama from Shakespeare to Southerne.* Baton Rouge: Louisiana State University Press, 1987.

Bartels, Emily C. "Imperialist Beginnings: Richard Hakluyt and the Construction of Africa." *Criticism* 34 (1992): 517–38.

Basse, William. *The Poetical Works of William Basse.* Ed. R. Warwick Bond. London: Ellis and Elvey, 1893.

Beal, Peter, comp. *Index of English Literary Manuscripts: Vol. 2, 1625–1700.* London: Mansell Publishing, 1987.

Beilin, Elaine V. *Redeeming Eve: Women Writers of the English Renaissance.* Princeton: Princeton University Press, 1987.

Belsey, Catherine. "Disrupting Sexual Difference: Meaning and Gender in the Comedies." In *Alternative Shakespeares,* ed. John Drakakis, 166–90. London: Methuen, 1985.

———. *The Subject of Tragedy: Identity and Difference in Renaissance Drama.* New York: Methuen, 1985.

Berger, John. *Ways of Seeing.* New York: Penguin, 1977.

Bhabha, Homi. "Signs Taken for Wonders: Questions of Ambivalence and Authority under a Tree outside Dehli, May 1817." In *"Race," Writing, and Difference,* ed. Henry Louis Gates, Jr. 163–84. Chicago: University of Chicago Press, 1986.

Blakeley, Allison. *Blacks in the Dutch World: The Evolution of Racial Imagery in a Modern Society.* Bloomington: Indiana University Press, 1993.

Bock, Philip K. *Shakespeare and Elizabethan Culture: An Anthropological View.* New York: Schocken, 1984.

Boime, Albert. *Art of Exclusion: Representing Blacks in the Nineteenth Century.* Washington, D.C.: Smithsonian Institution Press, 1990.

Boose, Lynda. E. " 'The Getting of a Lawful Race': Racial Discourse in Early Modern England and the Unrepresentable Black Woman." In *Women, "Race," and Writing in the Early Modern Period,* ed. Margo Hendricks and Patricia Parker, 35–54. London: Routledge, 1994.

Booth, Stephen, ed. *Shakespeare's Sonnets.* New Haven: Yale University Press, 1977.

Boyle, Robert. *Experiments and Considerations Touching Colours. . . .* 1664. Ed. Marie Boas Hall. New York: Johnson Reprint, 1964.

Brewer, Rose M. "Theorizing Race, Class and Gender: The New Scholarship of Black Feminist Intellectuals and Black Women's Labor." In *Theorizing Black Feminisms: The Visionary Pragmatism of Black Women,* ed. Stanlie M. James and Abena P. A. Busia, 13–30. New York: Routledge, 1993.

Brilliant, Richard. *Portraiture.* Cambridge: Harvard University Press, 1991.

Brome, Richard. *The English Moore; or, The Mock-Marriage.* Ed. Sara Jayne Steen. Columbia: University of Missouri Press, 1983.

Brown, Paul. " 'This thing of darkness I acknowledge mine': *The Tempest* and the Discourse of Colonialism." In *Political Shakespeare: New Essays in Cultural Materialism*, ed. Jonathan Dollimore and Alan Sinfield, 48–71. Manchester: Manchester University Press, 1985.

Browne, Thomas, Sir. *Pseudodoxia Epidemica; Or, Enquiries into very many received tenents and commonly presumed truths*. 1646. Ed. Robin Robbins. Oxford: Clarendon, 1981.

Brucioli, Antonio. *A Commentary upon the Canticle of Canticles*. Trans. Thomas James. London, 1598.

Bucher, Bernadette. *Icon and Conquest: A Structural Analysis of the Illustrations of Debry's "Great Voyages."* Trans. Basia Miller Gulati. Chicago: University of Chicago Press, 1981.

Bulwer, John. *Anthropometamorphosis: Man Transform'd; or, the Artificiall Changeling.* . . . London: William Hunt, 1653.

Cade, Toni. *The Black Woman: An Anthology*. New York: New American Library, 1970.

Campbell, Lorne. *Renaissance Portraits: European Portrait-Painting in the Fourteenth, Fifteenth, and Sixteenth Centuries*. New Haven: Yale University Press, 1990.

Carleton, Charles. *Royal Mistresses*. London: Routledge, 1989.

Cartelli, Thomas. "Prospero in Africa: *The Tempest* as Colonial Text and Pre-Text." In *Shakespeare Reproduced: The Text in History and Ideology*, ed. Jean Howard and Marion F. O'Connor, 99–115. New York: Methuen, 1987.

Cary, Elizabeth. *The Tragedy of Mariam, The Fair Queen of Jewry*. Ed. Margaret Ferguson and Barry Weller. Berkeley: University of California Press, 1994.

Cavell, Stanley. *Disowning Knowledge in Six Plays of Shakespeare*. Cambridge: Cambridge University Press, 1987.

Chapkis, Wendy. *Beauty Secrets: Women and the Politics of Appearance*. Boston: South End Press, 1986.

"The Character of a Town-Misse." 1680. In *The Old Book-Collector's Miscellany*, vol. 3, ed. Charles Hindley. London: Reeves and Turner, 1873.

Chew, Samuel C. *The Crescent and the Rose: Islam and England during the Renaissance*. New York: Oxford University Press, 1937.

Cleage, Pearl. *Deals with the Devil and Other Reasons to Riot*. New York: Ballantine Books, 1993.

Cleveland, John. *The Works of John Cleveland*. London, 1687.

Clissold, Stephen. *The Barbary Slaves*. New York: Barnes and Noble, 1977.

Cocks, Anna Somers. *An Introduction to Court Jewellery*. Owings Mills, Md.: Stemmer House, 1982.

Cohen, Walter. "*The Merchant of Venice* and the Possibilities of Historical Criticism." *ELH* 40 (1982): 765–89.

Collins, Patricia Hill. *Black Feminist Thought: Knowledge, Consciousness, and the Politics of Empowerment*. Boston: Unwin Hyman, 1990.

Collop, John. *The Poems of John Collop*. Ed. Conrad Hilberry. Madison: University of Wisconsin Press, 1962.

Constable, Henry. *Diana; or, The excellent conceitful Sonnets of H.C.* . . . London, 1594.

Cook, Ann Jennalie. *Making a Match: Courtship in Shakespeare and His Society*. Princeton: Princeton University Press, 1991.

Cook, M. A., ed. *Studies in the Economic History of the Middle East from the Rise of Islam to the Present Day: England to Egypt, 1300–1500.* New York: Oxford University Press, 1970.

Courtes, Jean Marie. Introduction to vol. 2 of *The Image of the Black in Western Art,* ed. Jean Devisse, 9–32. New York: William Morrow, 1979.

Crashaw, Richard. *The Delights of the Muses: Or, Other Poems written on severall occasions.* London, 1648.

———. *Steps to the Temple.* London, 1648.

Craton, Michael. *Sinews of Empire: A Short History of British Slavery.* Garden City, N.Y.: Doubleday, 1974.

Crenshaw, Kimberlè Williams. "Beyond Racism and Misogyny: Black Feminism and 2 Live Crew." In *Words That Wound: Critical Race Theory, Assaultive Speech, and the First Amendment,* ed. Mari J. Matsuda, Charles R. Lawrence III, Richard Delgado, and Kimberlè Williams Crenshaw, 111–36. Boulder, Colo.: Westview Press, 1993.

Cropper, Elizabeth. "The Beauty of Women: Problems in the Rhetoric of Renaissance Portraiture." In *Rewriting the Renaissance: The Discourses of Sexual Difference in Early Modern Europe,* ed. Margaret W. Ferguson, et al., 175–90. Chicago: University of Chicago Press, 1986.

Curtin, Philip D. *The Atlantic Slave Trade: A Census.* Madison: University of Wisconsin Press, 1969.

Dabydeen, David. *Hogarth's Blacks: Images of Blacks in Eighteenth-Century English Art.* Athens: University of Georgia Press, 1987.

Daniel, Samuel. *Delia and Rosamond Augmented, Cleopatra.* London, 1594.

Davenport, Doris. "The Pathology of Racism: A Conversation with Third World Wimmin." In *This Bridge Called My Back: Writings by Radical Women of Color,* ed. Cherríe Moraga and Gloria Anzaldúa, 85–90. New York: Kitchen Table, Women of Color Press, 1983.

Davidson, Basil. *The African Slave Trade.* Boston: Little, Brown, 1980.

———. *Black Mother: The Years of the African Slave Trade.* Boston: Little, Brown, 1961.

Davies, Godfrey. *The Early Stuarts, 1603–1660.* Vol. 9 of *Oxford History of England.* 16 vols. 2d ed. Oxford: Clarendon, 1959.

Davies, Kenneth Gordon. *The North Atlantic World in the Seventeenth Century.* Vol. 4 of *Europe and the World in the Age of Expansion.* 10 vols. Minneapolis: University of Minnesota Press, 1974.

Davis, Angela. *Women, Culture, and Politics.* New York: Vintage Books, 1990.

Davis, Natalie Zemon. *Society and Culture in Early Modern France: Eight Essays.* Reprint. Stanford: Stanford University Press, 1975.

Davis, Ossie. "The English Language Is My Enemy." *Negro History Bulletin* (April 1967): 3. Reprinted in *Revelations: An Anthology of Expository Essays by and about Blacks.* Needham Heights, Mass: Ginn, 1991.

deBeer, Edmond S. "King Charles II's Own Fashion: An Episode in Anglo-French Relations, 1666–1670." *Journal of the Warburg Institute* 2 (1938): 105–15.

Delacampagne, Christian. "Racism and the West: From Praxis to Logos." In *Anatomy of Racism,* ed. David Theo Goldberg, 83–88. Minneapolis: University of Minnesota Press, 1990.

Derrida, Jacques. "White Mythology: Metaphor in the Text of Philosophy." In *Margins of Philosophy,* trans. Alan Bass. Chicago: University of Chicago Press, 1982.

Dolan, Frances E. "Taking the Pencil out of God's Hand: Art, Nature, and the Face-Painting Debate in Early Modern England." *PMLA* 108 (1993): 224–39.

Donnan, Elizabeth. *Documents Illustrative of the History of the Slave Trade to America.* 4 vols. Washington, D.C.: Carnegie Institute of Washington, 1930.

Donne, John. *Poems, &c., by John Donne.* London, 1669.

Douglas, Mary. *Purity and Danger: An Analysis of the Concepts of Pollution and Taboo.* London: Routledge, 1978.

Douglas, Mary, and Baron Isherwood. *The World of Goods.* New York: Basic Books, 1979.

Drew-Bear, Annette. "Face Painting in Renaissance Tragedy." *Renaissance Drama* 12 (1981): 71–93.

duCille, Ann. "The Occult of True Black Womanhood: Critical Demeanor and Black Feminist Studies." *Signs: The Journal of Women in Culture and Society* 19, no. 3 (Spring 1994): 591–629.

Duffield, Ian, and Jagdish S. Gundara, eds. *Essays on the History of Blacks in Britain: From Roman Times to the Mid-Twentieth Century.* Brookfield, Vt.: Avebury, 1992.

Duncan-Jones, Katherine. *Sir Philip Sidney: Courtier Poet.* New Haven: Yale University Press, 1991.

Dyer, Richard. "White." *Screen* 29 (1989): 44–64.

Earle, Peter. "English Society." In *Stuart England,* ed. Blair Worden, 23–48. Oxford: Phaidon Press, 1986.

Eden, Richard. *The Decades of the New Worlde or West India. . . .* London, 1555.

Edwards, Paul. "The Early African Presence in the British Isles." In Duffield and Gundara.

Erickson, Peter. "Profiles in Whiteness." *Stanford Humanities Review* 3 (1993): 98–111.

——. "Representations of Blacks and Blackness in the Renaissance." *Criticism* 35, no. 4 (1993): 499–528.

——. *Rewriting Shakespeare, Rewriting Ourselves.* Berkeley: University of California Press, 1991.

Ernst, Kris. "Notes on Renaissance Cameos and Intaglios." *Metropolitan Museum Studies* (1930).

Evans, Joan. *English Jewellery from the Fifth Century A.D. to 1800.* London: Methuen, 1921.

Evans, Malcolm. "Deconstructing Shakespeare's Comedies." In *Alternative Shakespeares,* ed. John Drakakis, 67–94. London: Methuen, 1985.

Evelyn, John. *The Diary of John Evelyn.* Ed. E. S. deBeer. 6 vols. Oxford: Clarendon, 1955.

Fanon, Frantz. *Black Skin, White Masks.* 1952. Trans. Charles Lam Markmann. New York: Grove, 1982.

Felder, Cain Hope. *Troubling Biblical Waters: Race, Class, and Family.* Maryknoll, N.Y.: Orbis Books.

Feinberg, Nona. "Mary Wroth and the Invention of Female Poetic Subjectivity." In *Reading Mary Wroth: Representing Alternatives in Early Modern England,* ed. Naomi J. Miller and Gary F. Waller, 35–66. Knoxville: University of Tennessee Press, 1991.

Ferguson, Margaret. W. "Juggling the Categories of Race, Class, and Gender: Aphra Behn's *Oroonoko.*" In *Women, "Race," and Writing in the Early Modern Period,* ed. Margo Hendricks and Patricia Parker, 209–24. London: Routledge, 1994.

Fichter, Andrew. "*Antony and Cleopatra:* 'The Time of Universal Peace.'" *Shakespeare Survey* 33 (1980): 99–111. .

Fiedler, Leslie A. *The Stranger in Shakespeare.* New York: Stein and Day, 1972.

Fields, Barbara Jeanne. "Slavery, Race, and Ideology in the United States of America." *New Left Review* 181 (May/June 1990): 95–118.

File, Nigel, and Chris Power. *Black Settlers in Britain: 1555–1958.* London: Heinemann, 1981.

Fineman, Joel. *Shakespeare's Perjured Eye: The Invention of Poetic Subjectivity in the Sonnets.* Berkeley: University of California Press, 1986.

Fleming, Juliet. "Dictionary English and the Female Tongue." In *Enclosure Acts: Sexuality, Property, and Culture in Early Modern England,* ed. Richard Burt and John Michael Archer, 290–325. Ithaca: Cornell University Press, 1994.

Fletcher, Giles. *Licia, or Poemes of Love. . . .* London, 1593.

Fletcher, John. *Rule a Wife and Have a Wife.* Oxford, 1640.

Forneron, Henri. *Louise de Kéroüalle, Duchess of Portsmouth, 1649–1734: Society in the Court of Charles II.* London: Sonnenschein, 1891.

Foucault, Michel. *Power/Knowledge: Selected Interviews and Other Writings, 1972–1977.* Trans. and ed. Colin Gordon et al. New York: Pantheon Books, 1980.

Fradenburg, Louise Olga. *City, Marriage, Tournament: Arts of Rule in Late Medieval Scotland.* Madison: University of Wisconsin Press, 1991.

Franklin, Wayne. *Discoverers, Explorers, Settlers: The Diligent Writers of Early America.* Chicago: University of Chicago Press, 1979.

Fraser, Antonia. *King James.* New York: Knopf, 1975.

——. *Royal Charles: Charles II and the Restoration.* New York: Knopf, 1979.

Froude, James Anthony. *English Seamen in the Sixteenth Century.* New York: Scribner's, 1906.

Frye, Marilyn. *The Politics of Reality: Essays in Feminist Theory.* Trumansburg, N.Y.: Crossing Press, 1983.

Fryer, Peter. *Staying Power: The History of Black People in Britain.* London: Pluto Press, 1984.

Fumerton, Patricia. *Cultural Aesthetics: Renaissance Literature and the Practice of Social Ornament.* Chicago: University of Chicago Press, 1991.

Furber, Holden. *Rival Empires of Trade in the Orient, 1600–1800.* Vol. 2 of *Europe and the World in the Age of Expansion.* 10 vols. Minneapolis: University of Minnesota Press, 1976.

Galenson, David W. *Traders, Planters, and Slaves: Market Behavior in Early English America.* Cambridge: Cambridge University Press, 1986.

Gates, Henry Louis, Jr., ed. *Reading Black, Reading Feminist: A Critical Anthology.* New York: Penguin, 1990.

——. "Writing 'Race' and the Difference It Makes." In *"Race," Writing, and Difference,* ed. Henry Louis Gates, Jr., 1–20. Chicago: University of Chicago Press, 1986.

Giddings, Paula. *When and Where I Enter: The Impact of Black Women on Race and Sex in America.* New York: Morrow, 1984.

Gilman, Sander L. *Difference and Pathology: Stereotypes of Sexuality, Race, and Madness.* Ithaca: Cornell University Press, 1985.

Gilroy, Paul. *"There Ain't No Black in the Union Jack": The Cultural Politics of Race and Nation.* Chicago: University of Chicago Press, 1987.

Goldberg, David Theo, ed. *Anatomy of Racism.* Minneapolis: University of Minnesota Press, 1990.

Goldberg, Jonathan. "Fatherly Authority: The Politics of Stuart Family Images."

In *Rewriting the Renaissance: The Discourses of Sexual Difference in Early Modern Europe,* ed. Margaret W. Ferguson et al., 123–44. Chicago: University of Chicago Press, 1986.

Golding, Arthur, trans. *The xv Bookes of P. Ovidius Naso, entitled Metamorphosis . . .* (Ovid). London: Robert Walde-grave, 1587.

Gordon, D. J. "The Imagery of Ben Jonson's *The Masque of Blacknesse* and *The Masque of Beautie.*" *Journal of the Warburg and Courtauld Institutes* 6 (1943): 122–41.

Greenblatt, Stephen. *Marvelous Possessions: The Wonder of the New World.* Chicago: University of Chicago Press, 1991.

——. *Renaissance Self-Fashioning: From More to Shakespeare.* Chicago: University of Chicago Press, 1980.

——. *Shakespearean Negotiations: The Circulation of Social Energy in Renaissance England.* Berkeley: University of California Press, 1988.

Greville, Fulke. *The Life of the Renowned Sir Philip Sidney.* New York: Scholars' Facsimiles and Reprints, 1984.

Grewal, Shabnam, et al., eds. *Charting the Journey: Writings by Black and Third World Women.* London: Sheba Feminist Publishers, 1988.

Griffin, Susan. "The Sacrificial Lamb." In *Racism and Sexism: An Integrated Study,* ed. Paula S. Rothenberg, 296–305. New York: St. Martin's, 1988.

Guilpin, Edward. *Skialetheia. Or, a Shadowe of Truth, in certain Epigrams and Satyres.* London, 1598.

Hakluyt, Richard. *Discourse of Western Planting.* Vol. 2 of *The Original Writings and Correspondence of the Two Richard Hakluyts.* London: Hakluyt Society at Cambridge University Press, 1935.

——. *Diverse Voyages touching the Discoverie of America.* 1582.

——, ed. *The Principal Navigations, Traffiques and Discoveries of the English Nation.* 8 vols. Reprint. London: J. M. Dent & Sons, 1962.

Hall, Kim F. "Guess Who's Coming to Dinner? Colonization and Miscegenation in *The Merchant of Venice,*" *Renaissance Drama* n.s (1992): 87–111.

——. "'I rather would wish to be a Black-moore': Beauty, Race, and Rank in Lady Mary Wroth's *Urania.*" In *Women, "Race," and Writing,* ed. Margo Hendricks and Patricia Parker, 178–94. London: Routledge, 1993.

——. "Reading What Isn't There: 'Black' Studies in Early Modern England." *Stanford Humanities Review* 3 no. 1 (1993): 23–33.

Hall, Joseph. *Salomons divine arts, of ethickes, politickes, oeconomicks. . . .* London, 1609.

Hall, Stuart. "New Ethnicities." In *Black Film, British Cinema,* ed. Kobena Mercer, 27–30. London: Institute of Contemporary Arts, 1988.

Hampden, John. *Francis Drake, Privateer; Contemporary Narratives and Documents.* University: University of Alabama Press, 1972.

Hartwell, Abraham. trans. *A reporte of the kingdome of Congo, a region of Africa, and of the Countries that border rounde the same.* London, 1597.

Helgerson, Richard. *Forms of Nationhood: The Elizabethan Writing of England.* Chicago: University of Chicago Press, 1992.

Henderson, Mae Gwendolyn. "Speaking in Tongues: Dialogics, Dialectics, and the Black Woman Writer's Literary Tradition." In *Reading Black, Reading Feminist: A Critical Anthology,* ed. Henry Louis Gates, Jr., 116–44. New York: Meridian Books, 1990.

Herbert, Edward. *The Poems of Lord Herbert of Cherbury.* Oxford: Clarendon, 1923.

Herbert, George. *The Complete Works in Verse and Prose of George Herbert.* 3 vols. Ed. Alexander Grosart. London, 1874.

Herford, C. H., and Percy Simpson. *Ben Jonson.* 11 vols. Oxford: Clarendon, 1925.

Higginbotham, Evelyn Brooks. "African-American Women's History and the Metalanguage of Race." *Signs: The Journal of Women in Culture and Society* 17 no. 2 (Winter 1992): 251–74.

Hirst, Derek. *Authority and Conflict: England, 1603–1658.* Cambridge: Harvard University Press, 1986.

Hodge, John L. "Equality: Beyond Dualism and Oppression." In *Anatomy of Racism,* ed. David Theo Goldberg, 89–107. Minneapolis: University of Minnesota Press, 1990.

hooks, bell. *Ain't I a Woman: Black Women and Feminism.* Boston: South End Press, 1981.

——. "critical interrogation: talking race, resisting racism." In *Yearning: Race, Gender, and Cultural Politics,* 51–55. Boston: South End Press, 1990.

——. "feminism: a transformational politic." In hooks, *Talking Back: thinking feminist*thinking black,* 19–27. Boston: South End Press, 1989.

——. *Feminist Theory: From Margin to Center.* Boston: South End Press, 1984.

——. "overcoming white supremacy: a comment." In hooks, *Talking Back: thinking feminist*thinking black,* 112–19. Boston: South End Press, 1989.

Howard, Jean E. "Crossdressing, the Theatre, and Gender Struggle in Early Modern England." *Shakespeare Quarterly* 39 no. 4 (1988): 18–40.

Howarth, David. *Lord Arundel and His Circle.* New Haven: Yale University Press, 1985.

Hughes-Hallett, Lucy. *Cleopatra: Histories, Dreams, and Distortions.* New York: HarperCollins, 1990.

Hull, Gloria, Patricia Bell Scott, and Barbara Smith. *All the Women Are White, All the Men Are Black, but Some of Us Are Brave: Black Women's Studies.* New York: Feminist Press, 1982.

Hulme, Peter. *Colonial Encounters: Europe and the Native Caribbean, 1492–1797.* New York: Methuen, 1986.

Hunter, George K. *Dramatic Identities and Cultural Tradition: Studies in Shakespeare and His Contemporaries.* New York: Barnes and Noble, 1978.

Huntley, Frank Livingstone. *Bishop Joseph Hall and Protestant Meditation in Seventeenth-Century England: A Study with Texts of "The Art of Divine Meditation" (1606) and "Occasional Meditations" (1633).* Binghamton, N.Y.: Center for Medieval and Early Renaissance Studies, 1981.

Hutton, Ronald. *Charles II: King of England, Scotland, and Ireland.* Oxford: Clarendon, 1989.

Hyde, Lewis. *The Gift: Imagination and the Erotic Life of Property.* New York: Vintage, 1983.

Jameson, Fredric. *The Political Unconscious: Narrative as a Socially Symbolic Act.* Ithaca: Cornell University Press, 1981.

JanMohamed, Abdul R. "The Economy of Manichean Allegory: The Function of Racial Difference in Colonialist Literature." In *"Race," Writing, and Difference,* ed. Henry Louis Gates, Jr., 59–87. Chicago: University of Chicago Press, 1986.

Jardine, Lisa. *Still Harping on Daughters: Women and Drama in the Age of Shakespeare.* Totowa, N.J.: Barnes and Noble, 1983.

Johnson, Barbara. *A World of Difference.* Baltimore: Johns Hopkins University Press, 1987.

Jones, Ann Rosalind. *The Currency of Eros: Women's Love Lyric in Europe, 1540–1620.* Bloomington: Indiana University Press, 1991.

———. "The Self as Spectacle in Mary Wroth and Veronica Franco." In *Reading Mary Wroth: Representing Alternatives in Early Modern England,* ed. Naomi J. Miller and Gary Waller, 135–53. Knoxville: University of Tennessee Press, 1991.

Jones, Ann Rosalind, and Peter Stallybrass. "The Politics of *Astrophil and Stella.*" *Studies in English Literature* 24 no. 1 (1984): 53–68.

Jones, Eldred. *The Elizabethan Image of Africa.* Charlottesville: University of Virginia Press, 1971.

———. *Othello's Countrymen: The African in English Renaissance Drama.* London: Oxford University Press, 1965.

Jones, Howard Mumford. *O Strange New World: American Culture: the Formative Years.* New York: Viking, 1964.

Jonson, Ben. *Ben Jonson: The Complete Masques,* ed. Stephen Orgel. New Haven: Yale University Press, 1969.

Jordan, Winthrop. *White over Black: American Attitudes toward the Negro, 1550–1812.* Chapel Hill: University of North Carolina Press, 1968.

Kamps, Ivo, ed. *Shakespeare Left and Right.* New York and London: Routledge, 1991.

Kaplan, Paul H. D. *The Rise of the Black Magus in Western Art.* Ann Arbor, Mich: UMI Research Press, 1985.

Kelly, Anne Cline. "The Challenge of the Impossible: Ben Jonson's *Masque of Blackness.*" *College Language Association Journal* 20 no. 3 (1977): 341–55.

Kermode, Frank, et al., eds. *The Oxford Anthology of English Literature.* New York: Oxford University Press, 1973.

King, Deborah. "Multiple Jeopardy, Multiple Consciousness: The Context of a Black Feminist Ideology." *Signs: The Journal of Women in Culture and Society* 14, no. 1 (1988): 42–72.

King, Henry. *The English Poems of Henry King, D.D.* ed. Laurence Mason. New Haven: Yale University Press, 1914.

King, John N. *Tudor Royal Iconography: Literature and Art in an Age of Religious Crisis.* Princeton: Princeton University Press, 1989.

Kingsley, Garland Jane. "British Empire." Vol. 4 of *Encyclopaedia Britannica.* 11th ed. London: *Encyclopaedia Britannica,* 1910.

Kinsley, James, ed. *The Poems of William Dunbar.* Oxford: Clarendon, 1979.

Kolodny, Annette. *The Lay of the Land: Metaphor as Experience and History in American Life and Letters.* Chapel Hill: University of North Carolina Press, 1975.

Kopytoff, Igor. "The Cultural Biography of Things: Commoditization as a Process." In *The Cultural Life of Things: Commodities in Cultural Perspective,* ed. Arjun Appadurai, 64–91. New York: Cambridge University Press, 1990.

Krishna, Bal. *Commercial Relations between India and England, 1601–1757.* London: Routledge, 1924.

Lamb, Mary Ellen. *Gender and Authorship in the Sidney Circle.* Madison: University of Wisconsin Press, 1990.

———. "Women Readers in Mary Wroth's *Urania.*" In *Reading Mary Wroth: Representing Alternatives in Early Modern England,* ed. Naomi J. Miller and Gary Waller, 35–66. Knoxville: University of Tennessee Press, 1991.

Lanyer, Aemilia. *The Poems of Aemilia Lanyer: Salve Deus Rex Judæorum.* Ed. Susanne Wood. New York: Oxford, 1993.

Le Corbeiller, Clare. "Miss America and Her Sisters: Personifications of the Four Parts of the World." *Metropolitan Museum of Art Bulletin* 19 (April 1961): 209–23.

Lee, Sidney. *Elizabethan Sonnets.* 2 vols. New York: Cooper Square, 1964.

Leo Africanus, Johannes. *A Geographical Historie of Africa.* Trans. and ed. John Pory. London, 1600.

Lerner, Gerda. "Comment: Martin Bernal's *Black Athena.*" *Journal of Women's History* 4 (1993): 90–94.

Levin, Harry. *The Power of Blackness: Hawthorne, Poe, Melville.* New York: Knopf, 1958.

Lipson, Ephraim. *The Economic History of England.* 4th ed. 3 vols. London: A. and C. Black, 1947.

Locke, Alain LeRoy. *The Negro in Art: A Pictorial Record of the Negro Artist and of the Negro Theme in Art.* New York: Hacker Art Books, 1968.

Loomba, Ania. *Gender, Race, Renaissance Drama.* Manchester and New York: Manchester University Press, 1989.

Lorde, Audre. "A Burst of Light: Living with Cancer." In *A Burst of Light: Essays by Audre Lorde,* 49–134. Ithaca: Firebrand, 1988.

——. *Sister Outsider: Essays and Speeches by Audre Lorde.* Trumansburg, N.Y.: Crossing Press, 1984.

Lott, Eric. "Love and Theft: The Racial Unconscious of Blackface Minstrelsy." *Representations* 39 (Summer 1992): 23–50.

Lovelace, Richard. *The Poems of Richard Lovelace.* Ed. C. H. Wilkinson. Oxford: Clarendon, 1930.

Lust's Dominion. In *A Select Collection of Old English Plays,* ed. Robert Dodsley. 15 vols. London: Reeves and Turner, 1874–76,

Maltby, William S. *The Black Legend in England: The Development of Anti-Spanish Sentiment, 1558–1660.* Durham, N.C.: Duke University Press, 1971.

Mandeville, Sir John. *The Travels of Sir John Mandeville.* Ed. A. W. Pollard. New York: Dover, 1964.

Mannix, Daniel P., and Malcolm Cowley. *Black Cargoes: A History of the Atlantic Slave Trade, 1518–1865.* New York: Viking, 1962.

Marcus, Leah. *Puzzling Shakespeare: Local Reading and Its Discontents.* Berkeley: University of California Press, 1988.

Mark, Peter. *Africans in European Eyes: The Portrayal of Black Africans in Fourteenth- and Fifteenth-Century Europe.* Syracuse: Maxwell School of Citizenship and Public Affairs, Syracuse University, 1974.

Markham, Gervase. *The Poem of Poems, or Sions Muse, Contayning the divine Song of King Salomon, divided into eight Ecologues.* London, 1596.

Marotti, Arthur. "'Love Is Not Love': Elizabethan Sonnet Sequences and the Social Order." *English Literary History* 49 (1982): 396–428.

Masten, Jeff. " 'Shall I turne blabb?': Circulation, Gender, and Subjectivity in Mary Wroth's Sonnets." In *Reading Mary Wroth: Representing Alternatives in Early Modern England,* ed. Naomi J. Miller and Gary Waller, 35–66. Knoxville: University of Tennessee Press, 1991.

McCoy, Richard C. *Sir Philip Sidney: Rebellion in Arcadia.* New Brunswick: Rutgers University Press, 1979.

McDowell, Deborah E. "New Directions for Black Feminist Criticism." In *The New*

Feminist Criticism: Essays on Women, Literature and Theory, ed. Elaine Showalter, 186–99. New York: Pantheon Books, 1985.

McElwee, William. *The Wisest Fool in Christendom: The Reign of King James I and VI.* London: Faber and Faber, 1958.

Mengel, Elias, ed. *Poems on Affairs of State: Augustan Satirical Verse, 1678–1714.* 7 vols. New Haven: Yale University Press, 1963.

Mercer, Kobena, ed. *Black Film, British Cinema.* London: Institute of Contemporary Arts, 1988.

Meyer, Gerard Previn. "The Blackamoor and Her Love." *Philological Quarterly* 17 (1938): 371–76.

Miers, Suzanne, and Igor Kopytoff, eds. *Slavery in Africa: Historical and Anthropological Perspectives.* Madison: University of Wisconsin Press, 1977.

Miller, Christopher L. *Blank Darkness: Africanist Discourse in French.* Chicago: University of Chicago Press, 1985.

Miller, Jacqueline T. *Poetic License: Authority and Authorship — Medieval and Renaissance Contexts.* New York: Oxford University Press, 1986.

Miller, Naomi J. "Engendering Discourse: Women's Voices in Wroth's *Urania* and Shakespeare's Plays." In *Reading Mary Wroth: Representing Alternatives in Early Modern England*, ed. Naomi J. Miller and Gary Waller, 35–66. Knoxville: University of Tennessee Press, 1991.

——. " 'Nott much to be marked': Narrative of the Woman's Part in Lady Mary Wroth's *Urania.*" *Studies in English Literature: 1500–1900* 29 no. 1 (Winter 1989): 121–37.

Milton, John. *Reformation Touching Church Discipline.* Vol. 1 of *The Complete Prose Works of John Milton*, ed. Don M. Wolfe. 8 vols. New Haven: Yale University Press, 1953.

Montrose, Louis A. " 'Eliza, Queene of Shepheardes,' and the Pastoral of Power." *English Literary Renaissance* 10 no. 2 (Spring 1980): 153–82.

——. "The Elizabethan Subject and the Spenserian Text." In *Literary Theory/Renaissance Texts*, eds. Patricia Parker and David Quint, 303–40. Baltimore: Johns Hopkins University Press, 1987.

——. "*A Midsummer Night's Dream* and the Shaping Fantasies of Elizabethan Culture: Gender, Power, Form." In *Rewriting the Renaissance: The Discourses of Sexual Difference in Early Modern Europe*, ed. Margaret W. Ferguson et al., 65–87. Chicago: University of Chicago Press, 1986.

——. "The Work of Gender in the Discourse of Discovery." *Representations* 33 (1991): 1–41.

Morrah, Patrick. *Prince Rupert of the Rhine.* London: Constable, 1976.

Morrison, Toni. *The Bluest Eye.* New York: Washington Square, 1970.

——. *Playing in the Dark: Whiteness and the Literary Imagination.* Cambridge, Mass.: Harvard University Press, 1992.

Mukerji, Chandra. *From Graven Images: Patterns of Modern Materialism.* New York: Columbia University Press, 1983.

Murdoch, Kenneth B. *The Sun at Noon: Three Biographical Sketches.* New York: Macmillan, 1939.

Nahoum-Grappe, Véronique. "The Beautiful Woman." Trans. Arthur Goldhammer. In *A History of Women: Renaissance and Enlightenment Paradoxes*, ed. Natalie Zemon Davis and Arlette Farge, 85–100. Cambridge, Mass.: Harvard University Press, 1993.

Newman, Karen. " 'And wash the Ethiop white': Femininity and the Monstrous in *Othello.*" In *Shakespeare Reproduced: The Text in History and Ideology,* ed. Jean Howard and Marion O'Connor, 141–62. New York: Methuen, 1987.

Ngugi wa Thiong'o. "National Identity and Imperialist Domination: The Crisis of Culture in Africa Today." In *Barrel of a Pen: Resistance to Repression in Neo-Colonial Kenya,* 87–100. Trenton, N.J.: Africa World Press, 1983.

Nichols, John. *Progresses of King James I.* 2 vols. London, 1828.

Nixon, Rob. "Caribbean and African Appropriations of *The Tempest.*" *Critical Inquiry* 13 no. 3 (Spring 1987): 557–78.

Noble, Jeanne. "Bitches Brew." In *Beautiful, Also, Are the Souls of My Black Sisters: A History of Black Women in America,* ed. Jeanne Noble, 313–44. Englewood Cliffs, N.J.: Prentice-Hall, 1978.

Notestein, Wallace. *The English People on the Eve of Colonization,* 1603–1630. New York: Harper, 1954.

Ogilby, John. *Africa.* London, 1688.

Orgel, Stephen. *The Jonsonian Masque.* Cambridge: Harvard University Press, 1965.

———. "Prospero's Wife." In *Rewriting the Renaissance: The Discourses of Sexual Difference in Early Modern Europe,* ed. Margaret W. Ferguson et al., 50–64. Chicago: University of Chicago Press, 1986.

———, ed. *The Renaissance Imagination: Essays and Lectures by D. J. Gordon.* Berkeley: University of California Press, 1976.

Oxford English Dictionary. 2d ed. Oxford: Clarendon, and New York: Oxford University Press, 1989.

Pardes, Ilana. *Countertraditions in the Bible: A Feminist Approach.* Cambridge: Harvard University Press, 1992.

Parker, Patricia. *Literary Fat Ladies: Rhetoric, Gender, Property.* London: Methuen, 1987.

Parks, George Bruner. *Richard Hakluyt and the English Voyages.* New York: F. Ungar, 1961.

Pembroke, Lady Anne Clifford Herbert. *The Diaries of Lady Anne Clifford,* ed. D. J. H. Clifford. Wolfeboro Falls, N.H.: A. Sutton, 1992.

Pennington, Loren E. *Hakluytus Posthumus: Samuel Purchas and the Promotion of English Overseas Expansion.* Emporia, Kans.: Emporia State Teacher's College Graduate Division, 1966.

Pepys, Samuel. *The Diary of Samuel Pepys.* 11 vols. Ed. Robert Latham and William Matthews. Berkeley: University of California Press, 1970.

Peterson, Richard. "Icon and Mystery in Jonson's *Masque of Beautie.*" *John Donne Journal* 5 nos. 1–2 (1986): 169–99.

Piedra, Jose. "Literary Whiteness and the Afro-Hispanic Difference." In *The Bounds of Race: Perspectives on Hegemony and Resistance,* ed. Dominick LaCapra. Ithaca: Cornell University Press, 1991.

Prager, Carolyn. " 'If I Be Devil': English Renaissance Responses to the Proverbial and Ecumenical Ethiopian." *Journal of Medieval and Renaissance Studies* 17 no. 2 (1987): 257–79.

Prat, William, trans. *The Discription of the Countrey of Aphrique.* Ed. Lillian Gottesman. New York: Scholars' Facsimiles and Reprints, 1972.

Pratt, Mary Louise. *Imperial Eyes: Travel Writing and Transculturation.* New York: Routledge, 1992.

Princely Magnificence: Court Jewels of the Renaissance, 1500–1630. London: Debrett's Peerage, 1980.

Purchas, Samuel. *Hakluytus Posthumus; or, Purchas His Pilgrimes: Contayning a History of the World in Sea Voyages and Land Travells by Englishmen and others.* 20 vols. New York: Macmillan, 1905.

Puttenham, George. *The Arte of English Poesie; Contriued into Three Bookes: the First of Poets and Poesie, the Second of Proportion, the Third of Ornament.* 1589. Kent, Ohio: Kent State University Press, 1970.

Quilligan, Maureen. "The Constant Subject: Instability and Authority in Wroth's *Urania* Poems." In *Soliciting Interpretations: Essays in Seventeenth-Century Poetry*, ed. Elizabeth D. Harvey and Katharine Eisaman Maus, 307–35. Chicago: University of Chicago Press, 1990.

——. "Lady Mary Wroth and Family Romance." In *Unfolded Tales: Essays on Renaissance Romance*, ed. George Logan and Gordon Teskey, 257–80. Ithaca: Cornell University Press, 1988.

——. *The Language of Allegory: Defining the Genre.* Ithaca: Cornell University Press, 1979.

——. "Sidney and His Queen." In *The Historical Renaissance: New Essays on Tudor and Stuart Literature and Culture*, ed. Richard Strier and Heather Dubrow, 171–96. Chicago: University of Chicago Press, 1988.

Rabb, Theodore K. *Enterprise and Empire: Merchant and Gentry Investment in the Expansion of England, 1575–1630.* Cambridge: Harvard University Press, 1967.

Rackin, Phyllis. "Androgyny, Mimesis, and the Marriage of the Boy Heroine on the English Stage." *PMLA* 102 no. 1 (1987): 29–41.

——. "'Shakespeare's Boy Cleopatra': The Decorum of Nature and the Golden World of Poetry." *PMLA* 87 no. 2 (1972): 201–12.

Ragussis, Michael. "Representation, Conversion, and Literary Form: *Harrington* and the Novel of Jewish Identity." *Critical Inquiry* 16 no. 1 (1989): 113–43.

Raleigh, Sir Walter. *History of the World.* London: printed for Walter Burre, 1614.

Rawley, James A. *The Transatlantic Slave Trade: A History.* New York: Norton, 1981.

Revett, Eldred. *Selected Poems: Humane and Divine.* Ed. Donald M. Friedman. Liverpool: Liverpool University Press, 1966.

Roberts, Josephine. "Labyrinths of Desire: Lady Mary Wroth's Reconstruction of Romance." *Women's Studies* 19 no. 2 (1991): 183–92.

Roche, Thomas, Jr. "*Astrophil and Stella*: A Radical Reading." In *Sir Philip Sidney: An Anthology of Modern Criticism*, ed. Dennis Day, 185–226. Oxford: Clarendon, 1987.

Rowse, A. L. *The Expansion of Elizabethan England.* New York: St. Martin's, 1955.

Rubin, Gayle. "The Traffic in Women: Notes on the 'Political Economy' of Sex." In *Toward an Anthropology of Women*, ed. Rayna P. Reiter, 157–210. New York: Monthly Review, 1975.

Sackville-West, Vita. *Knole and the Sackvilles.* London: Heinemann, 1922.

Said, Edward W. *Orientalism.* New York: Pantheon Books, 1978.

Salzman, Paul. *English Prose Fiction, 1558–1700: A Critical History.* Oxford: Clarendon, 1985.

Sanders, Ronald. *Lost Tribes and Promised Lands: The Origins of American Racism.* Boston: Little Brown, 1978.

Sandoval, Chela. "Feminism and Racism: A Report on the 1982 National Women's

Studies Conference." In *Making Face/Making Soul* = *Haciendo Caras: Creative and Critical Perspectives by Feminists of Color*, ed. Gloria Anzaldúa, 55–71. San Francisco: Aunt Lute Books, 1990.

Scarisbruck, Diane. "Anne of Denmark's Jewellery: The Old and the New." *Apollo* 123 (April 1986): 228–36.

Scobie, Edward. *Black Britannia: A History of Blacks in Britain.* Chicago: Johnson Publishing Company, 1972.

Scott, Joan W. "The Evidence of Experience." In *The Lesbian and Gay Studies Reader*, ed. Henry Abelove, Michele Aina Barale, and David M. Halperin, 397–415. New York: Routledge, 1993.

Scott, Walter, ed. *A Collection of Scarce and Valuable Tracts* [*Somer's Tracts*]. 2d ed. 15 vols. London, 1809.

Shakespeare, William. *A Midsummer Night's Dream.* Ed. Harold Brooks. New York: Methuen, 1979.

——. *The Riverside Shakespeare.* Ed. G. Blakemore Evans. Boston: Houghton Mifflin, 1972.

——. *The Tempest.* Ed. Stephen Orgel. Oxford: Clarendon, 1987.

Shyllon, F. O. *Black Slaves in Britain.* London: Oxford University Press, 1974.

Sidney, Sir Philip. *An Apologie for Poetrie.* London: for Henry Olney, 1595.

——. *The Countess of Pembroke's Arcadia.* New York: Penguin, 1982.

——. *The Poems of Sir Philip Sidney.* Ed. William A. Ringler. Oxford: Clarendon, 1962.

Skura, Meredith Anne. "Discourse and the Individual: The Case of Colonialism in *The Tempest.*" *Shakespeare Quarterly* 40 (1989): 42–69.

Smith, Barbara. "Toward a Black Feminist Criticism." In *The New Feminist Criticism: Essays on Women, Literature and Theory*, ed. Elaine Showalter, 168–85. New York: Pantheon Books, 1985.

Smith, Paul. *Discerning the Subject.* Minneapolis: University of Minnesota Press, 1988.

Smith, Valerie. "Black Feminist Theory and the Representation of the 'Other.' " In *Changing Our Own Words: Essays on Criticism, Theory, and Writing by Black Women*, ed. Cheryl A. Wall, 38–57. New Brunswick: Rutgers University Press, 1989.

——. "Split Affinities: The Case of Interracial Rape." In *Conflicts in Feminism*, ed. Marianne Hirsch and Evelyn Fox Keller. New York: Routledge, 1990.

Snowden, Frank M., Jr. *Before Color Prejudice: The Ancient View of Blacks.* Cambridge: Harvard University Press, 1983.

——. *Blacks in Antiquity: Ethiopians in the Greco-Roman Experience.* Cambridge: Harvard University Press, 1970.

Spenser, Edmund. *The Yale Edition of the Shorter Poems of Edmund Spenser*, ed. William A. Oram et al. New Haven: Yale University Press, 1989.

——. *A View of the Present State of Ireland.* Ed. W. L. Renwick. Oxford: Clarendon, 1970.

Spooner, Brian. "Weavers and Dealers: The Authenticity of an Oriental Carpet." In *The Social Life of Things: Commodities in Cultural Perspective*, ed. Arjun Appadurai, 195–235. New York: Cambridge University Press, 1990.

Stallybrass, Peter. "Patriarchal Territories: The Body Enclosed." In *Rewriting the Renaissance: The Discourses of Sexual Difference in Early Modern Europe*, ed. Margaret W. Ferguson et al., 123–44. Chicago: University of Chicago Press, 1986.

Stallybrass, Peter, and Allon White. *The Politics and Poetics of Transgression.* Ithaca: Cornell University Press, 1986.

Steensgaard, Neils. "Trade of England and the Dutch before 1750." In *The Rise of Merchant Empires: Long Distance Trade in the Early Modern World, 1350–1700*, ed. James D. Tracy. Cambridge: Cambridge University Press, 1990.

Stone, Lawrence. *The Causes of the English Revolution, 1529–1642*. New York: Harper and Row, 1972.

Strickland, Agnes. *Lives of the Queens of England*. 16 vols. Philadelphia: G. Barrie and Son, 1902.

Strong, Roy. *The English Renaissance Miniature*. London: Thames and Hudson, 1983.

——. *Gloriana: The Portraits of Queen Elizabeth I*. London: Thames and Hudson, 1987.

——. *Splendor at Court: Renaissance Spectacle and the Theater of Power*. Boston: Houghton Mifflin, 1973.

Sundelson, David. "So Rare a Wonder'd Father: Prospero's *Tempest.*" In *Representing Shakespeare: New Psychoanalytic Essays*, ed. Murray M. Schwartz and Coppélia Kahn, 33–53. Baltimore: Johns Hopkins University Press, 1980.

Swift, Carolyn Ruth. "Feminine Identity in Lady Mary Wroth's *Urania.*" *English Literary Renaissance* 14 no. 3 (1984): 328–46.

Taylor, Don. *The British in Africa*. New York: Roy Publishers, 1964.

Tennenhouse, Leonard. *Power on Display: The Politics of Shakespeare's Genres*. New York: Methuen, 1986.

Thirsk, Joan, and J. P. Cooper, eds. *Seventeenth-Century Economic Documents*. Oxford: Clarendon, 1972.

Tietze-Conrat, Erica. *Dwarfs and Jesters in Art*. Trans. Elizabeth Osborn. New York: Phaidon, 1957.

Tilley, Morris P. *A Dictionary of Proverbs in England in the Sixteenth and Seventeenth Centuries*. Ann Arbor: University of Michigan Press, 1950.

Todorov, Tzvetan. *The Conquest of America: The Question of the Other*. Trans. Richard Howard. New York: Harper, 1982.

Tokson, Elliot. *The Popular Image of the Black Man in English Drama, 1550–1688*. Boston: G. K. Hall, 1982.

Traub, Valerie. "The (In)significance of 'Lesbian' Desire in Early Modern England." In *Erotic Politics: Desire on the Renaissance Stage*, ed. Susan Zimmerman, 150–69. New York: Routledge, 1992.

Tuan, Yi-Fu. *Dominance and Affection: The Making of Pets*. New Haven: Yale University Press, 1984.

Tuke, Thomas. A treatise against painting and tincturing of Men and Women. . . . London, 1616.

Van Noren, Linda, and John Pollack, eds. *The Black Feet of the Peacock: The Color Concept "Black" from the Greeks through the Renaissance*. Lanham, Md.: University Presses of America, 1985.

Van Sertima, Ivan. *They Came before Columbus: The African Presence in Ancient America*. New York: Random House, 1976.

Vaughan, Alden T., and Virginia Mason. *Shakespeare's Caliban: A Cultural History*. New York: Cambridge University Press, 1991.

Verlinden, Charles. *The Beginnings of Modern Colonization: Eleven Essays with an Introduction*. Trans. Yvonne Freccero. Ithaca: Cornell University Press, 1970.

Veeser, H. Aram, ed. *The New Historicism*. New York: Routledge, 1989.

Vickers, Nancy. "'The blazon of sweet beauty's best': Shakespeare's *Lucrece.*" In *Shakespeare and the Question of Theory*, ed. Patricia Parker and Geoffrey Hartman, 95–115. New York: Methuen, 1985.

——. "Diana Described: Scattered Women and Scattered Rhyme." In *Writing and Sexual Difference*, ed. Elizabeth Abel, 95–110. Chicago: University of Chicago Press, 1982.

Vilar, Pierre. *A History of Gold and Money 1450–1920*. Trans. Judith White. Atlantic Highlands, N.J.: Humanities Press, 1976.

Walker, Alice. *In Search of Our Mother's Gardens: Womanist Prose*. New York: Harcourt Brace Jovanovich, 1983.

Wall, Cheryl A. "Introduction: Taking Positions and Changing Words." In *Changing Our Own Words: Essays on Criticism, Theory, and Writing by Black Women*, ed. Cheryl A. Wall, 1–15. New Brunswick: Rutgers University Press, 1989.

Wallace, Michele. "Variations on Negation and the Heresy of Black Feminist Creativity." In *Reading Black, Reading Feminist: A Critical Anthology*, ed. Henry Louis Gates, Jr., 52–68. New York: Penguin, 1990.

Waller, Gary. "Mary Wroth and the Sidney Family Romance: Gender Construction in Early Modern England. In *Reading Mary Wroth: Representing Alternatives in Early Modern England*, ed. Naomi J. Miller and Gary Waller, 35–66. Knoxville: University of Tennessee Press, 1991.

Wallerstein, Immanuel. *The Modern World System: Capitalist Agriculture and the Origins of the European World-Economy in the Sixteenth Century*. 2 vols. New York: Academic Press, 1974.

Walvin, James. *The Black Presence: A Documentary History of the Negro in England, 1555–1860*. New York: Schocken, 1972.

Warburton, Eliot. *Memoirs of Prince Rupert and the Cavaliers*. 3 vols. London: Richard Bentley, 1849.

Washington, Joseph E. *Anti–Blackness in English Religion: 1500–1700*. New York: Edwin Mellen Press, 1984.

Waterhouse, Ellis. *Painting in Britain, 1530–1790*. Baltimore: Penguin Books, 1953.

Watson, A. M. "Back to Gold—and Silver." *Economic History Review* 20 no. 1 (April 1967): 1–34.

Weatherill, Lorna. "A Possession of One's Own: Women and Consumer Behavior in England, 1660–1740." *Journal of British Studies* 25 no. 2 (April 1986): 131–56.

Webster, John. *The Devil's Law-Case*. Ed. Frances A. Shirley. Lincoln: University of Nebraska Press, 1972.

——. *The White Devil*. Ed. J. R. Mulryne. Lincoln: University of Nebraska Press, 1969.

Weeks, Jeffrey. *Sex, Politics, and Society: The Regulation of Sexuality since 1800*. New York: Longman, 1981.

Weever, John. *Epigrammes in the Oldest Cut and Newest Fashion*. London, 1599.

Welsford, Enid. *The Court Masque*. Cambridge: Cambridge University Press, 1927.

Willan, Thomas Stuart. *Studies in Elizabethan Foreign Trade*. Manchester: Manchester University Press, 1959.

Williams, Ethel Carleton. *Anne of Denmark, Wife of James VI of Scotland, and James I of England*. New York: Longman, 1970.

Williams, George, ed. *The Complete Poetry of Richard Crashaw*. New York: New York University Press, 1972.

Williams, Noel H. *Rival Sultanas: Nell Gwynn, Louise de Kéroualle, and Hortense Mancini*. London: Hutchinson, 1915.

Williams, Patricia. *The Alchemy of Race and Rights: Diary of a Law Professor.* Cambridge: Harvard University Press, 1991.

Williams, Sherley Anne. "Some Implications of Womanist Theory." In *Reading Black, Reading Feminist: A Critical Anthology,* ed. Henry Louis Gates, Jr., 68–75. New York: Penguin, 1990.

Williamson, James A. *Sir John Hawkins: The Time and the Man.* Oxford: Clarendon, 1927. Reprint. Westport, Conn: Greenwood, 1970.

Wilson, Thomas. *The Art of Rhetorique.* London, 1585.

——. *The Rule of Reason, Conteinying the Arte of Logique.* Richard S. Sprague. Northridge, Calif: San Fernando State College Foundation, 1972.

Witherspoon, Alexander MacClaren. *The Influence of Robert Garnier on Elizabethan Drama.* New Haven: Yale University Press, 1925.

Woodbridge, Linda. "Black and White and Red All Over: The Sonnet Mistress amongst the Ndembu." *Renaissance Quarterly* 40 no. 2 (Summer 1987): 247–97.

Worden, Blair, ed. *Stuart England.* Oxford: Phaidon Press, 1986.

Wright, Abraham. *Parnassus Biceps, or Severall Choice Pieces of Poetry.* London, 1656.

Wroth, Mary. *The Countess of Montgomerie's Urania.* London, 1621.

——. *The Poems of Lady Mary Wroth.* Ed. Josephine Roberts. Baton Rouge: Louisiana State University Press, 1983.

Young, Lisa. "A Nasty Piece of Work: A Psychoanalytic Study of Sexual and Racial Difference in 'Mona Lisa.' " In *Identity: Community, Culture, Difference,* ed. Jonathan Rutherford, 188–206. London: Lawrence and Wishart, 1990.

Yuval-Davis, Nira, and Floya Anthias, eds. *Woman-Nation-State.* New York: St. Martin's Press, 1989.

Index

Adelman, Janet, 70n
Aeneid, 153
Aesthetic tradition
  non-racial interpretations of, 1, 69–71
  racialization of, 4–6, 41–42, 182
African cultures/people, 6–8
  and apes, 236, 238
  association with white women, 49–50, 244,
    247, 248
  and classical antiquity, 215, 217
  as curiosities, 11
  as decorative signifiers, 23–24
  disdain for, 30–31, 34, 44
  as disordered, 26–27, 38, 39–40, 63,
    156
  and geography, 26–28, 61, 156
  as grotesque bodies, 26, 157
  new historicist analysis of, 14–15
  and origins of blackness, 11–13
  symbolic functions of, 13–14, 203
  in *The Tempest*, 151
  See also Blackness; Cross-cultural contact;
    Portraiture; Travel narratives; *specific
    topics*
African trade, 3, 23
  and African presence in England, 11
  and Americas, 16, 17, 62–63n
  and aristocratic identity, 18, 65–66
  and coral, 253n
  development of, 16–22
  and jewel exchanges, 222
  and portraiture, 227
  and slave trade, 17–18, 19–22
  and visual culture, 212
  See also Cross-cultural contact; Imperialist
    expansion; Slave trade
Ainsworth, Henry, 111
Allegory, 64
Amazons, 35n, 39, 42–43, 85, 173, 217

Americas
  and African trade, 16, 17, 62–63n
  interracial desire issue in, 121n, 143
  and new historicism, 260n
  and origins of blackness, 94
  and slave trade, 81, 121n
  and sunburn, 93–94
  in travel narratives, 46–47
  and wealth, 81, 232n
Amoretti (Spenser), 78, 81–82, 91–92
Andrews, Kenneth R., 16, 17, 18
Androgyny, 241
Animals, 50–51, 52–53, 247
Anne of Denmark
  and *Masque of Blackness*, 128, 129, 134, 135,
    136
  portraiture, 238–39, 247
  See also James I
Anthias, Floya, 125
Antonie (Sidney), 184
Antony and Cleopatra (Shakespeare), 74, 97, 137–
    38, 153–60
Anzaldúa, Gloria, 255
Apollo, 63
Apology for Poetry (Sidney), 76–77, 109–10
Appadurai, Arjun, 212n
Appiah, Anthony, 3–4n, 13n, 255
Aristocratic bloodlines, 164, 172
  and Cleopatra, 155
  and commodification of women, 22
  and dark/light polarity, 142
  and English identity, 9, 125, 165
  and female subjugation, 34, 143, 148–49
  and female transgression, 34, 144n, 158, 163
  and imperialist expansion, 159–60
  and James's legitimacy, 150, 163
  and marriage, 22, 125, 159–60, 219
  and sunburn, 102
  See also Interracial desire; Marriage

Aristocratic identity
  and African trade, 18, 65–66
  and jewel exchanges, 215, 219, 222
  and language, 144
  and lyric poetry, 65–66
  and otherness, 14–15n
  and portraiture, 226–27
  and wealth, 163–64
  See also Aristocratic bloodlines; Class; English
    identity
Arundel, Lady, 242
Ashley, Maurice, 230n
Ashton, Robert, 127, 139
Astrophel and Stella (Sidney), 73–77
  contemporary responses to, 117
  dark/light polarity in, 108
  and literary influence, 74–77, 93
  and Sidney's imperialist involvement, 66, 73–
    74, 80
  sunburn in, 75, 92, 92–93, 98–99, 100–102
  wealth in, 79–80, 82–83, 84, 86
  whitening in, 67–68, 92

Bacon, Sir Francis, 120, 214
Bakhtin, Mikhail, 26
Baldwin, William, 114
Balibar, Etienne, 6n
Barbary Company, 18
Barne, George, 50–51
Barnes, 107
Bartels, Emily, 32, 48n, 49
Barthelemy, Antony Gerard, 7, 128–29, 132, 134,
  188, 189, 230n
Basse, William, 62–64, 70, 76, 97, 115
Beauty. *See* Blackness as beautiful; Fairness
Beilin, Elaine V., 204
"Bella Mora, La," 65–66
Belsey, Catherine, 2, 70, 71–72, 125, 144n, 167,
  180n, 181
Berger, John, 251
Best, George, 11–12, 145, 260
Bhabha, Homi, 51n
Black feminism, 15, 254–58, 261–65, 267–68
Blackness
  and chaos, 26–27, 63, 118
  and class, 100, 125
  in court tradition, 128–29
  cultural relativism in, 13, 26
  as dangerous, 65, 153–54
  and death, 4–5, 227
  double functions of, 188–89
  and female competition, 100, 134–35
  incidence of references to, 1–2
  male, 92–93, 100–101, 106
  as mystery, 40, 41, 42, 43, 47–48, 119, 120
  as necessary to whiteness, 9, 12, 22, 197, 240,
    247–48
  non-racial interpretations of, 1, 69–71
  and otherness, 64, 67, 183–84
  and sexuality, 28, 34, 90, 97, 130, 160, 169,
    189, 240
  and slavery images, 19, 20
  terminology, 7–9
  as undesirable, 12–13, 22, 132–33, 205, 207

  See also African cultures/people; Dark/light
    polarity; Whiteness; *specific topics*
Blackness as beautiful, 117, 132, 240
  and cosmetics, 87–89, 116, 130–31, 168–69
  and female transgression, 90
  and female writing, 205–6, 207, 209, 210
  impossibility of, 205–6
  and male poetic power, 67, 69, 110–11
  and materiality, 118–19
  and misogyny, 90
  and privileging of blackness, 117–18
  and resistance to racism, 71n
Blakely, Allison, 3n, 14, 238n, 244
Blazons, 81–82
  and competition, 170
  and female gaze, 192
  and slave trade, 19, 20, 24
  and wealth, 81–82
  and whitening, 113–14, 116
Bodin, John, 60
Body, 27, 51–53
  "classical," 52, 53
  dismemberment of female, 65, 69, 108, 112–
    13, 118
  as disordered, 45
  and English identity, 45
  and geography, 27–28, 61, 79
  grotesque, 26, 157
  and materiality, 118
  sexual characteristics, 52n
  and slave trade, 121
  and wealth, 81–82
  See also Cosmetics; Fairness; Sexuality; Sunburn
Boime, Albert, 5–6, 213–14
Boose, Lynda, 259
Booth, Stephen, 69–70
Boyle, Robert, 95n, 96
Brewer, Rose M., 256, 257–58
Brilliant, Richard, 226
Brome, Richard. *See English Moore, The*
Browne, Sir Thomas, 26, 87–88, 154n
  and origins of blackness, 12–13, 41, 94–95, 96,
    120
  Pseudodoxia Epidemica, 12–13, 41, 95
Brucioli, Antonio, 112
Bulwer, John, 87–89, 95n

Calvert, Cecil, 232, 233, 235
Calvert, George, 232, 234
Calvin's Case, 127
Carleton, Dudley, 129, 130, 132
Carby, Hazel, 263
Cary, Elizabeth, 100, 184–85
Cavell, Stanley, 160
Cecil, William, 20, 21
Charles I, 18n, 236–38
Charles II, 235, 242, 247–52
Charles V, 83
Chew, Samuel C., 103
Chivalry, 201–3, 210
Christian, 254
Christian conversion
  and imperialist expansion, 54–58, 76, 123
  in lyric poetry, 63, 64

Christian conversion *(cont.)*
  and materiality, 119–20
  and sunburn, 95–96, 98
  and travel narratives, 54–58, 63, 123
  and wealth, 64, 119–20
  and whitening, 114–15
  See also Christianity
Christianity
  and blackness as beautiful, 110
  and class, 171
  dark/light polarity in, 4–5, 48, 69, 103, 108, 111n
  See also Christian conversion
Class
  and Christianity, 171
  and fairness, 181–82, 198–99
  and language, 147
  and marriage, 210
  mobility, 148, 161–62, 170–71, 174n
  and otherness, 197
  and portraiture, 238, 248
  and sexuality, 158
  and sunburn, 100
  and white hands, 210, 248
  and whiteness, 209, 210, 248
  See also Aristocratic bloodlines; Aristocratic identity
Cleage, Pearl, 256
Cleopatra, 153–58, 182–87
Cleveland, John, 119, 210, 274–75
Clifford, Lady Anne, 13n, 137
Climate, 96. *See also* Sunburn
Collins, Patricia Hill, 15n, 180n, 256
Collop, John, 120, 279–80
Colonialism, 4
  and Africa as disordered, 28, 39–40
  and Amazons, 85
  and Cleopatra, 155
  "contact zone," 151–53
  and female subjugation, 50–51
  and literary influence, 79
  and racist/prejudicial thought, 6–7
  and visual culture, 228, 230, 232, 235
  and whitening, 218
  See also Imperialist expansion
Company of Adventurers of London Trading into Parts of Africa, 21
Competition
  and African trade, 17–18, 19–21
  female, 100, 134–35, 180–81, 184–85, 199–201, 241n
  and literary influence, 78–79, 84
  and slave trade, 121
  and travel narratives, 44, 55
  and wealth, 170
Constable, Henry, 84–85, 104
Cook, Ann Jennalie, 86n
Cosmetics, 86–92, 116, 130–31, 168–69, 182n
Countess of Montgomerie's Urania, The (Wroth), 177–78, 187–210
  admiration in, 190
  blackness as beautiful in, 205–6, 207, 209, 210
  blackness as undesirable in, 205, 207
  class in, 197, 198–99
  dark/light polarity in, 196–98, 206
  female abandonment in, 193–95
  female competition in, 199–201, 202
  female resistance in, 204–5
  female transgression in, 195–96
  identity formation in, 188n
  male characters' status in, 200–203, 206–7
  and *Masque of Blackness*, 187
  and *Othello*, 190
  religious difference in, 189–91
  sunburn in, 192–93
  white hands image in, 208–10
  whitening in, 203–4
Countess of Pembroke's Arcadia, The (Sidney), 179–80, 198–99, 203n, 204
Crashaw, Richard, 114–15, 285
Crenshaw, Kimberlé, 258
Cropper, Elizabeth, 241–42
Cross-cultural contact
  "contact zone," 151–53
  and creation of Great Britain, 126–27
  and Egypt, 155
  and English identity, 11
  and interracial desire, 63–64, 108–10, 124–25, 140, 145–47
  and language, 145–46
  and marriage, 149
  and sunburn, 93–94
  and travel narratives, 61, 123–24, 152
  and whitening, 71, 139–40
  See also Interracial desire; Travel narratives
Cross-dressing, 169, 172–74, 181
Cyprus, 190

Dabydeen, David, 241, 253
D'Agar, Jacques, 248
Daniel, Samuel, 154–56, 184
Dark/light polarity, 8–9
  and animals, 50–51, 52–53
  as arbitrary, 197–98
  and aristocratic bloodlines, 142
  and black experience, 257, 264
  and chaos, 48
  and Christian symbolism, 4–5, 48, 69, 103, 108, 111n
  and disorder, 48, 63
  and English identity, 9, 157
  and female pairs, 179–80
  gendered nature of, 8–9, 50–53, 134
  in lyric poetry, 69–71, 72, 108
  and projection of self, 196–97
  racialization of, 2–3
  and religious difference, 48–49
  sunburn as liminal space in, 92, 93, 94, 96, 97, 101–2, 118
  in travel narratives, 48, 63
  in visual culture, 213–14
  See also Blackness; Fairness; Sunburn; Whiteness; *specific topics*
Davis, Angela, 15
Davis, Ossie, 265, 266
Decades of the Newe Worlde (Gomora), 41–42, 108
Deconstructionism, 2
de Kéroüalle, Louise Renée, 247–49, 250–53

Dekker, Thomas, 85n
Denbigh, Earl of, 230–32
Derrida, Jacques, 72, 73
Devil's Law-Case, The (Webster), 131, 160–66, 167, 174–75
Diana, 217, 219
Dido, 153, 155, 159
Discourse of Western Planting (Hakluyt), 54
Discoverie of Guiana (Raleigh), 187
Discription of Aphrique, The (Prat), 38–39, 53–54, 60
Disraeli, Benjamin, 110
Dogs, 247n
Dolan, Frances, 87, 89
Donnan, Elizabeth, 19, 20, 21
Donne, John, 79, 80–81, 199–200
Douglas, Mary, 27, 28, 82n
Drake, Sir Francis, 18–19, 50, 74, 152, 222–26
Drama, 174–76. *See also specific plays*
Drayton, Michael, 78, 101
Dryden, John, 160
Dualisms, 2–3, 6, 151, 264. *See also* Dark/light polarity
duCille, Ann, 257n, 263
Dudley, Robert, 20
Dunbar, William, 128, 271
Duncan-Jones, Katherine, 73, 74, 80n
Dyer, Richard, 180, 240, 247

East India Company, 18n, 121
Eden, Richard, 41–42, 108
Edward IV, 19n
Egypt, 155–56. *See also* Cleopatra
Elizabeth I
  and African presence in England, 176
  African trade under, 17–21, 73, 74
  and Diana, 217
  and English identity, 124, 126
  expulsion of Moors, 14
  and fairness, 222
  and jewel exchanges, 217, 218–21, 226
  male anxiety about power of, 22, 158n, 226
  and marriage, 124
  nationalism under, 154
  and Sidney, 73, 74
  and Solomon, 109
  and wealth, 157
English identity, 3, 66
  and aristocratic bloodlines, 9, 125, 165
  and blackness as dangerous, 154
  and body metaphors, 45
  and cross-cultural contact, 11
  and cross-dressing, 173
  and dark/light polarity, 9, 157
  and disorder, 53–54, 140–41
  and futility, 175–76
  and interracial desire, 125
  and lyric poetry, 78
  and marriage, 124–27
  and nationalism, 66, 77–79, 110n, 126, 154
  and otherness, 140–41
  and portraiture, 235–36

  and travel narratives, 32, 54
  and wealth, 82–83
  and whiteness, 12, 133–34, 136
  See also Aristocratic identity; Imperialist expansion
English Moore, The; or, the Mock-Marriage (Brome), 166–75, 189
Enloe, 9
Erickson, Peter, 22, 209, 248, 256n, 261
Evans, Joan, 215
Evans, Malcolm, 115
Evelyn, John, 9
Exotic. *See* Otherness

Faerie Queene, The (Spenser), 37, 192, 193
Fairness, 177–78
  and black feminism, 264
  and blackness as undesirable, 12–13, 22, 132–33, 205, 207
  and class, 181–82, 198–99
  commodification of, 85–86, 90, 116
  and critical avoidance of race issue, 8, 70
  and female competition, 100, 134–35, 180–81, 184–85
  and female resistance, 204–5
  and female transgression, 36
  and imperialist expansion, 3, 4
  and jewel exchanges, 219, 222
  and male poetic power, 115
  and marriage, 86–87
  and portraiture, 240–41
  and sunburn, 94, 98, 181
  See also Dark/light polarity; Whitening
Fanon, Frantz, 71n, 211
Feinberg, Nona, 106, 193
Female subjugation
  and aristocratic bloodlines, 34, 143, 148–49
  and class mobility, 170–71
  and control of sexuality, 33–34, 37–38, 118, 143, 148–49, 165–66
  and imperialist expansion, 37–38, 50–51
  and whitening, 107, 137, 174
Female transgression
  and adventuring, 195–96
  and aristocratic bloodlines, 34, 144n, 158, 163
  and cosmetics, 89, 90, 91
  and cross-dressing, 172–74
  and Elizabeth I, 22, 158n, 226
  and fairness, 36
  and female writing, 107
  and imperialist expansion, 43, 153–54
  and interracial desire, 154–55
  and Nile, 157
  and otherness, 22, 76, 153–54
  and paternal absence, 166–67
  and Phaeton, 63
  and pregnancy/fertility, 136–37, 158
  and religious difference, 39, 104–5
  in travel narratives, 25–26, 32–37, 38–39, 42–43
  and war, 35n
  and wealth, 162–63

Female transgression *(cont.)*
  and whitening, 115, 137
  See also Female subjugation
Female writing, 107–8n, 177–87
  and blackness as beautiful, 205–6, 207, 209,
    210
  class in, 181–82
  Cleopatra in, 155, 182–87
  competition in, 180–81, 184–85
  dark/light pairings in, 179–80
  interracial desire in, 183–84, 185–87
  negotiated position in, 178–79, 182
  religious difference in, 189–91
  and resistance, 178
  and sunburn, 105–7, 181, 206–7
  and whitening, 107, 203–4
  See also Wroth, Lady Mary
Feminism. *See* Black feminism
Ferguson, Margaret, 184, 185n, 260
Fiedler, Leslie, 8n
Fineman, Joel, 71, 89, 105
Fleissner, Robert, 117, 118
Fleming, Juliet, 145
Fletcher, Giles, 78, 99, 195
Food imagery, 138–39, 156n
Forneron, Henri, 251n
Foucault, Michel, 60, 72–73, 261n
Fradenberg, Louise, 202–3
Fraser, Antonia, 134n
Frobisher, Martin, 19
Frye, Marilyn, 179n
Fryer, Peter, 3–4, 9, 85n, 176, 217
Fumerton, Patricia, 139n, 146–47, 215

Gates, Henry Louis, Jr., 144, 182, 255, 257
Geertz, Clifford, 14n, 16
Gender. *See* Cosmetics; Fairness; Female
    subjugation; Female transgression; Sexuality;
    Women; *specific topics*
Genesis, 48, 95–96, 118, 244
Geographical Historie of Africa (Leo Africanus), 27,
    28–40
  disdain for African cultures/people in, 30–31,
    44
  economic exploitation in, 39–40
  editorial ordering in, 29–30, 31–32, 40–41, 61
  Egypt in, 155–56
  female transgression in, 34–37, 43
  and imperialist seduction, 60
  religious difference in, 30, 48–49
  sexuality in, 30–31, 32–34
Giddings, Paula, 121, 143
Gilman, Sander L., 34, 108, 140–41, 175, 240,
    260
Gilroy, Paul, 12
Goldberg, Jonathan, 236–37, 238
Gold Coast, 19
Goody, Jack, 242
Greece, ancient, 3n
Greenblatt, Stephen, 14–15n, 30n, 33n, 37, 59,
    140, 193
Gresley jewel, 218–21

Greville, Fulke, 73–74
Grewal, Shabnam, 7n
Griffin, Susan, 141, 142–43
Guilpin, Edward, 90, 271–72
Guinea, 17
Guinea Company, 21, 121
Gypsies, 154n

Hakluyt, Richard. *See Principal Navigations . . .*
Hakluytus Posthumus, or Purchas His Pilgrimes
    (Purchas), 48, 54, 55–58, 63n, 105, 123–24,
    232
Hall, Joseph, 97, 110–11
Hall, Stuart, 11
Harrington, Sir John, 138–39, 140, 158
Hartwell, Abraham, 40–44, 51, 61, 120
Hawkins, John, 19, 20, 21
Hawkins, Sir William, 24
Helgerson, Richard, 55, 66
Henrietta Maria, 236–38, 248n
Herbert, Edward, 120, 276–79
Herbert, George, 96, 117–19, 120–22, 214, 273–
    74
Herbert, Mary, 73
Herbert, Thomas, 103
Hic-Mulier, 173
Higginbotham, Evelyn Brooks, 255
History of the World (Raleigh), 58
Hodge, John, 6n
Holinshed, Raphael, 125
hooks, bell, 15, 156n, 230, 255, 256, 257n, 264,
    265–66
Howard, Frances, 137
Howard, Jean, 173, 174n
Hudson, Jeffrey, 238
Hughes-Hallet, Lucy, 183
Hulme, Peter, 140n, 151, 152
Hunter, G. K., 75
Hyde, Lewis, 244

Imperialist expansion, 3–4
  and Africa as disordered, 28, 39–40
  and Africa as mysterious, 47–48
  and Americas, 16, 17, 46–47
  and animals, 51, 52–53n
  and aristocratic bloodlines, 159–60
  and artist, 74
  as cannibalism, 44
  and capitalism, 82n
  and Christian conversion, 54–58, 76, 123
  and classical antiquity, 215, 217
  and class mobility, 148
  and competition, 17–18, 19–21, 44, 55, 78–79,
    84, 121, 170
  and creation of Great Britain, 127, 133
  and cross-cultural contact, 123–24, 145–47
  and disorder, 25, 28, 148
  and economic exploitation, 39–40
  and editorial ordering, 44–45
  and fairness, 3, 4
  and female abandonment, 189, 193–95
  and female subjugation, 37–38, 50–51

Imperialist expansion *(cont.)*
  and female transgression, 43, 153–54
  and jewel exchanges, 214–15, 217, 218, 222
  and language, 75, 145–47
  and marriage, 86–87, 124, 142, 149
  and portraiture, 228, 230, 232, 235
  and sexuality, 37–38, 59–61, 102
  and Solomon story, 108, 113, 139–40
  and sunburn, 192–93
  and whitening, 138–39
  See also African trade; English identity;
    Interracial desire; Slave trade; Wealth
India, 80–81, 85n, 230n, 232
Inheritance. *See* Aristocratic bloodlines
Interracial desire, 22, 141
  and African presence in England, 11
  and cross-cultural contact, 63–64, 108–10, 124–
    25, 140, 145–47
  and Dido, 153
  and English identity, 125
  and female transgression, 154–55
  in female writing, 183–84, 185–87
  impossibility of, 206
  and language, 143–45
  and otherness, 206
  and rape threat, 142–43, 150–51, 160
  and slavery, 121n
  in Song of Songs, 108–10, 140
  and Spain, 145, 222
  and sunburn, 95
  See also Aristocratic bloodlines; Marriage;
    Sexuality
Ireland, 7, 145–47
Islam, 30, 49, 57–58, 103, 104, 138–39. *See also*
  Religious difference

James I
  and African presence in England, 176
  African trade under, 21, 65n
  and aristocratic bloodlines, 150, 163
  and English identity, 133
  excesses of, 138–40, 158, 238
  fascination with otherness, 23, 127–28, 137–38,
    176, 193
  gender in court of, 134–37, 193
  and male poetic power, 137, 170
  and marriage, 124–25, 126–27
  nationalism under, 154
  as Solomon, 58, 138–39
  and *The Tempest*, 143n
Jameson, Fredric, 1, 196
JanMohamed, Abdul R., 25, 52–53n, 230
Jardine, Lisa, 163
Jeffords, Susan, 259
Jewel exchanges, 213, 214–26
  and African trade, 222
  and aristocratic identity, 215, 219, 222
  Drake pendant, 222–26
  and Elizabeth I, 217, 218–21, 226
  and fairness, 219, 222
  Gresley jewel, 218–21
  and imperialist expansion, 214–15, 217, 218,
    222

  and public/private self, 218–19
  and slave trade, 120–21
  and whitening, 218
Jews, 39
John II (Portugal), 19n
Johnson, Barbara, 2
Joint-stock companies, 18
Jones, Ann Rosalind, 99, 179, 197
Jones, Inigo, 129
Jonson, Ben, 248. *See also Masque of Beauty; Masque
  of Blackness*
Jordan, Winthrop, 2, 9, 41, 70n, 96, 103, 238,
  244n

Kelly, Anne Cline, 131n, 136
Kermode, Frank, 157
King, Deborah, 258
King, Henry, 118, 176
King, John, 109
Kolodny, Annette, 79
Kopytoff, Igor, 213
Krishna, Hal, 89

"Lady of May, The" (Sidney), 200
Lamb, Mary Ellen, 178, 208, 210
Language
  and aristocratic identity, 144
  and cross-cultural contact, 145–46
  and imperialist expansion, 75, 145–47
  and interracial desire, 143–45
  and wealth, 147–48
  and whitening, 67
  and white supremacy, 265–67
  See also Literary influence; Male poetic power
Lanyer, Aemilia, 155, 183–84
Le Courbeiller, Clare, 232n, 253n
Lee, Sidney, 107
Leicester, earl of, 18
Leo Africanus, Johannes. *See Geographical Historie of
  Africa*
Lerner, Gerda, 6n
Lévi-Strauss, Claude, 251
Life of Sir Philip Sidney, The (Greville), 73–74
Literary influence, 74–79, 174n
  and competition, 78–79, 84
  and sunburn, 75, 93, 100, 106–7
Locke, Alain, 237
Lok, John, 20, 50–51
Loomba, Ania, 137, 142, 143, 154, 156n, 158n,
  263
Lorde, Audre, 7–8, 15
Lott, Eric, 257
Lovelace, Richard, 282–84
Love's Labour's Lost (Shakespeare), 13, 70n
  cosmetics in, 90–91, 130–31
  male poetic power in, 67, 69, 115
  religious difference in, 103
  whitening in, 67, 69, 90–91
Lust's Dominion; or, the Lascivious Queen, 97
Lyric poetry, 62–92, 108, 116–22
  allegory in, 64
  and aristocratic identity, 65–66

Lyric poetry *(cont.)*
and authors' imperialist involvement, 66, 73–74, 80
and blackness as beautiful, 67–68, 87–89, 90, 117–19
blackness as mystery in, 119, 120
Christian conversion in, 63, 64
and competition, 84
cosmetics in, 87–92, 116
dismemberment of female body in, 65, 69, 108, 112, 118
and English identity, 78
Eurocentric beauty in, 132–33
and linguistic order, 66, 71, 72–73, 75–77
and literary influence, 74–79, 93, 100, 106–7
male poetic power in, 66, 67, 69, 90–92, 98–99, 115–16
materiality in, 118–20
mercantile concerns in, 79–80
nationalism in, 66, 77–79, 110n
and slave trade, 120–21
sunburn in, 75, 92–93, 98–99, 100–102
and travel narratives, 63, 64–65
wealth in, 64, 79–85, 86, 119–20
whitening in, 62–63, 66–69, 71–72, 90–91, 92, 115–16
See also Song of Songs; Sunburn

Madonna portraits, 253
Male poetic power, 135–36
and blackness as beautiful, 67, 69, 110–11
and cosmetics, 90–92
in Song of Songs, 110–11, 113–14
and sunburn, 98–99
and whitening, 66, 67, 69, 90–92, 113–14, 115–16, 131, 169–70
Mandeville, Sir John. *See Travels of Sir John Mandeville*
Mark, Peter, 242
Markham, Gervase, 107, 111–12
Marotti, Arthur, 66, 80, 82
Marriage
and aristocratic bloodlines, 22, 125, 159–60, 219
and class, 210
and cross-cultural contact, 149
and English identity, 124–27
and imperialist expansion, 86–87, 124, 142, 149
and portraiture, 236–37
and wealth, 86–87, 161
See also Cross-cultural contact; Interracial desire
Marston, John, 188, 189
Mary, Queen of Scots, 19
Masque of Beauty (Jonson), 137, 140
male poetic power in, 115, 135–36, 170
Masque of Blackness (Jonson), 128–40
and *The English Moore*, 166, 169, 171–72, 174
and female transgression, 136–37, 205
male poetic power in, 115
and orientalism, 137–38
Queen Anne's patronage of, 128, 129, 134–36

and *Urania*, 187
and Mary Wroth, 105–7
Masten, Jeff, 107–8n
McDowell, Deborah, 262–63
Merchant of Venice, The (Shakespeare), 85, 165, 166, 207
foreign trade in, 23, 85
marriage in, 87, 161
sunburn in, 94
wealth in, 174
Midsummer Night's Dream, A (Shakespeare), 22–24
blackness as undesirable in, 1, 22, 70n, 207
female competition in, 180
foreign trade in, 23, 85
otherness in, 230, 232
white hands image in, 209
Miller, Christopher, 2n, 29n, 109n, 175
Miller, Naomi, 188n, 210
Milton, John, 1, 2
Miscegenation. *See* Interracial desire
Montrose, Louis, 22, 27–28n, 65, 67, 83, 226
Moors, 7, 14, 32n, 57
Morrah, Patrick, 228
Morrison, Toni, 14, 15–16n, 133, 263, 264–65
Mothers, 149–50
Mukerji, Chandra, 212

Nahoum-Grappe, Véronique, 86, 87
National boundaries. *See* Aristocratic bloodlines; English identity
Netscher, Constantyn, 242
New historicism, 14–15, 259–60
Newman, Karen, 8n
Nietzsche, Friedrich, 196
Nile, 27, 156–57
Noah, 54–55

O'Connor, Marion, 267
Ogilby, John, 253n
Old Arcadia (Sidney), 80n
Orgel, Stephen, 128, 134n, 135, 143n, 150, 153
Orientalism, 110, 137–40
Origen, 112
Origins of blackness
and Americas, 94
and blackness as beautiful, 131
and blackness as mystery, 120
and climate, 96
and cosmetics, 87–88
and infection, 11–12
and Phaeton, 63
and stability of whiteness, 12–13
and sunburn, 94–97
and travel narratives, 42
Otherness
and African cultures/people, 7
and allegory, 64
and aristocratic identity, 14–15n
and Cleopatra, 183–84
and colonialism, 230
and English identity, 140–41
and female transgression, 22, 76, 153–54

Otherness *(cont.)*
and interracial desire, 206
Jacobean fascination with, 23, 127–28, 137–38, 176, 193
and language, 67, 143–46
non-racial constructions of, 8n
and origins of blackness, 11
and portraiture, 230, 232, 236, 237
and projection of self, 196–97
and racist/prejudicial thought, 11–12, 141
and religious difference, 13, 103
and sameness, 94, 96, 175
and sexuality, 30–31, 182–83
and travel narratives, 32
and wealth, 83–84, 157

Palmers, Barbara Villiers, 246–48, 251
Pamphilia to Amphilanthus (Wroth), 191, 197–98
Pardes, Ilana, 112
Parker, Patricia, 22, 27, 65, 93, 124, 136, 175
Parrots, 232, 244
Pennington, Loren, 55
Pepys, Samuel, 212n
Peterson, Richard, 136n
Petrarchan rhetoric, 65, 106–7, 132–33, 168, 206, 240. *See also* Lyric poetry
Phaeton, 63, 96–97
Piedra, José, 146n
Plutarch, 160, 184
Polygamy, 42
Poole, Walton, 280–82
Portraiture, 226–39
and African trade, 227
and aristocratic identity, 226–27
association of women and African slaves in, 244, 247, 248
blackness as death in, 4–5, 227
blackness as necessary to whiteness in, 247–48
carnivalesque in, 237–38
and Charles II, 248–51
class in, 238, 248
and English identity, 235–36
and fairness, 240–41
and female competition, 241n
and female pathology, 241
and ideal beauty, 241–42
and imperialist expansion, 228, 230, 232, 235
and marriage, 236–37
offering in, 230, 238, 242–44
otherness in, 230, 232, 236, 237
and slave trade, 226, 228, 230
and teaching strategies, 268
and wealth, 157, 211–12, 232, 235, 251, 253
Portugal, 16–21
Pory, John, 29–32, 35n, 39, 48–49, 61
Poststructuralism, 2
Power
and linguistic order, 72–73
and racist/prejudicial thought, 6–7, 28
and sexuality, 37–38
See also Imperialist expansion; Male poetic power
Prager, Carolyn, 66, 67n
Prat, William, 29n, 53–54, 60

Pratt, Mary Louise, 152
Pregnancy/fertility, 75, 85, 93, 136–37, 158. *See also* Aristocratic bloodlines
Principal Navigations, Voyages, and Discoveries of the English Nation (Hakluyt), 11, 29, 44–53, 63, 118
Africa as mysterious in, 47–48
Americas in, 46–47, 62–63n
animals in, 50–51, 52
and aristocratic identity, 66
body metaphors in, 45, 51–53
gender in, 49–51
imperialist seduction in, 60, 61
otherness in, 32
and Purchas, 55
and stability of whiteness, 12, 51–53
wealth in, 82–83
writing as burden in, 44–45
Prostitution, 240
Ptolemy, 95
Purchas, Samuel. *See Hakluytus Posthumus, or Purchas His Pilgrimes*
Puttenham, George, 1, 2, 9

Quilligan, Maureen, 64

Rabb, Theodore K., 16, 65
Race issue, critical avoidance of, 254–55, 258–61
and aesthetic tradition, 1, 69–71
and fairness, 8
and power of language, 266–67
Racialism, 1, 3–4, 8n, 96, 182. *See also* Racist/prejudicial thought; *specific topics*
Racist/prejudicial thought, 6–7, 14, 28
in English language, 265–67
and otherness, 11–12, 141
and rape threat, 142–43
See also specific topics
Ragussis, Michael, 56
Rainolds, Henry, 117, 275
Raleigh, Lady, 242
Raleigh, Sir Walter, 27–28n, 49, 187
and Christian conversion, 54–55, 58
and Solomon, 109
and wealth, 82–83
writing as burden in, 45
Rape, 142–43, 150–51, 160
Religious difference
and female transgression, 39, 104–5
in female writing, 189–91
and otherness, 13, 103
and sunburn, 95–96, 98, 103–5
in travel narratives, 30, 48–49, 103
See also Christian conversion
Reporte of the Kingdome of Congo, A (Hartwell), 40–44, 51, 61, 120
Revett, Eldred, 119–20, 284, 285–90
Rich, Penelope, 137
Rich, Robert, 21
Richards, Beah, 267
Roberts, Josephine, 188n
Roche, Thomas, Jr., 108
Royal African Companies, 18n, 121
Royal Company of Adventurers Trading into Africa, 18

Rubin, Gayle, 123
Rupert, Prince, 228–30, 248

Sackville-West, Vita, 13
Said, Edward, 110, 138
Salve Deus Rex Judaeorum (Lanier), 155, 183–84
Salzman, Paul, 193
Sandoval, Chela, 178–79
Scobie, Edward, 240, 247
Scott, Joan W., 23, 256
Sexuality
    and blackness, 28, 34, 90, 97, 130, 160, 169, 189, 240
    control of male, 148
    and cosmetics, 90
    and imperialist expansion, 37–38, 59–61, 102
    and otherness, 30–31, 182–83
    and power, 37–38
    in Song of Songs, 112–13
    and sunburn, 101–2
    in travel narratives, 30–31, 59–61
    voyeurism, 60
    and wealth, 157–58
    See also Female subjugation; Female transgression; Interracial desire; Marriage; Women
Shakespeare, William, 1, 22–24, 157, 165
    aristocratic identity in, 219, 222
    blackness as dangerous in, 153–54
    blackness as undesirable in, 1, 22, 70, 207
    class in, 181
    cosmetics in, 90–91, 130–31
    and *The English Moor*, 166
    female abandonment in, 195
    female competition in, 180, 181
    female materiality in, 118
    female transgression in, 157
    foreign trade in, 23, 85
    linguistic difference in, 148
    and linguistic order, 77
    male poetic power in, 67, 69, 115–16
    marriage in, 87, 161
    and *Masque of Blackness*, 166
    otherness in, 8n, 206, 230, 232
    religious difference in, 103, 104–5
    sunburn in, 94, 97, 102
    teaching, 266–67
    and *Urania*, 190
    wealth in, 157–58, 174
    white hands image in, 209, 210
    whitening in, 67, 69, 90–91, 115–16
Shakespeare's works
    Much Ado about Nothing, 100, 148, 195
    Othello, 8n, 70n, 181, 190, 206, 210
    The Rape of Lucrece, 60, 61, 65n, 74
    Romeo and Juliet, 148
    Titus Andronicus, 70n
    Troilus and Cressida, 248
    Two Gentlemen of Verona, 181
    See also Antony and Cleopatra; Love's Labour's Lost; Merchant of Venice, The; Midsummer Night's Dream, A; Tempest, The
Sheba, 108–9, 111n, 140
Shephearde's Calender (Spenser), 100

Sidney, Mary, 184
Sidney, Sir Philip, 200, 203n, 204
    imperialist involvement of, 18, 66, 73–74
    on Song of Songs, 109–10
    See also Astrophel and Stella
Skura, Meredith, 151–52
Slave trade, 17–18, 19–22
    and lyric poetry, 120–21
    and pregnancy/fertility, 85
    and visual culture, 19, 120–21, 212–13, 222n, 226, 228, 230
    and wealth, 81
    See also African trade
Smith, Barbara, 262
Smith, Paul, 198n
Smith, Valerie, 150–51, 257, 258
Snowden, Frank, 3n
Solomon, 58, 108–9, 113, 138–40. *See also* Song of Songs
Song of Songs, 107–16
    beauty of whiteness in, 52, 251
    and blackness as beautiful, 110–11, 132, 207, 209, 240
    female dismemberment in, 108, 112–13
    and imperialist expansion, 108
    and interracial desire, 108–10, 140
    male poetic power in, 110–11, 113–14
    sunburn in, 97–98
    whitening in, 110–11, 113–14, 139
    See also Solomon
Spain, 16, 19
    and interracial desire, 145, 222
    James I's policy towards, 126
    and otherness, 17, 83–84
    and religious difference, 57
    wealth of, 83–84, 108
Spenser, Edmund, 62, 192, 193
    female subjugation in, 37–38
    on linguistic difference, 145–47
    and literary influence, 78
    male poetic power in, 67, 91–92
    sunburn in, 100
    wealth in, 81–82, 84
Spivak, Gayatri, 263
Stallybrass, Peter, 52n, 53n, 99, 170–71, 181, 238
Stone, Lawrence, 126
Strong, Roy, 215n, 217, 222
Stuart, Lady Arabella, 137, 169n
Sunburn, 53, 92–107
    and blackness as beautiful, 118
    and class, 100
    and cosmetics, 90
    and cross-cultural contact, 93–94
    and cultural difference, 97–98
    and female writing, 105–7, 181, 206–7
    and imperialist expansion, 192–93
    and interracial desire, 95
    and literary influence, 75, 93, 100, 106–7
    and male poetic power, 98–99
    and men, 100–101, 106
    and origins of blackness, 94–97
    and religious difference, 95–96, 98, 103–5
    and sexuality, 101–2

Sundelson, Eric, 148
Swift, Carolyn Ruth, 198

Tempest, The (Shakespeare), 141–45, 147–53, 190
    aristocratic bloodlines in, 142, 143, 148–49,
        150, 159
    class in, 147, 148, 238
    cross-cultural contact in, 151–53
    Dido in, 153, 155, 159
    dualisms in, 151
    interracial desire in, 141, 142–43, 150–51, 153,
        160
    language and imperialism in, 145–47
    linguistic difference in, 143–45
    maternal absence in, 149–50
    wealth in, 147–48
Tennenhouse, Leonard, 154
Thirsk, Joan, 21
Tilley, Morris P., 100
Todorov, Tzvetan, 82, 84, 232
Tokson, Elliot, 117
Tragedie of Cleopatra, The (Daniel), 154–56
Tragedie of Mariam, The (Cary), 100, 184–85
Traub, Valerie, 36n, 37
Travel narratives, 25–61, 63
    Africa as disordered in, 26–27, 38, 39–40, 156
    Americas in, 46–47, 62–63n
    animals in, 50–51, 52
    and apes, 238
    blackness as mystery in, 40–43, 47–48
    body metaphors in, 26, 27, 45, 51–53, 61
    cannibalism in, 43–44
    and Christian conversion, 54–58, 63, 123
    cross-cultural contact in, 61, 123–24, 152
    danger in, 65
    disdain for African cultures/people in, 30–31,
        44
    dismemberment of female body in, 65
    economic exploitation in, 39–40
    editorial ordering in, 29–30, 31–32, 40–41, 61
    and England as disordered in, 53–54
    and English identity, 32, 54
    female transgression in, 25–26, 32–37, 38–39,
        42–43
    foreign sexuality in, 30–31
    gender in, 49–51
    geography in, 26–28, 30, 61, 156
    as imperialist seduction, 59–61
    and instability of whiteness, 13, 51–53
    and lyric poetry, 63, 64–65
    racialization of aesthetic tradition in, 41–42
    religious difference in, 30, 48–49, 103
    writing as burden in, 44–45
    writing as travel in, 29, 46
Travels of Sir John Mandeville, 26–28, 30, 45, 52n,
        55, 56, 59, 109n
Tuan, Yi-Fu, 212, 217, 241n, 247n

Urania. See Countess of Montgomerie's Urania, The
Urania, or The Woman in the Moon (Basse), 62–64,
        70, 107n, 115

van Linschoten, Jan Huygen, 232
Van Noren, Linda, 110–12

Vaughan, Alden T., 142, 151
Vaughan, Virginia, 142, 151
Verlinden, Charles, 16
Vickers, Nancy, 60, 65, 69, 170, 240
View of the Present State of Ireland, A (Spenser), 145–
        47
Visual culture
    and cosmetics, 87, 88
    dark/light polarity in, 213–14
    Sheba in, 111n
    and slave trade, 121, 212–13
    wealth in, 211–12
    See also Blazons; Jewel exchanges; Portraiture

Wall, Cheryl, 263
Wallace, Michele, 254, 264
Waller, Gary, 194
Wallerstein, Immanuel, 83
Walsingham, Francis, 73
Waterhouse, Ellis, 232
Wealth, 79–85, 157
    and aristocratic identity, 163–64
    and Christian conversion, 64, 119–20
    and class mobility, 161–62
    and commodification of women, 22, 23, 79–82,
        84, 90, 150–51
    and competition, 170
    and cosmetics, 87
    and English identity, 82–83
    and fairness, 85–86, 90, 116
    and female transgression, 162–63
    and language, 147–48
    loss of, 174
    and marriage, 86–87, 161
    and materiality, 119–20
    and paternal absence, 167
    and portraiture, 157, 211–12, 232, 235, 251,
        253
    and sexuality, 157–58
    and Solomon, 58, 108
Weatherill, Lorna, 242
Webster, John. *See Devil's Law-Case, The; White
        Devil, The*
Weeks, Jeffrey, 261n
Weever, John, 272–73
Weller, Gary, 184, 185n
Welsford, Enid, 128
West Africa Company, 18n
West Indies, 18n, 19, 21, 121, 127
White Devil, The (Webster), 131, 175, 188–89
Whiteness
    blackness as necessary to, 9, 12, 22, 197, 240,
        247–48
    and body, 52
    and Christianity, 171
    and class, 209, 210, 248
    and cosmetics, 87
    and English identity, 12, 133–34, 136
    as grief, 106
    instability of, 13, 51–53
    interrogation of, 15, 257, 264–65
    and linguistic order, 66, 71, 72–73
    as male construct, 179n
    and reason, 180

Whiteness *(cont.)*
  white hands image, 208–10, 248
  See also Fairness; Whitening
Whitening, 62–63, 66–69, 71–72, 259–60
  as Christian conversion, 114–15
  and cross-cultural contact, 71, 139–40
  and female subjugation, 107, 137, 174
  and female transgression, 115, 137
  and female writing, 107
  in female writing, 107, 203–4
  gender specificity of, 134
  and imperialist expansion, 138–39
  and jewel exchanges, 218
  and male poetic power, 66, 67, 69, 90–92,
    113–14, 115–16, 131, 169–70
  in Song of Songs, 110–11, 113–14
White supremacy, 4, 265–66
Whitewashing. *See* Whitening
Whitney, Geoffrey, 68
Willan, Thomas Stuart, 17, 18, 21
Williams, Bishop, 139
Williams, Ethel Carleton, 128, 136, 137
Williams, Noel H., 251n
Williams, Patricia, 15, 71, 254, 262, 266
Williamson, James, 16, 19
Willoughby d'Eresby, Lord, 4–5, 227
Wilson, Thomas, 3, 100
Witherspoon, Alexander, 184

Women
  commodification of, 22, 23, 79–82, 84, 90,
    150–51
  competition between, 100, 134–35, 180–81,
    184–85, 199–201, 241n
  dismemberment of, 65, 69, 108, 112–13, 118
  and geography, 27–28n, 61, 79
  honor of, 167–68
  and imagination, 89
  as marginal, 49–50
  pregnancy/fertility, 75, 85, 93, 136–37, 158
  as usurpers, 91
  See also Aristocratic bloodlines; Cosmetics;
    Female subjugation; Female transgression;
    Female writing; Interracial desire; Marriage;
    Whitening
Wonder of Women, The; or, The Tragedy of Sophonisba
  (Marston), 188, 189
Woodbridge, Linda, 80
Wright, Abraham, 280
Wroth, Lady Mary, 105–7, 107–8n, 137.
  See also Countess of Montgomerie's Urania, The
Wyatt, Sir Francis, 65–66

Young, Lisa, 171
Yuval-Davis, Nira, 9, 125

Zepheria, 85–86, 90, 94, 99, 107